DIVINE CONTINGENCY

THEOLOGIES OF DIVINE EMBODIMENT IN MAXIMOS THE CONFESSOR AND TSONG KHA PA

Divine Contingency

Theologies of Divine Embodiment in Maximos the Confessor and Tsong kha pa

Thomas Cattoi

Gorgias Press
2008

ISBN 978-1-59333-970-8

GORGIAS PRESS
180 Centennial Ave., Suite 3, Piscataway, NJ 08854 USA
www.gorgiaspress.com

Library of Congress Cataloging-in-Publication Data
Cattoi, Thomas.
 Divine contingency : theologies of divine embodiment in Maximos the Confessor and Tsong kha pa / Thomas Cattoi. -- 1st Gorgias Press ed.
     p. cm.
 Includes bibliographical references.
 1. Incarnation--Comparative studies. 2. Maximus, Confessor, Saint, ca. 580-662.
3. Tson-kha-pa Blo-bzan-grags-pa, 1357-1419. 4. Christianity and other religions--Dge-lugs-pa (Sect) 5. Dge-lugs-pa (Sect)--Relations--Christianity. I. Title.
 BT220.C25 2008
 230'.14092--dc22

                    2008026782

TABLE OF CONTENTS

PREFACE:
THE CHALLENGE OF CONTINGENCY

The thought of Jean Paul Sartre is perhaps an unlikely starting point for a reflection on Christology and spirituality in a multicultural, multireligious world. The French philosopher had little patience with organized religion, or indeed, with religion of any kind. His thought gave it for granted that faith in a God or a First Maker was a relic of the past—a relic which bolstered an unjust and ultimately doomed social structure. Sartre's profound pessimism leaves nothing beyond the reach of its suffocating embrace: friendship and love are absent from his gloomy and depressing world, where interpersonal relationships are inevitably marked by exploitation and hostility.

If we turn to Sartre's work *La Nausée*, the worldview we find is unrelentingly bleak. The main character, a man called Roquentin, experiences feelings of repulsion and disgust when he looks at the roots of a chestnut tree. Everything is obscene and threatening; the world is "brute and nameless," the superabundance of its elements is sickening and overwhelming. Despite all our attempts to penetrate its significance, the world's utter pointlessness persists relentlessly, almost mockingly. For Sartre, the only redeeming quality of this epiphany of the absurd is that it sets Roquentin apart from the "bourgeois fools" whose consciousness is "dulled," and who cannot help seeing the world as "solid." The bourgeois is perfectly at home in the world; Roquentin's horror for le *visqueux* saves him at least from a destiny of inauthenticity and bad faith.[1]

In her work *Sartre: Romantic Rationalist*, the British novelist and philosopher Iris Murdoch wonders whether Roquentin's pose of moral superiority is actually justified. He might well be more sensitive than the superficial bourgeoisie; but why is it that the "contingent superabundance" of the

---

[1] Jean Paul Sartre, *Nausea* (trans. L. Alexander; New York: New Directions Publishing Corporation, 1969), 126–9.

world must be seen as nauseating? Roquentin deplores the utilitarian attitude that sees the world only as "material," but he is incapable of offering any constructive solution, and he retreats into an attitude of aristocratic hauteur. Murdoch ascribes Sartre's contempt for the contingent to a morbidly defensive egocentricity; it is no surprise, then, if *l'enfer, c'est les autres*.[2] But perhaps, Murdoch suggests, the superabundance of the world might be experienced differently; it might even be a source of joy. Murdoch suggests that contingent reality is more fruitfully approached as a lesson in the insignificance of the observer, who eventually realizes that she is not at the center of the world.

This Copernican revolution often begins in rather unexpected ways. In her novel *Bruno's Dream*, Murdoch suggests that it is through the experience of love that many people are ripped out of their egocentric cocoon, until even the experience of earthly love is left behind.[3] One eventually learns to "be in love with the separate world and the separate people it contains," even if this love is somehow less ardent, and less personal. If one is truly capable of love, one does not need to withdraw from the world's 'messiness', or fear the indeterminacy of one' consciousness, besieged by contingency on all sides. To counter Sartre's obsession with viscosity, Murdoch resorts to an analogous aqueous metaphor: to face the world with balance and inner detachment is like jumping into water, surrendering to creation's "mysteriously supportive properties." Becoming an authentically spiritual person is perhaps like learning to swim: one must "surrender a rigid, nervous attachment to the upright position," and abandon oneself to the surrounding waters.[4]

For the Christian theologian, Sartre's fear of contingency indicates his ultimate contempt for our creaturely condition. After all, the serpent's temptation in the garden, "you shall be like God, knowing good from evil," suggests an analogous desire to escape from our condition, marked by unavoidable illness, old age and death. As a consequence of the fall, the created order becomes a menace, something that threatens our survival and against which we need protection. In this uncertain world, the power of *eros* offers little solace: earthly love is fickle, it is often marred by conflict and

---

[2] Iris Murdoch, *Sartre: Romantic Rationalist* (Tonbridge, UK: Viking Press, 1987), 15–19.

[3] Iris Murdoch, *Bruno's Dream* (London, Penguin, 1970), 292, *passim*.

[4] See Peter J. Conradi, *The Saint and the Artist: A Study of Iris Murdoch's Works* (New York: HarperCollins, 2001), 134–8.

strife. Murdoch's intuition that "love" was the answer was right: but where can one find a love which is so strong that nothing in the world will over-shadow or extinguish it?

It is not within ourselves that we shall find the medicine to heal Roquentin's *nausée*, but in the pages of Paul's Letter to the Philippians. There, we are told that Christ, "though he was in the form of God, did not regard equality with God something to be grasped," but "emptied himself, taking the form of a slave, coming in human likeness."[5] Surely, there can be no better example of "surrender of one's upright position" than Christ's own *kenōsis*.[6] He was not repelled by our creaturely condition, but freely chose to embrace it, and to die on the cross: he swam in the ocean of con-tingency, but ultimately was not swallowed by it. The incarnation signals that Christ opts for finitude over infinity, suffering over impassibility, agapic love for one's suffering neighbor over self-absorption; he shows us that the way towards a more fulfilled humanity necessarily goes through marginality and asceticism.

The same apostle Paul tells us in 1 Cor 2:14–15 that the "spiritual man" (*anēr pneumatikos*) is not someone looking for *recherché* inner states, or seeks refuge in a proudly independent interiority. Rather, what "he" sets out to do is to serve the community and its needs; spirituality is not something that one *does*, but something that one *is*. Roquentin and Paul's "spiritual man" are the paradigms of two different types of spirituality: one which refrains from contingency and companionship, the other which embraces them and turns them into channels of divine grace. Christ's incarnation shows that salvation is the result of a prolonged work of self-purification which cannot be accomplished in isolation, but actually culminates in what Iris Murdoch terms the "ethics of unselfing."

The temptation to look in the depths of the soul for shelter from a menacing world has perhaps never been as strong as today. Unfortunately, one quickly realizes that the soul is more a labyrinth than a refuge, and all too often its twists and turns conceal unconfessed yearnings and desires, which turn our best intentions to their service. Instead of serving our neighbor in her needs, we expect tributes from the outside world; instead of letting our reason control our passions, we allow the latter to subjugate the former. The agony at Gethsemani shows us that Christ could accomplish

---

[5] Phil 2:6–7.

[6] Iris Murdoch also develops this theme in her novel *Nuns and Soldiers* (Reprint ed. London: Penguin, 2002), 104–108.

what no one had ever been able to do: turn our will finally and permanently towards God. Our desires for radical independence make us less than human; our submission to God makes us partake of the divine. In this way, paradoxically, the promise of the serpent is fulfilled: at the end, *erimus sicut Deus*. The malaise engendered by Roquentin's chestnut is not cured by the tree of good and evil; it is the tree of the cross that bears the fruit of immortality.

This study will explore the way in which the Christian understanding of incarnation presupposes and sustains a theology of contingency, or, in other words, a belief in the salvific import of the created order in its infinite variety and difference. Our starting point will be the Christology of Maximos the Confessor (580–662), a Greek Father who lived towards the end of the Patristic period, and whose writings offer us a remarkable synthesis of the theological controversies of the first centuries. The question will then be: what is it that makes Maximos' theology of contingency specifically Christian? How does it differ from other theological or philosophical systems that view contingent reality as intrinsically meaningful and valuable? In order to answer this question, I will engage in a comparative experiment, and juxtapose Maximos' Christology to the Buddhological speculation of Tsong kha pa (1359–1427), a Tibetan master who authored some of the most important systematic expositions of Buddhist doctrine. Both Maximos and Tsong kha pa favored a form of spirituality that was deeply appreciative of the created order, in the case of the former, and of conventional reality, in the case of the latter. A joint reading of these two authors will enable Christian theologians to rediscover how the teaching of incarnation invests the created order with a salvific dignity that is not paralleled by any other tradition. This study will thus adumbrate the contours of a Christian theology of contingency, and, in line with Frank Clooney's injunctions in *Hindu God Christian God*, the resulting theology will be systematic, constructive, and comparative.[7]

In her early novel *The Bell*, Iris Murdoch's voice speaks through the voice of one of her characters, who claims that "all failures are ultimately failures in love." Our inability to appreciate the contingent, and the retreat into an attitude of rarefied disdain, is most likely such a failure. The voice of Maximos the Confessor tells us that an exclusive focus on the interior life may be a temptation, perhaps even an affront to the kenotic outpouring of

---

[7] See Francis X. Clooney S.J., *Hindu God Christian God: How Reason Helps Break Down the Boundaries Between Religions* (Oxford: Oxford University Press, 2001), Ch. 1.

agapē that began in the incarnation. Our world bears the marks of sin, but this is no justification to abandon it to its doom. The bombed city of London that is the theatre of many scenes in Murdoch's *Under the Net* is a metaphor for the redundant contingency of our world, which is wounded, chaotic, often lacking in harmony and beauty. During one of his peregrinations in this novel, the protagonist Jack Donaghue blurts out: "I hate contingency. I want everything in my life to have a sufficient reason."[8] Unfortunately, or more likely fortunately, we will never get altogether rid of contingency; thus, it might be worthwhile to see whether contingency does not have a sufficient reason already. This reason we might be unable to see, but a reason nonetheless, thanks to which whatever we fail to understand becomes an encouragement, a comfort, a gift.

The incarnation is the reason why Christians continue to hope beyond hope in a possible redemption of this world, even when everything seems to point in the opposite direction. It is quite apposite that Murdoch's quip should concern a city; a city is the dwelling place of a multitude, and it is the celestial city of Jerusalem, not the Garden of Eden, which descends from heaven in the Book of Revelation.[9] In this city, "arrayed like a bride," God and his lamb dwell eternally with humanity, and all of creation is united in a celestial liturgy, where everything is where it should be, and goes where it should go.

Thomas Cattoi

---

[8] Iris Murdoch, *Under the Net* (New York: Penguin, 1977), 24. See also Jamieson Ridenhour, "*I Know the City Well*: The Metaphysical Cityscape in Iris Murdoch's *Under the Net*," online: *Literary London Journal* 1, 1 (2003): http://homepages.gold.ac.uk/london-journal/march2003/ridenhour.html.

[9] See Maximos the Confessor, *Mystagogy*, 2 (PG 91: 667–671); Hans Urs von Balthasar, *Truth Is Symphonic: Aspects of Christian Pluralism* (trans. G. Harrison; San Francisco: Ignatius Press, 1987), 7–18.

1 DIALOGUE OR ENSTASY?
SPIRITUAL TRANSFORMATION ACROSS DIFFERENT TRADITIONS

In his work *Mystical Theology*, Mark McIntosh argues that the divide between theology and spirituality will debilitate the former no less than the latter, leaving them incapable of critiquing and sustaining each other. The task of the theologian is to uproot Christian theology from the sheltered terrain of philosophical argumentation and to force it to attend in silence to the murmur of the divine speech. Ch. 5 of his work suggests that to find some clues as to the manner to overcome this impasse, we ought to look at the Passion narratives in the Gospel.[1]

We know how, in the last hours of his earthly life, Christ is asked by the Jewish authorities over and over again to provide evidence for his Messianic claims. Jesus, however, chooses to remain silent. Even on Golgotha, some onlookers mock him and ask him to come down from the cross, but the only answer they receive is the sight of a body in the throes of agony. At the foot of the cross, however, there are other characters: John, the disciple "whom Jesus loved," Jesus' mother Mary, and a group of other women, who had followed Jesus during his ministry, attending to his needs and to those of his disciples. The identity of these women is blurred; we are not sure about their number, or their real names. We do know, however, that it is to them that Jesus chooses to manifest himself on the morning of the resurrection. Their path is one of contemplation and action, both flowing from familiarity with the mystery that unfolds in their midst.

For McIntosh, the moral of the story is quite clear. The irruption of divine reality is unsettling; it upends our assumptions about the world, and confronts us with painful aspects of reality that we would be more than willing to forget. By participating in a life of discipleship, McIntosh tells us, one can find out what remains hidden to the doctors of the law, who had clear expectations of what the Messiah had to be like, and yet, according to

---

[1] Mark McIntosh, *Mystical Theology*, Ch. 5: "The Trinity and Divine Suffering," 151–87.

the Gospel narrative, failed to recognize him. The more one realizes one's fundamental inadequacy, the more one realizes that speculative reflection is often powerless, and that what is needed is a growing readiness to *listen* to what the mystery has to say. Within the Christian tradition, spiritual experiences that bear the mark of authenticity take always the form of a dialogue with God: the anguished awareness of one's finitude and mortality seeks a higher power that welcomes us in its embrace.

The question, of course, is how Christians of later ages should imitate the example of these pious women, and make sure that spirituality does not degenerate into mawkish sentimentality or the mechanical performance of practices that have no real transformative effect. My suggestion is that one looks for guidance in the writings of those who before us have found solace in the lived practice of spirituality, and for whom their spiritual experiences have become the source for theological reflection. How will we choose, however, from the bewildering variety of texts that have come down to us from past centuries, representing myriads of different approaches to the spiritual life? Among the life-style options on sale in the supermarket of post-modernity, "spirituality" seems to occupy quite a few shelves, many of which carry products of every imaginable origin. Christianity has lost its traditional monopoly, and now faces the competition of all sorts of purveyors of inner peace, whose success is often proportional to the vigor with which they advertise their alleged "Eastern" origin. Even the most adventurous seeker will often be at a loss for criteria to distinguish the authentic from the commercial, the real expression of a tradition from its marketed version.

THE SILENT GROUND: IDENTITY OR RELATION?

In his *Skizzen sur Theologie*, Hans Urs von Balthasar draws some useful distinctions, to which we will often return in the course of this study. The German theologian observes that, as soon as the ancient polytheistic myths started to recede into the background, humanity started to interpret its own religious experiences in terms of a descent into multiplicity followed by a return into unity (*Aufstieg/Abstieg*).[2] Platonism is thus an ancient philosophical expression of this desire to flee a world burdened by individuality and multiplicity. Von Balthasar argues that Christianity has taken up and tran-

---

[2] Hans Urs von Balthasar, *Skizzen zur Theologie*, V (Einsiedeln: Johannes Verlag, 1986), 104–105; 228–240; 360; *et al.* (Vol. V of *Explorations in Theology*, no English translation yet available).

scended (*aufgehoben*) this Platonic dialectic; in the Christian version of *Aufstieg/Abstieg*, however, the ascent of the individual responds to the kenotic self-disclosure of the eternal Word. In this perspective, there is an irreducible difference between Christianity's dialogical nature, where the terms of spiritual practice follow God's initiative, and the alternative desire for an autonomously attained self-transcendence. Anthropocentric experiments of the latter sort, which enthrone the human self as ultimate judge and arbiter, are the ultimate instance of *hybris*.[3]

Von Balthasar is adamant in his conviction that humanity's aspiration towards the ultimate is only fulfilled in the communion with a divine reality that remains totally, irreducibly *other*. Spirituality is the form that this encounter takes: an encounter that results in the gradual transformation of the individual who receives this particular grace, and who perhaps will now seek to share her experience with her community. Any distinction between a theology of the intellect for the few, and a mysticism of the affections for the masses, entirely misses the point. In a Christian perspective, God's self-disclosure in the incarnation engages all aspects of the human person, touching the mind as well as the heart. The theological endeavor, which uses language, concepts, arguments, and all sorts of tools from the armory of philosophy, is part of the individual's integrated response to God's invitation to intimacy. In the third volume of his *Theologik*, von Balthasar contrasts this approach to the pining of Advaita Vedanta practitioners for a primordial ground (*Urgrund*) that is also absolute emptiness (*Ungrund*) and absence of speech (*Unwort*). Here, the goal is the individual's un-becoming (*Entwerdung*), where everything drowns in the abyss of infinity, and words and concepts merge with the primordial silence. There is no escape from the ultimate choice that faces all mystics: either enter into a dialogue with the divine, or lose yourself in the *analogia identitatis*.[4]

The women at the foot of the cross whom McIntosh extols as paradigms of the spiritual life show us clearly that Christian discipleship consists of two mutually sustaining parts: an attitude of receptiveness towards the divine speech, and our response to it, as we let ourselves be shaped by its beauty. In light of von Balthasar's earlier considerations, perhaps McIntosh

---

[3] Raymond Gawronski, S.J., *Word and Silence: Hans Urs von Balthasar and the Spiritual Encounter between East and West* (Edinburgh: T&T Clark, 1995), 5–40.

[4] Hans Urs von Balthasar, *Theologik*, Vol. 3, *Der Geist der Wahrheit* (Einsiedeln: Johannes Verlag, 1987), 100–101. See also the English translation *Theo-logic*, Vol. 3, *The Spirit of Truth* (trans. by G. Harrison; San Francisco: Ignatius Press, 2005).

is right when he suggests that one should discontinue the use of the term "mysticism," burdened as it is with solipsistic overtones, and replace it with "contemplation." Theology is then based on the contemplation of what we already believe, yet do not fully understand, or have not fully integrated into our own personal experience. The trademark of a good spirituality, and thus of a good theology, is the fundamental willingness to face the *real*, rather than our projections or fears. The writings of the mystics, who have drawn on their spiritual experience to develop their own theological vision, remain signposts which mark the way towards a deeper communion with God, towards a fuller life.[5]

The practice of reading texts where spirituality and theology form a deeper synthesis is thus the starting point for a theology that integrates the intellectual and the affective aspect, seeks to be in continuity with the tradition, but is not afraid to be constructive. Theologians who study these texts are not merely interested in the historical context that influenced their composition, or the philosophical or literary influences that may be detected in the style of writing. In the words of Frank Clooney, theologians actually believe in "some transcendent (perhaps supernatural) reality, the possibility of an (usually fact of) a normative revelation, and in the need to make practical decisions and life choices which have a bearing on salvation."[6] The texts that are the starting point for a constructive theological experiment are then read out of a "concern" for these beliefs. In fact, it is this very concern that induces theologians to question the modes of discourse employed by the texts, and perhaps to reformulate them, or merely to present them in a different light.[7]

While these considerations may have been valid in earlier times as well, they become all the more compelling as Christianity is increasingly viewed as one option among the many that crowd the religious market. Jacques Dupuis' and Paul Knitter's work on Christian theologies of religious pluralism show the extent to which contemporary informed believers feel challenged by the competing truth claims of different religious traditions, and as

---

[5] Mark McIntosh, *Mystical Theology*, 68–69, on this tendency to divorce "mysticism" from reality.

[6] Frank X. Clooney S.J., *Theology after Vedanta: An Experiment in Comparative Theology* (Albany, N.Y.: SUNY Press, 1993), 4–5.

[7] Frank Clooney discusses this hermeneutical question in *Seeing Through Texts: Doing Theology Among the Srivaisnavas of South India* (Albany, N.Y.: SUNY Press, 1996).

such seek to develop a theological rational for this on-going diversity.[8] As Clooney again points out, whenever a theologian, who is committed to a particular truth claim, encounters a different version of this truth in another religious tradition, he or she will experience a tension between fidelity to the truth which one has known and experienced, and vulnerability to the truth which is encountered in this new context.[9] At this point, one might be tempted to move the theological endeavor to a neutral place where every commitment is suspended, so as to maintain an attitude of equal respect for all religious positions even if they appear to contradict each other. Very soon, one will see that this strategy is self-defeating. If one seriously engages a truth claim that challenges previously held beliefs, one shall never again be able to hold on uncritically to these beliefs. The writings of an author who questions the validity of one's religious beliefs can wound you deeply, and the scars after the struggle may never heal. With the scars, however, comes also wisdom; a wisdom that does not seek to imprison challenging religious tradition within the categories of the uninspired or the demonic, but acknowledges their claims as partners in a conversation across different faiths.

SPIRITUAL PRACTICES, SPIRITUAL TEXTS

If one is truly committed to a particular religious tradition, one will not be able to ignore claims that appear to question its truthfulness or accuracy. If it is truly the case, as we said earlier, that the trademark of a good theology is the willingness to face the real, without being derailed by one's fears, a good theology will necessarily engage these competing claims. While a scholar of comparative religion, or comparative spirituality, might simply wish to study particular texts to understand the broader phenomenon of religious experience, comparative theologians will be rooted in a particular context and their goal will be a deeper understanding, or appreciation, of the beliefs of their original community. As a result, one's belief will not change, but one will experience them differently, and their particularity will be all the more evident after they are compared to an equally particular, though not identical, position.

---

[8] See Jacques Dupuis, *Towards a Christian Theology of Religious Pluralism* (Maryknoll, N.Y.: Orbis, 2006); Paul F. Knitter, *Introducing Theologies of Religion* (Maryknoll, N.Y.: Orbis, 2006).

[9] This is a theme that is developed throughout Clooney's work. See the already mentioned *Hindu God Christian God*, esp. Ch. 1–2, 4.

The central role of competing particularities needs to be stressed, lest we are tempted to let go of those areas of our tradition that appear to conflict with the claims of others, and are left with a fabricated synthesis which does not represent anyone's position. The nature of ultimate reality, or the problem of salvation, or the import of mystical experience are more than just elements in a text; they are existential questions that demand to be faced. If one agrees that an increase in theological knowledge is possible, one should welcome the insights that one gains as one probes different traditions and explores how they offer answers to these existential questions. Finally, but perhaps most importantly, comparative theologians should be ready to discern where the two traditions take positions that cannot be reconciled with each other. One should always be willing to *learn*, but, at the same time, one should also be ready to *judge*.

In light of these considerations, I would like to think of this work as an experiment in comparative theology, whose goal is a deeper understanding of the position of Christian theology on the salvific role of contingent reality. The project will underscore the inner unity between spiritual practice and the project of speculative theology, while also stressing the inextricable link between a theology of incarnation and a theology of the created order. Following the methodology outlined by Frank X. Clooney in *Theology After Vedanta*, I will begin outlining a specific Christian instance of a theology of contingency, explore an analogous theology as developed in a particular school of Tibetan Buddhism, and eventually return to the Christian starting point to explore the similarities as well as the less obvious differences between the two positions. My work will focus on the writings of the Greek Father Maximos the Confessor (580–662) and the Tibetan thinker and monastic reformer Tsong kha pa (1357–1419).[10] These two authors, who lived centuries and thousands of miles apart in cultures that most likely never came in contact with each other, reflected on the salvific value of the natural order in response to currents within their own tradition that were incompatible with their understanding of God's, and the Buddha's, active intervention in the world. In so doing, we will effectively compare two debates on the correct understanding of divine embodiment, the first sur-

---

[10] For a chronology of Maximos' life and works, see Hans Urs von Balthasar, *Cosmic Liturgy: The Universe According to Maximos the Confessor* (trans. by Fr. B. Daley, S.J. San Francisco: Ignatius Press, 2003), 74–80. The life and cultural background of Tsong kha pa are introduced by Robert Thurman in *The Central Philosophy of Tibet: A Study and Translation of Jey Tsong khapa's 'Essence of True Eloquence'* (Princeton, N.J.: Princeton University Press, 1984), 63–89.

rounding the Christological definition of Chalcedon and its implications for the spiritual practice of the individual, the second concerning the notion of *nirvāna* and the debates on the relationship between the Buddha's different bodily manifestations. The final part of this work will highlight the extent to which the Christian understanding of incarnation arguably sustains a stronger sacramental reading of the created order than the Tibetan Buddhist vision. At the same time, I will also suggest that familiarity with the Tibetan Buddhist tradition helps Christian theology to retrieve a deeper appreciation for contingency as a gift that shapes our spiritual itinerary.

The theological synthesis of Maximos the Confessor emerged out of the desire to articulate theologically, but also to promote and facilitate Christian spiritual practice. Maximos achieved this by a creative and innovative use of tools forged by the tradition of Origenist spirituality under the philosophical tutelage of Hellenist Neo-Platonism. Maximos appropriated many elements of Origenist spirituality as it had developed in the Evagrian school, but at the same time he also subjected it to a severe critique, highlighting what in his opinion amounted to the inability of Origenism to account for the intrinsic value of the created order.[11] The eventual decision of the Third Council of Constantinople in 681 to enshrine Maximos' teaching as a normative expression of the Christian faith expressed two centuries earlier at Chalcedon marked the final demise of the Origenist school of spirituality. At the same time it also signaled that centuries of Christological controversy were drawing to an end, and that a consensus had developed, which saw the incarnation as the ultimate glorification of human nature, and thus of human experience as a whole. The lingering Evagrian suspicion for the created order, as well as the Monophysite tendency to blur the distinction between Christ's humanity and divinity, are superseded by Maximos' commitment to a diversity of nature secured by a unity of person.[12]

---

[11] For an overview of the relation between Maximos and Evagrios, see Andrew Louth, *The Origins of the Christian Mystical Tradition: From Plato to Denys* (Oxford: Oxford University Press, 1981); Polycarp Sherwood OSB, *The Earlier Ambigua of St. Maximos the Confessor* (Studia Anselmiana 36. Rome: Herder, 1955). The issue will be discussed extensively in Ch. 3 and 4.

[12] The Council of Chalcedon asserted that Christ's two natures were united in an undivided and yet unconfused manner (*adiairetōs kai asygchytōs*), whereas monophysites accepted the full humanity of Christ *before* the union, but claimed that *after* the union the humanity was deified and somehow *absorbed* into the divinity. See Jaroslav Pelikan, *The Christian Tradition: A History of the Development of Doctrine*, Vol. 1: *The Emergence of the Catholic Tradition (100–600)* (Chicago and London: University of

Maximos assimilates the Platonic lesson inasmuch as in his spiritual theology contemplation entails an intellectual no less than an affective transformation. At the same time, however, the thrust of the contemplative experience at the basis of his theology is unfailingly Christological; the *kenōsis* of the Son is the paradigm of our duty to let go of our self-centered desires, which obscure our understanding of the divine plan. Maximos' understanding of the ascetic endeavor concurs with von Balthasar's reading of the Christian vocation as ultimately a vocation to attentiveness.[13] The created order must not be feared, but embraced, since it conveys God's invitation to a greater intimacy with him. In the earthly life of the eternal Word, this intimacy is carried to an unprecedented level, leading humanity to the very core of divine life and accomplishing its irreversible transfiguration. The ordered reality of the cosmos that takes flesh in the person of Christ shows that the dichotomy between theology and spirituality, speculation and affectivity, rests on a false opposition: the wisdom that discerns God's presence in creation is the same that discerns God's hypostatic indwelling in Christ, who transforms and redeems our humanity beyond all expectation.

The same von Balthasar who, in his *Cosmic Liturgy*, laid the foundations for Maximos' rediscovery, systematically contrasts the transformative power of Christian practice and the alleged sterility of non-Christian forms of spirituality. In this perspective, if the incarnation models humanity's response to God's call to partnership, a spiritual practice which is not patterned on Christ will necessarily be deficient.[14] The reservations voiced by von Balthasar towards the end of *Theo-drama* are not infrequent. In his major work on Orthodox spirituality, the Rumanian theologian Dumitru Staniloae shows no hesitation in viewing the Buddhist search for *nirvāna* as an ultimately selfish and egotistic pursuit, which isolates the individual from

---

Chicago Press, 1971), 271–277; also Leontius of Byzantium, *Against the Nestorians and the Eutychians* 2 (PG 86a: 1329).

[13] Hans Urs von Balthasar, *Prayer* (San Francisco: Ignatius Press, 1986), Ch. 2.

[14] Hans Urs von Balthasar was one of the main figures behind the "rediscovery" of Maximos the Confessor in the middle of the twentieth century, and in his turn he was greatly influenced by Maximos' own vision. To this day, von Balthasar's monograph *Cosmic Liturgy* (trans. by Fr. Brian Daley, S.J.; San Francisco: Ignatius Press, 2003) remains one of the most important and insightful studies of Maximos' thought.

the needs of her neighbor.[15] The 1989 letter to the Bishops of the Catholic Church *On Some Aspects of Christian Meditation* similarly dismissed the claim that forms of spirituality developed outside the Judeo-Christian purview possess any transformative potential. This letter's offhand dismissal of vaguely labeled "Buddhist practices" is accompanied by the claim that Westerners' increasing attraction to the meditative practices of "Eastern" religions reflects the wish to escape a reality that poses *demands* on human freedom.[16] The implication is that Christianity educates the individual to discern God's presence and will in creation, whereas Buddhism owes its relative success among the more affluent Western élites to its readiness to pander the contemporary fashion for emotionalism and subjectivism.

From this perspective, the theology of incarnation that underpins the writings of Maximos the Confessor would seem to epitomize all that Buddhism allegedly rejects, such as attentiveness to reality and to the need of the other. This construal of Buddhism, however, is grossly inaccurate, perhaps deliberately so. After all, the contention that Asian religions fail to be engaged in the world and seek refuge in an attitude of passivity conveniently serves as an apologetic prop for the enduring hegemonic designs on the part of Euro-American Christianity. If Hinduism and Buddhism have proved incapable of educating the consciences of Asian populations, what better solution than replace these traditions with Christianity? The notion of Christianity as midwife of enlightened modernity is even enjoying an unexpected revival in the ranks and file of the Christian Right. Fortunately, even a cursory acquaintance with the actual teachings of Asian religions about the nature and purpose of spiritual practice shows us the extent to which such sweeping generalizations are misleading, or simply mistaken. Buddhist practice is far more than a spiritualizing flight from the senses, and certainly does not advocate a retreat into the depths of a self, who is utterly indifferent to the world's suffering. Nor does Buddhist philosophy call for a rejection of speculative reasoning; on the contrary, it underscores the intrinsic unity of ethical and epistemic purification, so that the mind which is no

---

[15] Dumitru Staniloae, *Orthodox Spirituality* (South Canaan, Pa.: Saint Tikhon Seminary Press, 2003), 188–189. Staniloae talks of the Buddhists' desire for a condition of "egotistic apathy."

[16] See the *Letter to the Bishops of the Catholic Church on Some aspects of Christian Meditation* issued by the Congregation for the Doctrine of the Faith on October 15th, 1989, Section III ("Erroneous Ways of Praying"); or the remarks on Buddhism in Card. Joseph Ratzinger, 'Inter-religious Dialogue and Jewish-Christian Relations,' *Communio* 25, no. 1 (1998): 29–41.

longer obfuscated by desire may finally intuit the emptiness of reality. The Mahāyāna tradition of Buddhism goes even further and asserts that spiritual practice is based on the simultaneous cultivation of wisdom and compassion, through which one may aid all sentient beings to attain enlightenment.

If Maximos the Confessor viewed theology as the expression of an encounter with the living Christ, Buddhist philosophy is also the articulation of a transformative experience of reality that requires a profound personal commitment. The Tibetan rendition of Mahāyāna, itself divided into a variety of schools, strongly emphasizes the role of selfless service in helping one draw closer to the mystery at the core of reality.[17] The Pauline conviction that authentic spirituality is only possible within the ambit of the ecclesial community is echoed by the Tibetan conviction that the pursuit of wisdom and compassion is sustained by the merits of all members of the *sangha*. In both traditions, the *communio sanctorum* embraces those who fight the good battle on this earth; it also extends to those who enjoy the heavenly company of the saints, or dwell with the bodhisattvas in the pure realms. The virtue of charity, however, develops over time no less than the habit of compassion; openness to experience in the totality of its factors eventually uncovers the layers of self-deception with which we sideline the more unsavory truths about the human condition. What Simon Weil called the virtue of *attention* takes the form of *theōria* for Maximos the Confessor, and contemplation of conventional reality for Tsong kha pa. In the Tibetan tradition, the universe where we exist is itself a manifestation of Buddhahood, overflowing with compassion for sentient beings, be they friends or enemies, human or non-human.[18]

In both traditions, contingency is a vehicle of grace; it is not the punishment for a primordial fall, as later Origenists were inclined to think, but, in the words of Gregory of Nyssa, it is like a pair of wings that lift us towards the divine. Maximos' understanding of the hypostatic union strongly emphasizes how the divinity of the Word suffuses and transfigures his humanity, which encompasses both the soul and the body. The body, with all its limitations, is a paradigm of contingency, which in all its manifestation is very much a *pharmakon* in the classical meaning of the term: a medicine which heals if used with caution, but which may also kill if inattentively em-

---

[17] Paul Williams, *Mahāyāna Buddhism* (New York: Routledge, 1989), Ch. 1–3.

[18] This is the ultimate rationale behind the Mahayana teaching on the Buddha bodies, which we will explore in greater detail in Ch. 6. For an introductory overview, see Paul Williams, *Mahāyāna Buddhism* (New York: Routledge, 1989), 167–84.

ployed. Theravada Buddhism was deeply suspicious of our embodied condition; the purpose of practice was a spiritualizing flight from the senses. Tsong kha pa, however, shares the Mahāyāna belief in the propedeutic value of the body, which is invested with a salvific potential: all the more so, if the body belongs to the Buddha, whose life was the ultimate paradigm of wisdom and compassion. Tsong kha pas critical attitude towards schools of Tibetan Buddhism such as rNying ma, which argued for the immediate character of enlightenment, reflected his conviction that the mastery over one's intellect and desires is only attained over time, as the limitations of one's embodied condition would only allow for a gradual intuition of *nirvāna*.[19] Much as the incarnate Word offers the hermeneutic key to the Christocentric nature of the cosmos, the life of the Buddha provides the cues that disclose the intrinsically benevolent character of conventional reality.

Theological reflection, in this perspective, is inextricably linked with *praxis*. The desire of the ecclesial community to spread the good news of the Gospel overflows into repeated, ever provisional attempts to articulate its experience of the divine. In the same way, speculative reflection on the *dharma* flows from the compassion of Buddhist practitioners towards sentient beings. Theology is not authentic if it is not, at some deeper level, an expression of love; McIntosh's fascination with the silent women at the foot of the cross reminds us that theology flows from an experiential, and indeed a loving familiarity with the mystery, which is present in the midst of our fallen world. This attitude informed the work of early Christian writers, whose ultimate allegiance did not go to philosophical systems or doctrinal definitions, but to their encounter with the mystery in Christ. But perhaps, in our day and age, we need to become acquainted with a different tradition to rediscover what is truly particular to our own; and the writings of the Buddhist masters can come to our aid.

NECESSARY JUDGMENTS? PARTICULARITY AND THE CHALLENGE OF DIFFERENCE

The earlier discussion of competing theological particularities underscored the importance for comparative theologians of their readiness to be challenged by the truth no matter where the latter is found to be present. As such, the task of the comparative theologian goes beyond listing points of

---

[19] For an overview of the rNying ma position, see Reginald A. Ray, *Secrets of the Vajra World: The Tantric Buddhism of Tibet* (Boston, Mass. & London: Shambala, 2002), 294–324.

agreement and disagreement between different texts or beliefs. If a comparison is to foster dialogue and reciprocal understanding, it is necessary to formulate a judgment about what constitutes an *irreducible difference*. What is it that makes Christian spiritual theology specifically Christian? Is the transformative character of Christian spirituality a culturally determined rendition of mystical experience, or is it a reflection of particular Christian beliefs? A comparative reading of Maximos' and Tsong kha pa's spiritual theologies will help us answer these questions. Tsong kha pa's version of Buddhism agrees with Maximos in viewing the world of matter as a support for practice, but also underscores its ultimately impermanent character. In the world of the Tibetan master, one must engage conventional reality, and eventually let go; the highest insight has no place for contingency and plurality. For Maximos, instead, God has intended creation as God's eternal dwelling place; the natural order sustains us on our way to salvation, but will be there in the eschaton as the universe is transfigured.

This comparison will show how the Chalcedonian understanding of divine embodiment, while bearing a surprising resemblance to Tsong kha pa's reflections on Buddha nature, entails a much stronger reading of the sacramental value of reality than is ever possible in the Buddhist tradition. If Christian theology is fundamentally incarnational and dialogical, it may not promote spiritual practices where one seeks the ultimate dissolution of the self. As one engages a different religious tradition, the first-order judgment on what a particular text entails must be accompanied by a second-order judgment on whether its claims about ultimate reality are compatible with analogous Christian claims. Theological texts, of course, are not to be treated in the same way in which a natural scientist may treat the specimens in his laboratory. Any experimentally backed observation, if contradicted by new evidence, ought to be discarded, whereas a theological claim does not automatically lose value if faced by an opposing affirmation. However, even the theologian who encounters such tensions between religious traditions must sometimes acknowledge that their accounts of the ultimate nature of reality are not compatible with each other. This means that the Christian theologian must be ready to *critique* claims made by a Buddhist author if these do not dovetail with her theological starting point.

Such a model of theological dialogue through texts is bound to be controversial, if only because it presupposes that theological discourse does not merely exist within the self-contained boundaries of a tradition, but is also ontologically grounded within reality. As Paul Knitter asks towards the end of his work *Introducing Theologies of Religion*, post-modernity's fascination with the role of language in shaping our worldview risks turning into a sort of linguistic determinism, where language effectively prevents us from seeing things differently.[20] One may accept the rather obvious claim that a theological system is a hermeneutic paradigm that offers an all-encompassing explanation of reality, but one may be reluctant to concede that such paradigms are utterly self-enclosed systems which bear no relationship to reality, or which may not even have any objective referent at all! The consequence of what George Lindbeck calls "intratextuality"—the claim that one may view reality from a particular standpoint alone—is to make dialogue between different religious standpoints a virtual impossibility.[21] If dialogue is impossible, then one may at most adopt an attitude of all-embracing tolerance, underscoring what are the perceived "common elements" between the religions that may sustain a shared concern for social justice. To affirm contemporary standards of political correctness, however, may come at a high cost for one's own integrity. The distinctiveness of the Christian message, and indeed of any religious message, is lost as one tries to make it fit broader cultural sensitivities; and as Knitter warns us, a similar strategy effectively shortchanges the world where we live, which is in desperate need of the alternative vision offered by Christianity.[22]

Fortunately, a defensive retreat into a supercilious superiority is not the only alternative to postmodern reductionism. Paul Griffiths's 1991 study, provocatively titled *An Apology for Apologetics*, concedes that it is the nature of each religious viewpoint to be comprehensive, and to argue for the intrinsic superiority of its own meta-narrative.[23] All religious believers, if they truly are such, will affirm the higher explanatory power of their position. For Griffith, this does not entail a renewed legitimation of the partial fulfillment model of dialogue that views Christianity as the summit, towards which all religious traditions, and indeed all their practitioners, unconsciously tend. One may defend one's tradition without for that reason subjugating the religious other to one's "power claim," or, what is the greatest risk, failing to *listen* to what the other has to say. As such, Knitter tells us, inter-religious dialogue must assume an apologetic dimension, in the original sense of the word: one ought to argue for, and defend, the truth that

---

[20] Paul Knitter, *Introducing Theologies of Religion* (Maryknoll, N.Y.: Orbis Books, 2006), 224.

[21] George A. Lindbeck, *The Nature of Doctrine: Religion and Theology in a Post-liberal Age* (Philadelphia: Westminster Press, 1984).

[22] Paul Knitter, *op. cit.*, 183.

[23] Paul Griffiths, *An Apology for Apologetics: A Study in the Logic of Inter-religious Dialogue* (Maryknoll, N.Y.: Orbis Books, 1991).

one claims, since this truth *matters*, for me no less than for anybody else. If, as we said earlier, theology is born out of love, this very same love will induce one to do all in one's power so that everybody can have the same transformative encounter with the divine mystery that one was fortunate to make.

In light of these considerations, I would like to view this project as an apologetic exercise, in the sense that I intend to show how the notion of divine embodiment that Maximos embraces lays the foundations for a theology of contingency which is truly conducive to human flourishing. This does not entail a dismissive attitude towards the Buddhist understanding of the natural order, but merely an awareness of the differences that set the two systems apart, as well as an appreciation of what the implications of the two systems are for spiritual practice. James L. Fredericks' reflections in *Faith among Faiths* express a similar conviction that "a better understanding of the meaning of Christianity" is "the real goal" of the exercise of comparative theology, which takes the form of a dialogical engagement of the other.[24] Fredericks does however go further, and he expresses a deep skepticism about the possibility to build a systematic theology of religions upon the insights gained from inter-religious conversation. In this perspective, comparative theology would be a sort of truncated apologetics, which offers good reasons for choosing an option over another, but becomes most reticent when it comes to present an overall picture of how the claims of different religious systems relate to each other. In an earlier article published in 1995, Fredericks had already expressed his conviction that "abandoning attempts to erect a systematic theology of religions may be difficult for Christian theologians to accept," but "honesty to our current situation requires this of us."[25] Paul Knitter appears to approve this methodological stance when he quips that, instead of seeking to understand other religions on the basis of Christian teachings, one might view "other religions" as "microscopes" with which one looks at the data of Christianity.[26]

My objection at this point, however, is that the very project of comparative theology appears to founder unless a rationale is provided that accounts for our decision to engage another tradition in dialogue. It is not

---

[24] James L. Fredericks, *Faith among Faiths: Christian Theology and Non-Christian Religions* (New York: Paulist Press, 1999), 166–70.

[25] James L. Fredericks, "A Universal Religious Experience? Comparative Theology as an Alternative to a Theology of Religions," *Horizons* 22 (1995): 83–4.

[26] Paul Knitter, *op. cit.*, 205.

after all surprising, when believers convinced to possess the fullness of the truth go on to claim that non-Christian religions are at best expressions of the human need for meaning and comfort. This is the position developed by Karl Barth in his *Church Dogmatics*. There, Barth contends that all "the true and the good and the beautiful" that one finds in "almost all religions" does not change the "judgment" of divine revelation: "religion is unbelief," it seeks to replace God's self-disclosure with a human artifact that is devoid all value.[27] While Barth would eventually nuance this position and affirm the presence of "other lights" beyond the boundaries of Christianity, not a few Evangelical Churches remain committed to the earlier position outlined in *Church Dogmatics*, which effectively dismisses dialogue as a misguided endeavor. In order to move beyond this impasse, it is then necessary to ground comparative theology in a broader vision which at least ascribes *some* propedeutic value to "the religious other."

Fredericks' critique of theology of religions very much sounds like George Eliot's mocking portrayal of Casaubon's "key of all mythologies" in *Middlemarch*. In a subtle attack on the hybris of intellectuals who have lost touch with reality, Eliot tells us the story of an old Anglican clergyman, Rev. Casaubon, who has spent the latter part of his life trying to write a systematic explanation of all the mythological and religious beliefs ever held by humanity. At his death, all that is found on his desk is a series of fragments; and as his young widow Dorothea tries to put them together into some sort of coherent whole, she quickly grows discouraged, and eventually leaves her plan behind. In this perspective, the history of Christian theology has been full of characters resembling Casaubon.[28] In this perspective, Justin Martyr's use of the *logoi spermatikoi* in his *Apologies*; Irenaeus' use of the Noachic covenant as the template for God's continued action outside the Judeo-Christian story; or Rahner's famous teaching on "anonymous Christianity," are all instances of "armchair theology," whose grandiose explanatory visions reflect the desire to accommodate everything within one's own system.[29] These models, which view Christianity as the fulfillment of the reli-

---

[27] Karl Barth, *Church Dogmatics* (Edinburgh: Clark, 1956), I, 2, 299–300.

[28] George Eliot, *Middlemarch: A Study of Provincial Life* (New York: Penguin, 2003).

[29] These authors share a Christocentric understanding of the cosmos, where the incarnate Christ is the interpretive key for the whole arc of human history. See for instance Ireneus, *Adversus Haereses* 3, 18 (PG 7a: 932–938); Justin Martyr, *Apologia Prima* 46 (PG 6: 397–400); Karl Rahner, *Foundations of Christian Faith* (Herder and Herder, 1982), Ch. 6.

gious aspirations of humanity, suffer from a fundamental flaw: they never truly engage the claims of the other traditions.

It is easily conceded that fulfillment theories are like Procrustean beds; one's theological limbs will hardly escape undamaged. The question is whether, faced by unconvincing meta-narratives on one hand, and a radical exclusivism on the other, the only viable solution is merely a suspension of judgment, and claim that no theology of religion is possible "at present." The lack of a theological rationale will make the theological credential of comparative theology look dubious; the much vaunted distinction between comparative theology and the discipline of comparative religions will evaporate in front of a programmed reluctance to engage in what I earlier called "second-order judgments" on irreducible differences. A scholar without any religious commitment might engage in a reading of Maximos the Confessor and Tsong kha pa and explore the points of contact between their respective visions, and do in so in a way that does not differ substantially from a theologian wishing to engage in inter-religious dialogue, but intending to abstain from any judgment as to the value of diverging claims on ultimate reality.

My suggestion is that the drawbacks of the fulfillment model do not warrant a radical rejection of theology of religions, but should serve as an incentive to develop alternative models that respect the integrity of different traditions without subordinating them to a Christian imperialist design. In other words, what other traditions teach us about the meaning and goal of individual existence, and their beliefs as to the ultimate purpose of the cosmos, should not be read as a mere *preparatio Christi*, but as gateways to different aspects of ultimate reality. Heim's Trinitarian theology of religious ends is thus a welcome alternative to the allegedly inescapable choice between an inclusivist meta-narrative and a post-modern pluralist stance. On one hand, Heim is not afraid to take the claims of different traditions seriously; in his view, theological discourse is not a mere linguistic exercise, but an attempt to articulate authentic experiences that transcend the boundaries of language.[30] On the other hand, Heim contends that the Christian model of salvation as communion with a personal God is unable to account for the diversity of eschatological fulfillments that different traditions present as their goal, and he therefore questions inclusivist paradigms that postulate the eventual occurrence of a universal acceptance of Christianity. The Vaiś-

---

[30] S. Mark Heim, *Salvations: Truth and Difference in Religions* (Maryknoll, N.Y.: Orbis Books, 1995), 140–52.

navite Hindu who engages in *bhakti* devotional practices, the Mahāyāna Buddhist who has taken the *bodhisattva* vow, or the Eastern Orthodox ascetic who structures his life around the recitation of the Jesus prayer, they are not all unconsciously moving towards the same spiritual goal; they are seeking different religious ends, or, to use Heim's term, different "salvations." Human beings are not moving towards the same eschatological horizon; they have different goals, and all these goals can foster human flourishing.

Heim's contention is that the ends which various religious traditions offer as "alternative human fulfillments" diverge because they foster "different relations with God."[31] God's Trinitarian nature ensures a multiplicity of dimensions within ultimate reality, which ground the different religious ends, and effectively make possible forms of human flourishing that are independent of Christian "salvation." At first, some might dismiss this position as a stealthy, and perhaps not even too subtle re-introduction of an inclusivist meta-narrative. Heim, however, is not claiming that all relationships with the divine draw their significance from the presence of Christ in non-Christian religions (as in Rahner), or even that alternative religious goals are intrinsically defective (as claimed by magisterial documents such as *Dominus Jesus*).[32] God's "withdrawal" from creation is what ensures human self-determination, and this allows humans to decide whether to believe in God's existence, and whether they believe that God's attitude towards creation is one of benevolence or indifference. W. Rowe's notion of "epistemic distance" in his discussion of Hick's religious epistemology may actually indicate this "open space" left by God's withdrawal, leaving us free to shape our relationship with the divine.[33]

This form of "orientational pluralism," to use Heim's own words, ensures that God's Trinitarian nature as a whole provides the foundations for a theology of religions, avoiding the tendency of inclusivist models to focus on the presence in other traditions of either the Logos or the Spirit, and thus to present the other persons of the Trinity as "economic or secondary representations of that reality." Heim is quite happy, on the other hand, to pause and reflect on the dialectic relationship of the personal and the im-

---

[31] S. Mark Heim, *op. cit.*, 181.

[32] See Congregation for the Doctrine of the Faith, *Declaration "Dominus Jesus" on the Unicity and Salvific Universality of Jesus Christ and the Church*, at www.vatican.va.

[33] W. Rowe, "Paradox and Promise: Hick's Solution to the Problem of Evil," pp. 11–124 in H. Hewitt Jr. (ed.), *Problems in the Philosophy of Religion: Critical Study of the Work of John Hick* (New York: St. Martin's Press, 1991).

personal within divine reality, which in his opinion is mirrored in the variety of religious ends. Patristic Trinitarian theology viewed in the unity of substance the antidote to the fragmentation of polytheism, and in the Trinity of persons the final revelation of divine plurality that was already intuited in the old dispensation. For Heim, the perichoretic exchange of the divine substance between the three persons is the outer boundary of the divine life, a sort of impersonal dimension of God's being that in the Hebrew Scriptures is unveiled in extraordinary events such as the theophany on Sinai, or is perceived in the majesty of nature. Asian traditions such as Hinduism or Buddhism, whose goal is the dissolution of the self in the impersonal embrace of the cosmos, would then be rooted in this aspect of the divine life. The outer personal expression of the divine life, which takes the form of God's self-disclosure through the medium of Scripture or other prophetic utterances, would be the backbone of the Jewish and Islamic tradition, which emphasize God's intervention in specific times and places.

While Christianity shares with the other Abramitic religions an attitude of prayerful attentiveness to God's will, Heim contends that, of all religious traditions, Christianity alone enables its practitioners to share in the inner life of God. Through the person of Christ, the relation of intimacy and love shared by the three persons of the Trinity is broadened to include humanity, whose members are then in some way able to experience God's love and shape their lives accordingly. In this sense, Heim reintroduces a hierarchy of ends, claiming that the Christian end is fuller and more conducive to human flourishing. Yet, unlike Rahner, Heim is not interested in tracing "pointers" in other religions that are fulfilled in Christ; for him, engaging another religious tradition is valuable as it discloses an additional dimension of the divine life. In this way, Christians might be able to find some of the "more truth" that Jesus promises to his disciples as the Gospel of John draws to a close, something that complements or integrates some of the truth that they already knew *in speculo et aenigmate*. It is then possible to claim that God's presence within the religions of the world is also as an invitation to the Christian church to leave behind the certainties of the past and explore how God brings all of humanity in some form of relation with divine life in its different aspects.

While I believe that Heim's model may offer a viable alternative to the fulfillment model or the pluralist paradigm, I do not wish to suggest that this model is not vulnerable to criticism, or that it represents the only acceptable form of theology of religions. In fact, Heim's association of different religious traditions with different aspects of God's Trinitarian life lacks nuance, and offers an overly simplistic understanding of what "Abramitic" or "Asian" religions actually teach. May one truly affirm that "Islam" or "Judaism" focus on the outer dimension of God's life, if one considers the century-long history of Sufism or the innumerable schools of Jewish mysticism? Surely, the writings of Rumi and the Hassidic masters were also seeking to establish a deeper level of communion with the divine. In a similar way, the claim that "Hinduism" and "Buddhism" focus on the impersonal dimension of divine life is also problematic. The intricate sacrificial rites of the Vedic period and the theological reflection on the cosmic role of ritual typical of Mimamsa philosophy are much closer to what Heim calls the "outward aspect" of God's self-revelation. At the same time, the *bhakti* tradition of later Hinduism, as well as the devotion towards the Buddhas, the bodhisattvas and the lamas, show clearly that certain currents within the "Asian" traditions also engage the "personal dimension" of divine life. Finally, familiarity with the Christian tradition shows clearly how numerous Christian mystics such as Gregory of Nyssa or Meister Eckhart did experience the depths of divinity as an impersonal abyss, which had no limits or bounds.[34]

These objections to Heim's model, however, do not touch upon his crucial contention. This is the claim that religious pluralism is a sacramental sign of God's Trinitarian being, and that different religious traditions relate differently to the various dimensions of God's life. My contention is that religious traditions are far too complex and multifaceted to establish one-to-one correspondences between individual religious traditions, or practices, and specific dimensions of the Trinity. At the same time, a version of Heim's model that is less epistemologically ambitious but remains committed to the Trinitarian grounding of religious pluralism may provide a framework for inter-religious conversations that avoids the overly systematizing tendencies deplored by Fredericks no less than Lindbeck's reduction of theological claims to discourse. The task of comparative theology would then also fill the gaps of the initial picture, seeking to establish how particular elements of the different religious traditions illumine specific aspects of the divine life. The role of second order judgment would then be crucial in adjudicating between different religious experiences and insights, associating them with what Heim terms the "impersonal" dimension of the divine life, or the various ways in which God's "personal" reality may interact with

---

[34] See Gregory of Nyssa, *De Vita Moysis* (PG 44: 298–434); Bruce Milem, *The Unspoken Word: Negative Theology in Meister Eckhart's German Sermons* (Washington DC: Catholic University of America Press, 2002).

individual practitioners. In this perspective, theology of religions is the starting point, as well as the point of arrival of the comparative enterprise, providing it with a theological rationale as well as an overarching direction.

My particular project, which seeks to uncover the distinctive character of a Christian theology of contingency, presupposes that speculative reflections from other traditions on the salvific value of the natural order illumine and deepen our understanding of how God interacts with humanity even outside the boundaries of Christianity. Tsong kha pa's reflection on the soteriological import of conventional reality and the central role in his system of the teaching of the Buddha bodies may be taken as engaging God's impersonal *and* personal dimension in a way which Heim's original model would be at pains to accommodate. Yet, even as the Trinity remains the lynchpin of this approach to theology of religions, the central role of divine embodiment in both Maximos the Confessor and Tsong kha pa forces us to reconfigure our comparison, and to view it as the locus where the differences between the two systems will come to the fore. The Chalcedonian teaching of hypostatic union that is the backbone of Maximos' reflections induces us to view Tsong kha pa's theology of conventional reality as a form of *attenuated*, or weaker, sacramentalism, than the one sustained by Maximos' vision.

In this perspective, what distinguishes the two approaches is not that Maximos' spiritual theology fosters a personal relationship with the divine, while Tsong kha pa's understanding of practice acquaints practitioners with God's impersonal aspect. Rather, both approaches engage the dialectic of personal and impersonal that characterize the divine life, but they do so in different ways; it is the task of the comparative theologian to explore in what ways these approaches overlap, and in which ways they differ. At the end of my comparison, we should be able to argue for the ultimate coherence of the Christian vision, while also appreciating the integrity of the Tibetan "religious end" as a spiritual reality that yields an insight into the divine life.

2 AND HIS KINGDOM WILL HAVE AN END: EVAGRIOS PONTIKOS AND THE FLIGHT FROM PLURALITY

The *Vita Sabae* by Cyril of Scythopolis is first and foremost a hagiographic work; the biography of perhaps the greatest figure of early Palestinian monasticism, it turns what must have been a relatively uneventful life into an edifying tale, recounting Saba's extraordinary ascetic feats in the depths of the Judean desert. During the last years of Saba's life, the region of Palestine was troubled by what would later become known as the Origenist crisis. Origen, of course, had died almost three hundred years earlier; indeed, the heyday of the Origenist school of spirituality, led by Evagrios Pontikos and his disciples, had also been over for almost two centuries. For a long time, the theological attention of the Christian East had been directed to the Christological controversies on the manner of the hypostatic union, which the Council of Chalcedon in 451 had not been able to placate entirely. In Palestine and Egypt, in fact, the aftershocks of that Council were visible to all; the Jacobite and the Coptic church had severed communion with the local Patriarchs of Jerusalem and Alexandria, accused of having betrayed the Cyrillian theology ratified at Ephesus. Yet, in the middle of the fifth century, long-buried controversies were given a new lease of life, and the virulence of the disputes was such that it even reached the monks of the wastes of the Judean deserts.[1]

In 531, the 92 year old Saba, who had been living at Mar Saba since 484, left his seclusion to appear in front of the emperor Justinian. Saba was concerned that certain long forgotten Origenist teachings were back in fashion, and that Nonnus, the abbot of another Palestinian foundation and one of the leading supporters of these ideas, had gained the favor of the court.

---

[1] See John Meyendorff, *Christ in Early Christian Thought* (Crestwood, N.Y.: St. Vladimir's Seminary Press, 1975), Ch. 3, 47–69, for a discussion of the Origenist crisis.

Different accounts of the events have survived; it is possible that Cyril, eager to pile praise on Saba, exaggerated his role in Justinian's ensuing turnaround. In any case, Justinian penned his treatise *Adversus Origenem*, and a formal condemnation of a number of propositions taken from Origen's own works was pronounced by the synod of Constantinople (*synodos endēmousa*) in 543. In his *Institutiones*, Cassiodorus mentions that Pope Vigilius of Rome approved of these condemnations, which ten years later would be ratified once more by the fifth ecumenical council.

In fact, renewed sensitivity to the more troublesome aspects of Origenism was not unrelated to the on-going disputes on the manner in which the person of Christ could simultaneously accommodate a human and a divine nature. The Nestorian controversy that had precipitated the Council of Ephesus reflected a deep-seated reluctance on the part of some thinkers to envisage anything beyond a unity by association (*synapheia*) between human nature and the eternal Word of God. Nestorius' uncle, Theodore of Mopsuestia, had argued for a weak form of the union throughout his writings, and while the full-fledged "Two-Sons" Christology that some ascribed to Nestorius was really a forced reading of his position, the tendency to drive a wedge between the distinct *ousiai* posed a variety of problems that monastics like Saba could not afford to ignore. If the eternal Logos was not truly united to our humanity, how could the latter be truly saved? Conversely, if the Word of God had chosen to enter into a union of association with a single human being, did this mean that only this man, out of all humanity, had truly been freed from sin? In a sense, of course, it made little sense to use Origen's positions in support of either Cyrillian or Nestorian Christology, since Origen, as a pre-Nicene author, did not even hold on to the teaching of *homoousia*. Yet, his claim in *De Principiis* that the Word of God had assumed a pre-existent human soul—rather than a human body, or humanity in general—could be read as supporting a looser understanding of incarnation than the one affirmed at Chalcedon.

The role of Origen in shaping the development of Christian theology was unparalleled, and, as Meyendorff points out in his survey of the development of Christology in the East, a majority of Christian authors would continue to hold him in the highest regard despite the condemnation that aspects of his thought would eventually garner.[2] To this purpose, some have argued that the more "problematic" aspects of Origen's cosmology and anthropology were only a minor element in his theological vision, but

---

[2] John Meyendorff, *Christ in Early Christian Thought*, 48–9.

they were unfortunately taken out of their context and given a new lease of life by a group of misguided followers known as "vulgar Origenists." While there is some truth to this distinction, and while few would trace the full extent of Evagrios' eschatological quirks in his *Kephalaia Gnostika* to Origen's original vision,[3] it is undeniable that many of Origen's writings lend themselves quite easily to unorthodox interpretations. While Harl's 1958 study of Origen claimed that the sixth-century re-emergence of Origenism was due to disciples who were "less intelligent than the master" and insisted on the more questionable parts of his writings, Meyendorff actually views these "questionable" traits as crucial parts of Origen's own thought.[4] The dispute, which had already torn apart the Egyptian church at the turn of the fifth century and exacerbated the difficult relations between the Alexandrian see and its provincial subordinates, did not concern Origen's Christological subordinationism, or his more idiosyncratic speculations on different orders of rational beings, but rather hinged on the role played by the material order in God's plan for the cosmos, and therefore in the spiritual life of the individual. Origen's emphasis on the noetic dimension of the spiritual life was a useful resource for those who opposed the more "incarnational" Christocentrism ratified at Chalcedon.

INDIVIDUAL FREEDOM AND THE PROVIDENTIAL COSMOS

The divide between a more "intellectual" and a more "Chalcedonian" theology of the spiritual life constitutes the horizon against which Maximos' own theology would develop in the course of the seventh century. Indeed, Maximos' own vision would be developed largely as a reaction to the Origenist tendencies that lingered in many monastic circles, and that was ultimately incompatible with the Christological consensus of the last two councils. One could argue that, without the Origenist crisis of the sixth century, Maximos' synthesis might have never emerged. For this reason, it is necessary to chart the main points of contention between these two competing

---

[3] See for instance Evagrios Pontikos, *Kephalaia Gnostika*, Book 6, in *Les Six Centuries des 'Kephalaia Gnostica' d'Évagre le Pontique* (trans. A. Guillaumont; Paris: Firmin Didot, 1958), where we are told that at the end of times, rational beings will "create new worlds." Guillaumont's work contains the critical edition and the translation of two Syriac versions of this work, which differ slightly in the wording, but only occasionally in the content.

[4] Marguerite Harl, *Origène et la fonction révélatrice du Verbe incarné* (Paris: Seuil, 1958), 103–20; John Meyendorff, *op. cit.*, 51.

visions, which entail radically distinct approaches to individual spiritual practice.

Origen's own theology of history was developed as a response to the Stoic position that viewed the universe as controlled by blind laws indifferent to humanity.[5] A distinctive preoccupation with the purposive nature of the cosmos was a characteristic that Origen shared with other Christian authors of the first centuries, such as Justin Martyr, who saw Stoic philosophy as one of the greatest threats to the Christian teaching of providence (*pronoia*).[6] For Origen, the history of the cosmos is itself an exercise in divine pedagogy (*paideusis*), whereby God discloses his will to humanity and manifests his desire to be known. Throughout his major work *De Principiis*, Origen argues that the fortunes of the world are not ruled by chance, and that God takes the closest interest in our individual conduct.[7] Without freedom, the spiritual dignity of humanity is utterly lost, since our rational nature entails the ability to choose between alternative courses of action, which God rewards accordingly.[8] Indeed, one must also hold for certain that our present condition in life is largely the result of our earlier choices.

Origen's concern with individual self-determination colors his theological reflections on the origin and the destiny of the universe, but the re-

---

[5] The literature on Origen' theology of history is immense, and inevitably highlights the tension between Origen's vision and later doctrinal developments. Eugène de Faye, in Part 3 of *Origène, sa vie, son oeuvre, sa pensée* (Bibliothèque de l'École des Hautes Études en Sciences Religieuses, 37, 43, 44. Paris: Éditions Leroux, 1923–8) goes as far as to claim that Origen holds no doctrine of redemption. Hal Koch, in *Pronoia und Paideusis, Studien über Origenes und sein Verhältniss zum Platonismus* (New York: Garland Publications, 1979), argues that Origen's soteriology is a personal rendition of themes from the philosophy of Plotinus, and as such it is fundamentally incompatible with the testimony of Scripture. Similar reservations are expressed by Rowan A. Greer in his introduction to *Origen: An Exortation to Martyrdom, Prayer, and Selected Works* (Classics of Western Spirituality, Mahwah, N.J.: Paulist Press, 1979). A more charitable approach seems to characterize Hans Urs von Balthasar's *Origen, spirit and fire: a thematic anthology of his writings* (Washington DC: Catholic University of America Press, 1984).

[6] David E. Hahm, *The Origins of Stoic Cosmology* (Columbus, Ohio: Ohio University Press, 1977); for the relation between early Christian theology and Stoicism, see Jaroslav Pelikan, *Christianity and Classical Culture: the Metamorphosis of Natural Theology in the Christian Encounter with Hellenism* (New Haven: Yale University Press, 1993), 19, 28.

[7] Origen, *De Principiis*, 1, 8, 2 (PG 11: 176–7).

[8] Origen, *De Principiis*, 2, 9, 6 (PG 11: 230–1).

sulting theological vision is quite different from what one might expect from a Christian theologian. On one hand, in his *Commentarium in Mattheum*, Origen is very critical of the Gnostic worldview, which claimed that all beings were created with an unchangeable spiritual, a psychic, or a rational nature (*physis*).[9] Origen found this position unacceptable. For the Gnostics, the ontological divide between God and his creatures did not merely entail that the former was immutable, whereas the latter were subject to change.[10] Rather, the chief distinction hinged on God's unqualified freedom, while created beings were severely limited in their choices by their different *physeis*, which placed them firmly within different "orders" of creation. At this point, one might expect Origen to get rid entirely of the different *physeis*, as incompatible with the testimony of Scripture. This is not however what he chooses to do. In contrast with the Gnostic position, Origen argues that all souls were initially created equal, but because of the use they made of their nature, they developed in different ways, and this constant move up and down the ladder of the different *physeis* characterizes our existence as created beings.[11] In the first chapters of *De Principiis*, Origen insists that this makes us responsible for our destiny; at the beginning of creation, rational beings who cultivated their familiarity with God became angels, and those heavy with egotism became demons.[12]

The question at this point is *how* this ontological change actually takes place, and whether according to Origen it is ever possible to attain a measure of ontological stability. Where should we find guidelines to discern which type of behavior is conducive to spiritual growth, and which is actually detrimental? Even more crucially, if whatever spiritual growth one may attain is only fleeting and provisional, and nothing prevents one from sliding back to sin, is the ascetic life at all worth pursuing? It is to answer objec-

---

[9] Origen, *Comm. Matt.* 10 (PG 13: 835–40).

[10] This is an important theme in many works of the Middle-Platonic period, with which Origen was most likely familiar. See for instance Plutarch, *De Iside et Osiride* (Loeb Classical Library, Vol 5, Cambridge, Mass.: Harvard University Press, 1936), 363–387. The influence on Origen of Hellenist treatments of the immutability of God is discussed in Jean Daniélou, *Origen*, 87–89; Eugène de Faye, *Origène, sa vie, son oeuvre, sa pensée*, 122, 137–141.

[11] Origen, *De Principiis*, 2, 9, 6 (PG 11: 230–1).

[12] Origen, *De Principiis*, 1, 3, 8; 1, 8, 1 (PG 11: 154–5; 176). The teaching that our souls constantly change even as they receive their being from God at every moment would be a major theme in the cosmology of Athanasios of Alexandria; see *Contra Arios*, Or. 3 (PG 26:321).

tions of this sort that Origen develops his doctrine of the Logos, which then spills over into his theology of the created order. God has not left humanity without cues or guidance, and it is the eternal Word of God through whom we are to learn what is God's ultimate plan for the cosmos, and for humanity.

The late classical period was swarming with all sorts of intricate cosmological systems, where archons and syzyges, angels and demons ruled over different spheres of the universe, and served as intermediary between the divine and the human realm. Irenaeus' *Adversus Haereses* enables us to gain some familiarity with the cosmology of the Valentinian Gnostics, a mind-boggling system of self-generating entities that assemble and disassemble in ever-changing arrangements.[13] Echoes of this system are not entirely absent from Origen, who clearly believed that angelic beings were in charge of different parts of the cosmos and could aid or thwart our spiritual progress.[14] At the same time, the one intermediary between God and humanity is the eternal Logos, who is chief among all spiritual creatures, and who is directly subject to the Father. The Logos rules over the cosmos and guides it to its ultimate goal; it is the Logos who becomes incarnate in Christ. Origen's Logos is a regulative intelligence as well as a personal entity; every rational entity in the universe possesses its own *logos*, but all these *logoi*, in their infinite variety, are subordinate to the Logos with a capital "L." The *Commentarium in Johannem* expatiates on the cosmic role of the Logos, who is in charge of the smooth functioning of the universe; yet, the Logos stops short of being fully divine. Reflecting on the prologue of the fourth gospel, Origen writes that the Father alone is worthy of being called God *ho theos* ("God"); the Son may be called *theos* ("god"), as he is the first to share God's divinity by participation, "but not more than that."[15] Later on in the same work, Origen even claims that the distance between the Father and the Son is greater than the distance between the Son and creation.[16] There is only one mediator, and even he is not fully identical with God.

The opposition between the One and the Many that characterizes the early pages of the *Commentarium in Johannem* clearly retrieves Plotinus' notion of the One, who is utterly behind the reach of human discourse, but turns

---

[13] Irenaeos, *Adversus Haereses*, Book 2 (PG 7a: 437–841).

[14] See Origen, *Contra Celsum* 7, 6 (PG 11: 1427); on the doctrine of the guardian angels, which is sometimes traced to Porphyry, see Paul Boyancé, "Les deux démons personnels dans l'antiquité grecque et latine," *RevPhil* (1935): 189–202.

[15] Origen, *Comm Jo* 2, 2 (PG 14: 107).

[16] Origen, *Comm Jo*. 13, 25 (PG 14 : 439).

the Soul of the World towards itself and entrusts it with the government of the cosmos.[17] The natural order is a pedagogical devise, whose purpose is to lead us back to God; indeed, the variety and multiplicity of creation would never have come into existence if rational beings had not turned away from their eternal source in the first place. In line with Neo-Platonic cosmology, Origen insists that the fall took the form of a descent into the sensible, and that redemption is a return to the noetic; good spirits yearn to lose their individuality in the embrace of the lost primordial unity (*henas*), whereas evil ones are attached to their separate identity and seek to preserve it as long as they can.[18] Our embodied condition is thus a punishment as well as a medicine; if our will is attuned to God's will, even matter can become an instrument conducive to the good.[19]

How does the Logos redeem us? Ruling over this world of multiplicity, the Logos seeks to bring back all the *logikoi* to their original—purely noetic—condition. The purpose of history, therefore, is a return to the henad, whose fragmentation led to the emergence of the cosmos. Like a shepherd mindful of his flock, the Logos goes out to look for the lost sheep, ready to face unforeseeable dangers so that no one is ever lost. For Origen, the incarnation of the Logos consists primarily in a descent into the realm of multiplicity, but the incarnation is merely an episode in God's overall pedagogy, and cannot be understood in isolation from it. In his reflections on John's gospel, Origen argues that our redemption is closely connected with the Logos' own "aspects" (*epinoiai*) or "theorems" (*theōrēmata*), which rational beings gradually apprehend as they advance in their spiritual life.[20] At the outset of *De Principiis*, Origen argues that all these "aspects" have a soteriological function; some relate to the cosmic role of the Logos (Wisdom, Truth, Life), whereas others refer to his earthly mission (Bread of Life, True Vine, Lamb of God).[21] Echoing the letter to the Ephesians, Origen talks of the "unfathomable riches" of the Logos, to indicate that one will partake in his mystery to the extent that one has left behind one's attachment to things

---

[17] See *Enneads*, 5, 1, in Plotinus, *Enneads* (Loeb Classical Library, Cambridge, Mass., 1968–88).

[18] Origen, *De Principiis*, 2, 9, 1–2 (PG 11: 225–227); also Hal Koch, *Pronoia and Paideusis*, 37–50.

[19] Origen, *Comm. Matt.* 15, 24 (PG 13: 1323); *Hom in Lev.* 13, 14 (PG 12: 548), on the "bread of proposition."

[20] Origen, *Comm. Jo.*, 2 (PG 14: 103–109).

[21] Origen, *De Principiis*, 1 (PG 11: 115–81).

of this world.[22] When the Logos dwelt among men, his "earthly" attributes were disclosed to all his disciples, but only few were chosen to ascend the mountain and witness his transfiguration in glory.[23]

The type of "knowledge" (*gnōsis*) that familiarity with the Logos communicates is of course far deeper than the mere apprehension of specific "truths." When Origen uses the term "Gnostic," he refers to the transformative knowledge emerging in contemplation, signaling that mysticism is not a mere intellectual exercise. Harl warns readers of Origen that the anthropology of the latter does not drive a wedge between intellect and affections, and that in his worldview familiarity with the Logos has an intellectual as well as an ethical dimension.[24] Operating with a taxonomy of authorities that encompasses the testimony of Scripture as well as the Hellenist tradition, Origen re-organizes Christian anthropology according to a model that blends Pauline and Platonist elements, and that envisages contemplation (*theōria*) as the basis of spiritual progress.[25] Famously, Plato had distinguished three elements within the soul: the intellect (*nous*), the incensive faculty (*thymos*), and concupiscence (*epithymia*). Origen, for his part, adopts the Pauline distinction between spirit (*pneuma*), soul (*psychē*), and body (*sōma*), but Plato's threefold distinction turns into a template for the way in which the *nous* takes charge of the lower functions of the soul. Since the latter were attached to the soul after the fall and mediate between the intellect and material reality, the "truths" which *theōria* discloses about the "aspects" of the Logos translate into ethical injunctions for the *nous*, which learns how to use material reality in a way that is conducive to one's overall spiritual development.

In this perspective, human existence is a constant struggle as the *nous* chooses whether to yield to the "wisdom of the flesh" (the *phronema tēs sarkos* of Rom 8: 6), or follow the indications of the Logos. In his reading of *De Principiis*, Crouzel argues that Origen does not understand the various elements of the soul as ontologically distinct realities, but as tendencies inscribed within the person, who always wavers between the call of the spirit

---

[22] Origen, *Contra Celsum* 6, 77 (PG 11: 1414).

[23] Origen, *Comm. Matth.* 12, 36 (PG 13: 1066), on the Transfiguration.

[24] Marguerite Harl, *Origène et la fonction révélatrice du Verbe incarné*, Ch. 1.

[25] Arguably, Origen's chief allegiance is to the Pauline understanding of the human person, even as he blends it with Paltonic elements. In the fourth century, the school of Evagrios will reverse the order of priorities. See H. Crouzel, *Origen* (Edinburgh: T&T Clark, 1989), 87–88.

and the attractions of the flesh.[26] Whether Crouzel is right or not, what matters is that Origen views our connection with the material world as inherently fraught with danger; without the knowledge that comes from familiarity with the Logos, one will be unable to restrain one's passions and become a victim of one's desires. In *De Principiis*, we are told that God actually withdraws the *pneuma* from the damned, leaving their souls and body to suffer for the consequences of sin.[27]

Later authors such as Gregory of Nyssa would of course share Origen's earlier preoccupation with inner purification, which is a necessary prerequisite for a union with the divine. This purification has therefore an ethical, but also an ontological dimension: Eastern theology often uses the language of "image" (*eikōn*) to indicate the divine mark which from the moment of birth sets us apart from the animal world, and resorts to the term "likeness" (*homoiōsis*) to suggest the condition of the glorified individual who has reached the highest level of spiritual practice. Origen does not deploy this terminology, and chooses to emphasize the importance for spiritual practice of the soul becoming aware of its intimate kinship with the divine.[28] As Daniélou points out in his study of Origen, the *Commentarium in Canticum* conflates the classical injunction to "know oneself" (*gnōthi seauton*) and the Christian command to love and serve God. The Scriptural admonition, "if you know not yourself, o most beautiful among women, arise and follow the steps of the flock," becomes a warning to the soul, which must acknowledge its spiritual nature, lest the passions take over the *nous* and one starts behaving like an irrational animal.[29]

THE *NOUS* AND THE CREATED ORDER: ASCENT THROUGH *GNŌSIS*

The propedeutic activity of the Logos, which envelops the cosmos and culminates in the incarnation, introduces the individual soul into a deeper relationship with the divine. Its signs scattered throughout the universe are like the pillar of light that accompanied the Hebrews through the desert

---

[26] Henri Crouzel, *Théologie de l'image de Dieu chez Origène* (Théologie 34. Paris: Aubier/Montagne, 1956), ch. 3.

[27] Origen, *De Principiis* 2, 10, 7 (PG 11: 239–40); see also *Hom. Matt.* 62 (PG 13: 1698), and *Com. Rom.* 2, 9 (PG 14: 892).

[28] Origen, *Hom. Gen.* 1 (PG 12: 145) and 13 (PG 12: 229).

[29] Jean Daniélou, *Origen*, 296; Origen, *Comm. in Cant*, Prologue (PG 13: 75–76). This study is somewhat dated, but it still contains a number of valuable insights.

until they reached the Promised Land; indeed, all the stages of the journey from the Red Sea Sinai to the river Jordan are taken to symbolize the gradual ordering of the passions by the *nous*.[30] This intellectual initiation (*noetikē eisagogē*) ensures that rational beings may themselves partake in the pedagogical work of the Logos, and help their fellow *logikoi* in their ascent towards God.[31] Marguerite Harl objected that Origen's vision was problematic, since he barely considered the possibility of setbacks, as if the soul never passed through shadows in its advance towards the light.[32]

It was not Origen's emphasis on the intellectual dimension of spiritual practice, however, that would become suspect in the eyes of later writers; indeed the notion of *theōria* developed in *De Principiis* and the Scriptural commentaries would become the basis for later reflection on the spiritual value of contemplation. What would be seen as increasingly problematic would be Origen's tendency to view the soul's kinship with God as almost a natural property, so that spiritual practice does not truly entail a progress, but rather a *retrieval* of a virtual identity with the divine. It is this emphasis on a return to a lost condition of perfection, rather than a progress towards an eschatological reality, that becomes increasingly problematic as the church focuses more and more on the historical event of the incarnation, and less on the acquisition of *gnōsis*.

In the fourth century, however, Origen's emphasis on the noetic dimension of practice would be developed further in the writings of Evagrios Pontikos, who would also attempt a systematic reflection on the ontological relationship between God and the *nous*. Indeed, the Origenist revival of the sixth century that led to Saba's intervention with emperor Justinian owed more to Evagrios' thought than to Origen's original insights. Despite spending the earlier part of his life in Constantinople, where he attended the second ecumenical council and was made a reader by Basil the Great, Evagrios' spirituality was eminently monastic, reflecting his familiarity with the ascetic practices of the Egyptian desert. Indeed, his writings go even further than Origen's in seeing one's struggle with the passions as the litmus test of Christian life, without which one's apprehension of the world is necessarily

---

[30] See Origen, *Hom. on Numbers*, 27 (PG 12: 780–801), where the section on the different stages of the journey carries the title *De mansionibus filiorum Israel.*

[31] Walther Völker, *Das Vollkommenheitsideal des Origenes* (BHTh 7. Nendeln: Kraus Reprint, 1966), 30–42.

[32] Marguerite Harl, *Origène et la fonction révélatrice du Verbe incarné*, Ch. 2–4; also Origen, *Comm in Cant* 1, 3 (PG 13: 94–100). For Origen, the possibility of a 'dark night of the soul' does not seem to exist.

distorted by our sinful desires. It is what Evagrios understands to be the highest goal of the spiritual path, however, that many saw as problematic, in the fourth century, and even more in the sixth.

Following Origen's threefold division of the ascetic life in the *Commentarium in Canticum*, Evagrios claims that the Christian faith has a "practical," a "natural," and a "theological" component (*ek praktikēs kai physikēs kai theologikēs sunestos*).[33] In this perspective, the individual has to undergo a process of inner purification before he or she can engage in contemplation of the natural world, and only at the end of one's inner journey can one apprehend the divine mystery at the core of the cosmos. Analogously, Evagrios talks of three different levels of knowledge: a "practical philosophy" (*praktikē philosophia*) which results in the practice of the virtues, a "natural philosophy" (*physikē philosophia*) which discloses the inner workings of creation, and a final insight into the divine reality. While later authors would use the term *theōria* to indicate all levels of contemplation, Evagrios tends to associate it more closely with the highest stage of one's spiritual journey, claiming that "only those that are pure are worthy of *theōria*."[34] Yet another distinction is that between "kingdom of heaven" (*basileia tōn ouranōn*, the term favored by Matthew) and "kingdom of God" (*basileia tou theou*, the term favored by Luke). In *Praktikos* 2–3, the former indicates a state of dispassion (*apatheia*), "together with true knowledge of what exists" (*meta gnōseōs tōn ontōn alēthous*)[35]; in the Epistle of Basil, the latter is "the contemplation of the very essence of divinity" (*autēs tēs theotētos theōria*).[36] For Evagrios, spiritual practice entails a move from a condition of ignorance to a condition of awareness, where "false knowledge" (*pseudonymos gnōsis*) is superseded by familiarity with the divine plan.

Origen's ambiguity towards material creation, which can be a support as well as a hindrance for inner progress, may also be detected in the writ-

---

[33] Evagrius Pontikos, *Praktikos*, 1 (PG 40: 1221); also in Evagrius Ponticus, *The Praktikos and Chapters on Prayer* (trans. J. E. Bamberger OCSO; Kalamazoo, Mich.: Cistercian Publ., 1981), 15. Origen thought that Proverbs, Ecclesiastes, and the Song of Songs corresponded to three phases of the soul's ascent.

[34] Evagrios, *Kephalaia Gnostika*, 4, 90, in *Les Six Centuries des 'Kephalaia Gnostica'* d'Évagre le Pontique (trans. A. Guillaumont; Paris: Firmin Didot, 1958), 174–175. The term "divine philosophy" (*theologikē philosophia*) is never used.

[35] Evagrios, *Praktikos*, 2–3 (PG 40: 1221–1222); also in Evagrius Ponticus, *The Praktikos and Chapters on Prayer*, 15–16.

[36] Evagrios, *Eighth Epistle—Epistle to Basil* (PG 32: 257). Admittedly, Migne ascribes this epistle to Basil himself.

ings of Evagrios included in the *Philokalia*. In fact, Evagrios' reflections on spiritual practice reflect a deep concern that entanglement with mental images of the material world may block or indeed reverse one's spiritual progress, causing a return to virtually "pagan" practices. We know from various sources that, towards the end of the fourth century, a dispute had broken out in Egypt between monks who thought it helpful to support one's inner prayer with mental images of the Godhead, and others who thought this a deplorable anthropomorphism.[37] Evagrios, of course, thought that no images of the Godhead were at all possible, and that those who still relied on them grossly misunderstood the purpose of spiritual practice. In his *153 Texts on Prayer*, Evagrios warns his readers that they ought to "approach the immaterial in an immaterial manner (*asōmatōs*)," and that "demons" seek to trick us, presenting to our intellect some "strange and alien form (*morphē*)"; they make us imagine that "the deity is there," when in fact "the deity does not possess quantity and form."[38]

Like Origen, Evagrios believes in the soteriological value of the natural order, and is read to acknowledge that contemplation of its structure helps the soul advance towards God. At the same time, Evagrios' writings eagerly stress that in order to reach *theōria*, the soul must "no longer dally with dispassionate thoughts about various things," since even the dispassionate contemplation (*apathetikē theōria*) of created things "impresses their forms upon the intellect and keeps it away from God."[39] The dialectic of unity and particularity is again rooted in the eternal Logos, who "gives being" to the "inner essences" (the *logoi*) of created things. Yet, where for Origen knowledge of the *logoi* already gave a partial insight into the mystery of the Logos, Evagrios is adamant that knowledge of the Logos can only arise "in the state of prayer" after knowledge of creation has been left behind.[40] This pure prayer (*proseuchē*), which uses no verbal or visual supports, is the privi-

---

[37] Glenn F. Chestnut, *The First Church Histories. Eusebius, Socrates, Sozimen, Theodoret and Evagrius* (Macon, Ga.: Mercer University Press, 1998), Ch. 7–8. The tension between anthropomorphite and anti-anthropomorphite monks reflected the tension between the more educated, urban Christians and the rural areas where pagan customs survived for a longer time. This division would become permanent after the schism of the Coptic church that followed Chalcedon. See also Elizabeth A. Clarke, *The Origenist Controversy—The Cultural Construction of an Early Christian Debate* (Princeton, N.J.: Princeton University Press, 1992), 55–57.

[38] Evagrios Pontikos, *153 Texts on Prayer*, 67–68, in *Philokalia*, Vol. 1, 63.

[39] Evagrios Pontikos, *153 Texts on Prayer*, 57, in *Philokalia*, Vol. 1, 62.

[40] Evagrios Pontikos, *153 Texts on Prayer*, 51–2, in *Philokalia*, Vol. 1, 61–62.

lege of those who attain dispassion, whereas less advanced souls must rely on words and images and thus resort to discursive prayer (*psalmotēs*). The implications of this deep cautiousness towards verbal and visual supports is rooted in Evagrios' peculiar Christology, which is developed particularly in the work known as *Kephalaia Gnostika*. In Book 3 of this work, whose Greek original is no longer extant and which survives in two Syriac versions, all that existed at the beginning of time was a "pure intellect" (*gymnos nous*), created in the image of God. Later, this *nous* chose to descend into "movement" (*kynesis*), and acquired a sort of "thickness" (*pachytēs*) which would develop into material creation. While Evagrios never says that matter is intrinsically evil, he is ready to assert that the origin of matter is the conscious decision to assert one's separateness from God.[41] Like Origen, Evagrios does not emphasize the role of the divine image or its obfuscation because of sin, but in the *Letter to Melania*, he notes that, after the fall, the *nous* assumed "the image of animals," becoming in fact worse than brute beasts, which are at least incapable of sin and deceit.[42] The addition of an "animal" aspect to human intelligence (*to logistikon*) refers of course to the appetitive and incensive parts of the soul (*to thymikon* and *to epithymētikon*), which Evagrios, like Origen, derives from Plato. In the context of this tragic deviation from God's initial plan, Christ is said to be the only rational creature that preserved his unity with God at all times, and as such never defiled the purity of his *nous*. In becoming incarnate, Christ's soul did acquire its passible part (*pathētikon*) like every other soul, but always retained full control over the passions. As in Origen's writings, Christ's death and resurrection do not figure prominently in Evagrios' theology; indeed, one could say that they are in no way more important than any other event in Christ's earthly life. What matters is that Christ assumed our humanity and gave us a paradigm of a perfectly rational existence, where the *nous* reins in the horses of the passions and guides the soul to its proper destination.

Evagrios' understanding of the pedagogical role of the Logos is analogous to that developed by Origen in *De Principiis*, where the function of the Logos is to uncover the real essence (or *logos*) of every aspect of reality.

---

[41] Evagrios, *Kephalaia Gnostika*, 3, 6–8: see also 6, 20, on "movement," in *Les Six Centuries des 'Kephalaia Gnostica'*, 100–101, 224–225.

[42] Evagrios, *Letter to Melania*, 6, in Martin Parmentier, "Evagrius of Pontus' 'Letter to Melania'," in Bijdr 46 (1985): Part I, 2–38 (this section contains an English translation of the letter).

Evagrios, however, differs from Origen in two chief respects. On one hand, he underscores how the move from a distorted to a correct perception of the *logoi* entails a process of noetic discrimination (*diakrisis*). In order to adjudicate between different thoughts (*logismoi*) about reality, the *nous* must be able to discern which are of demonic origin, which are ethically neutral, and which are prompted by the Logos and the angels that serve him. Evagrios discusses this theme in his *Texts on Discrimination in Respect of Passions and Thoughts*, using the example of gold.[43] Neutral (human) thoughts about gold bring to the mind images (*eidōla*) of the precious metal, without any attendant passion or greed. Demonic thoughts use the same images to suggest the wealth and pleasures that come from possession of gold. Finally, angelic thoughts suggest how gold might be deployed to the greater glory of God according to the examples that are given in Scripture.[44] Demons are constantly seeking to distract ascetics suggesting *logismoi* that might be neutral or even angelic in other men (such as marriage and the begetting of children), but become sinful if they are entertained by someone who chose to flee the world.[45] For Evagrios, the Pauline warnings that liken this world to a context in an arena (1 Cor 9:24), or call us to wrestle against "the rulers of the darkness of this world" (Eph 6:12) suggest that the struggle for knowledge is indeed a cosmic one, involving the angelic and the demonic hosts.[46]

At the same time, as we already mentioned, Evagrios drives a thicker wedge between knowledge of the individual *logoi* (even if this knowledge belongs to the angelic type) and knowledge of the eternal Logos, who is their ground and yet surpasses them all. *Diakrisis*, which is nothing else but the *discretio spirituum* of later epochs, is only a preliminary stage, after which one should let go of *logismoi* completely. Inner vigilance (*nēpsis*) will enable one to become invulnerable to the temptations that might arise from images (*eidōla*), until the images themselves fade away, and one may ascend to "pure prayer" (*kathara proseuchē*) where one may commune with God. In his *Texts on Discrimination*, Evagrios claims that the kingdom of God was fore-

---

[43] Evagrios, *Texts on Discrimination in Respect of Passions and Thoughts*, in *Philokalia*, Vol. 1, 38–52.

[44] Evagrios, *Texts on Discrimination in Respect of Passions and Thoughts*, 7, in *Philokalia*, Vol. 1, 42–3.

[45] Evagrios, *Antirrhetikos*, 1, 30; 1, 56, in Evagrio Pontico, *Contro i pensieri malvagi - Antirrhetikos* (Italian trans. from Syriac G. Bunge and V. Lazzeri; Magnano, Comunita' di Bose: Ed. Qiqajon, 2005), 26; 42.

[46] Evagrios, *Texts on Discrimination in Respect of Passions and Thoughts*, 5, in *Philokalia*, Vol. 1, 41–2.

shadowed by the vision of the elders, who ascended Mount Sinai with Moses, and "saw the God of Israel: and under His feet there appeared to be a pavement of sapphire, as clear as the sky itself" (Ex 24:10). For Evagrios, our *nous*, when it has shed all images, is *itself* the kingdom of God, and it contemplates its own nature "like a sapphire, or the kingdom of heaven."[47]

THE *KEPHALAIA GNOSTIKA* AND THE DISSOLUTION OF INDIVIDUALITY

There is in Evagrios a deep correspondence between the cosmic dimension of the universe and the interior dimension of the individual; the inner events that mark the ascent of the *nous* towards God mirror the cosmos' movement towards its final goal in God's plan. While remaining in broad continuity with Origen's belief that material creation is a *pharmakon* which did belong to God's original intention, Evagrios tends to understand the emergence of the universe as a gradual process set in motion by the rational beings themselves as they decided to be separate from God. In the *Kephalaia Gnostika*, we are told that everything was created for the purpose of knowing God, though "in the order of being," some things came to exist before others; "more ancient than the first things" (the rational beings, or *logikoi*) "is knowledge (*gnōsis*)," and "more ancient than the second things" (the bodies) "is movement (*kynesis*)."[48] Origen had of course been perfectly aware that his account did not dovetail with Scripture. Yet, he had argued that inconsistencies with the letter of the text should not be a cause of concern, since Scripture also conceals a deeper spiritual meaning that is only accessible to a few.[49] Evagrios follows a similar strategy, and Book 2 of the *Kephalaia Gnostika* associates the creation account of Scripture with the creation of the "second things," claiming that the earlier creation of rational beings was not recorded by Genesis.[50]

Since Evagrios uses the term soul (*psychē*) to refer to the *nous* as it mingles with the body, one might exonerate him from the charge of asserting

---

[47] Evagrios, *Texts on Discrimination* 18, in *Philokalia*, Vol. 1, 49. There are striking similarities between Evagrios' notion of the *nous* and the teaching of the Buddha nature in Mahāyāna Buddhism, to which we will return in a later chapter.

[48] Evagrios, *Kephalaia Gnostika*, 1, 50, in *Les Six Centuries des 'Kephalaia Gnostica'*, 40–41.

[49] Origen, *Hom. Gen.* 15, 5 (PG 12: 244).

[50] Evagrios, *Kephalaia Gnostika*, 2, in *Les Six Centuries des 'Kephalaia Gnostica'*, 44–98.

the pre-existence of souls; yet, in spite of a few terminological differences, Evagrios' account is largely congruent with Origen. In Book 3 of the same work, Evagrios writes that the soul is nothing but the *nous* which has fallen from unity because of negligence (*ameleia*), and has "descended to the realm of action (*praktikē*)" because of its "lack of vigilance (*aphylaxia*)."[51] The *Letter to Melania* similarly argued that, in its nature (*physis*), substance (*ousia*), and order (*taxis*), the intellect is one, but it descended into plurality because of a mistaken use of its self-determination.[52] While the eternal Logos is always turned towards God (*pros ton theon*), the individual *nous* "turned its face away from Unity"; negligence led to movement, and this entailed ignorance.[53] The prologue of the Gospel of John is one more proof of the fact that the Logos was not "negligent," and thus preserved the fullness of *gnōsis*. The fact that some *nooi* moved further away from God than others is the reason behind the existence of *diversity*: like Origen, Evagrios envisages a whole hierarchy of beings, who inhabit different regions of the universe.[54] Yet, again echoing *De Principiis*, Evagrios also insists that creation's "names and modes," which of course are a consequence of movement, are also a channel of grace.[55] The body might be the tomb of the soul (*taphos de psychēs sōma*), but it is a tomb from which, like Christ, one can rise again.[56]

If, on one hand, the endpoint of the universe is the restoration of the lost unity, the individual soul, on the other hand, may *anticipate* this restoration through an inner experience of communion with the Godhead. In the *Kephalaia Gnostika*, one finds again the teaching on the *logoi* and the mental images that is developed in the writings on spiritual direction that are included in the *Philokalia*; this time, however, this inner struggle is rooted within a vast cosmic movement from unity to multiplicity, and back. The path of inner reintegration, which seeks to reorder the passions and attain

---

[51] Evagrios, *Kephalaia Gnostika*, 3, 28, in *Les Six Centuries des 'Kephalaia Gnostica'*, 108–109.
[52] Evagrios, *Letter to Melania*, 6, in Parmentier, "Evagrius of Pontus' Letter to Melania'," 2–38.
[53] Evagrios, *Kephalaia Gnostika*, 3, 22, in *Les Six Centuries des 'Kephalaia Gnostica'*, 106–107.
[54] Evagrios, *Kephalaia Gnostika*, 2, 26, in *Les Six Centuries des 'Kephalaia Gnostica'*, 70–71.
[55] Evagrios, *Kephalaia Gnostika*, 1, 51, in *Les Six Centuries des 'Kephalaia Gnostica'*, 40–43.
[56] Origen, *Exegetica in Psalmos* (PG 12: 1445). The passage comments on Psalm 48.

knowledge of the divine, views the culmination of this path in terms that would be familiar to Western Scholastic thinkers: in the words of Evagrios, "our God is the very source of intelligibility" (*ho de Theos ēmōn auto ginōskomenon estin*).[57] God *is* non-conceptual, non-discursive knowledge; whoever attains this condition has attained knowledge of the divine, and indeed, may be said to partake in the divine nature.

The crucial question at this point is the nature of the Logos' role in effecting the restoration of the universe, as well as the nature of our relationship with the Logos. In light of the years that Evagrios spent in Constantinople and his close acquaintance with some of the leading theologians of the time, it is quite surprising how little the Christological and Trinitarian controversies of the time seem to figure in his reflection; yet, where Origen espoused a form of Christological subordinationism, where not even the Logos truly knows the Father, Evagrios effectively adopts the Nicene position, and states that, unlike the fallen *logikoi*, the Son alone knows the Father as he is.[58] The Logos' rule over the *logikoi* is like that of a pedagogue adapting his teaching style to the level of his pupils; as such, once rational beings all attain *gnōsis*, material creation will exhaust its role, and return to the original undifferentiated condition. If the soul that sheds verbal and visual supports is an instance of realized eschatology, the actual last days of humanity will also unfold in two distinct stages: the resurrection of the flesh at the end of times will be a prelude to a final restoration, when multiplicity and bodiliness disappear entirely. For Evagrios, this return to the *gymnos nous* is suggested by the passage in 1 Cor 15:28, where we are told that at the end of times, Christ will put all his enemies under his feet, and then hand over the kingdom to the Father. For Evagrios, Christ's "feet" are the practice of the virtues and the contemplation of the *logoi*, whereas Christ's kingdom is the period during which multiplicity has the upper hand over unity, and thus creation remains separate from God.[59]

The implications of this position, however, are troubling. The letters of Barsanuphios of Gaza, who lived two centuries after Evagrios, show us how deeply monastic life had been influenced by the Evagrian teaching on *diakrisis*, but also how profoundly the tension was felt between the cosmol-

---

[57] Evagrios, *Kephalaia Gnostika*, 1, 3; 35, in *Les Six Centuries des 'Kephalaia Gnostica'*, 16–17; 32–33.

[58] Evagrios, *Kephalaia Gnostika*, 3, 1, in *Les Six Centuries des 'Kephalaia Gnostica'*, 98–99.

[59] Evagrios, *Kephalaia Gnostika*, 6, 15, in *Les Six Centuries des 'Kephalaia Gnostica'*, 222–223.

ogy and anthropology of Evagrios, and the orthodoxy that had taken shape after Nicaea and Chalcedon. During the fourth and the earlier part of the fifth century, when Christological doctrine had yet to take the shape it would eventually assume in the wake of the Nestorian controversy, there was still a measure of latitude as to what determined the boundaries of acceptable Christological belief. After Chalcedon however, any form of theology or spirituality that did not assert the radical ontological distinction between the individual human person and Christ would become increasingly suspect.[60] This is what makes the *Kephalaia Gnostika* so problematic, much more than the texts included in the *Philokalia*, where little, if any Christology is actually present. If at the end of time all the *logoi* disappear, and we may all have the same knowledge of the Father as the eternal Logos, what is the difference between the eternal Logos and each one of us? As co-heir of Christ's kingdom, a purified *nous* has an ordered understanding of created reality as long as the latter subsists. Later on, as it ascends to the highest *gnōsis*, it contemplates the primeval Unity towards which the Logos is eternally turned. Ultimately, the difference between the Logos and the *logoi* is entirely eliminated; spiritual practice may grant one a *praegustatio* of this unity already in this life, even as its final attainment is postponed to the eschaton.

As early as the fourth century, Theophilos had accused Evagrios in his *Paschal Letter* of denying the eternal kingship of Christ which even Pilate and the Jews (at least implicitly) had accepted.[61] The considerably higher Christology of the fifth and sixth century would be even more reluctant to accommodate such a view, which effectively reduced the incarnation to a passing episode in the history of the cosmos. After all, if the ultimate purpose of the divine pedagogy was the surpassing of the created order, why did the eternal Logos choose to become incarnate in the first place? On one hand, the New Testament never mentions the final shedding of corporeality; indeed, if one takes the Gospel narratives at face value, Jesus' discussion with the Sadducees about the woman who had seven husbands seems to indicate that he, along with the Pharisees, accepted the belief in a bodily resurrection.[62] On the other hand, if the kingdom of the *logoi* will pass away,

---

[60] Barsanuphios' letters were edited by Nicodemos the Agiorite and published in 1816 under the title *Spiritual Letters*, but they are also found in Migne. For the passage in the letters discussing Evagrios, see PG 86a: 892–901.

[61] Theophilos, *Paschal Letter* (CSEL 55: 160–165); see also Elizabeth Clark, *The Origenist Controversy*, 112–113.

[62] Matt 22:23–33; see also Ez 37:1–14; 2 Mac 7 (and the longer version in 4 Mac 8–14:10).

this means that the Logos assumed humanity only for a time, rather than for all eternity; and that in fact the Logos as a separate reality will cease to be completely.[63] As the second council of Constantinople would identify the principle of Christ's subjectivity with the Second Person of the Trinity, Evagrios' position would necessarily be seen as heretical.

In terms of the life of the individual Christian, Evagrios' position would question the very purpose of asceticism and self-denial. Book 4 of *Kephalaia Gnostica*, Evagrios concedes that, in the realm of natural contemplation, some souls are more advanced than others. Yet, "in the final unity, there shall be no heads and no subjects, since all shall be gods."[64] Since the multiplicity of creation will pass away, the very notion of numbers will fade away, leaving only an undifferentiated, purely noetic reality.[65] In his *Commentary on Ephesians*, Jerome, preoccupied with hierarchies of merit, had noted the detrimental consequences of such a doctrine, which viewed no ultimate difference between the strictest ascetics and the most deprived demons.[66] In addition to this, by the sixth century it was also felt that the Evagrian position effectively challenged the sacramental nature of the Christian church, where the spiritual life of the individual was increasingly ordered to a visible hierarchical structure. If the goal of spiritual practice is to attain communion with the divine in the depths of the dispassionate *nous*, what is the use of partaking of the body of Christ in the Eucharist? Evagrios' works on the spiritual life included in the *Philokalia* make no reference to a common liturgical life at all, and portray individual monks who pursue their struggle with the passions in complete solitude, as if the church's Trinitarian and Christological beliefs were only marginal accretions. The renewed controversy around the time of Saba and Justinian reflected a fear that Evagrios' spiritual theology could foment a sort of ecclesial anarchy, where each monk would be his own master, and the orthodox teaching on the incarnation would be questioned or even ignored.

The Chalcedonian definition that by the sixth century had become the starting point of Christological reflection famously emphasized the utter

---

[63] Later, we will see that this comes close to the Christology developed by John Keenan in his *The Meaning of Christ: a Mahāyāna Christology* (Albany, N.Y.: SUNY Press, 1989).

[64] Evagrios, *Kephalaia Gnostika*, 4, 51, in *Les Six Centuries des 'Kephalaia Gnostica'*, 126–127; see also 3, 72, at 158–159.

[65] Evagrios, *Kephalaia Gnostika*, 1, 7, in *Les Six Centuries des 'Kephalaia Gnostica'*, 18–9.

[66] Jerome, *Commentary on Ephesians* 2 (PL 26: 524–528).

consubstantiality of the Son with the Father, on one hand, and with human-ity, on the other. The presence of two different natures resting in one hy-postasis ensured that Christ could be seen as sharing our human nature without in any way jeopardizing his uniqueness as the eternal Son of the Father. In the *Kephalaia Gnostika*, the absence of precise terminology results in a Christology that oscillates between an adoptionist view strongly influ-enced by Origen, and a position where Christ is not ontologically distinct from individual rational beings.[67] In the former case, Christ is not naturally part of the Godhead; the divine nature is the spring whence *gnōsis* eternally flows, and Christ is the "tree of life" that is eternally drinking from that source; the descent of the Spirit at the Jordan was the "gnostic unction," whereby Christ was assimilated to the Godhead.[68] In the latter case, Christ is the vessel of the eternal Logos, who *is* the "substantial knowledge" (*gnōsis ousioudēs*) promised by God; the difference between Christ and us is that he was the first to have received this celestial inheritance.[69] By the sixth cen-tury, many practitioners of Evagrian spirituality had come to deny any es-sential difference between Christ and the purified *nous* for the individual, developing a position known as *isochristism*.[70] Book 5 of the *Kephalaia Gnostika* contains perhaps the most startling statement of the whole Eva-grian *corpus*: at the end of time, every *logikos* will become another Christ, and thus another God, with the ability to *create other worlds*.[71]

For Origen as well as for Evagrios, the created order is at best a sup-port, and at worst a hindrance for the spiritual progress of the individual, who must eventually let go of all references to the material world. This spirituality is a spirituality of *retrieval*, rather than progress; it seeks to re-cover a forsaken noetic identity with the divine, rather than progress to-wards a deeper communion with God. It is also an eminently *contemplative*

---

[67] See Antoine Guillaumont, *Les 'Kephalaia Gnostica' d'Évagre le Pontique et l'histoire de l'Origénisme chez les Grecs et chez les Syriens* (Paris: Seuil, 1962), 147–160.

[68] Evagrios, *Kephalaia Gnostika*, 4, 8; 5, 69, in *Les Six Centuries des 'Kephalaia Gnostica'*, 138–139; 206–207.

[69] Evagrios, *Kephalaia Gnostika*, 4, 9; 6, 14, in *Les Six Centuries des 'Kephalaia Gnostica'*, 138–139; 222–223.

[70] Antoine Guillaumont, *Les 'Kephalaia Gnostica' d'Évagre le Pontique*, 152–160. Another term used for the followers of Evagrios was *protoctists*, indicating their be-lief that all rational beings (*logikoi*) had been created together at the beginning of the universe.

[71] Evagrios, *Kephalaia Gnostika*, 5, 81, in *Les Six Centuries des 'Kephalaia Gnostica'*, 211. This claim, however, is only found in *one* of the two extant Syriac versions.

spirituality: the drama of salvation is played out almost entirely on the stage of one's soul, and the practice of the virtues always takes second place to the pursuit of *gnōsis*. Finally, it is a spirituality of *union*: the mystic who attains pure prayer anticipates within time the union with God that is the destiny of all rational beings. Any form of ontological *difference*, or diversity, is a provisional reality; the goal is to return to Unity.

In light of these considerations, it is difficult to agree with Karl Rahner, when in an early article he notes that the ultimate goal of Evagrian spirituality is the contemplation of the triune God.[72] Von Balthasar comes closer to the mark when in the first volume of *The Glory of the Lord*, he concedes that Evagrios was a genuine mystic, but observes that "he tends towards the boundary of the Buddhist," for whom "forms" are merely "concepts to be overcome."[73] As Raymond Gawronski reminds us in his study of von Balthasar's encounter with the East, the great theologian of "form" (*Gestalt*) could not but feel deeply uncomfortable with Evagrios' Neo-Platonic flight to the Absolute and what he called its "Asiatic peculiarities" (*Asiatismen*).[74] The belief that all the *logoi* of creation should disappear leaving behind a sort of luminous emptiness is for Balthasar a mockery of true "Christian discipleship" (*Nachfolge Christi*), which he believes is better summed up by the Scriptural injunction to take up one's cross. Hagiography, in this perspective, is a better guide to spiritual practice than treatises on *diakrisis*; in the lives of the saints we are confronted by individuals, who let their own existence be transformed by the love of God.

Mackintosh's position echoes von Balthasar's at this point. The women at the foot of the cross did not "let go" of the incarnate Logos or the community of his disciples; in their lives, contemplation and charity were forever intermingled, and neither could supersede the other. The *Kephalaia Gnostika* demotes the created order to a theatre of shadows, from which souls do not flee through an "ecstasy to a Thee," but through an

---

[72] Karl Rahner, "Die geistliche Lehre des Evagrius Pontikus," in ZAM (1933): 22. If one were to consider only the works contained in the Philokalia, this claim might still be accommodated, but the eschatology of the *Kephalaia Gnostika* clearly develops in a different direction.

[73] Hans Urs von Balthasar, *Herrlichkeit-Schau der Gestalt* (Einsiedeln: Johannes Verlag, 1988), 529–530. See also the English translation *Seeing the Form. The Glory of the Lord: a Theological Aesthetics*. San Francisco: Ignatius Press, 1982.

[74] Hans Urs von Balthasar, *Skizzen zur Theologie*, II (Einsiedeln: Johannes Verlag, 1971), 133.

"enstasy to a God"—a God, who "dwells in the inner spirit (*geistesinnig*)."[75] The 6th century condemnation of Origenist spirituality, which Saint Saba hoped would bring peace to his unruly monks in the Judean desert, ensured that this vision would be definitely superseded by the more incarnational theology and spirituality of Chalcedon.

---

[75] Hans Urs von Balthasar, *Herrlichkeit-Schau der Gestalt*, 257.

3 THE REDEMPTION OF PLURALITY: MAXIMOS THE CONFESSOR AND THE CHRISTO-CENTRIC COSMOS

Throughout *Kosmische Liturgie*, von Balthasar's work on Maximos the Confessor, the German theologian reiterates how the key of Maximos' theology is his retrieval of the Chalcedonian understanding of hypostatic union and its use as hermeneutic key to interpret the purpose of the cosmos and human history. In the person of Christ, humanity and divinity attain an equilibrium that upends all human attempts at interpreting reality, and reveals once and for all the dialectical structure of God's eschatological plan, which does not suppress individuality and difference, but rather invests them with the greatest imaginable salvific potential. In this perspective, the task of Christian theology is to articulate the deposit of faith as it rests on the tension between transcendence and immanence, necessity and contingency, absolute and relative.

The purpose of this study is to explore the manner in which Christian theology articulates the notion of divine embodiment and thereby asserts the sacramental dignity of the created order. Maximos' position on this question differs radically from the position embraced by Origen and Evagrios, since Maximos, unlike the figures discussed in the last chapter, turns to his understanding of Christology to assert the salvific value of variety and difference. In the writings of Maximos, ontological diversity is a resource, and individuality never dissolves into impersonality; the theandric mystery of the incarnation is the ground of a prodigious comic synthesis, where the distinctness of humanity is ratified by its indwelling in the eternal Logos.

THE EMBODIED COSMOS: CHRISTOLOGY AS SYNTHESIS OF KNOWLEDGE

"Synthesis" is indeed the key word to understand Maximos' work, and at the outset of *Kosmische Liturgie*, "synthesis" is said to be "the interior form" of Maximos' work.[1] Many scholars concur with von Balthasar's judgment, even if, as noted by the French scholar Philipp G. Renczes, they tend to use this term in different ways, each of them emphasizing a specific aspect of Maximos' thought.[2] For Alois Grillmeyer, the eminent historian of Christian thought, the synthetic character of Maximos' theology consists in an ability to appropriate the insights of the earlier philosophical tradition, and deploy them to illumine the profound reasonableness of divine revelation.[3] For Lars Thunberg, Maximos' theology is synthetic because it eschews the separate discussion of "different entities, such as we know in Western medieval scholastic tradition"; his goal is to offer a remedy to the ever present danger of theological fragmentation.[4] Hans Urs von Balthasar, for his part, claims that what is truly "synthetic" in Maximos' theology is his ability to view the tension between opposing terms as leading to a higher truth, or disclosing a higher theological insight. The vision of cosmic history that emerges from the pages of *Kosmische Liturgie* is clearly influenced by 19th century German philosophy: a re-enchanted universe from the pages of Schelling moves unfailingly towards higher goals, in a Hegelian drama of setbacks and triumphs.

Grillmeyer, Thurnberg and von Balthasar all read Maximos from the perspective of theologians who are familiar with the orthodox "rule of faith" enshrined at Nicaea and Chalcedon. Indeed, in light of the fact that

---

[1] Hans Urs von Balthasar, *Cosmic Liturgy*, 56–65. For a chronology of Maximos' life and works, see Hans Urs von Balthasar, *Cosmic Liturgy: The Universe According to Maximos the Confessor* (trans. by Fr. B. Daley, S.J. San Francisco: Ignatius Press, 2003), 74–80.

[2] Vittorio Croce, *Tradizione e ricerca. Il metodo teologico di san Massimo il Confessore* (Milano: Vita e Pensiero, 1974), 12–20; Philipp Gabriel Renczes, *Agir de Dieu et liberté de l'homme- Recherches sur l'anthropologie théologique de saint Maxime le Confesseur* (Paris: Cerf, 2003), 13–16.

[3] Alois Grillmeyer, *Le Christ dans la tradition chrétienne*, II, 1, *Le Concile de Chalcédoine (451), Réception et opposition (451–513)*, Cogitatio Fidei, 154 (Paris: Cerf, 1990). See also the English translation published as *Christ in Christian tradition*, (Louisville, Ky.: Westminster/John Knox Press, 2002).

[4] Lars Thunberg, *Man and the cosmos—The Vision of St. Maximus the Confessor* (Crestwood, N.Y.: St. Vladimir's Seminary Press, 1985), 31.

Maximos' own understanding of the hypostatic union would become the theological centerpiece of the third Council of Constantinople in 682, it would seem that no one could have better "orthodox" credentials. In his survey of Chalcedon's *Rezeptiosgeschichte*, Grillmeyer notes how Maximos succeeds in appropriating the insights of the earlier philosophical tradition, deploying them to illumine the profound reasonableness of divine revelation.[5] Grillmeyer sees Maximos' work as bringing to a close an epoch of protracted intellectual struggle for the doctrinal articulation of the faith, an epoch that had witnessed the struggle of Athanasios for the Nicene dogma, the Cappadocian elaboration of Trinitarian teaching, and Cyril's reflections on the incarnation.

All these insights are reaffirmed and recapitulated in Maximos' *Ambigua* (also known as *Difficulties*) and his *Quaestiones ad Thalassium*, sweeping works that reflect on Scripture and the writings of earlier writers to underscore the inner congruence of the Christian vision. As Thurnberg stresses, Maximos is convinced that the entirety of his theological vision, which ranges from Christology to anthropology and ecclesiology, is fully implied by the most unassuming passage of Scripture, and is also present, at least implicitly, in the writings of earlier fathers such as Gregory of Nazianzos or Cyril of Alexandria. For Maximos, as for Gregory of Nyssa before him, exegesis is an exercise in spiritual pedagogy; familiarity with the inexhaustible meanings of Scripture sustains our spiritual progress no less than it deepens our grasp of revelation.[6]

Presenting Maximos as "merely" a champion of orthodoxy, however, might result in underestimating the startling originality of his thought, as well as his creative appropriation of themes and concepts from authors whose overall theological vision he actually critiques. On one hand, Maximos' vision is in profound continuity with the Patristic conviction, according to which human reason cannot *create* new theological truths, but merely

---

[5] Alois Grillmeyer, *Le Christ dans la tradition chretienne* (II, 1), 31. See also the English translation published as *Christ in Christian tradition* (Louisville, Ky.: Westminster/John Knox Press, 2002).

[6] See Assaad Kattan, *Verleiblichung und Synergie: Grundzüge der Bibelhermeneutik bei Maximos Confessor* (Suppl. To Vigiliae Christianae, 63. Leiden and Boston: Brill, 2003), 20–32; also, Paul Blowers, *Exegesis and Spiritual Pedagogy in Maximus the Confessor: An Investigation of the Quaestiones ad Thalassium* (Notre Dame, Ind.: University of Notre Dame Press, 1991).

explore the faith delivered to humanity once and for all.[7] On the other hand, the fact that our reason (*logos*) is modeled on the eternal Word (*Logos*) that is forever active in the cosmos indicates that we may strive for a deeper and more comprehensive understanding of this faith.[8] In this perspective, the theological *virtue* of synthesis consists in the ability to get acquainted with one aspect of the divine truth and discern how this particular aspect is tied with all others, as well as with every aspect of human knowledge.[9]

Since the Logos is present in all aspects of the universe and grounds them epistemologically no less than ontologically, all affirmations about the structure of the universe and its relationship with God contain a sparkle of the intelligence that sustains the world. If this is the case, a theologian may recover those elements in concurrent accounts that are in conformity with the Logos, even if these elements are then put at the service of a system that is incompatible with one's vision. This is what Maximos does as he sets out to critique the spirituality of the Evagrian School, and simultaneously retrieves elements of its anthropology and spirituality as building blocks for his own system. The Pauline warning "prove all things, and hold fast all that is good" (*panta dokimazete, to kalon katechete*, 1 Th 5:21) is an injunction Maximos applies to human experience no less than to the writings of the earlier fathers, such as, in his case, Evagrios Pontikos.

Maximos' Christological *Aufhebung* of Evagrian spirituality and his si-multaneous commitment to a cosmological vision can be seen as bringing to a close the centuries-long process, whereby Christian theology appropri-ated the lesson of Hellenist philosophy and used it to articulate the faith found in the Scriptures. In his major study *Christianity and Classical Culture*, Jaroslav Pelikan charts the earlier phases of this dialectic, without which the Nicene Creed as well as Chalcedonian Christology would not have been possible. Pelikan focuses on the development of Trinitarian doctrine in the fourth century, and observes that the three great Cappadocian thinkers (who become four with Macrina the Younger) viewed themselves as "squarely in the tradition of Classical Greek culture," while also sensing that

---

[7] In *Opuscula 9* (PG 91:128b), Maximos asserts the normative character of the teaching of the "inspired Fathers of the Catholic Church and of the Five Holy Ecumenical Synods." As such, any theologian must confront an unchanging "de-posit of faith" and may not depart from it in any way.

[8] In *Q.Th.* 64 (PG 90: 709b), Maximos argues that divine revelation is free of contradiction and cannot but confirm whatever we apprehend correctly in any field of knowledge.

[9] See also Philipp Gabriel Renczes, *Agir de Dieu et liberté de l'homme*, 16–19.

they were also called to "critique" that tradition.[10] Examples of this fundamental ambiguity towards the philosophical tradition are numerous. In the
funeral oration for Basil of Caesarea, for instance, Gregory of Nazianzos
extols his friend's virtues as an orator and a philosopher alongside his dedi-
cation to the priesthood; in another oration, however, he severely critiques
Greek religious observances as well as the myths and fables of the pagan
tradition.[11] In the same way, Gregory of Nyssa claims in *Against Eunomios*
that the truth of the Christian faith is guaranteed by the testimony of pagan
philosophers,[12] but argues that Christians have nothing to learn from the
work of dramatists who wrote theatrical compositions based on Greek mythology.[13] Hellenist philosophers set out to study *the nature of things*; by so
doing, as taught by the Letter to the Romans, they could get an intimation
of the divine. The Church Fathers, who had received an excellent education
and had mastered the writings of the classics, knew quite well that Hellenist
philosophy had gained important insights into the nature of the cosmos. As
thinkers who were first and foremost Christian believers, they also knew,
however, that Hellenist speculation on cosmology and anthropology had to
go through the sieve of divine revelation in order to become a useful tool
for the construction of a Christian theology.

Maximos the Confessor lived and wrote at a much later period, when
the great pagan schools of rhetoric and philosophy had become a distant
historical memory. The academy at Athens where Basil and Gregory had
studied had been closed by Justinian some ten years before the same emperor had turned his attention to the Evagrian controversy, and the study of
classical authors such as Plato and Aristotle was becoming the province of
an ever more restricted circle of scholars. Yet, Maximos' theological system
is closer to the Cappadocians than a distance in time of three hundred years
might let us think. Like the Cappadocians, Maximos thought that a study of
the natural order could buttress and confirm divine revelation, as it would

---

[10] Jaroslav Pelikan, *Christianity and Classical Culture—The Metamorphosis of Natural
Theology in the Christian Encounter with Hellenism* (New Haven, Conn: Yale University
Press, 1993), 9.

[11] Gregory of Nazianzos, *Orationes* 2, 95 (PG 35: 497). See also Paul F. Fedwick, *Basil of Caesarea on Education*, Toronto: Pontifical Institute of Medieval Studies,
1983.

[12] Gregory of Nyssa, *Contra Eunomium*, 1 (PG 45: 308).

[13] Gregory of Nyssa, *Contra Eunomium*, 12 (PG 45: 1119–1120). This develops
the earlier diatribe of Justin martyr in the *First Apology*, who is full of admiration for
Greek thought, but claims that Greek myths are the inventions of demons.

evidence God's economic activity in creation; yet, like Gregory of Nazianzos, Maximos believed that no exploration of the cosmos, no matter how
insightful, could fully disclose the mystery of God. To use a term that
would come in vogue many centuries later in the Christian vocabulary,
natural theology plays an important role as *praeparatio Christi*, as long as its
practitioners do not overstep the mark and convince themselves that the
insights of natural theology might substitute the deliverances of revelation.
The Trinitarian orations, chiding the hybris of the Eunomians, warn us that
the "fullness of reason" (*logou plērōsis*) is only attained through "faith"
(*pistis*).[14]

Another major point of contact between Maximos and the Cappadocians is their shared conviction that the order of nature is an important
source of information to determine the boundaries of ethical conduct. Like
Origen and Evagrios, the Cappadocians appropriate Plato's notion of reason as the charioteer trying to break the unruly horses of our passions; indeed, they come closer to Plato than to Evagrios when they stress that
without sensuality the intellect in charge of the soul's chariot would in fact
be incapable of any spiritual progress.[15] The models of virtue proposed by
Greek culture, however, could not satisfy the Cappadocians or Maximos,
inasmuch as imitation of Homeric or Stoic "virtue" (*aretē*) did not draw one
closer to God. Hector and Diogenes might have mastered their inner
drives, but they were unaware of the fact that human reason is a gift from
God whose ultimate purpose is to make us acquainted with Him. In his
work *De Anima et Resurrectione*, Gregory of Nyssa show us his sister reflect
on the regulative role of the intellect as it reorders our disordered passions,
but Macrina's encomium of human rationality, while echoing Plato, builds
on a Christian understanding of the soul as the locus of the divine image
that is the source of the intellective faculty.[16] While Evagrios' reflections on
diakrisis find no counterpart in the writings of the Cappadocians, Evagrios
shares with the latter a deep conviction that a dispassionate apprehension of
created reality is a prerequisite for ethical progress, and thus for a full flow-
ering of our potential as individuals created in God's image.

From the perspective of Cappadocian natural theology that Maximos
embraces, natural contemplation and reflection on human conduct are not

---

[14] Gregory of Nazianzos, *Orationes* 29, 21 (PG 36: 101).
[15] See also J. Warren Smith, *Passion and Paradise: A Study of Theological Anthropology in Gregory of Nyssa*, New York: Crossroads Publ., 2004.
[16] Gregory of Nyssa, *De Anima et Resurrectione* (PG 46: 21–25).

merely two different functions of human reason, but two mutually supporting and integrating aspects of our response to God's self-disclosure. Indeed,
through natural contemplation God also reveals that men and women differ
from other creatures because they are endowed with rationality and freedom: and it is through rationality and freedom that one can first discern and
finally co-operate with God's design for the universe. In the third century,
Origen's rejection of the pagan notion of "fate" (*tychē*) had led him to
counter the determinism of earlier Stoic cosmologies with a notion of history as an exercise in divine providence; and more than a hundred years
later, this notion could be traced in the writings of Evagrios no less than in
Basil's conviction in the *Haexameron* that the cosmos was ordered by the
eternal Logos, and the latter played a crucial pedagogical role in disclosing
God's plan. Indeed, for all these authors, what is crucial is that, if we are to
respond to God's invitation and bring our ethical conduct in line with the
injunctions of the eternal Word, we must possess the ability to respond
freely; if such ability is disfigured by sin, we must do our utmost to retrieve
it. The ability to discern God's mark in creation is thus inextricably linked
with the ability to take a correct ethical decision; to use the terminology that
Immanuel Kant would develop some fourteen centuries after the Cappadocians, there is no distinction between pure reason, which analyses the phenomenal world, and practical reason, which is the instrument of the individual's self-determination.

This ethical dimension of the connection between cosmology and anthropology entails that every individual who can discern God's plan in the
universe can co-operate with Gods' own plan. In the preface to *De Hominis
Opificio*, Gregory of Nyssa points out that the ability to contemplate, but
also to leave a mark on creation is indeed what constitutes the divine image.[17] This position, which views *praxis* as no lower an activity than *theōria*,
entails a far greater appreciation of the salvific value of the created order
than was ever contemplated by the Origenist or the Evagrian systems. *De
Hominis Opificio* and the *Kephalaia Gnostika* equally stress the importance of
discerning order and purpose in the multiplicity of creation, but the former
differs from the latter as it asserts that plurality is neither ontologically, nor
ethically inferior to unity. If the kingdom of the *logoi* is destined to disappear, no human effort, no matter how great, will survive the eschatological
suppression of difference. The Cappadocian Fathers insist on the contrary
that from its very inception, the universe was conceived as a *composite* (*synthe-*

---

[17] Gregory of Nyssa, *De Hominis Opificio*, Preface (PG 44: 125–128).

tos) unity, destined to remain such for all eternity.[18] The composite nature of man, who belongs to the material no less than the spiritual realm, is a reflection of the structure of the cosmos, and indeed it can be said that man is himself a sort of second world, reflecting the inner structure of creation.

Writing in the first half of the seventh century, Maximos is eager to stress the continuity of his position with the earlier tradition, but while the Cappadocian Fathers, writing before Chalcedon, were more directly focused on Trinitarian doctrine, Maximos' writings are also characterized by an overarching Christological thrust. On one hand, Maximos' treatment of textual hermeneutics in his *Quaestiones ad Thalassium* underscores the primacy of the spiritual sense—and the parenetic role of exegesis—in broad congruence with the example of Origen's use of Scripture.[19] On the other hand, the different *Ambigua* start off as commentaries to passages from the writings of Gregory of Nazianzos, and it is the latter that afford Maximos the inspiration for some of his most adventurous theologizing. Maximos' goal is to show the ultimate ontological congruence between the fundamental structure of the cosmos, the dynamic interplay of humanity and divinity in the incarnate Christ, and the embodied character of individual spiritual life.

For Maximos, as for the Cappadocian Fathers, God utterly transcends the created order, but he alone comprehends it fully; in his providential wisdom he guides the cosmos to its eschatological transfiguration. Spiritual life cannot result in a renewed awareness of our identity with the divine; while this is the assumed goal of practice in the *Kephalaia Gnostika*, Maximos follows Gregory of Nyssa in postulating an unbridgeable gasp between humanity and the Godhead.[20] The knowledge of self that is nurtured by *theōria* and *praxis* rather discloses our *affinity* with the divine; contemplation and the virtues make us understand that our condition of rational, and yet embodied creatures is a gift from God, which enables us to *understand* the structure of the universe, and *use* it to foster God's glory. Macrina the Younger, with words that are an implicit critique of the Origenist position, insist that the body and the soul were created at the same moment in time.[21] The incarnate Christ, who shared our human nature while remaining hypostatically

---

[18] See for instance Basil of Caesarea, *Haexameron* I (PG29b: 4–27).

[19] Paul M. Blowers, *Exegesis and spiritual pedagogy in Maximus the Confessor: An Investigation of the Quaestiones ad Thalassium* (South Bend, Ind.: Notre Dame University Press), 1991.

[20] Gregory of Nyssa, *De Hominis Opificio*, 16 (PG 44: 180).

[21] Gregory of Nyssa, *De Hominis Opificio*, 16 (PG 44: 180).

united with the Father, provides the hermeneutic key of the universe, show-ing that multiplicity and contingency, and thus our embodied condition, have a part in the divine plan. The tension between unity and multiplicity is not oppositional, but integrative; contingency is invested with eschatological significance because Christ made it his own, and his own it shall remain even after the world as we know it has come to an end.

INTERPRETING TABOR: THE TRANSFIGURATION AS HERMENEUTIC EVENT

Maximos' exegesis of the Transfiguration narratives is one of the highest points of the whole of the *Ambigua*. With considerable linguistic and con-ceptual virtuosity, Maximos presents the cosmic order as an intimation of the divine wisdom which is revealed in Scripture and which becomes fully manifest in Christ, in an endless dialectic of concealment and disclosure. Let us now examine an excerpt from *Amb. 10*, and see in greater detail how Maximos uses Origenist and Chalcedonian elements to develop his Chris-tological vision.[22]

> Thus, [...] even some of Christ's disciples, to whom it befell, thanks to their pursuit of virtue (*di'aretēs epimeleian*), to ascend and be raised to-gether with Him to the mountain of His manifestation, as they saw Him transfigured and inaccessible because of the light of His countenance, overawed by the splendor of His garments (*tē tōn esthēmatōn lamprotēti kataplēktoi*) and intuiting that He had become all the more venerable in virtue of the honor that was attributed to Him by those who stood on either side of Him (meaning Moses and Elijah), passed from the flesh to the spirit (*apo tēs sarkos eis to pneuma*) even before shedding their carnal life, through the supersession, wrought in them by the Spirit, of the ac-tivities that are in conformity to sensation (*tē enallagē tōn kat'aisthēsin ener-geiōn, en autous to pneuma enērgēse*);[23] indeed the spirit had lifted the pas-sionate impediments (*tōn pathōn ta kalymmata*) which thwarted their no-

---

[22] This *Ambiguum* begins with a discussion of an excerpt of Gregory of Na-zianzos, *Or* 21, 2 (PG 35: 1084–1086), where Gregory argues that the practice of "philosophy" enables material creation to become one with God; see Maximos the Confessor, *Amb. 10* (PG 91: 1108a). Maximos develops this theme further by em-phasizing the pedagogic role of *theōria*.

[23] This theme of "energetic supersession" is crucial to Maximos' understanding of *theōsis*. See Jean-Claude Larchet, *La divinisation de l'homme selon Saint Maxime le Confesseur* (Paris: Editions du Cerf, 1996), 582–93; also *Amb. 20* (PG 91: 1237c–1240a).

etic activity. Thanks to Him, after they purify their spiritual and their bodily senses, they apprehend the spiritual *logoi* of the mysteries that are disclosed to them (*tōn paradeichthentōn mysteriōn tous pneumatikous ekpaideuontai logous*). Thus, the most blessed splendor that shone as the rays of the sun from Christ's own countenance—indeed, it vanquished the power of the eye—, this they mystically apprehended as a symbol of His divine nature, which is beyond the intellect and sensation and substance and knowledge (*hyper noun kai aisthēsin kai ousian kai gnōsin*).

In knowing that He had neither form nor comeliness,[24] and that the enfleshment of the Logos concerned One who is fairer than the sons of men,[25] they were led to understand that He was in the beginning, and that He was with God and He was God,[26] and through an exercise of theological apophasis that exalted Him as being utterly uncontained by all (*pasin achōrēton*), they were gnostically lifted to the glory as of the Only Begotten of the Father, full of grace and truth. And the whitened garments bore the symbol of the words of Holy Scripture (*ta de leukathenta himatia tōn rēmatōn tēs agias graphēs pherein*), inasmuch as the words then became to them clear and transparent and luminous, and were grasped without any obscure enigma and shadow of symbol, and revealed the hidden concept of the things there suggested (*ton en autois onta te kai kalyptomenon paradēlounton logon*), as they [the disciples] threw themselves into the plain and correct gnosis of God and freed themselves of the passion that is turned to the world and the flesh; or they [the garments] were the symbol of created reality itself (*tēs ktiseōs autēs*), a symbol that entailed the suppression of the vulgar conjecture (*rhyparas hypolēpseōs*) which until then seemed to transpire from it.

This [the vulgar delusion] was the belief of men who were victims of delusion and were chained solely to the sensation (*tōn ēpatēmenōn kai monē aisthēsei prosdedemenōn*) wrought by the wise variety of the different forms that constituted it, [a variety] which on the contrary, like a garment, signified according to analogy the dignity of that world which carried the power of the creating Logos (*tēn tou genesiourgou logou dynamin*).[27] Both things which we are saying, in fact, shall be adapted to this text, since the latter, as is logical, is on our account concealed in uncertainty in

---

[24] Is. 53:2.
[25] Ps. 44:3.
[26] John 1:1.
[27] Maximos the Confessor, *Quaestiones ad Thalassium* 25 (PG 90: 332 ac). The contemplation of nature (what Gregory of Nazianzos called "philosophy") discloses the presence of the Logos.

both these senses, so that we do not dare unworthily to turn to the reality which we cannot comprehend, such as the Logos in the case of Holy Writ, and to the Creator and maker and fashioner (*ōs ktistēs kai poiētēs kai technitēs*) in the case of creation. For this reason I claim that he who wants to direct in a blameless manner his right conduct towards God has absolute need of the gnosis that comes from Scripture in the Spirit, and of the natural contemplation (*physikēs theōrias*) of the things according to the Spirit, so that the two laws, which are equal in honor (*isotimous*) and teach the same things—I mean the natural law and the written law (*ton te physikon kai ton grapton*), neither of which is superior or inferior to the other—can show, as is logical, that he who loves wisdom in a perfect manner becomes a lover of perfect wisdom.

(Amb. 10, PG 91: 1125d-1128d)

What happens here? At the top of Mount Tabor, the apostles are granted a vision of the glory of God incarnate, as for a moment the mutual exchange of properties between the humanity and the divinity of Christ is made manifest to their eyes. It is not only the face of Christ that is transfigured, however, but also his clothing, and for Maximos this Scriptural detail lends itself to two different—though mutually complementary— interpretations. On one hand, Christ's garments indicate the words of Scripture in which the eternal Logos lies hidden, but which, through the grace of God, enable the receptive soul to discern the presence of Christ in both the Old and the New Testaments. On the other hand, they also indicate creation in the inexhaustible variety of its forms, a prism through which one can discern the power of the Logos who directs the cosmos towards its ultimate goal. In the Transfiguration, we are invited to contemplate prayerfully the inner consistency of the law of nature and of the law of Scripture, both of which find their lynchpin in the eternal wisdom of God; to borrow a term favored by von Balthasar, the mystery of the cosmos and the mystery of Scripture have revealed their ultimate Christic form, which alone sets the term for a coherent hermeneutics.

For Origen and his followers, the ontological distinction (*diaphora*) between the different components of creation, as well as their unceasing transformation and movement (*kinēsis*) are symptoms of a fundamental disorder, a wound that must be healed.[28] For Maximos, on the other hand, the

---

[28] Maximos the Confessor, *Amb. 7* (PG 91: 1089b); also Polycarp Sherwood, OSB, *The Earlier Ambigua of St. Maximus the Confessor and His Refutation of Origenism* (Studia Anselmiana 36. Rome: Herder, 1955), Ch.1–2; also Lars Thunberg, *op. cit.*, 81–3. In *Ep. 2* (PG 91: 36c), Maximos notes that love brings man to authentic *stasis*,

incarnation is the incontrovertible guarantee of the soteriological value of the created order. The belief that creation has been raised to the dignity of God's own dwelling sits uneasily with any cosmology that demotes matter to a mere consequence of, or support for, sin. The backbone of spiritual practice consists in the ability to contemplate (*thaumazein*) the Christocentric nature of reality; but the very fact that each aspect of the cosmos has its ontological foundation and ultimate significance in Christ ensures that variety and difference in creation are part of God's salvific design.

Maximos' resort to the doctrine of the *logoi spermatikoi* connects him, of course, to the Origenist and Evagrian tradition which in its turn goes back all the way to Plato's *Timaeus*.[29] Maximos' understanding of the mediation of the eternal Logos, however, significantly differs from that of earlier authors, and enables him to reach very different conclusions while resorting to the same conceptual tradition. While in the first century of our era Philo had identified the *logoi* with the essences of all things dwelling in the mind of God, the Neo-Platonic tendency to envisage the *logoi* as static realities was then challenged by the Pseudo-Denys. In *De Divinis Nominibus*, the latter assimilated them to the divine will, or more precisely viewed them as different expressions of this will, giving rise to different components of creation.[30] In questioning the Platonic ascription of ontological superiority to *stasis*, the Pseudo-Denys was already moving beyond the Origenist account of creation. Maximos follows the Pseudo-Denys and claims the variety and the complexity of the cosmos as flowing from God's own will; in this way, he undercuts the Origenist position that construes material creation as a remedy to sin.

Even more crucially, Maximos goes on to explain how the distinct *logoi* are in relation (*anaphora*) both with the eternal Logos and with the incarnate Christ. The organizing principle of this relation is of course Chalcedonian Christology. In the hypostatic union humanity and divinity co-exist "without division and without confusion" (*adiairetōs kai asynchytōs*), but the two

---

but this *stasis* is the culmination of spiritual practice, and not something that pre-existed creation.

[29] For Plato, time is "movement," whereas eternity is "fixed" in unity. See Plato, *Timaeus* (trans. by Donald Zeyl. Indianapolis, Ind.: Hackett Publishing Company, 2000), 37d.

[30] See Pseudo-Denys, *De Div Nom* 2, 4 (PG 4: 216–9); 10, 3 (PG 4: 385–90). See also Hans Urs von Balthasar, *Cosmic Liturgy: The Universe According to Maximos the Confessor* (trans. by Brian Daley, S.J. San Francisco: Ignatius Press, 1961), 136, note 3.

ousiai cannot subsist without the hypostasis of the eternal Word; in the same way, all aspects of creation mix and interact without confusion, but their *logoi* draw meaning and purpose from the Logos.[31] In *Amb. 10*, the eighteen different interpretations of the Transfiguration narrative reveal the extent to which the Chalcedonian dialectic of unity and plurality can provide a template for an intelligent retrieval of centuries of cosmological speculation, but they also show that a theology of spiritual practice cannot be developed ignoring man's fundamentally embodied reality.

We know from history that Maximos was one of the chief actors in the prolonged Christological controversies that were tearing apart the Christian East in the sixth century. The Armenian Church and large sections of the Coptic Church had refused to accept the Chalcedonian dogma, and over the following two centuries all that had been accomplished by the various attempts at reunion was to ensure that the manner of the hypostatic union continued to be the lynchpin of theological debate.[32] Maximos' theology of Christ's wills and operations was developed out of his conviction that the monothelite controversy was not a marginal theological issue, but affected the very core of the Christian understanding of incarnation, Christ's full and complete assumption of a human nature wounded by sin. In his study of Maximos' critique of monothelitism, Demetrios Bathrellos notes how the Rumanian theologian Dimitru Stăniloae traces monothelite Christology to Origen's mistrust of human motion (*kinēsis*).[33] The association of the will with the hypostatic rather than the natural dimension is seen as indicative of a reluctance to envisage *change* as part of nature, rather than a later unfortunate addition. Maximos postulates a human will in Christ to stress that ethical self-determination (*autexousiotēs*) is an intrinsic part of being human, and that no part of our nature was left out of Christ's redeeming work.

Gregory of Nyssa had already implied as much when discussing the providential role of our "garments of skin," noting that "the changeable

---

[31] This use of the Chalcedonian dialectic of unity and plurality as an interpretive paradigm for cosmology, as well as spirituality and anthropology, is discussed by Adam G. Cooper throughout his study *The Body in Saint Maximus the Confessor: Holy Flesh, Wholly Deified* (Oxford: Oxford Early Christian Studies, 2005).

[32] See Lars Thunberg, *Microcosm and Mediator: The Theological Anthropology of Maximus the Confessor* (2nd ed. Chicago and La Sale, Ill.: Open Court, 1995), 36–40, on the relationship between Maximos and Neo-Chalcedonianism.

[33] Demetrios Bathrellos, *The Byzantine Christ: Person, Nature and Will in the Christology of St. Maximus the Confessor* (Oxford Early Christian Studies. Oxford: Oxford University Press, 2005), 89.

character of our nature, which earlier seemed an obstacle, has become a wing in our flight towards the height."[34] Maximos retrieves the Cappadocian position and views the ability of the individual to determine one's destiny as an integral part of God's plan for creation, established from all eternity and now revealed in Christ. Indeed, as Maximos presupposes a belief in the fundamental ontological freedom of the individual, the notion of providence (*pronoia*) in *Amb. 10* is accompanied by the notion of judgment (*krisis*), as well as the possibility of different outcomes that Evagrios effectively ruled out. God shall confer eternity (*aei einai*) to the outcome of our choices; the episode of the agony in the garden, where Christ wills our salvation with a human will, is indicative of the extraordinary dignity of our freedom.[35] In *Amb. 42*, the hypostatic union is presented as the manifestation in the flesh of the guiding principle of the comic order, who chooses to enter time so as to provide us with an example of what makes a human existence worthy of the divine favor.[36]

If we go back to the *Amb. 10* , we can see how the faculty of deliberation (*gnōmē*), healed from the consequences of sin, rescues the inner self from fragmentation, ordering every activity to the greater glory of God:

> […] And the mixture and the composition of beings are like the symbol of our deliberation (*gnōmē*). Deliberation, in fact, uniting itself to the virtues (*kratheisa gar autē tais aretais*) and uniting the virtues to itself, can also put together a world that is most worthy of God (*theoprepestaton*). And position is the teacher of the behavior (*ethous*) that conforms to deliberation since it must remain firm in what has appeared to be good; thus behavior sets itself up in opposition, in no way allows circumstances to move it in any way from its position in conformity to reason. And joining on the other hand position to movement and mixture to difference, they [the saints] have indivisibly (*adiairetōs*) distinguished[37] the substance of the cosmos into being and difference and movement, and thinking that by reasoning in an inventive and appropriate manner (*epinoian*)[38] it is

---

[34] Gregory of Nyssa, *De Perfecta Christiani Forma* (PG 46: 285).
[35] Maximos the Confessor, *Amb. 10* (PG 91: 1133bc-1136a).
[36] Maximos the Confessor, *Amb. 42* (PG 91, 1316b).
[37] An obvious Chalcedonian reference.
[38] See also Maximos the Confessor, *Amb. 7* (PG 90: 1077c). The term *epinoia*, ultimately of Stoic origin, indicates for Origen the modality, whereby our mind perceives the multiplicity of the Son, in opposition to the unity of the Father. See Origen, *Comm in Matt*, 10, 17 (PG 13: 876–880), where our *epinoiai* of Christ are opposed to his hypostasis.

possible to see the Cause in created things, they have reverently understood that this is to be, and to be wisely, and to live (*einai kai sophōn einai kai zōn einai*). [....] And yet, attentively beholding creation from the point of view of position alone, they united into three the five modes of spiritual contemplation which we have mentioned, acknowledging that creation, with its inner *logos*—taking into account the heaven and the earth and all that is contained therein—,[39] is teacher of ethical and natural and theological philosophy.

Here one may see how Maximos builds upon Origen's and Evagrios' earlier reflection and yet integrates it into the Chalcedonian system. The propaedeutic role of the incarnation had of course been present in Origen's corpus, but Origen insisted on driving a wedge between the incarnate manifestation of the Logos and the fullness of its mystery. In the *Homiliae in Leviticum*, for instance, Origen implied that, in the highest stages of spiritual progress, contemplation of the Word made flesh would be superseded by contemplation of the divine Wisdom which is eternally veiled in mystery.[40] Similarly, as we saw earlier, Evagrios thought that the incarnate Christ had been the first to receive the "gnostic unction" making him equal to the eternal Word, but thought the mysterious reality of God was yet higher than the mystery of the Logos. For Maximos, on the other hand, there is *nothing* which is higher than the incarnate Christ, to whom all *logoi* of creation incessantly point. One might object that in *Amb. 20* he chides those who do not let the Word "return to the Father," clinging to the outer form like Mary Magdalene on Easter morning. Yet, Maximos does not enjoin a spiritualizing flight from the senses. What he is doing is to warn against forgetting that the material channel of revelation is not identical with the mystery it discloses. The words of Holy Scripture, or the shining garments of Tabor, simultaneously reveal and conceal the eternal Word, much as the forms and shapes of the natural world both manifest and veil their creator.

It is thus not the case, as in Evagrios, that the knowledge of the *logoi* should be left behind in order to ascend to the highest degree of familiarity with the divine: the knowledge of whatever was created through Christ "is naturally and fittingly revealed through Him (...) while He is known to be

---

[39] Again a Stoic definition; see Roberto Radice, *I Frammenti degli Stoici Antichi* (Milano: Bompiani, 1999), 612.

[40] Origen, *Hom Lev.*, 4, 6 (PG 12: 473–475); a similar opinion is expressed in the *Comm. Jo.*, 1, 8 (PG 14: 33–36). This concern would resurface in Calvin's notion of *extra calvinisticum* (the mystery of the incarnate Christ was finite and thus it was not *capax infiniti*).

separate from the order of creation, it is His desire that the *logoi* of every-thing intelligible and sensible are made known together with Himself."[41]
Amb. 10 shows that there is no knowledge which surpasses the knowledge of Christ:

> we shall also know those *logoi*—evidently the last ones we can reach—of which we have received creation as teacher, and the five modes of con-templation (*pente tēs theōrias tropous*) joined to them, by means of which the saints have divided creation devotedly collecting the five mystical *logoi* which are contained therein. They have divided creation into sub-stance (*ousian*), movement (*kinēsin*), difference (*diaphoran*), mixture (*krasin*) and position (*thesin*).[42] They said that three of these *logoi* served preeminently to divine gnosis, so that they could lead us to it: they are the one according to substance (*kat'ousian*), the one according to move-ment (*kata kinēsin*) and the one according to difference (*kata diaphoran*). By means of them God makes Himself known to men, who can deduce from things the proofs of the fact that God is creator and provider and judge (*ōs dēmiourgou kai pronoētou kai kritou*). To educate us to virtue and to familiarity with God, I mean the one according to union and the one according to position (*ton kata krasin kai ton kata chrēsin*), because the man who is formed by them becomes God (*ho anthrōpos theos ginetai*), un-dergoing his being in God[43] as a consequence of existing reality (*to theos einai pathōn ek tōn ontōn*), and seeing by the intellect the manifestation of God flowing from His goodness in its entirety, and logically conforming himself to this most pure goodness. That indeed which the pure intellect sees through pious gnosis by means of its nature, the pure intellect can also undergo, because through virtue the pure intellect (*ho katharos nous*) becomes that in its very self (*touto kai pathein dynatai*).
>
> (*Amb. 10*, PG 91: 1133a-1133b; 1136b-c)

---

[41] Maximos the Confessor, *Amb. 10* (PG 91: 1156a).

[42] The five modes of contemplation are a re-elaboration of a theme already present in Evagrios Pontikos; see Antoine Guillaumont, *Les Six Centuries des Kepha-laia Gnostika d'Évagre le Pontique* (Paris: Firmin-Didot, 1958), 1, 27, whose original model might well be the five "categories" of Plato's *Sophist* (trans. by Eva Brann. Newburyport, Mass.: Focus Publishing/R. Pullins Company, 1996) 254d-255c. See also Lars Thunberg, *op. cit.*, 72, and Andrew Louth, *Maximus the Confessor. The Early Church Fathers* (London and New York: Routledge, 1996), 23–6.

[43] Maximos the Confessor, *QTh 22* (PG 90: 320cd); also Pseudo-Denys, *De Div Nom*, 2, 9 (PG 3: 647–6488).

Here, we see that the hypostatic union explodes the dichotomy between apophasis and kataphasis; what is concealed is revealed through negation, and what is revealed is concealed through attribution.[44] The *logoi* of creation and the *logoi* of Scripture disclose in equal manner God's on-going involvement with creation; their ultimate correspondence is underscored by the fact that both of them provide instruction for those who, seeking to please God, wish to lead a virtuous life. The *logoi* of *ousia* aid the human mind to discern God's creative activity; the *logoi* of *dynamis* and *heterotēs* indicate God's providence, as well as His eschatological commitment to preserve the plurality of the cosmos. What ultimately matters, however, is that through the *logoi*, God offers ethical guidance to humanity, and in the earthly life of Christ, He provides us with a pattern we can contemplate (through *theōria*) and imitate (through *praxis*).[45]

In this perspective, spiritual practice acquires a twofold purpose. On one hand, it does *not* seek to restore a forsaken noetic purity, but rather it strives to accomplish a harmony between the different faculties of the individual while respecting their specific character. On the other hand, it sets out to transform the fragmentation (*diairesis*) of creation into a harmony that respects diversity (*diaphora*).[46] In this vein, *Amb. 41* illustrates on the scope of our moral agency and emphasizes the soteriological potential of the interaction between the composite nature of humanity and the complexity and variety of the cosmos:[47]

> "Man therefore did not move (*ou kekineto*) by turning to the reality that is unmoved (*to akinēton*), which was its beginning (I mean God), thereby obeying his nature, in conformity to which he had been created (*physikos, ou dedemiourgeto*); rather, he moved himself turning to the things that were subject to him, and which God had given him the order to rule (*autos theothen archein epetagē*). Thus, man, of his own free will, moved ignorantly (*anoetos*) against nature." Thus he made a perverse use (*parachrēsamenos*) of the natural power that had been given him to unite the things that were divided (*pros henōsin tōn diērēmenōn*) according to their origin, and used it

---

[44] Maximos the Confessor, *Amb. 10* (PG 91, 1129cd).

[45] This is the chief argument of Maximos' work *Liber Asceticus* (PG 90: 911–958). See also Maximos the Confessor, *The Ascetic Life and the Four Centuries on Charity* (trans. by Polycarp Sherwood, OSB. Mahwah, N.J.: Paulist Press, 1955).

[46] Walter Voelker, *Maximus Confessor als Meister des geistlichen Lebens* (Wiesbaden: F. Steiner, 1965), 471–89.

[47] Maximos the Confessor, *Amb. 41* (PG 91: 1304a–1307).

instead to divide those that were united, and thus he almost returned wretchedly into non-being.[48]

The cosmic work of mediation between the different *logoi* is of course inaugurated by the incarnation of the eternal Logos:

> This is why natures are renewed (*kainotomountai physeis*),[49] and, paradoxically, that which is beyond movement in its nature moves, so to speak, remaining unmoved (*kinoumenon akinētos*), and God becomes man to save the man who had perished and unites in himself the fragments (*ta rhēgmata*) of the total nature that because of man had been scattered, and showing the universal *logoi* of partial things that had become manifest (*tous epi merous propheromenous logous*) and thanks to which is accomplished the union of what is separate, he fulfils the great counsel (*tēn megalēn boulēn*) of God the Father, recapitulating in Himself all the things, those in heaven and those in earth, since in fact it had also been in Him that they had been created.[50] And surely, after having begun—by moving from the division that is in us—to the general reunification of all things in himself (*eis eauton anakephalaiōsas ta panta*), He becomes perfect man, on our account coming from us and like us, having all our characteristics in a complete manner, with the exception of sin… […]

(Amb. 41, PG 91: 1308c-1309a)

Our task is then to imitate Christ's mediatorial work and to continue it in our everyday life. Where Origen and Evagrios saw the Logos as mediating between unity and multiplicity with the aim of restoring the former, for Maximos the task of Christ is to heal differences without erasing them. In this way, where the goal of the Origenist mystic is to escape contingent realities into the undifferentiated realm of the *nous*, Maximos' theology of the spiritual life enjoins a far more optimistic engagement of the creation, which has been invested with an unprecedented dignity. In *Amb. 41*, Maximos lists five different aspects of our mediatorial work, all of which reconcile different aspects of the natural order: the two sexes, the inhabited *oikoumenē* and the rest of the world, the earth and the heavens, the created and the uncreated.[51] In line with his Chalcedonian commitment, Maximos en-

---

[48] See also Maximos the Confessor, *Amb. 7* (PG 91: 1084d–1085a).

[49] Gregory of Nazianzos, *Or.* 39, 13 (PG 36: 347–50) on the unification of opposites.

[50] Is 9, 5; Eph. 1,10; Col 1, 16.

[51] Maximos the Confessor, *Amb. 41* (PG 91: 1304d-1313b). See also Lars Thunberg, *Man and the Cosmos: The Vision of Saint Maximus the Confessor* (Crestwood,

visages the multiplicity of the visible as a prism making the invisible (i.e., the divine) ultimately accessible to human beings; resorting to a Rahnerian expression, we could say that for Maximos the *logoi* of creation constitute the grammar of our infinite possibilities of self-expression, whereby we learn to echo God's own incarnate speech.

DIACHRONIC REDEMPTION: CONTEMPLATING THE INCARNATE WORD

An implication of the Christocentric nature of Maximos' theology is that, compared with the vision that underpins Origenist spirituality, Maximos views the redemption as a process that unfolds *in time*. The mystery of our salvation begins in the humdrum of our daily life, but its fruits are carried into eternity. As argued by Heinzer in his study of Maximos' Christology, a tendency exists to view the doctrinal controversies following Chalcedon as merely unfolding what was implicit in the conciliar definitions. Yet Heinzer notes how the Chalcedonian definition did not consider that the incarnation of Christ had a diachronic as well as a synchronic dimension, touching our nature as well as the way in which this nature evolves *through time*.[52] According to Oscar Cullman, the Classical, or better the Stoic expression of time was the circle, while its Scriptural counterpart was the ascending line.[53] The assertion of an eternal intellectual world and the belief in the cyclical return of rational created beings to their noetic origin could not easily accommodate the drama of the incarnation, but it could certainly welcome the Origenist vision and its yearning for a lost unity. Among those who, like Evagrios, were sympathetic to the notion of a cyclical universe, the importance of *theōria* would always outweigh that of *praxis*, since *theōria* enabled the individual to transcend her embodied condition and to enter an ever accessible, disembodied state free from the shackles of temporality. Maximos' incarnational approach, on the other hand, is based on a tension between the past and the future. The latter does not, indeed, it *cannot* reproduce the for-

---

N.Y.: St. Vladimir's Seminary Press, 1997), 80–91. These five forms of mediatorial work are not to be confused with the five *logoi* that keep creation together and that are discussed in *Amb. 10.*

[52] Felix Heinzer, *Gottes Sohn als Mensch: die Struktur des Menschseins Christi bei Maximus Confessor* (Freiburg: Universitätsverlag, 1980), 12–20.

[53] Oscar Cullman, *Christ and Time: The Primitive Christian Conception of Time and History* (Louisville, Westminster/John Knox Press, 1950), 36.

mer, since every individual life leaves its mark on the evolution of the cosmos.

In this more dynamic perspective, the *logoi spermatikoi* are still the Christological ground of our existence, but they are not a fixed blueprint setting the boundaries of our being. Rather, as one can see in *Amb. 42*, each *logos* is a matrix for a process of development, which is potentially present from the beginning, and involves a spiritual as well as the material dimension:

> Now [...] every noetic and every sensible nature (*noētē te kai aisthētē*)—in other words every simple and every composite one (*ēgoun haplē kai synthetos*)—whatever is its mode, never obtains partially the beginning of its generation to being, nor can it subsist only in half (*ex ēmiseias moiras hyphistasthai*). But if it is a composite nature, it immediately subsists, whole and perfect in the perfection of its parts, and has no interval of time (*kata ton chronon diastasin*)—no matter how long—among its constitutive parts, in relation to itself or one with the other. If instead it is a simple nature, in other words noetic, in the same way it subsists immediately of its own nature together with its perfect *logoi* (*hama tois eautēs aparaleiptos logois*), immediately perfect, absolutely no time in any way keeps it separate from its specific *logoi*.[54] And in fact never in the past nor in the present nor in the future shall there ever exist among the things a nature that is in its own *logos* that which now it is not, nor it is now or shall it be later that which before it was not. In fact the production and the substantiation in conformity to the *logoi* of those things, whose *logoi* obtained from God perfection together with existence (*para tō Theō hama to einai to teleion eschon*), admit of absolutely no addition and no subtraction from what they effectively are [...]
>
> (*Amb. 42*, PG 91: 1345a-1345c)

While Stoic philosophy could envisage the cosmos as an effectively self-sufficient system, Maximos insists that creation exists only by participation (*metochē*) in the divine wisdom. By establishing an indestructible ontological link between the Logos and our human condition, a ground is established for a participation in the divine life where our individuality is wholly retained; on the other hand, by presenting the divine mystery as surpassing

---

[54] Maximos is here anticipating the Scholastic discussions on the unity of the substantial form of Christ. See Jean-Pierre Torrell O.P., *Saint Thomas Aquinas*, Vol. I, *The Person and His Work* (Washington: Catholic University of America, 2005), 187–91.

the limits of human knowledge, Origen's belief in further falls engendered by satiety (*koros*) is ruled out.[55]

Another, fundamental, difference between the Origenist approach and Maximos' theology of the spiritual life is the latter's emphasis on the role of agapic love in fostering communion with God. In the *Disputatio cum Pyrrho*, Maximos defends his conviction that our fundamental moral agency (*hē kata physin autexousiotēs*) is a natural faculty which mirrors the divine freedom; through this faculty, we know that we were created in the divine image.[56] Yet, while Evagrios seems to have little interest in the role of the ecclesial community, Maximos emphasizes the communitarian dimension of spiritual practice, which finds expression in the mutual practice of charity, and—as we will see later in greater detail—in the celebration of the liturgy.[57] Charity (*agapē*) supersedes knowledge (*gnōsis*) as the goal of ordered human existence; divine likeness can only be attained if *theōria* is accompanied by *praxis*. The incarnation of the eternal Word reveals the Christocentric structure of the cosmos; first and foremost, however, it is an act of selfless love, and it is this selfless love that we are to imitate.

In his 1952 study of this theme in Maximos the Confessor, Hausherr searches his writings of Maximos for various references to love of self (*philautia*), and goes on to chart Maximos' understanding of this notion as the root of inner spiritual disintegration.[58] Love of self makes human beings unresponsive to God's love. It gradually erodes their ability to love God and to love their neighbor, locking them in an attitude of sterile self-centeredness. Even if the divine image is inscribed in the *logos* of humanity, love of self destroys "the outward manifestation of its unity."[59] Contemplation of the signs scattered by the eternal Logos in creation does then serve as an antidote to love of self. Overcoming this effective addiction to fragmentation, one may acquire a habit of self-giving love which reintegrates one's personality after the pattern of Christ.

The opening of the *Capita de Charitate* points out that the love which is attained when we are no longer attached to the things of this world make us

---

[55] See also Polycarp Sherwood OSB, *op. cit.*, 181–92.

[56] Maximos the Confessor, *Dispute with Pyrrhus* (PG 91: 324 d).

[57] Lars Thurnberg, *The Man and the Cosmos—The Vision of St. Maximus the Confessor*, 94–96.

[58] Irénée Hausherr, *Philautie. De la tendresse de soi à la charité selon Saint Maxime le Confesseur* (Rome: Pont. Institutum Orientalium Studiorum, 1952).

[59] Lars Thurnberg, *The Man and the Cosmos—The Vision of St. Maximus the Confessor*, 95.

more receptive to divine knowledge (*gnōsis tou theou*) above everything else.[60]
There is still an emphasis on the role of *theōria* as in Evagrios, but the notion that charity is the highest mark of our affinity with God signals a clear
move away from Origenist spirituality. As Völker notes in his work on
Maximos' spiritual theology, the *Liber Asceticus*' greater agapic and Christocentric thrust is fundamentally dialogical, and implies that such a dialogical
dimension marks even the highest stages of *gnōsis*. On one hand, the Evagrian influence on Maximos is particularly strong as he outlines the importance of discrimination: the eight-fold classification of the vices, as well as
Plato's theory of the three-tiered soul, is virtually identical to Evagrios' own
discussion of these themes.[61] On the other hand, unlike Evagrios, Maximos
does not believe that the goal of practice is to shed the lower levels of the
soul, but rather that the noetic and the sensitive dimension should reach a
condition of harmonious equilibrium. The renewed appreciation of difference that we have seen mark Maximos' cosmology is also evident in his
construal of the dynamics of the human soul. The ontological drive to *stasis*
which dominates Origen's universe is turned here into an impulse to reach
God through the practice of the virtues, which are nothing but our passions
ordered to their original goal.

For Maximos, human freedom is always embedded and circumstantial;
our ontological structure compels us to practice the virtues (*physei men gego-
namen pros aretēn*),[62] and it is quite clear that there can be no ascetic life that
doe not unfold according to the fundamental law of nature (*kata nomon phy-
seōs*).[63] Developing a position that is already present in the *Stromata* of Clement of Alexandria, Maximos claims that sinful behavior is ultimately the

---

[60] Maximos the Confessor, *Capita de Charitate* 1, 1, in *Philokalia*, Vol. 2, 53 (PG
90: 961).

[61] Maximos the Confessor, *Liber Asceticus*, 19 (PG 90: 935–936) where, in the
words of the "old man" (perhaps Sophronios), love, self-mastery, and prayer are
the virtues associated with the three parts of the soul. See also Maximos the Confessor, *The Ascetic Life and the Four Centuries on Charity* (trans. and intro. P. Sherwood,
OSB; London: The Newman Press, 1955), 114.

[62] Walther Völker, *Maximus Confessor als Meister des geistlichen Lebens*, 204; 292–
300.

[63] Maximos the Confessor, *Amb.* 5 (PG 91: 1057 c). A similar claim is made by
Maximos in *Q.Th 40* (CCSG 7: 192), where it is claimed that the way in which virtues are to be practiced (*tōn aretōn hoi nomoi*) was inscribed in our nature by God
from the beginning (*kata physin ex archēs theothen egraphēsan*).

consequence of ignorance about our embodied condition.[64] Maximos uses the term *gnōmē* to indicate the deliberative process which precedes moral decisions, and which is vulnerable to mistakes as long as one is not fully attuned to one's nature. Arguably, Maximos' construal of spiritual practice as an exercise in gnomic reform based on the contemplation of the created order constitutes a defense of natural law approaches to ethics against the modern tendency to view morality as wholly determined by culture and as virtually independent from our given psycho-physical constitution. In this perspective, Pyrrhos' notion of hypostatic will must be rejected as it severs the link between moral autonomy and humanity's *logos*, and turns ethical deliberation into an arbitrary exercise of choice.[65]

As we noted earlier, however, Maximos' dynamic understanding of the *logoi* is meant to ensure that the latter do not restrain individual development, but actually offers guidelines for fuller flourishing. Admittedly, however, the question remains as to how the demands of the *logos* may in practice be reconciled with the desire for originality and self-expression. According to Polycarp Sherwood, one may find an answer in Maximos' work *Liber Asceticus*, which in tone and purpose closely resembles the Evagrian treatises on monastic life in the first volume of the *Philokalia*. Sherwood focuses on the distinction between *logos* and *tropos*, which for him, as for von Balthasar, is closely related to the distinction between nature and person.[66] In this perspective, the person (or hypostasis) *uses* human nature to pursue his or her diverse existential goals, and *tropos* is the term that indicates the manner of this "use" (*chrēsis*). Bernardo de Angelis suggests that not only is it the case that the hypostasis determines the *tropos*, but the *tropos* also shapes the hypostasis and effectively determines the type of person that we are going to be.[67] Of course, Christ's divine hypostasis used our

---

[64] Clement of Alexandria, *Stromateis* 6, 17 (PG 9: 370–374).

[65] Of course, Phyrros did not see the implications of his position this way, since, in his mind, the will was not an essential capacity to Christ's human nature, but belonged more properly to the divine person who was the subject of each and every one of Christ's acts. It is only when one follows Maximos' arguments that one sees the extent to which this Christological thinking impoverishes human agency.

[66] Polycarp Sherwood OSB, introduction to Maximos the Confessor, *Liber Asceticus*, 82.

[67] Bernardo De Angelis, *Natura Persona e libertà- l'antropologia di Massimo il Confessore* (Quaderni dell'Assunzione. Rome, Armando Editore, 2002), ch. 2.

humanity in the most perfect manner, and thus gave us an example of the ideal *tropos*.

Sherwood resorts to the Scholastic categories of "natural" and "supernatural" to distinguish between our use of human nature and Christ's own use in the hypostatic union. This is probably more indicative of Sherwood's Thomistic inclinations rather than of Maximos' understanding of the use of "nature," which rather allowed for a whole variety of uses. In Christ, humanity's fundamental orientation to God is fulfilled to the utmost degree, and our human will is fully conformed to the divine will. In every other individual, the degree to which the *gnome* is attuned to God's plan varies in relation to our degree of success in the inner combat that accompanies spiritual practice. The endless variety in human destinies reflects humanity's irreducible freedom; our fundamental orientation towards good or towards evil arises "out of the choice of the volitional faculty" (*kata proairesin en tō thelēmati*).[68]

In this perspective, the spiritual combat that in Evagrios was carried out in virtual isolation from the world becomes a constant *imitatio Christi*. While for Evagrios the condition of inner equilibrium was characterized by utter detachment, in the *Capita de Charitate* Maximos closely associates *apatheia* with *agapē* or *charis*. Both of them are the result of self-control, which overturns love of self thanks to faith in God (*pistis tō theō*).[69] In the latter part of the *Liber Asceticus*, Maximos argues that Scripture calls Christians to fear but first and foremost to love God, in the certainty that our trust in Him shall eventually be vindicated.[70] As love predisposes us to knowledge of God, and this helps us love God more deeply, spiritual practice is akin to a virtuous circle: the gnostic experiencing of what was earlier believed through faith strengthens one's resolve to persevere in *praxis*, and this lets us penetrate ever more deeply into the divine mystery.

In the *Liber Asceticus*, the long inner struggle that leads to *apatheia* and self-control (*egkrateia*) mirrors and continues the battle waged by the incarnate Word against the forces of evil.[71] As the elder says at the opening of

---

[68] Maximos the Confessor, *Capita de Charitate* 4, 13, in *Philokalia*, Vol. 2, 101–102 (PG 90: 1051–1052).

[69] Maximos the Confessor, *Capita de Charitate* 1, 2, in *Philokalia*, Vol. 2, 53 (PG 90: 961–962).

[70] Maximos the Confessor, *Liber Asceticus*, 28–30 (trans. P. Sherwood), 119–121 (PG 90: 933–936).

[71] Maximos the Confessor, *Liber Asceticus*, 5 (trans. P. Sherwood), 105–106 (PG 90: 913–916).

the *Liber Asceticus*, by taking flesh from the Virgin, the Word of God set an example by his life, and did do so out of love for humanity.[72] As usual, noetic contemplation of Christ's actions provides us with an *exemplum* teaching us how to discriminate between good and evil. Christ's three temptations in the desert, for instance, are paradigmatic of the three things (food, wealth, and reputation) where individuals are most vulnerable to the lures of the devil.[73] Even more significantly, the devil is said to have tempted Jesus to transgress the commandment of love, making him confront the spiteful Pharisees, but Jesus endured their mockery and preferred to die on the cross rather than fail to love his neighbors. In the context of Christian *praxis*, there can be no contradiction between love of God and love of neighbor, since Christ practiced both to the utmost.[74]

The spiritual program of the *Liber Asceticus* accompanies the contemplation of the incarnate Christ in continuous meditation on the Word of God, though in this text the latter is certainly subordinated to the former. The brother's anxious entreaties as to the way to attain inner peace induce the elder to explain the connection between familiarity with Scripture and the practice of the virtues engendered by fear of God; reading how David and later Paul could resist temptation helps us in our struggle with the passion. The elder's resort to the Neo-Platonic three-tiered template setting the intellective part of the soul over and against the vegetative and sensitive parts is thus integrated by citations from Scripture illustrating the reasonableness of the Lord's commandments, in such a way that the lower parts of the soul are not crushed, but thrive insofar as they are properly ordered towards the higher soul.[75] As in Evagrios, the goal of prayer is to purify the *nous* from all attachment to material things and to unite it with God in unceasing prayer; for Maximos, however, it is desire (*erōs*) that inclines our mind to seek union with the Godhead once it has been reoriented to its true goal. Thus, *theōria* and *praxis* are to be pursued simultaneously; contemplation of the Word furnishes the guidelines for the practice of the virtues, but

---

[72] Maximos the Confessor, *Liber Asceticus*, 3 (trans. P. Sherwood), 104–105 (PG 90: 913–914).

[73] Maximos the Confessor, *Liber Asceticus*, 10 (trans. P. Sherwood), 108–109 (PG 90: 919–920).

[74] Maximos the Confessor, *Liber Asceticus* (trans. P. Sherwood), 12; 15, 110; 111–112 (PG 90: 921–922; 923–924).

[75] Maximos the Confessor, *Liber Asceticus* (trans. P. Sherwood), 24, 116–117 (PG 90: 929–930).

the practice of the virtues introduces one to ever deeper degrees of contemplation.

THE ESCHATOLOGICAL BANQUET: THE ENDS OF CONTEMPLATION AND THE KNOWLEDGE OF GOD

It should be clear by now that Maximos' work accomplishes a fundamental Christocentric turn in the understanding of *theōria*. The *Ambigua* and the *Liber Asceticus* signal that Origen's appropriation of Classical natural theology has now been supplemented by a specifically Christian vision, where the incarnate Word becomes the ultimate hermeneutical key of the created order. The constant perusal of Scripture also becomes an instance of *theōria*, and possesses as transformative and integrative a potential as the unmediated contemplation of the cosmos, since both Scripture and the cosmos derive their inner structure from the eternal Word. In this perspective, Sherwood's claim that *theōria* "may be omitted" from spiritual practice on the ground that "natural contemplation" is not explicitly mentioned in the *Liber Asceticus* appears misguided; for Maximos, *theōria* is not coterminous with contemplation of the created order, but it embraces a broader set of activities that reflect the activity of the eternal Logos in the cosmos and in human history, in space as well as in time.[76] For Evagrios, the chief purpose of *theōria* was to undercut ignorance, while for Maximos, it is the purification of our *erōs*; a soul torn apart by disordered desires is no less incapable of loving than of knowing God. Since the hypostatic union is the highest instance of God's love for the human race, our love for God grows by the extent to which we put into practice what the incarnation teaches about our common humanity.[77]

Maximos' indebtedness to Evagrian spirituality resurfaces in texts where the relation of *theōria* and *praxis* is discussed more systematically; in the *Capita de Charitate*, where Maximos outlines the relation between spiritual practice and our assimilation into the divine nature, we find echoes of Evagrios' preoccupation with mental images. Maximos' approach, however, indicates how far the theological reflection on the created order has moved from the time of the anthropomorphite controversy in the 4th century. *Theōria* is seen as the beginning of deification; as we grow more and more at-

---

[76] Polycarp Sherwood OSB, introduction to *St. Maximus the Confessor—the Ascetic Life and the Four Centuries on Charity*, 87–88.

[77] Jean-Michel Garrigues, *Maxime le Confesseur: La charité, avenir divine de l'homme* (Paris: Beauchesne, 1976), 22–30.

tuned with God's intended plan for the cosmos, we begin to co-operate with it and are thereby assimilated into the divine nature. Through contemplation we attain inner re-integration, but we also imitate the eternal Logos, inasmuch as we collect in our *nous* the *logoi* of all created things and thus bring it, so to speak, to an inner spiritual union. By the time of Maximos, the teaching of the *logoi tōn ontōn* and of their pre-existence in the eternal Logos had gained a secure foothold in the tradition of Christian cosmological speculation. The Pseudo-Denys notes that the *logoi* of each individual nature dwell in the Logos "in an unconfused union" (*kata asugchyton henōsin*), serving as exemplars for all that exists;[78] when, in the *Capita de Charitate*, Maximos notes that rational natures know God by apprehending the harmonious wisdom (*sophia*) of creation,[79] he is effectively echoing Gregory of Nyssa's claim in the *Hexaemeron* that in every work of creation (*pragma*) one can discern God's "wise and creative power" (*logos sophos kai technikos*).[80] Thus, natural contemplation directs the mind's gradual ascent towards God, which is the ultimate *aitia* of all that exists; at the same time, true knowledge of God can only be attained leaving behind all forms and shapes, since, as Evagrios warned in the treatise *On Prayer*, the mind has to regain utter simplicity to experience the One who is utterly beyond composition.

Bearing this in mind one can understand the rationale informing Maximos' claim that the effect of observing the commandments is to "free from *pathos* our conceptual images of things," while the effect of "spiritual reading and contemplation" is to "detach the intellect from form and matter."[81] The person who strives to imitate Christ's earthly conduct can then discern the divine plan in creation and view its individual components with dispassion; if we do not misuse the conceptual images of things, we shall not make a wrong use of the things themselves.[82] At the same time, a

---

[78] Pseudo-Denys, *De Divinis Nominibus* 5, 7 (PG 4: 821 ab).

[79] Maximos the Confessor, *Capita de Charitate* 3, 24, in *Philokalia*, Vol. 2, 86 (PG 90: 1023–1024).

[80] Gregory of Nyssa, *Hexaemeron* (PG 44: 73). See also the discussion in Walther Völker, *Maximus Confessor als Meister des geistlichen Lebens*, 304–305, which goes further back in time and, alongside Gregory of Nyssa's explicit reference to Philo, also mentions Plato's assertion in the *Timaeus* of an existing correspondence between the *kosmos aisthētos* and the *kosmos noētos*.

[81] Maximos the Confessor, *Capita de Charitate* 2, 4, in *Philokalia*, Vol. 2, 65 (PG 90, 983–984).

[82] Maximos the Confessor, *Capita de Charitate* 2, 73; 78, in *Philokalia*, Vol. 2, 77–78 (PG 90, 1007–1008; 1009–1010).

deeper penetration into God's mystery makes us leave the created order behind; thus Maximos can talk of two different "highest stages" of prayer: one for those "who have not advanced beyond the practice of the virtues," and one for those "leading the contemplative life."[83] There is an obvious Evagrian echo in the notion that images conveyed by the senses or by memory may lead us astray, while dispassion leads to discrimination;[84] and of course Maximos, like Evagrios, sees pure prayer as the ultimate goal of practice. Maximos, however, never *dismisses* the practice of the virtues as finally devoid of value; on the contrary, the fact that it is presented as one of *two* "highest forms" of prayer evidences how Maximos views the ordered use of creation as integral to the Christian vocation. The cosmology of Evagrios' *Kephalaia Gnostika*, exclusively postulating an eschatological return to a purely noetic reality, had little patience for the use of a reality that was destined to ultimate dissolution.

In both the *Liber Asceticus* and the *Capita de Charitate*, *theōria* appears to be both the *terminus a quo* and the *terminus ad quem* of *praxis*. The latter strives to make good use of human nature as well as of creation on the basis of the cues scattered by the divine wisdom; at the same time, it is also the route laid down by God to ensure that every individual might enjoy an everlasting communion with Him. The dialectic of *logos tēs ousias* and *tropos tēs hyparxeōs* is evident in the *Capita de Charitate*'s contention that rational natures participate in God's being through their essence and in God's goodness through their will.[85] Again, the utter simplicity of God, in whom being and goodness are essential properties, is contrasted to the composite nature of man, in whom goodness is attained only through a deliberate use of one's faculties in accordance with nature. In God, there is no distinction between *logos* and *tropos*; in man, the *tropos* is what enables the individual to develop the potential of the image of God in his *logos* and thereby attain the divine likeness.

Maximos' notion of *praxis* involves both the body and soul, in the same way as both body and soul are involved in *theōria*; it is with the aid of the senses that we form images of external reality, and it is through our

---

[83] Maximos the Confessor, *Capita de Charitate* 2, 6, in *Philokalia*, Vol. 2, 65–66 (PG 90, 985–986).

[84] Maximos the Confessor, *Capita de Charitate* 2, 26, in *Philokalia*, Vol. 2, 69 (PG 90, 991–992).

[85] Maximos the Confessor, *Capita de Charitate* 3, 25, in *Philokalia*, Vol. 2, 86–87 (PG 90, 1023–1024).

body that we leave our imprint on creation.[86] An intelligent use of conceptual images and of their corresponding physical objects redirects both soul and body away from all impurity; as such, the first of the two highest stages of prayer, associated with the virtues, deifies the body, while the second, associated with knowledge of God, deifies the soul.[87] The deification of the individual is the culmination of a dialectic involving God's offer of His love and the human reception to it; as such, it is a dialectic that involves the gnomic synergy of two freedoms. Once more, the hypostatic union provides the paradigm of our response to the divine love; in the person of Jesus Christ our human will is perfectly conformed to the will of God, so that our humanity, whose *ousia* necessarily unfolds in an act of intentional self-realization, comes to partake in God's wisdom and goodness.

The Origenist understanding of God's providential activity underpinned an eschatological vision where our bodies were eventually shed and where the individual's retrieval of his noetic communion with the Godhead was the benchmark of the divine judgment. Maximos, however, not only sees the union of soul and body as analogous to the union between God and humanity, but in *Amb.* 7 envisages *theōsis* as a state where both soul and body partake in the divine nature, the soul gaining immutability (*atrepsia*), and the body, through the mediation of the soul, gaining immortality (*athanasia*).[88] Such a perspective is ultimately incompatible with the Evagrian yearning for apokatastasis and effectively undercuts the Origenist understanding of divine providence (*pronoia*) and judgment (*krisis*) of Evagrios' *Kephalaia Gnostika*.[89] For Maximos, the notion of final restoration would evacuate God's gift of creation of any purpose and it would also demean human moral autonomy. God did not create the universe so as to remedy

---

[86] Maximos the Confessor, *Capita de Charitate* 4, 10, in *Philokalia*, Vol. 2, 101 (PG 90, 1049–1050), where it is said that our intelligible and our sensible nature share in the apprehension of created reality. See also Maximos the Confessor, *Amb.* 7 (PG 91: 1084 a), where the deified man is said to be the one who "has attained the [divine] likeness through the virtues" (*tēn di'aretōn prostheis exomōiosin*).

[87] Maximos the Confessor, *Capita de Charitate* 3, 1, in *Philokalia*, Vol. 2, 83 (PG 90: 1017–1018).

[88] Maximos the Confessor, *Amb.* 7 (PG 91: 1088 c).

[89] Maximos the Confessor, *Amb.* 10 (PG 91: 1133 ab); *Capita de Charitate* 4, 17–21, in *Philokalia*, Vol. 2, 102 (PG 90: 1051–1052); also Andrew Louth, *Maximus the Confessor*, 112, notes 45–46. For Evagrios' treatment of *pronoia* and *krisis*, see Evagrios, *Kephalaia Gnostika*, 1, 27, in *Les Six Centuries des 'Kephalaia Gnostica' d'Évagre le Pontique*, 28–29.

the fall of some pre-existent souls, but brought creatures into existence so that they might participate in Him "in proportion to their capacity" and He might in His turn "rejoice in their works."[90] We noted earlier how the goal of practice is to heal all divisions (*diaireseis*) within each individual, as well as within the larger human family, but this must be accomplished by means of "true faith" *and* "spiritual love." Within each individual, Maximos distinguishes a natural potentiality (*einai*), an intentional operation (*eu* or *kakōs einai*), and God's ratification of its outcome (*aei einai*), noting that the *logoi* of this third reality belongs to us only by God's grace.[91]

In this perspective, divine judgment does not roll back history to the beginning, but separates individuals on the basis of their fundamental orientation to good and evil, which, in turn, reflects how they responded to the commandment of love. This is a triumph of plurality, much as Origen and Evagrios postulated a triumph of undifferentiated oneness. Jerome's preoccupation with hierarchies of spiritual merit, which had led him to remonstrate against Evagrios' eschatological egalitarianism, is preempted by Maximos' assertion in the *Capita de Charitate* of a final division of humanity into the moral categories of "godly" and "ungodly."[92] God's judgment on the use we have made of our nature shall reflect the way in which we have engaged in *theōria* and *praxis* over the course of our lives. If the choice between loving God in one's neighbor or loving oneself in *philautia* hinges on whether one is willing to take one's cues from the created order, spiritual progress effectively mirrors one's readiness to let the insights disclosed by *theōria* consistently inform one's moral choices. As Maximos reminds us in the *Capita de Charitate*, those who are anointed with the oil of contemplation and who partake of the table of the virtues will one day drink from the cup of divine knowledge.[93]

---

[90] Maximos the Confessor, *Capita de Charitate* 3, 46, in *Philokalia*, Vol. 2, 90 (PG 90: 1029–1030). The Scriptural reference is to Ps. 104:31.

[91] Maximos the Confessor, *Capita de Charitate* 3, 23, in *Philokalia*, Vol. 2, 86 (PG 90: 1023–1024).

[92] Maximos the Confessor, *Capita de Charitate* 3, 26, in *Philokalia*, Vol. 2, (PG 90: 1023–1024).

[93] Maximos the Confessor, *Capita de Charitate* 3, 2, in *Philokalia*, Vol. 2, (PG 90: 1017–1018).

4 *MOIRA THEOU*:
SPIRITUAL TRANSFORMATION AND THE
BOUNDARIES OF IDENTITY

Introducing his work on St. Silouan the Athonite, one of the greatest figures of contemporary Orthodox spirituality, Larchet argues that the "spontaneous and immediate character" of Silouan's writings would never have been possible without the forty years of spiritual combat which the saint underwent on Athos. This struggle presupposed "the assiduous practice of the commandments, the long and methodical combat against all passions, as well as the patient acquisition of all virtues, *fruits of the synergy of human effort and divine grace.*"[1] For Larchet, Silouan's condition of inner balance and tranquillity constitutes the hard-won culmination, and not the beginning, of the spiritual path. Christ's promise that human beings can be saved and deified is still valid today; yet, it is only possible if one is ready to face a harsh and protracted struggle.[2]

The notion of synergy used by Larchet is a constant Leitmotif in the writings of Eastern Christian authors, and indeed it is a crucial theme in Maximos' works. In this chapter we will see how the reciprocity of human and divine effort in the process of deification constitutes the lynchpin of Maximos' understanding of *theōsis*. The synthetic character of his vision, which was already commented upon earlier, finds its most complete expression in the perfect congruence between the hypostatic union and the trans-

---

[1] Jean-Claude Larchet, *Saint Silouane de l'Athos* (Paris: Cerf, 2001), (my translation and italics). St. Silouan the Athonite (1866–1938) was canonized in 1987, and his work was published and made known by his disciple, the Archimandrite Sophrony (1896–1993). The notion of "spiritual combat" owed its popularity among Athonite monastics not only to its frequent mention in the *Philokalia*, but also to the popular treatise *Spiritual combat* by Lorenzo Scupoli, republished in the early 19th century thanks to the efforts of St. Nikodemos of the Holy Mountain and the Kollyviades Fathers.

[2] St. Silouan, *Wisdom from Mount Athos: The Writings of Staretz Silouan, 1866–1938* (trans. R. Edmonds; Crestwood, N.Y.: St. Vladimir's Seminary Press, 1974), 24–30; 115.

figuration of individual humanity, which finds its destination in the assembly of the celestial Jerusalem.

For Maximos, the pursuit of *theōria* and *praxis* are nothing but the human response to the gift of creation, according to the model of the incarnate Christ. Balthasar's assertion that creation as a whole is a question expecting a response from human freedom is ultimately no different from Maximos' conviction that the way in which we use the "common humanity" we received from God plays *the* crucial role in determining our destiny.[3] According to Evagrios, spiritual growth culminated in a return to an undifferentiated ontological unity. Maximos' vision, on the contrary, allows the adventure of human life to have a plurality of conclusions. His theology of *theōsis* underscores the transformative character of spiritual practice; it also grounds the enduring quality of such transformation, which culminates in an endless dialogue of love between God and the individual.

In the course of this chapter, we shall see how the perichoretic exchange between humanity and divinity in the person of Christ is once more the pattern for our gradual assimilation into the divine nature. This assimilation never takes the form of a re-absorption, but in line with Maximos' respect for particularity, operates through the very finiteness of our human reality. The *aei eu einai* ("eternal well-being"), which God promises to humanity, bears the marks of our moral choices, in the same way as Christ's glorious body—we are told—reigns in heaven with his wounds.

USING THE *PATHĒ*: CHRIST'S APPROPRIATION OF THE PASSIONS AND THE RESTORATION OF MORAL AUTONOMY

In the introduction to the *Quaestiones ad Thalassium*, Maximos gives us what comes closest to an account of his understanding of the fall.[4] In line with earlier writers, Maximos argues that the human failure to attain its natural potential is due to the individual having turned his or her faculties and efforts towards something other from their natural goal—in other words, to one's letting an unnatural love of self (*philautia*) take precedence over love of God. In *Ep.2*, the same theme is developed from a slightly different an-

---

[3] See von Balthasar's *Cosmic Liturgy*, 12–26, passim; also Geoffrey Wainwright, "Eschatology," in Edward T. Oakes, S.J., and David Moss, eds., *The Cambridge Companion to Hans Urs von Balthasar*, Cambridge: Cambridge University Press, 2004, 113–128.

[4] Maximos the Confessor, Introduction to the *Quaestiones ad Thalassium* (CCSG 7: 29).

gle, noting that, while the devil induced humanity to forsake the joys of the spirit for the pleasures of the flesh, we still carry full responsibility for the fall, as God had endowed us with the strength necessary to resist any temptation.[5] Indeed, the fall and humanity's subsequent entanglements in the passion of the flesh are not merely accompanied by a measure of suffering proportioned to the transgression,[6] but also by a loss in the ability to discern between good and evil and effectively by a loss in freedom, which somehow reduces the ontological chasm between human nature and the animal kingdom.[7] Maximos' account of the fall privileges a sense of regret for the abdication of our—divinely given—mediatorial role in creation.

As noted already, one of Maximos' chief preoccupations was to establish an ontological grounding for our condition as morally autonomous beings. The Stoic determinist understanding of the universe as an enclosed system entailed that the conduct of rational beings was framed by a relentless cycle of identical creations, leaving the individual the mere freedom to make the same moral choices an infinite number of times. For Maximos, Origen's solution to this problem was dissatisfactory, since it replaced an absolute, unconditioned determinism with a post-lapsarian variant where one's own moral choices after the fall could do nothing to change one's own eschatological condition. What would be the point of *autexousiotēs* (self-determination), if individual choices played no role in shaping one's own ultimate destiny?[8] Maximos' intuition was that his theological vision needed to ground the *transformative* character of spiritual practice, but also to give reasons for believing that the outcome of such practices would be eschatologically *enduring*—and thus would not be ultimately vain.

---

[5] Maximos the Confessor, *Ep. 2* (PG 91: 396 b).

[6] The dialectic of *hēdonē-odunē* is central to Maximos' understanding of the post-lapsarian state, which could only be exploded by the incarnation of Christ. See Maximos the Confessor, *Q.Th 61* (CCSG 22: 82–86), especially his discussion of the virgin birth in connection with the death of Christ.

[7] Maximos the Confessor, *Q.Th.1* (CCSG 7: 47). Of course, animals are not called to work out their deification, but, as part of the created order, they are not excluded from the world to come.

[8] George Boys-Stones, "The truest account: Origen in defense of Christian allegory" (paper delivered at the annual meeting of the SBL, San Antonio, Tex, November 21, 2004), 6–9. I thank Dr. Boys-Stones for his readiness to share his insights on the matter. One could add that *apokatastasis* erases all spiritual *loss* as well, bringing everyone "up" to the same level.

In *Amb. 45*, Maximos goes back to a late oration by Gregory of Nazianzos to argue that God did not create human nature in the fullness of its potentiality, but chose instead to allow every individual to make use of it, according to his or her inclination.[9] Thunberg rightly critiques Hentjes' claim that, for Maximos, Adam's exalted state was no different from divine likeness.[10] The divine image had been planted in him as a seed, as it would be the case with every member of the human race; in the same way, Adam was no exception from God's disposition that the divine likeness can only be realized through the free exercise of will. Our forefather had thus the possibility to attain a far higher perfection than the one bestowed on him in the garden, and if now humanity suffers the consequences of the fall, it is because he forsook this opportunity and directed his will towards the pleasures of the flesh. The treatise *De Vita Moysis* by Gregory of Nyssa already envisaged spiritual practice in terms of an itinerary from *eikōn* to *homōiosis*.[11] Maximos emphasizes the Christological dimension of this progression, so that spiritual practice is identified with *Nachfolge Christi* and the whole cosmos is transformed as a result. Deification is not only an anthropological reality, but the eventual destiny of the universe, which God conceived from all eternity and finally disclosed in the incarnation.[12]

In the *Capita Theologiae et Oeconomiae*, Maximos retrieves the Origenist notion of the Logos as the fullness (*plērōma*) of all individual *logoi*, arguing

---

[9] Maximos the Confessor, *Amb. 45* (PG 9: 1353–1354). The quote discussed here is taken from *Orationes* 45 by Gregory of Nazianzos (PG 36: 632 c).

[10] Lars Thunberg, *Microcosm and Mediator*, 145. The reference is to Jan Heintjes, "De opgang van den menschelijken geest tot God volgens sint Maximus Confessor," in *BiNJ* 6 (1943): 65–72.

[11] See for instance the conclusion of Gregory of Nyssa's *De Vita Moysis* (PG 44, 427–430). The same Gregory of Nyssa also notes in *Orationes de beatitudinibus* 1 (PG 44: 1200c) that "the goal of the virtuous life is the divine likeness" (*telos tou kat'aretēn biou estin hē pros ton theon homoiōsis*).

[12] See for instance Maximos the Confessor *Q.Th. 40* (PG 90: 396 bc), where it is said that "deification is the ineffable and ultimate *logos* of those things disposed by Providence for humanity," or even more explicitly in the *Orationis Dominicae Brevis Expositio* (PG 90: 873d), where we are told that "the deification of our nature is the work of the divine counsel." Jean-Claude Larchet, in *La Divinisation de l'Homme selon Saint Maxime le Confesseur* (Paris: Cerf, 1996), 83, opens his discussion of deification in Maximos with a quote from the *Life of the Virgin*, 51 ("the divine counsel was for the life and the deification of all"). See Maxime le Confesseur, *Vie de la Vierge* (trans. M.-J. van Esbroeck; Louvain: Ed. Peeters, 1986), 20–21, 41. Most other scholars, however, reject the ascription of this *Life* to Maximos.

that while Christ possessed it "by nature" (*kat'ousian*), man can acquire this fullness "by grace" (*kata charin*), provided that he cultivates wisdom and simultaneously engages in virtuous acts; indeed, neither *sophia* nor *aretē* are sufficient to procure it unless supported by the other.[13] As usual, Maximos appropriates an Origenist theme and simultaneously challenges its original meaning; in this case, an allegorical understanding of the Logos as the seat of all virtues furnishes Maximos with a link between the practice of *aretē* and the conscious imitation of the incarnate Christ. Admittedly, Clement of Alexandria had anticipated this move by claiming that the *plērōma* could be acquired by those following God's commandments.[14] Yet, Maximos' position differs from what we find in the *Stromateis*. His reflections on the nature of human freedom, as well as his considerations on sin and moral autonomy, ground the appropriation of the prerogatives of the Logos in the temporal manifestation of the Logos in Christ. It is only the hypostatic union which enables us to use humanity properly.

We must bear in mind that for Maximos, salvation and deification are distinct, and yet inextricably linked moments in the history of our salvation. Hans Urs von Balthasar,[15] and more recently Artemije Radoslavljevic,[16] claimed that for Maximos the incarnation would have taken place even without the fall, equating any assertion to the contrary to an instrumental understanding of Christ's life on earth.[17] In the same vein, Orthodox authors such as Florovsky and Nellas, when critiquing the theories of penal substitution developed in the Western Middle Ages, have not hesitated to

---

[13] Maximos the Confessor, *Capita Theologiae et Oeconomiae*, 2, 21, in *Philokalia*, Vol. 2, 141–2 (PG 90: 1133–1134).

[14] Clement of Alexandria, *Stromateis* 2, 2 (PG 8: 936–942).

[15] Hans Urs von Balthasar, *Cosmic Liturgy*, 252–70.

[16] See Artemije Radoslavljevic, "Le problème du 'présupposé' ou du 'non-présupposé' de l'Incarnation de Dieu le Verbe," in Felix Heinzer and Cristoph von Schönborn, eds., *Maximus Confessor. Actes du Symposium sur Maxime le Confesseur* (Fribourg-en-Suisse: Editions Universitaires, 1982): 193–206.

[17] In this respect, von Balthasar largely rehearsed an opinion that was common in the pre-war period among scholars of the Eastern Fathers. Madame Lot-Borodine asserted for instance that according to Maximos and "other Fathers," the eternal Word would have taken flesh even without the fall, with the only difference that he would not have been put to death. See Myrrha Lot-Borodine, "La doctrine de la déification dans l'Église grecque jusqu'au XI siécle," in *RHR* 105 (1932): 5–43.

list Maximos as one of their chief sources.[18] Subordinating the incarnation to the fall would seem to entail a change in God's plan, and we have already seen how strongly Maximos rejected any suggestion of a double-creation. This position seems also to be supported by the way he outlines the work of the Logos in a passage of *Q.Th 60* where the incarnate Christ is identified with "the mystery hidden from ages and from generations past," but now "manifested to his holy ones" so as to disclose the great counsel of God (*boulē tou theou*) that infinitely pre-exists all creation.[19] In this text, it is also claimed that the purpose of the incarnation is to *make known* the role of the Logos in the divine economy, which is to accomplish the deification of all beings by grace. Before the coming of Christ, God's plan for humanity was not fully revealed; humanity could at most resort to natural contemplation and get acquainted with the Logos' role in creating "the essence of all things."[20]

The incarnation, therefore, makes deification possible, by opening our eyes to the salvific nature of the created order. After the fall, the human condition was such that individuals were blind to the sacramental character of the cosmos and to its hints as to the manner of their conduct. The dramatic impact of sin is outlined in the *Orationis Dominicae*, when, pondering the consequences of Adam's transgression, Maximos remarks that sin had placed immortality beyond the reach of our forefather, and that only Christ's spiritual nourishment can bring us back to Adam's original condition.[21] According to *Amb. 7*, before the fall one could have acquired the divine likeness by a proper use of one's natural faculties, but after the fall the same goal could only be attained in another manner, which was "more paradoxical and more divine": God's "mystical coming" among humanity.[22] The word I translate as "manner" is *tropos*, which Maximos habitually juxtaposes to *logos*; and while the *logos* of human nature is forever fixed in the

---

[18] See Georges Florovsky, *The Byzantine Fathers of the Sixth to the Eighth century* (Crestwood, N.Y.: St. Vladimir's Seminary Press, 1987), 227, and Jean-Claude Larchet, *La Divinisation de l'Homme selon Saint Maxime le Confesseur*, 87–88. The theme is also amply discussed in Panaghiotis Nellas, *Deification in Christ. The Nature of the Human Person* (Crestwood, N.Y.: St. Vladimir's Seminary Press, 1987).

[19] Maximos the Confessor, *Q.Th 60* (CCSG 22: 73). The Scriptural quotation is from Col 1: 26.

[20] Maximos the Confessor, *Q.Th 60* (CCSG 22: 78–79).

[21] Maximos the Confessor, *Orationis dominicae brevis expositio* (PG 90: 897 b).

[22] Maximos the Confessor, *Amb. 7* (PG 91: 1097 cd).

mind of God, the *tropos* whereby we reach out for its goal is susceptible to change.[23]

As noted by Larchet, the fact that Maximos allows for different *tropoi* in the reception of grace does not mean that, in his system, the deification of the first man could have been accomplished independently of the incarnation.[24] The goal of each creature is to live according to its *logos*; the same *Amb. 7* allows for no exception when it asserts that all members of the human race who live in accordance with their nature are to become members of the eternal Word. Adam possesses the same human nature that we all share; if he had lived according to his *telos*, the Logos would have become incarnate in his members, as it is his desire with each one of us.[25] In the horizon of the divine plan, where the fall had been foreseen, the hypostatic union served both as the ultimate horizon of human perfection—including that of the first man—as well as the expression of the divine mercy towards fallen humanity. All deifying grace is the grace of the incarnate Christ, but, because of sin, it is only through the incarnation that we come to its full fruition. In other words, the Logos' coming into the flesh is not only what gives significance to human history, but also what enables it to unfold according to the divine plan.

Salvation, therefore, is not primarily an "ethical" condition where the individual's behavior is acceptable to God, but rather the presupposition of the process of deification.[26] If we turn to *Amb. 42*, we see that the miraculous manner of Christ's conception is given a particular emphasis, as it en-

---

[23] In this respect it is difficult to make sense of the claim of Demetrios Bathrellos, for whom Maximos believed that the hypostatic union accomplished the deification of an individual human *logos*. It is quite clear that, for Maximos, Christ had no human hypostasis, and thus did not possess the individual *logos* allotted to every human being, but only the *logos* of the human nature that we all share. Bathrellos' reading of Maximos' Christology leans towards the Antiochean versions of *homo assumptus*, with all the attendant problems. See Demetrios Bathrellos, *The Byzantine Christ: Person, Nature, and Will in the Christology of Saint Maximus the Confessor* (Oxford: Oxford University Press, 2005), 68 and 75.

[24] Jean-Claude Larchet, *La Divinisation de l'Homme selon Saint Maxime le Confesseur*, 94.

[25] Maximos the Confessor, *Amb. 7* (PG 91: 1097b).

[26] This is one of the fundamental flaws of Jean-Michel Garrigues' work *Maxime le Confesseur. La charité, avenir divine de l'homme*, where we find statements such as "for Maximos, deification and salvation coincide" (192), and where the "symphony of the wills" is effectively the highest goal of human life. Throughout his work, Garrigues consistently overlooks the ontological aspect of deification.

sures that the incarnate Word is not subject to the law of corruption.[27] Maximos is adamant that the eternal Logos assumes all imperfections burdening our nature as a consequence of the fall;[28] yet, the virgin birth ensures that he was not *under compulsion* to do so, since he was conceived "without passion" and was thus exempt from the accompanying pain. As such, he could *control* the consequences of the fallen human condition, making of them the use that he thought would be best, turning them into weapons for the deliverance of humanity.

As Foucault reminds us, the notion of using one's passions was shared by various currents in Hellenist thought;[29] Evagrios, for instance, did view the passions as corrupted virtues which spiritual practice could purify.[30] Where Maximos differs from previous thinkers is in his articulation of the link between the use of the passions and the redemptive work of Christ, and indeed of the even more crucial link between the practice of the virtues and the hypostatic union. Since Christ's humanity is eternally united to the Logos, this union guarantees that our deified humanity endures forever, according to the use we made of our passions. In our spiritual practice, we appropriate the fruits of the salvation wrought by Christ and we then proceed to be deified by the grace of Christ that, as we saw earlier, pervades the cosmos and the Christian scriptures.

The passages where Maximos ascribes *pathē* to Christ, and even contends that they possess a special salvific value, might seem to contradict the numerous instances where the Church Fathers pit the impassibility of the Christian God against the weaknesses and emotional excesses of the pagan deities.[31] In *Adversus Haereses*, Irenaeus had affirmed that affections and passions belong only to humans,[32] whereas Gregory of Nazianzos, who was one of Maximos' main authorities, insisted in the *Orationes Theologicae* that

---

[27] Maximos the Confessor, *Amb. 42* (PG 91: 1316c-1317a). Maximos plays here on the similarity and the distinction of *genesis* and *gennēsis* (generation).

[28] This is stated explicitly in Maximos the Confessor, *Ep. 15* (PG 91: 573b).

[29] See Michel Foucault, *The History of Sexuality: The Use of Pleasure* (New York: Vintage, 1990), Ch. 2.

[30] See for instance Evagrios, *Texts on Discrimination in respect of Passions and Thoughts*, 3–5, in *Philokalia*, Vol. 1, 39–41.

[31] See for instance Paul Gavrilyuk, *The Suffering of the Impassible God–The Dialectic of Patristic Thought* (Oxford Early Christian Studies. Oxford: Oxford University Press, 2004), Ch. 2, 47–64.

[32] Irenaeus, *Adversus Haereses*, 2, 13, 5 (PG 7a, 745a).

our creator was utterly untouched by our petty desires and concerns.[33] The appropriation and Christianization of the Stoic notion of *apatheia*, therefore, should be seen against the background of this critique of pagan notions of divinity. Yet, at the same time, the Church Fathers were faced by Scriptural references to God's anger or God's mercy, which did not easily fit with this assertion of divine detachment. Cassian or Augustine viewed these passages as modeled analogically upon human behavior to convey God's mysterious presence in history.[34] But can one still talk of analogy when we turn to the incarnate God, who "was found in human form," and "became obedient to the point of death" (Phil 2: 6–11)? The easy solution to this conundrum would be some form of Docetism, contending that the Son of God appeared to be subject to human *pathē*, but was truly untouched by suffering, or perhaps distinguishing a divine and a human subject in Christ; the former would have maintained its utter impassibility, whereas the latter would have experienced hunger or thirst, and eventually suffering and death.[35] Either of these options would have turned the incarnation into a sort of divine play (the *lila* of the Hindu *avatars*), reopening the chasm between humanity and divinity which the hypostatic union was meant to bridge.

Maximos is wholly in agreement with Gregory of Nazianzos' conviction that "what is not assumed is not redeemed," as well as with the general consensus, formed in the wake of the Arian controversy, that the Son's involvement with human suffering is in no way incompatible with his full-fledged divinity.[36] Earlier historians of Christian thought viewed "Antiochean" Christology as eager to secure Christ's humanity against the docetist inclinations of the Alexandrians, but more recent studies have brought out the extent to which Alexandrian Christological speculation was often at the

---

[33] Gregory of Nazianzos, *Orationes* 28, 11 (PG 36: 39–40).

[34] See for instance Cassian's *Institutes*, 8, 4, in John Cassian, *The Institutes* (trans. B. Ramsey, O.P.; New York and Mahwah, N.J.: Newman Press, 2000), 204–208. As noted by Paul Gavrilyuk (*The Suffering of the Impassible God*, 57), Augustine viewed divine wrath as "a human way of realizing the gravity of sin and the inevitability of divine judgment."

[35] The first position, shared by many currents of Gnosticism, is rebuked by Ireneus in *Adversus haereses*, 2, 17, 6 (PG 7a: 764 a-b). The second position is the main charge of Cyril of Alexandria against the Nestorians in Cyril of Alexandria, *On the Unity of Christ* (PG 75: 1255–1256; 1261–1262, *et passim*).

[36] See Gregory of Nazianzos, *Epistle CI 'Ad Cledonium'* (PG 37: 175–190); also Gregory of Nyssa, *Against Eunomios*, 3 (PG 45: 595–599), where it is stressed that the Godhead manifested on the cross is worthy of the same honor as the Father.

forefront in asserting the eternal Son as the subject of the sufferings of Christ against the Antiochean reluctance to ascribe *pathē* to the deity.[37] Maximos' traditional association with the Alexandrian school, rather than signaling a desire to subordinate Christ's humanity to the hypostasis of the Son, is indeed indicative of his conviction that the impassible divine nature truly suffered the pains of the flesh and made them his own. John McGuckin reminds us for instance that for Cyril of Alexandria, the incarnation of the Word amounted to a full appropriation (*oikeiōsis*) of human characteristics on the part of God;[38] Cyril is quite convinced that "for each human experience, you shall find in Christ whatever corresponds to it."[39]

On the strength of such assertions, Paul Gavrilyuk feels justified in claiming that Cyril's vision "brought to a fitting conclusion centuries of Patristic deliberation," eliminating all doubt as to the fact that "the very nerve center of the Gospel" lay in its assertion of God's utter involvement in the human condition.[40] Maximos is of course deeply indebted to Cyril; no author who wrote on Christology after the 5th century could ignore Cyril's theology of the unity of Christ. Yet, with Maximos, we go one step further. Christ's use of the human passions *is* the paradigm of spiritual practice; the incarnate Christ *is* the model of the deified state. Our ascetic efforts, so to speak, are *ennobled* by the fact that Christ himself chose to undergo them, and invested them with an unprecedented salvific power.

In Maximos' writings, the two turning points in Christ's appropriation of our passions are the temptations in the desert and the events surrounding his passion. In *Q.Th 61*, Maximos notes that Christ's assumption of the human passions, without the inclination to pleasure and the eagerness to avoid pain, enables him to employ them as weapons to free human nature from the power that they exercised over it.[41] In *Q.Th 21*, we are told that the passions attacked Christ hoping to induce him to act in a way contrary to his nature, but he was able to turn them into "victims of their own de-

---

[37] See John J. O'Keefe, "Impassible suffering? Divine passion and Fifth-Century Christology," *TS* 58 (1997): 39–60. By and large, Von Balthasar's *Kosmische Liturgie* is characterized by the old understanding of the distinction between the two schools.

[38] John McGuckin, *St Cyril of Alexandria: the Christological Controversy. Its history, theology, and texts* (Crestwood, N.Y.: St. Vladimir's Seminary Press, 1994), 201–05.

[39] Cyril of Alexandria, *In Ioannem* 8, (PG 74: 92b).

[40] See Paul Gavrilyuk, *The Suffering of the Impassible God*, 175.

[41] Maximos the Confessor, *Q.Th* 61 (CCSG 22: 87–89); see also Jean-Claude Larchet, *La Divinisation de l'Homme selon Saint Maxime le Confesseur*, 235–236.

ceit," freeing our human nature from their mortal sting.[42] The same text, perhaps echoing an earlier insight by Gregory of Nyssa,[43] notes that the final victory was accomplished as Christ accepted the challenge of the crucifixion; by feeding the powers of evil with his flesh, death was annihilated by the divinity that was hypostatically united to it, ensuring that men should no longer fear bodily dissolution. Through the *logos* of our humanity, we come to share the fruits of Christ's work, who has returned our nature to its condition before the fall. Christ dissolves the laws of nature that had been established by sin,[44] or, in other words, restored the divine image in us by freeing our nature from slavery to the passions, and from the fear of death.[45]

This is why Christ's human will plays such a crucial role in Maximos. For him, monothelitism is a docetist distortion of Chalcedon, which leaves us with a Christ who is less than fully human, and is effectively "pretending" (*dramatourgeōn*) to be such.[46] In *Op. 6*, reflecting on the soteriological significance of the agony in the garden of Gethsemani, Maximos concludes that Christ's suffering had to be the *human* suffering of the eternal Son. In this perspective, the expression of subordination to the divine will that Christ utters shortly before the passion does not refer to the submission of the Son to the will of the Father (since in the divine nature there is only one will). Rather, it refers to the human obedience of a divine person, who finally brings to completion the history of the gradual submission of our human *pathē* to the divine purpose. Through the human will, Christ's redemptive work embraces the totality of our condition, and heals our ability to use our will in conformity with our *logos*.

---

[42] Maximos the Confessor, *Q.Th* 21(CCSG 7: 129). The text adds also that Christ did this for our sake, and not his own, since he was not under the domain of the *pathē*.

[43] See Gregory of Nyssa, *In Orationem Catecheticam*, 32 (PG 45: 77–84).

[44] Maximos the Confessor, *Amb.* 31 (PG 91: 1276 b).

[45] Maximos the Confessor, *Q.Th*. 42 (CCSG 7: 289–90).

[46] See Iain R. Torrance, *Christology after Chalcedon: Severus of Antioch and Sergius the Monophysite* (Eugene, Ore.: Wipf and Stock, 1998). For a discussion of the background of the controversy, see François Marie Léthel, *Théologie de l'agonie du Christ: la liberté humaine du fils de Dieu et son importance sotériologique mises en lumière par saint Maxime le Confesseur*, (Théologie historique, 52. Paris: Beauchesne, 1979), 23–53. Here, Léthel distinguishes between the different shades of monothelitism that Maximos found himself opposing.

To use a very simple metaphor, Christ's salvific work functions analogically to the way in which vaccines against a particular disease get hold of the harmful principle that causes it and use it to protect the recipient against infection. The incarnation makes us resistant to the poison of the passions; the bite of temptation becomes harmless. The very frequency in Maximos' works of references to the restoration of our nature evidences the untenable character of those interpretations arguing that, for Maximos, Christ's salvific work had no ontological impact on our humanity, but merely an ethical impact on our conduct.[47] In fact, what Christ restored was our very *capacity* of exercising the moral autonomy that is an intrinsic part of the *logos* of our humanity.

SALVIFIC ANALOGY: THE UNIQUENESS OF CHRIST AND THE "REPEATED INCARNATIONS"

The question remains, however: to what extent can the spiritual practice of the individual actually imitate Christ's own life? In what measure can one truly imitate his life on earth? Is there an ultimate ontological limit, beyond which it is impossible to go? And if there is, what is its theological rational? The answer, for Maximos, is quite clear, and it differs substantially from the position adopted by Evagrios. For the former, there can never be a moment, when the practitioner fully attains the spiritual level, or the ontological condition, of the incarnate Logos. Deification discloses a different mode of using one's own individual nature, which is then glorified in its irreducible difference and contingency. For Maximos, salvation is communicated to all in an equal manner through the sacrament of baptism, but deification is achieved in proportion to our receptiveness to divine grace, and to our readiness (*diathesis*) to engage in consistent spiritual practice. In *Q.Th 59*, he states clearly that the deifying power of the Holy Spirit can operate in us only when our natural faculties have been purified from sin and we have attained an inner equilibrium.[48] Unless we set out to obey God's commandments and seek to do His will, we shall "never know the glory, which

---

[47] See Jean-Marie Garrigues' *Maxime le Confesseur*, but also, for instance, Endre von Ivanka's *Maximos der Bekenner. all-eins in Christus* (Einsiedeln: Johannes Verlag, 1961), and Bernardo De Angelis, *Natura, persona e libertà*. (Roma: Armando Editore, 2002).
[48] Maximos the Confessor, *Q.Th 59* (CCSG 22: 45, 49, 51, 67, *et passim*).

the Father keeps in store for those who love Him."[49] Indeed, it is Christ himself that takes over the individual; to the extent that we obey Christ's commandments, we become "other Christs."

In 1953, Dalmais pointed out that the practice of the commandments was the lynchpin of Maximos' theology of deification, but failed to articulate satisfactorily how Maximos established an ontological, and not merely an ethical link between the acquisition of the virtues and the hypostatic union. The same problem affects the works of Riou and Garrigues, whose interpretation of Maximos' soteriology is colored by their commitment to the Western notion of created grace.[50] Admittedly, there are passages that lend themselves to both readings, and at other times *theōsis* is connected with the grace donated to man in virtue of Christ's self-abasement.[51] Yet, other passages appear invested with a strong ontological thrust, and seem to envisage, so to speak, a *multiplicity of incarnations*. In the *Liber Asceticus*, for instance, the blessed are those who truly believed in Christ and thus, "through the practice of the commandments, have made *Christ himself come to live in them*."[52] This contention reflects Maximos' conviction that the eternal Word encompasses the *logoi* of the virtues, so that Christ actually becomes incarnate in all those who practice the commandments.[53] Similarly, the *Capita Theologiae et Oeconomiae* tell us that in virtue of the circumincession of Father, Son and Holy Spirit, the person who obeys the commandments becomes the mystical dwelling place of all three persons of the Trinity.[54]

---

[49] The *Orationis Dominicae Brevis Expositio*, for instance, implies that the mystery of God's love for His creation shall be kept hidden from those who choose to forego it. See for instance Maximos the Confessor, *Orationis Dominicae Brevis Expositio* (PG 90: 880b); see also Dalmais, "Un traité de théologie contemplative," 123–139.

[50] Irénée-Henry Dalmais, "La doctrine ascétique de saint Maxime le Confesseur, d'après le *Liber asceticus*," *Irén* 26 (1953): 25–36.

[51] See for instance, Maximos the Confessor, *Orationis Dominicae Brevis Expositio* (PG 90: 877a); or *Opuscula Theologica et Politica* 4 (PG 91: 57 ab), where "the Word deifies by grace those who undergo asceticism *of their own free choice*." For this tendency in general, see Jules Gross, *La divinisation du Chrétien d'après les Pères grecs* (trans. P. A. Onica; Anaheim, Calif.: A&C Press, 2002), 234–256.

[52] See Maximos the Confessor, *Liber Asceticus*, 34 (PG 90, 340 b).

[53] For a discussion of the issue of created vs. uncreated grace in Maximos, see Manuel Candal SJ, "La gracia increada del *Liber Ambiguorum* de San Maximo," OCP (1961): 131–149.

[54] Maximos the Confessor, *Capita Theologiae et Oeconomiae*, 2, 71, in *Philokalia*, Vol. 2, 154 (PG 90: 1156d).

The *Ambigua* highlight the connection between deification and obedience, noting that our own deification is patterned after Christ's self-emptying *kenōsis*.[55] As the eternal Logos encompasses the *logoi* of all virtues, following the commandments brings us closer to the transfigured humanity of Christ; ascetic practice entails a sort of "discipline of unselfing," whereby the individual bids farewell to his individual desires and inclinations, and which effectively parallels the kenotic self-emptying of the eternal Son. The reciprocity, or symmetrical relation (*antidosis*), between our ascent and Christ's descent, is yet a further instance of the synergy between the divine and the human initiative that shape the spiritual progress of the individual. In the *Letter* to John the Cubicularius, Maximos goes as far as claiming that God's incarnation in the virtues of the individual Christian reflect the character of the moral choices of the latter; thus, the unique and unchangeable Godhead becomes manifest in an infinite number of different and ever changing ways.[56]

This belief that ascetic practice accomplishes a gradual renewal of the incarnation might appear to echo the ancient "Christology by degrees" favored by authors such as Paul of Samosata, and later condemned as ultimately incompatible with the orthodox understanding of the incarnation.[57] In the text from the *Philokalia* quoted above, Maximos contends, for instance, that to the extent that "I remain imperfect and refractory, neither obeying God by practicing the commandments" (through *praxis*) "nor becoming perfect in spiritual knowledge" (through *theōria*), Christ "also appears imperfect and refractory," for "I diminish and cripple Him by not growing in spirit."[58] In this perspective, one might infer that the culmination of spiritual progress amounts to a condition where the ontological distinction between Christ and the practitioner is blurred, or where Christ is ultimately nothing else but the archetype of perfected humanity. Maximos' notion of *theōsis*, however, asserts the ultimacy of each individual *logos*, and construes the deification of humanity as an instance of "mystical symme-

---

[55] See for instance Maximos the Confessor, *Amb.* 31 (PG 91: 1276c); *Amb.* 48 (PG 91: 1364c).

[56] See Maximos the Confessor, *Ep.2* addressed to John the Cubicularius (PG 91: 408a). An English translation of this epistle is included in Andrew Louth, *Maximus the Confessor*, 84–94.

[57] About Paul of Samosata, see John A. McGuckin, Intro. to Cyril of Alexandria, *On the Unity of Christ* (Crestwood, N.Y.: St. Vladimir's Seminary Press, 1997).

[58] Maximos the Confessor, *Capita Theologiae et Oeconomiae*, 2, 30, in *Philokalia*, Vol. 2, 145 (PG 90: 1137d).

try," where one reverses and paradoxically renews the miracle of the hypostatic union. Man assumes the properties of the divinity, without in any way trespassing the unbridgeable ontological distinction between human nature and divine nature.

According to Larchet, deification marks "a change of order (*metataxis*), whereby man leaves behind the domain of earthly reality" and his nature is raised beyond its proper limits.[59] Deification is not a reality that can be accomplished without divine help: if this were the case, deification would no longer be the outcome of God's grace, but merely a manifestation of humanity's natural power (*dynamis*).[60] This is clearly impossible; according to *Q.Th 59*, humanity, no different in this respect from the other elements of created reality, possesses the *logos* of its own nature, but not the *logoi* of what goes beyond it or belongs to the supernatural realm.[61] The utter gratuitousness of *theōsis* is stressed over and over again. In the *Quaestiones ad Thalassium*, whenever deification is mentioned, Maximos emphasizes how the latter is something that human beings effectively *undergo*, and which is inextricably connected with divine grace. In *Q.Th 22*, we are told that we "*suffer* the transformation that by grace turns us into gods";[62] in *Q.Th 61*, we are reminded that in the gift of *theōsis*, we have received a grace which transcends the limits of our nature. While deification is given to us in different measures according to our dignity,[63] the *Philokalia* reminds us that we should

---

[59] Jean-Claude Larchet, *La Divinisation de l'Homme*, 563–564.

[60] Maximos the Confessor, *Amb.* 20 (PG 91: 1237ab).

[61] Maximos the Confessor, *Q.Th 59* (CCSG 22: 173).

[62] In Maximos the Confessor, *Q.Th 22* (CCSG 7: 141), we are told that the blessed are those who "undergo the gracious transformation that makes one into a god" (*paschontes tēn pros to theousthai chariti metapoiēsin*). The same passage goes on to say that "we do not accomplish [this change] ourselves, we suffer it, and for that reason we cannot be called 'makers of divinity'" (*ou poioumen, alla paschomen, kai dia touto ou legomen theourgoumenoi*).

[63] Maximos the Confessor, in *Q.Th 63* (CCSG 22: 173), commenting upon this, argues that in the candlestick on the right, one may contemplate the mystery of the incarnation "inasmuch as it accomplishes the supernatural deification accomplished by grace [...] of those who are saved" (*ōs energētikon tēs hyper physin chariti [...] tōn sōzomenōn theōseōs*); in *Q.Th 64* (CCSG 22: 197), it is said that our individual destiny is the mystery "of the grace of deification given in accordance to everyone's merit" (*tēs epaxiōs hekastou kata tēn theōsin charitos*).

beware lest we regard it as recompense for our good actions, instead of an expression of the divine "love for humanity" (*anthrōpophilia*).[64]

The question remains: how is it possible for our transfigured humanity not to forego its individual character even as it is taken over by God's deifying power? The apostle's assertion "I live, though it is no longer I, but Christ that lives in me" (Gal 2: 20) appears to identify the highest degree of the spiritual life with an effacement of the ego, which is yet more radical in the eschaton, when Christ becomes "all in all." If at the end of times our natural operation shall be replaced by God's own operation (*energeia*), does this imply that we shall leave part of our humanity behind? Similarly, and even more worrying in its theological implications, this final "energetic supercession" might suggest that throughout the whole of his earthly life the incarnate Christ was never endowed with a human operation, as he enjoyed the fullness of divinity from the very first moment of his conception.

Maximos, as always, develops his answer on the basis of Chalcedonian Christology, and his take on the question would become normative in the Eastern Orthodox tradition. Many centuries later, discussing the relation between the communication of idioms in Christ and the mystery of *theōsis*, Vladimir Lossky notes that for the Greek Fathers, the union of our humanity with God is merely *analogous* to the union of Christ's humanity to the second person of the Trinity.[65] The distinction between the divine essence and the divine energy that is typical of Eastern Orthodoxy is crucial to determine the extent to which a human intellect can penetrate into the mystery of God (postulating the inaccessibility of the divine essence); at the same time, it also to secure the historical uniqueness of the event of the incarnation, as opposed to the effects of deifying grace upon the rest of humanity. Our human nature can never bear the *fullness* of divinity, whereas the divine nature of Christ *could* bear the fullness of humanity. We thus have one single and perfect hypostatic union in the person of Christ, and a series of reversed, imperfect hypostatic unions in the persons of the deified mem-

---

[64] See Maximos the Confessor, *Capita Theologiae et Oeconomiae*, 1, 31, in *Philokalia*, Vol. 2, 120 (PG 90, 1094 d). The same text goes on to say that "the human intellect lacks the power to ascend and to participate in the divine illumination, unless God draws it up, in so far as this is possible for the human intellect" (*oudepote psychē dunatai pros gnōsin ektathēnai Theou, ei mē autos ho Theos sugkatabasei chrēsamenos hapsētai autēs, kai anagagē pros heauton*).

[65] See Vladimir Lossky, *The Mystical Theology of the Eastern Church* (Crestwood, N.Y.: St. Vladimir's Seminary Press, 1997), 104.

bers of the human race. Christ bore all the attributes of both natures; humans are never vouchsafed the fullness of the divinity.

Once it is clear that the hypostatic union and our own deification follow *analogous*, but not *identical* dynamics, one also understands that the relationship between human and divine operations in Christ differs from the similar relationship in deified individuals. In the former, from the very first instant of the incarnation, there is a synergy between the two operations, in the same way as there is a co-operation of the wills; thus, Christ acts both as man and as God, and accomplishes our salvation with the aid of his human operation, as is the case for instance at Gethsemani. In our case, on the other hand, our human operation is eschatologically "silenced," to the extent that we are transformed by the divine energy. As noted by Bausenhart in his study of Maximos' Christology, the Cyrillian paradigm of *oikeiōsis* meant that Christ had to be endowed with a human operation if he was to accomplish our deification.[66] In the case of Christ, both operations were present from the first moment of his earthly existence, since operations are a function of their respective natures. Where a nature is lacking or deficient, the corresponding operation is ordinarily not present; if at the eschaton deified humanity becomes the recipient and indeed the channel of the divine energies, it is only because of the "law of grace" that elevates—but does not destroy—the "law of nature." *Theōsis* does not deprive men of their nature, but the latter now operates in a divine manner, so that deified individuals become "by position" (*thesei*) what God is by nature (*physei*).[67] In this respect, Maximos comes close to the position of Karl Rahner in *Foundations*, where Rahner construes the whole of reality as the channel of God's self-expression, and views the exchange of properties in the person of Christ as paradigmatic of human destiny.[68]

---

[66] Guido Bausenhart, *"In Allem uns gleich außer der Sünde": Studies zum Beitrag Maximos des Bekenners zur alt-kirchlichen Christologie* (Tübinger Studien zur Theologie und Philosophie, 5. Mainz: Matthias-Grünewald-Verlag, 1992), 147–154; 172–8 (on the role of perichoresis).

[67] Maximos the Confessor, *Amb.* 7 (PG 91: 1088c).

[68] See for instance Karl Rahner, *Foundations of Christian Faith* (trans. W. V. Dych; New York: Crossroad, 1982), Ch. 6.1 ("Christology within an evolutionary view of the world"), 178–202. Of course, one could argue that Rahner is merely going back to an early Patristic tradition where the whole of reality is "graced." On the other hand, Rahner's position might be regarded as problematic if it is construed as implying that the hypostatic union and our own deification are *identical*.

If we turn to Sherwood's analysis of the early *Ambigua*, we see clearly how Maximos' understanding of deification completely debunks the Origenist position and presents deification as ontologically transformative. Throughout *Amb.* 7, which is based on a passage by Gregory of Nazianzos where human beings are called "parts of God" (*moira theou*),[69] Maximos argues that Gregory's claim, if interpreted correctly, does not support Origen's eschatological return to the henad; rather, it envisages the deification of humanity as the ultimate manifestation of God's care for His creation's particular realities. When Maximos writes that at the end of history, "one energy" shall be shared by God and by all the saints, this is not a concession to the Evagrian *reductio ad unum*. Rather, in Maximos' vision, this "operational supercession" is what guarantees our enduring identity. Origen's cosmos was locked in a cycle of creations, since the *logikoi* could not attain a "position" (*thesis*) that was "unchangeable in its stability on the good." In Maximos' creation, by contrast, the possibility of further falls is eliminated as the divine energy that fills deified individuals ensures that satiety (*koros*) no longer arises, by fixing their orientation to the good.[70]

Sherwood draws our attention to how Maximos nuances the Patristic metaphor of the iron exposed to the fire, deployed by Athanasios during the Arian controversy, and later by Cyril of Alexandria, so as to delineate the relation between Father and Son; in this context, this image illumines the ontological transformation of deified humanity.[71] The Chalcedonian preoccupation with "union without confusion" resurfaces in Maximos' terminology as he insists that the divine energy, enveloping and irreversibly transfiguring the individual person, does not modify the *logos* of our humanity.[72] This marks a significant distinction from Evagrian anthropology,

---

[69] See Gregory of Nazianzos, *Orationes* 14, 7 (PG 35: 865–868). According to Justinian's *Epistle to the Synod* (PG 86, 991a-c), this text was often used by 6th century Origenist monks to support their theory of the henad. See also Claudio Moreschini's version of *Ambigua*, 618, n. 4; Lars Thunberg, *Microcosm and Mediator*, 86, n. 7.

[70] Maximos the Confessor, *Amb.* 7 (PG 91: 1069c).

[71] See Polycarp Sherwood OSB, *The Earlier Ambigua of St. Maximos the Confessor* (Studia Anselmiana 36. Rome: Herder, 1955), 149–156.

[72] Maximos the Confessor, in *Q.Th 64* (CCSG 22: 237), emphasizes how "the law of grace" effects an irreversible transformation: "the law of grace is the law that transcends nature, transforming the nature [of men] without changing it" (*ho des charitos nomos hyper physin kathestēke logos, pros theōsin atreptōs tēn physin metaplattōn*), and "bestowing the permanence of good being" (*tēn tou aei eu einai diamonēn parechomenos*).

where the noetic element of our soul was set apart from its passible part and was alone destined to immortality; for Maximos, it is not only our *nous* that is deified, but also our sensitive and volitional faculties, since all three dimensions are part of our *logos*. On one hand, our *nous*, even if transformed by the Holy Spirit into "the semblance of another god,"[73] retains its own identity, and is not reabsorbed into the undifferentiated noetic reality of the *Kephalaia Gnostika*. On the other hand, deification is an event that affects the intellect as well as the body; our moral life encompasses both. Maximos' confidence in the eschatological endurance of our passible part is voiced in various passages, where we are reassured that nothing is too lowly for God's deifying power. In a late passage of *Quaestiones et dubia*, for instance, Maximos takes care to note that the divine energies shall not suppress any aspect of our humanity, but actually "reestablish" (*prothesei*) our vegetative and incensive functions on a new basis.[74]

Völker, when analyzing the philosophical presuppositions of Maximos' spiritual theology, seems to find this position of Maximos inconsistent with his overall vision. How can Maximos be committed to moral autonomy as an integral part of our *logos*, and yet postulate its effective cessation at the end of time?[75] Doucet answers this objection claiming that the individual's readiness to let his or her natural functions be subsumed by God's greater and more powerful operation is not just a sort of *Aufhebung*, but effectively amounts to a conscious acknowledgement of the ontological limit of human nature.[76] Already in the Pseudo-Denys, we find passages where those seeking perfection "deliberately" choose to "co-operate" with God, and "allow the divine operation to become manifest in them."[77] In the *Disputatio cum*

---

[73] Maximos the Confessor, in *Q.Th. 6* (CCSG 7: 69), points out that deification "transformed the *nous*, so that it could be called 'another god'" (*ton noun metepoiēsen, ōs allon einai theon nomisthēnai*).

[74] Maximos the Confessor, *Quaestiones et dubia* 57 (CCSG 10: 46).

[75] See Walther Völker, *Maximus Confessor als Meister des geistlichen Lebens*, 472–480.

[76] See Marcel Doucet, "Vues récentes sur les 'métamorphoses' de la pensée de saint Maxime le Confesseur," *Sciences et Esprit* 31.3 (1979): 269–291. Larchet is skeptical on this point : see Jean-Claude Larchet, *La Divinisation de l'Homme selon Saint Maxime le Confesseur*, 577.

[77] Of course, while the influence of the Pseudo-Denys is undeniable, Maximos' theological vision, unlike that of the Pseudo-Denys, is fundamentally Christocentric, and utterly preoccupied with the "redemption of the particulars." See *De Coelesti Hierarchia*, 3, 2 (PG 3: 165–6).

Phyrro, there is an almost direct echo of this claim when Maximos reminds his adversary of some Old Testament characters (such as Moses or David), who, even before the coming of Christ, voluntarily "laid down their operations" to become channels of the divine energy.[78] In *Amb. 7*, the cessation of our individual operation is construed as God's guarantee that our orientation to the good no longer gives way to sin; man's fundamental freedom (*autexousia*) is not suppressed, but an intentional effacement of this faculty is necessary if our nature is to be secured from the vagaries of change.[79]

In this way, what ensues after the eschaton is a sort of *passive* synergy between God and man, as opposed to the *active* synergy which characterized our life on earth. We noted earlier how Evagrios read the Pauline image of the Son handing over his kingdom to the Father as a Scriptural endorsement of his eschatological vision. In the *Quaestiones ad Thalassium*, this same image indicates the suspension of our operation, and the simultaneous co-optation into the divine nature of all deified individuals.[80] In this perspective, the Son's voluntary act of obeisance does not signal the return of the *logikoi* to the henad, but rather the definitive, voluntary submission to the Father of all rational beings, who henceforth reign with Him and the incarnate Logos. It is not difficult to see how Maximos' Chalcedonian commitments shape this eschatological vision: operational supercession establishes the union of the human and the divine nature, but this is not accompanied by "confusion" at the level of the *ousia*.[81] Similarly, as the Logos encompasses but also transcends all the *logoi* of creation, the Godhead envelops and transfigures all deified individuals within the boundaries of their nature, even if the essence of Godhead remains utterly inaccessible. The figure of Melchisedec, who tradition affirms had no father or mother or human ancestry, is particularly fitting to convey the image of a humanity which, to use

---

[78] Marcel Doucet, in the article quoted above, does refer to this passage, but evidently Larchet does not view it as a sufficiently convincing proof-text. See also Maximos the Confessor, *Disputatio cum Phyrro* (PG 91: 297a).

[79] Maximos the Confessor, *Amb. 7* (PG 91: 1076c).

[80] Maximos the Confessor, in *Q.Th.22*, (CCSG 7: 139), tells us that the union is achieved "according to the *tropos* of every individual" (*kata panta tropon*), "save only, of course, the identity with himself according to the *ousia*" (*chōris monēs dēlonoti tēs pros auton kat'ousian tautotētos*).

[81] See also Irénée-Henry Dalmais, "Saint Maxime le Confesseur et la crise de l'origénisme monastique," in George Lemaître, ed., *Théologie de la vie monastique: Études sur la tradition patristique* (Théologie, 49. Paris: Aubier, 1961), 416–424.

later Palamite terminology, is invited to "become uncreated,"[82] assuming by grace the idioms that are proper to God.

It may be interesting to note that certain Roman Catholic thinkers critical of the Eastern distinction between the divine essence and the divine energies (which would become the main focus of Palamite theology and spirituality) have objected to such an understanding of spiritual practice, arguing that it weakens the boundary between created and uncreated nature and effectively leads to pantheism. To avoid this problem, thinkers operating in the Thomist tradition have argued that each member of the human race is the recipient of a special grace *created* with the specific purpose of procuring his or her own individual salvation, which is accomplished without overstepping the boundary between human and divine.[83] Maximos' theological vision offers a possible response to these concerns. If deification was inscribed in the human *logos* from the beginning of creation, and the whole of the cosmos was geared towards the accomplishment of this goal, deification does not obliterate separate individual identities; on the contrary, only those who are transfigured by the divine energies experience humanity to its fullness.[84] It is actually the Evagrian position that comes closer to pantheism; *Amb. 41*, on the other hand, offers a clear Chalcedonian alternative to the eschatology of the *Kephalaia Gnostika*, claiming that we are destined to become one with God, without, however, any confusion at the level of the natures."[85]

There is one more aspect of the theology of "repeated incarnation" which is worthy of note. The undifferentiated noetic reality envisaged by

---

[82] The figure of Melchisedec plays an important role in Maximos' multi-layered reading of the transfiguration. See Maximos the Confessor, *Amb. 10* (PG 91: 1137bd).

[83] For this controversy, see Marie-Joseph Le Guillou, "Lumière et charité dans la doctrine palamite de la divinization," *Istina* 19 (1974): 329–338, critiquing the ideas of the *Hagioretic tome* by Palamas. Garrigues' work, as mentioned already, systematically distorts Maximos' thought so as to make it consistent with this notion of created grace. See his *Maxime le Confesseur. La charité, avenir divine de l'homme*, 186–87.

[84] This is a point that Eastern Orthodox authors are particularly fond of stressing. See for instance John Meyendorff, *Christ in Eastern Christian Thought*, 205.

[85] The emphasis on the idea that the union is "on the level of grace" (*kata tēn hexin tēs charitos*) and not on the level of nature serves of course to underscore that there is no confusion at the level of the essence, since nature encompasses both essence and the energies.

the *Kephalaia Gnostika* undercuts the very possibility of an enduring *dialogical* relationship between the creator and his creatures; indeed, the ultimate elimination of *alterity* undercuts the very possibility of *love*. Maximos' vision, securing that the deified individual preserves his distinct identity, ensures that the synergy of human effort and divine grace which begins in this life continues eternally in a dialogue of love. In this perspective, the gift of deification that we receive in the Son makes us "co-heirs with Christ" (*sygklēronomoi de Christou*); *theōsis* amounts to our *filial adoption* by God.[86] It is the eternal Son who accomplished the deification of the *logos* of humanity, making us children of the Most High; it is the same Son, who is the source and foundation of all our virtues, and who "takes flesh" in us as we progress on the spiritual path. Humanity comes therefore to enjoy the prerogatives of the Godhead, *inasmuch as they belong to the Son*. The contrast between divinity *kata physin* and *kata charin* is mirrored by the contrast between the One who is Son by nature and those who become God's children by grace.[87]

Some might object at this point that claiming to share in the deity *of the Son* might be incompatible with the belief that the three Persons of the Trinity share the same undivided essence, while also contradicting Maximos' association of Christ's wills and operations with their natures, rather than the hypostasis of the Word. This claim, however, asserts nothing more than the fact that the Son is the chief instrument of our salvation, and as such it is through the Son that we receive our share in the divine nature.[88] In the *Capita Theologiae et Oeconomiae*, the application to the incarnate Christ of the Old Testament expression "son of man" (*hyios tou anthrōpou*) is opposed (by *antistrophē*) to our adoption by the Father: "the divine Word, son of God the Father, became man and son of man so as to turn men into

---

[86] Maximos the Confessor, *Q.Th 59* (CCSG 22: 59), where the Scriptural reference is to Rm 8:17. See Larchet, *La Divinisation de l'Homme selon Saint Maxime le Confesseur*, 617–620, for a critique of Garrigues' notion of filial adoption, which again distorts Maximos' understanding of deification and sees filial adoption as the acquisition of a special (created) grace on our part. This co-inheritance is thus radically different from Evagrios' construal of this notion, where what is inherited *is* the Logos himself.

[87] See Maximos the Confessor, *Orationis Dominicae Brevis Expositio* (PG 90: 884–890); also *Amb. 10* (PG 91: 1121b).

[88] See Felix Heinzer, *Gottes Sohn als Mensch. Die Struktur des Menschseins Christi bei Maximus Confessor*, 173.

gods and sons of God."[89] Irénée-Henri Dalmais, also echoed by Heinzer, observes that how for Maximos, deification is ultimately synonymous with "a mode of filial participation in the relation of the Son to the Father."[90] In this way, Maximos' understanding of deification treads the difficult balance between the preservation of individual identity and its assimilation to the divinity, while also establishing the deified individual as partner in the incessant dialogue of love between Father and Son.

GLORIFIED PLURALITY: THE ROLE OF *AGAPĒ* AND THE CELESTIAL JERUSALEM

The question that remains to be answered is the role that our *restored* faculties play in the context of practice. How do natural contemplation and the practice of the virtues relate to the deified state? Is our eschatological condition so totally *other* that *theōria* and *praxis* are merely preparatory stages, or is the final mystical insight an intensified form of these practices? In the *Capita Theologiae et Oeconomiae* and the *Capita de Charitate*, these two aspects of spiritual practice are not mere preparatory stages; rather, *theōria* and *praxis* define our spiritual itinerary both in this life and in the next, where our individual effort will eventually be superseded by God's grace.

The presence of different stages of natural contemplation is present already in Origen's exegetical writings, where the virtues prepare one for natural contemplation, and the latter, in turn, prepare one for union with God, with precise boundaries marking one's progress from one stage to the next.[91] Evagrios' *Kephalaia Gnostika*, as well his writings included in the *Philokalia*, take up again this three-fold scheme, with *theōria praktikē* and *theōria physikē* paving the way to the highest stage of contemplation.[92] As re-

---

[89] Maximos the Confessor, *Capita Theologiae et Oeconomiae*, 2, 25, in *Philokalia*, Vol. 2, 143 (PG 90: 1136b).

[90] See Irénée-Henry Dalmais, "Maxime le Confesseur," in *Dictionnaire de spiritualité* X (1980): 836–847; also Felix Heinzer, *Gottes Sohn als Mensch*, 180–186. Jean-Claude Larchet (in *La Divinisation de l'Homme selon Saint Maxime le Confesseur*, 624) contends that deification is not equivalent to filial adoption, although the two always happen simultaneously. In view of the fact, however, that deified individuals receive the divine prerogatives inasmuch as they are the prerogatives *of the Son*, it would seem to me that the two views are substantially equivalent.

[91] See Origen, *Comm. in Canticum*, Prologue (PG 13: 61–82), where Proverbs, Ecclesiastes, and the Song of Songs refer to the three stages of the spiritual life.

[92] As noted for instance in Evagrios, *Kephalaia Gnostika*, 1, 10, in *Les Six Centuries des 'Kephalaia Gnostica'*, 20–21. There is also an earlier Hellenist tradition that

marked by Daniélou in his study of Gregory of Nyssa, the Cappadocian Fathers modify the scheme slightly, seeing the three stages as effectively parallel while also undermining the strict dichotomy between contemplation and the virtues.[93] Maximos, in his turn, retrieves Evagrios' scheme, adopts the Cappadocian correctives, and grounds the system in his theology of the hypostatic union. In this way, the deified state transfigures the intellect, while also transforming our psycho-physical faculties. The cosmos, together with Scripture and the life of the incarnate Word, offer cues as to our behavior, which eventually makes us worthy of the knowledge of God. In this perspective, one could almost talk of two different stages of *theōria*, mediated by *praxis*.

As observed by Völker, Maximos' terminological usage is not fully consistent; in most cases, *theōria* refers to the contemplation of creation, but occasionally it also indicates the higher mystical insight.[94] A term that is used to indicate both is *gnōsis*; while Evagrios identified *gnōsis* with the experience of union with one's noetic ground, Maximos distinguishes a lower *gnōsis*, whereby the *nous* gains an insight into created reality, and an *hypselotatē gnōsis*, whereby the *nous* is vouchsafed a partial apprehension of the divine reality.[95] The whole of the *Ambigua* are rife with references to this "ineffable" and "divine" *gnōsis*, towards which all earlier contemplation seemed to point. For Evagrios, the *nous* which has shed its corporal shell would be able to gaze into the depth of the divine mystery, which is beyond all form as well as beyond number and time; in this perspective, the *nous* is the locus of the highest mystical insight.[96] Maximos' position is more nuanced, but numerous passages emphasize the importance of leaving behind a "carnal" attitude towards the divine mystery. In a few passages of the *Capita Theologiae et Oeconomiae*, those who are attached to the *logoi* of the cosmos are ac-

---

sees ethics, physics, and logic as the three parts of philosophy; see for instance Pierre Hadot, *Philosophy As a Way of Life : Spriritual Exercises from Socrates to Foucault* (trans. by M. Chase; Oxford, U.K., and Cambridge, Mass: Blackwell Publ., 1995).

[93] Jean Daniélou, *Platonisme et théologie mystique. Essay sur la théologie spirituelle de Gregoire de Nysse* (2d ed.; Paris: Seuil, 1953), 22.

[94] See Walther Völker, *Maximus the Confessor als Meister des geistlichen Lebens*, 242–251. The author compares Maximos' terminology with Evagrios'.

[95] Maximos the Confessor, Prologue to *Quaestiones ad Thalassium* (CCSG 7: 19).

[96] See Evagrios, *Kephalaia Gnostika*, 4, 18–21, in *Les Six Centuries des 'Kephalaia Gnostica'*, 142–145.

cused of "keeping Christ in the flesh."[97] In *Amb. 10*, the second circumcision wrought by Joshua with stone knives is taken to symbolize the leaving behind of the knowledge of creation by those who are vouchsafed the vision of God.[98] Similarly, in *Amb. 21*, Paul's third heaven indicates the soul's final movement beyond the knowledge of the *logoi*.[99] Finally, the *Capita Theologiae et Oeconomiae* figuratively describe the highest mystical insight as "circumcision of circumcision," or "Shabbat of Shabbat." While circumcision indicates the soul's ability to contemplate created reality without the passions, this further stage indicates the stripping away even of the soul's "impassioned feelings" for creation.[100] Using an analogy, Maximos characterizes this final stage of spiritual progress as a "harvest of harvest," where the soul, following "the mystical contemplation of noetic realities," finally apprehends God.[101]

Maximos' position as to the ontological implications of this insight is however radically different from Evagrios', resting on a deeper disagreement as to the ontological nature and destiny of the *logoi*. As early as 1930, M. Viller noted how Maximos' spiritual theology, while retaining Evagrios' apophatic understanding of mystical knowledge, did not share the latter's belief in the inevitability of *elisio alteritatis*.[102] For Evagrios, the ultimate mystical insight effectively meant that our *nous* would dissolve in the uncreated divine mind, but for Maximos knowledge of the divine nature actually secures the separate existence of our *nous*. The *Capita Theologiae et Oeconomiae* observe that the Apostle's saying "We shall have Christ's *nous*" (1 Col 2:16) does not mean that our intellect shall be suppressed, nor that Christ's *nous* shall "perfect" our *nous* in the same way as grace perfects nature (an inter-

---

[97] Maximos the Confessor, *Capita Theologiae et Oeconomiae*, 2, 47 and 94, in *Philokalia*, Vol. 2, 148–9 and 161–2 (PG 90: 1145–6 and 1169–1170), quoted also in Hans Urs von Balthasar, *Kosmische Liturgie*, 553.

[98] Maximos the Confessor, *Amb.* 10 (PG 91: 1120a). Joshua (who in the Septuagint has the same name as Jesus) is also associated with the same theme in Maximos the Confessor, *Quaestiones et dubia* 2, 82 (CCSG 10: 164).

[99] Maximos the Confessor, *Amb.* 21 (PG 91: 1240b).

[100] Maximos the Confessor, *Capita Theologiae et Oeconomiae*, 1, 36–41, in *Philokalia*, Vol. 2, 121–122 (PG 90: 1097–8).

[101] Maximos the Confessor, *Capita Theologiae et Oeconomiae*, 1, 43–44, in *Philokalia*, Vol. 2, 122–3 (PG 90: 1099–1100).

[102] Marcel Viller, "Aux sources de la spiritualité de saint Maxime. Les œuvres d'Évagre Pontique," *RDAM* 11 (1930): 163–66.

pretation suggested by Garrigues),[103] but rather that Christ's *nous* shall illumine our intellect with the light of its knowledge, to the extent compatible with the limited nature of our *logos*.[104]

Later Byzantine authors, such as Symeon the New Theologian or Gregory Palamas, would emphasize the "visual" aspect of this apprehension, which hesychast literature associates with the uncreated light of Tabor.[105] Maximos' view can certainly be read as foreshadowing these later developments, inasmuch as he interprets the experience of the disciples at the Transfiguration as a foretaste of the beatific vision;[106] similarly, he echoes the Apostle's claim that the just shall see God face to face.[107] His position, however, comes close to Gregory of Nyssa in emphasizing the *intellectual* dimension of this insight, whereby the *nous* comes to experience the glory of God. The move beyond the *logoi* signals that knowledge of God is no longer mediated by created reality, and that our intellect comes into direct contact with the mystery of God. Of course, even if the *logos* of our nature was created so as to be receptive to this knowledge of the divine, its bestowal ultimately rests upon God's initiative; in the *Capita Theologiae et Oeconomiae*, we are reminded that the human intellect, lacking "the power to ascend," only attains *theologia* if the "rays of the divine light" deign to illumine it.[108]

This last qualification shows how much Maximos has distanced himself from the *Kephalaia Gnostika*, where the final noetic insight suppresses any distinction between the individual and the divine reality. Whenever the *Ambigua* point out that the object of *theologia* is not God *per se* (*kat'auton*), but

---

[103] See Jean-Marie Garrigues, "L'énergie divine e la grâce chez Maxime le Confesseur," *Istina* 19 (1974): 282–284.

[104] Maximos the Confessor, *Capita Theologiae et Oeconomiae*, 2, 83, in *Philokalia*, Vol. 2, 159 (PG 90: 1164–1165).

[105] See for instance Archbishop Basil Krivocheine, *In the Light of Christ. St. Symeon the New Theologian: Life-Spirituality-Doctrine* (Crestwood, N.Y.: St. Vladimir's Seminary Press, 1986), 382–6, on the theme of the uncreated, deifying light.

[106] Maximos the Confessor, *Q.Th 25* (CCSG 7: 165), where it is claimed that the ultimate destiny of every intellect is "to behold the true Word of God without seeing, and having shed every understanding and knowledge" (*pas nous [...]deon pasēs auton gymnon ennoias kai gnōseōs anommatōs horan ton alēthē theon logon*).

[107] Maximos the Confessor, *Capita Theologiae et Oeconomiae*, 2, 80, in *Philokalia*, Vol. 2, 158 (PG 90: 1161–1164).

[108] Maximos the Confessor, *Capita Theologiae et Oeconomiae*, 1, 31, in *Philokalia*, Vol. 2, 120 (PG 90: 1093–1096).

rather the *logoi* that are around Him, Maximos echoes Gregory of Nazianzos' critique of Eunomios' *technologia*, according to which the properly trained *nous* could gain an unlimited insight into the divine nature. When, in *Or. 40*, Gregory of Nazianzos gives an allegorical reading of the "fire before the Lord's countenance" in Exodus, he is underscoring that our intellect can only grasp the outer aspect of the divine essence. This conviction is no different from the claim by Gregory of Nyssa that the invisible God is seen through "certain realities" (the energies) that "move around Him."[109] While the *logoi* of created reality are the object of *theoria*, and the *logoi* of the uncreated energies are the object of *theologia*, our mind shall never know the *logos* of the divine essence. We are again confronted with the dialectic of unity and plurality that grounds all creation in the eternal Word; the same paradigm transferred to a higher ontological level enables Maximos to posit our intellectual apprehension of the divine reality, while securing its ultimate epistemological inexhaustibility.

Maximos does not resort to theme of divine darkness (*gnophos*), but his understanding of the utter remoteness of the divine essence echoes the apophatic reverence for the divine mystery that one finds in Gregory of Nyssa's *Vita Moysis*. At the same time, for Maximos the revelation of God's plan takes place on Tabor, not on Sinai; and it is not the Father's back that is revealed to the disciples, but the transfigured face of Christ. The divine light is mediated by the incarnate Christ, who explodes the dichotomy between apophasis and kataphasis; in this light we discern the *logoi* of creation and the *logoi* of the divine operations (or energies), both resting in the hypostasis of the eternal Son. *Q.Th. 8* observes that in the divine nature there is only one light according to the essence, though this light is threefold according to the hypostases.[110] The light of Christ is the vehicle whereby the *nous* attains the highest mystical insight, but also the very content of this insight; through this light we ascend to the world of unity and spirit which does not however suppress the world of plurality and form.

Indeed, it is this glorified plurality that we learn to see, as we advance on the spiritual path. In *Amb. 22*, for instance, we are reminded that the *logoi* of created reality are nothing but markers of God's presence in creation. The multiplicity of these *logoi* is bound to disorient those intellects that go

---

[109] Gregory of Nyssa, *Oratio de Beatitudinibus*, 6 (PG 44: 1268c-1270a); Gregory of Nazianzos, *Orationes* 40 (PG 36: 363–4; also 411–4). This is the root of the later Palamite distinction between essence and energies.

[110] Maximos the Confessor, *Q.Th 8* (CCSG 7: 77).

no further than form and matter, but this should be no cause for concern; as noted by the Pseudo-Denys, God remains one and undivided in all His manifestations, which follow a clear order and plan.[111] While the ontological transfiguration of the *nous* is accompanied by an intensified intellectual insight, the difference between created and uncreated works precedes our apprehension of it, since God's plan for the cosmos precedes the foundation of the world.[112] The *logoi* of creation reveal the works of God that have begun in time, whereas the *logoi* of the operations unveil *ta erga tou theou* that know no beginning and no end, such as His goodness or immortality.[113] Both sets of *logoi* rest in God; each set discloses God's plan to the extent compatible with our spiritual attainment.[114]

We saw in the last chapter how the *Liber Asceticus* presented Christ's life on earth as an object of contemplation setting the terms for *praxis*. The inextricable link between *gnōsis* and *agapē* does not cease at the eschatological level; given that natural contemplation is always accompanied by virtuous activity, the highest mystical insight is accompanied by a dialogue of love with God. In the same way as Christ turned water into wine at the wedding at Cana, God turns the water of *theōria* into the wine of *theologia*, introducing us to the joy of divine intimacy.[115] At the culmination of our spiritual path, we no longer love God through His creatures, but in His very being. While a certain degree of union with God is already realized in the earlier stages of

---

[111] Maximos the Confessor, *Amb.* 22 (PG 91: 1256a-1257c). The reference to the Pseudo-Denys in this *Ambigua* is to Pseudo-Denys, *De Divinis Nominibus*, 4, 2–3 (PG 3: 695–698).

[112] Some disagree on this matter, and insist in seeing only an epistemological distinction; see for instance Endre von Ivanka, *Plato christianus. La réception critique du Platonisme chez les Pères de l'Église* (Paris: Presses Universitaires de France, 1990), 280–286; Bernardo De Angelis, *Natura, Persona e Libertà: l'Antropologia di Massimo il Confessore*, Ch.2–3.

[113] See Maximos the Confessor, *Capita Theologiae et Oeconomiae*, 1, 48, in *Philokalia*, Vol. 2, 123 (PG 90: 1099–1102). The way to distinguish between the two is that the former "have non-being as prior to their being," whereas the latter do not.

[114] A further distinction between Maximos' personalism and Evagrios' position is that for Maximos God is the *source* of substantial knowledge (*gnōsis ousiōdēs*), whereas Evagrios effectively identifies God with it. See Lars Thunberg, *Microcosm and Mediator*, 355. With his theology of deification, Maximos completes the Christian assimilation of the Platonic notion of substantial knowledge, according to which those who gain a deeper insight into reality are necessarily transformed by this insight.

[115] Maximos the Confessor, *Q.Th 40* (CCSG 7: 266).

theōria, the stripping away of all references to created reality ensures that this union is now all the more intense, as we no longer see or love God through the mediation of creation.[116] The Evagrian understanding of creation made it difficult to accommodate the notion of a *gradual* union with God already in this world; even if a few individuals practicing stern asceticism can anticipate the eschaton already in this life, the ultimate mystical insight ordinarily emerges only when the intellect is withdrawn from creation. Maximos' readiness to envisage the *logoi* of this world as manifesting the divine plan means that for him deification can already begin in this life.

This different approach to plurality is reflected in a different approach to *apatheia*, which in Maximos acquires a much more active and relational dimension than in the Origenist school. For Evagrios, spiritual practice freezes the passions rooted in the lower part of the soul, so that they are no longer an obstacle to spiritual progress; for Maximos, the passions have the potential to become virtues, which, as we shall see below, secure our likeness to Christ, changing us into God's adopted children. In this perspective, our disordered love for the things of this earth, which takes the form of sexual desire, or craving for material possessions, is transformed into love for God; similarly, the anger that sometimes plagues our relationship with our neighbor is turned into zeal to do God's will in this world and the next. In this way, *apatheia* is not only compatible, but effectively entails a rightful exercise of our virtues, which at the end shall also become vehicles of the divine energies, and which already in this life help us to attain the divine likeness.[117] Even in the final, unitive state, where the Evagrian *nous* drowns in the sea of the henad, the intellect is carried towards God "on the wings of *agapē*."[118]

In this perspective, it is easy to make sense of Maximos' reading of the episode in Luke, when Christ sends his disciples to arrange a room for the Last Supper. In this passage, Peter and John, who are themselves taken to symbolize the active and the contemplative life, are first confronted by a man who carries a jar of water, and then, once they reach the house that Jesus has indicated, by the steward who shows them the room for the meal. In *Q.Th 3*, the man with the jar represents those who carry the grace of

---

[116] Jean-Claude Larchet, *La Divinisation de l'Homme selon Saint Maxime le Confesseur*, 516–17.

[117] Lars Thunberg, *Microcosm and Mediator*, 338–339.

[118] This is the expression used by Maximos the Confessor in *Capita de Charitate*, 2, 26, in *Philokalia*, Vol. 2, 69 (PG 90: 991–2).

God "on the shoulders of the virtues" (*tois ōmois tōn aretōn*), and who thereby reaches a stable condition of *apatheia* (the house). In the house, the steward represents those who have attained *theologia*, and are thus in constant converse with God; but even in this condition, where no barrier exists to the highest contemplative insight, the steward is still expected to practice the virtues so as to ensure that the eternal Logos can come into the house.[119] It is easy to see that for Maximos the man with the jar and the steward are effectively the same person, who has moved further on the path to perfection. Clearly, the whole scene is set up so as to present the Eucharist as the culmination of the intellectual and agapic dialogue between God and humanity.

In the *Ambigua*, Maximos highlights the intrinsic symmetry between Christ's kenotic descent and suffering, undertaken out of love for humanity, and our noetic ascent into the divine, sustained by a deepening love for God. At the crucifixion, Christ did not merely suffer in the body, but also in the soul and mind; both humanity and divinity were involved in the redemption of humanity. In *Amb. 47*, Maximos sees the detachment from material things and the dispassioned contemplation of their *logoi* prefigured in the crucifixion of Christ's *body*, whereas the leaving behind of created references reflects the crucifixion of Christ's *soul*. Finally, the injunction never to rest satisfied in our experience of the divine energies, but further to deepen our insight into the divine nature, is associated with the crucifixion of Christ's *mind*.[120] The fact that this third crucifixion never ends is a further indication of the fact that Maximos, unlike Evagrios, sees no conclusion in our gradual assimilation to the divine reality. Our individual identity is thus a dynamic reality, which is forever evolving even as it dwells securely in the divine love. Within each individual, Maximos distinguishes a natural potentiality (*einai*), an intentional operation (*eu* or *kakōs einai*), and God's ratification of its outcome (*aei einai*), noting that the *logoi* of this third reality belongs to us only by God's grace.[121] The blending of divinity and humanity in Christ ensures that in the deified individuals the union of soul

---

[119] Maximos the Confessor, *Q.Th. 3* (CCSG 7: 55–59).
[120] Maximos the Confessor, *Amb.* 47 (PG 91: 1360ad).
[121] Maximos the Confessor, *Capita de Charitate* 3, 23, in *Philokalia*, Vol. 2, 86 (PG 90: 1023–1024).

and body mirrors and repeats the glory of the incarnation, to the extent that we are receptive to divine grace.[122]

The ratification of individual identity, and the assertion of the enduring quality of ontological boundaries, ensures that glorified bodiliness is a fundamental characteristic of Maximos' eschatological horizon. In this perspective, any notion of "final restoration" would eliminate any purpose from creation, and it would also demean our moral autonomy. God did not create the natural order so as to punish some wayward souls, but brought creatures into existence, so that they could participate in Him "in proportion to their capacity" and He might in His turn "rejoice in their works."[123] The goal of practice is to heal the inner wounds (*diaireseis*) within each individual and within creation, by means of "true faith" *and* "spiritual love." These *diaireseis* are not erased, but are turned into fruitful distinctions (*diaphorai*) that lead to dialogue and growth, and actually ensure a plurality of outcomes. In this perspective, divine judgment does not roll back history to the beginning, but separates individuals on the basis of their fundamental orientation to good and evil, which, in turn, reflects how they responded to the commandment of love.

If we turn to Maximos' *Mystagogia*, we see a glorified plurality of embodied souls joining in the Church's liturgy of thanksgiving, which prefigures the celestial Jerusalem of the last day. Much as the individual straddles the divide between the sensible and the intelligible realm, and partakes of the divine under both aspects, the Church is a concrete as well as a spiritual reality, and it shares in the gradual deification of created matter.[124] In the words of Maximos, the *ekklēsia* is "an image of the world composed of visible and invisible substances,"[125] encompassing within itself "unity and diversity."[126] Within the church, everything is invested with a symbolic meaning. Within the building that is destined to the common acts of worship, the area assigned to the laity (the nave), is separate from the area assigned to the ministers (the sanctuary), mirroring the hypostatic union of humanity and

---

[122] The soul gains immutability (*atrepsia*), and the body, through the mediation of the soul, gains immortality (*athanasia*). See Maximos the Confessor, *Amb.* 7 (PG 91: 1088 c).

[123] Maximos the Confessor, *Capita de Charitate* 3, 46, in *Philokalia*, Vol. 2, 90 (PG 90: 1029–1030). The Scriptural reference is to Ps. 104:31.

[124] *Mystagogia* 2, 4 (PG 91: 667–71; 684).

[125] *Mystagogia* 2 (PG 91: 667): *eikōn esti tou ex horatōn kai aoratōn ousiōn hyphestōtos kosmou.*

[126] *Mystagogia* 2 (PG 91: 667): *henōsin kai diakrisin epidechomenēn.*

divinity. As the destiny of Christ's humanity is to be deified, in the same way the nave *is* the sanctuary in potency,[127] and as Christ's divinity is only known by us through his humanity, so is the sanctuary the nave in actuality, "by virtue of the principle of the sacred action (*mystagogia*) which is there accomplished."[128]

The Eucharist, of course, is the lynchpin of the church building. Both Eucharist and building mirror the incarnation, after which the entire cosmos is patterned according to God's plan. As the spiritual and the material world reflect each other in an endless game of mirrors, the Chalcedonian exchange of properties between the two *ousiai* reflects the ceaseless intercourse between the world of the higher powers, again prefigured by the sanctuary, and the realm of those who indulge the senses, again symbolized by the nave. Church buildings are places where the spiritual world becomes manifest within the sensible realm in an explicit manner, and for Maximos their architecture offers a secure hermeneutic tool to discern an order within the world. Churches are a symphony of symbols, alerting worshippers to the Christocentric thrust of the liturgy, no less than the Christocentric thrust of the cosmos. The Logos orders all things towards their proper goal; it maintains harmony (*diakosmēsis*) among the cosmos' different components.[129] Much as the labyrinths adorning the nave of Medieval cathedrals possessed a cruciform structure that helped visitors make sense of their ultimate purpose, the hypostatic union is the woof guiding us through the maze of signs.[130] And where but in the Eucharist should we look for a symbol of our transfigured identity in Christ?

---

[127] *Mystagogia* 2 (PG 91: 669): *hierateion men ton naon kata tēn dynamin.*

[128] *Mystagogia* 2 (PG 91: 669): *kai empalin naon to hierateion, kata tēn energeian tēs idias ton archon echon mystagōgias archēn.* As noted by George Berthold, this is one of the rare occasions when Maximos actually uses the term *mystagōgia* (rendered by Migne as *res sacra*) to indicate the Eucharist; see his *Maximus the Confessor: Selected Writings*, Note 33 to the *Mystagogia*, 217.

[129] See Irénée-Henri Dalmais, "La Théorie des 'Logoi' des Créatures chez S. Maxime le Confesseur," RSPT 36 (1952): 244–249. The term *diakosmēsis* most likely reveals Maximos' indebtedness to the Pseudo-Denys, who in *De Coelesti Hierarchia* 2, 1 (PG 3: 135–138) talks of the "ordered harmony" of the universe ruled by the Godhead.

[130] See the discussion of the Christian symbolism of the labyrinth in Craig Wright, *The Maze and the Warrior: Symbols in Architecture, Theology and Music* (Cambridge, Mass.: Harvard University Press, 2004), Ch. 1–3.

For Maximos, the consecrated bread and the wine prefigure the destiny of the natural order at the end of time, when Christ "will be all in all." At the same time, the different liturgical actions are interpreted as symbolizing different aspects of Christ's salvific work, which we, in our turn, are invited to emulate.[131] Thus, through the celebration of the Eucharist, the Church participates in Christ's mediatorial work, and helps bring about the transfiguration of created matter.[132] Much as the divinity of Christ reconfigures his humanity and yet respects its ontological distinctiveness, the practice of the virtues conforms the sensitive and incensive parts of the soul to the simplicity of the intellect, and yet does not subsume the passions into the *nous*.[133] The Chalcedonian preservation of plurality as a harmonious synthesis is suggested by the purposeful unity of altar, sanctuary, and nave, which are hierarchically ordered in mutual complementarity like the different phases of *theōria*.[134] Towards the end of the *Mystagogia*, the communication of the idioms that takes place in the hypostatic union is the model for the perichoretic relationship of the three forms of contemplation, which is symbolized by the great entrances of the synaxis; through this circular movement, the liturgical action taking place in the sanctuary moves back to the nave and embraces the congregation, making it partake of the mystery accomplished on the altar.[135]

Maximos' fondness for reciprocity (*paradosis*) ensures that the symmetry between divine self-bestowal and human response is reflected by a dialogical construal of spiritual practice: Christ's kenotic self-emptying and humanity's virtuous self-denial mirror each other, and whenever an individual succeeds in turning her passions into virtues, the Word once more becomes incarnate and turns her virtues into his own body. The liturgy is therefore the paradigm of what happens in our very selves; Evagrios Pon-

---

[131] *Mystagogia* 5–24 (PG 91: 687–718). Maximos' reading of the liturgy belongs to the vast corpus of allegorical readings of the liturgy in the Eastern tradition, the most famous of which is probably Nicholas Kabasilas' *Life in Christ* (*Peri tēs en Christō zōēs*), itself greatly influenced by Maximos. See Endre von Ivanka (ed.), *Das Buch vom Leben in Christus: Sakrament und Liturgie von Nikolaos Kabasilas* (translated into German by Gerhard Hoch. 2nd ed. Wien und Munich: Cura Verlag, 1966).

[132] *Mystagogia* 2, 4 (PG 91: 667–671).

[133] On Maximos' rendition of the Platonic division of the soul into three parts, see Irénée-Henri Dalmais, "Un traité de théologie contemplative: *Le Commentaire du Pater Noster* de saint Maxim le Confesseur," *RAM* 29 (1953): 123–39.

[134] Maximos the Confessor, *Capita de Charitate* 3, 2 (PG 90: 1017–8).

[135] *Mystagogia* 23 (PG 91: 698–702).

tikos had also talked of the virtues as readying our intellect for the presence of the divine, but for Maximos the eternal Logos descends into our flesh and makes it its own.[136] As such, the life of the individual Christian is itself a liturgy, no less awesome than what happens in the temples of the church; the Chalcedonian paradigm of unity in diversity not only affords a hermeneutic lens for the mystery of the real presence, but also explains the manner in which we are called to respond to God through the simultaneous pursuit of *theōria* and *praxis*.

Maximos' reading of the liturgy as a cosmic event making present the event of the incarnation and fostering its salvific impact throughout the created order rests on the conception of the universe as an intelligible reality which was one of the crucial concerns of the Cappadocian Fathers.[137] Yet, what is crucial here is that the liturgy is the highest response which transfigured humanity can offer to the God who has chosen freely to redeem us and introduce us into a dialogue of love with Him. Liturgy is synergy; liturgy is reciprocity and symmetry; liturgy is *theōsis*. In the Eucharist, created reality withdraws and lets God enter into reality and transform it; in our lives, we are invited to let go of self-love and let the eternal Word take flesh in us over and over again. Receiving the consecrated bread and the wine, we receive the guarantee of our incorruptibility, which plants in us a seed of immortality and invites us to gaze towards the "new heaven" and the "new earth" which God is preparing for us.

When in her work *After Writing* Catherine Pickstock presents the Eucharist as the guarantee of reality's meaning and purpose, and goes on to indict what she views as the subjectivism and reductionism of contemporary worship, her eschatological thrust is analogous to Maximos' longing for the celestial Jerusalem, whose manifestation will seal the deification of the

---

[136] Evagrios' texts collected in the *Philokalia* emphasize how the virtues purify the *nous* of the images of created reality and ready it for an experience of virtual unity with the divine; the incarnation plays hardly any role. See for instance Evagrios, *Outline Teaching on Asceticism and Stillness in the Solitary Life*, and *On Prayer: One Hundred and Fifty-Three Texts*, in Geoffrey E. H. Palmer, Philip Sherrard, and Kallistos Ware (eds.), *Philokalia*, Vol. 1 (London: Faber & Faber, 1979), 31–7 and 55–71. For Maximos' discussion of the continued presence of Christ after the incarnation, see *Capita Theologiae et Oeconomiae*, I, 54–55; II, 28–33 (PG 90: 1104; 1137–40).

[137] On the Cappadocians' qualified retrieval of the Hellenist notion of the cosmos as an ordered reality, see Jaroslav Pelikan, *Christianity and Classical Culture: The Metamorphosis of Natural Theology in the Christian Encounter with Hellenism* (New Haven, Conn.: Yale University Press, 1993).

cosmos begun in Christ.[138] While God glorifies us by letting us partake of the divine nature, we glorify God in preparing a fitting place in our intellect and flesh for him, who alone "returns all things to itself and gathers together whatever may be scattered."[139] It is only at the end of time that we shall truly be *moira theou*, but then we will also be truly ourselves, more than any stage of our earthly life could ever bear. The mysterious image of the wheels in Ezekiel's vision, which are forever interlocking and are forever distinct, is a symbol of the undivided harmony of Maximos' vision, where each element is preserved in its identity, and yet all components carry and are carried by the eternal Logos.[140]

---

[138] See Catherine Pickstock, *After Writing: The Liturgical Consummation of Philosophy* (Oxford: Blackwells, 1997), esp. Ch. 6 ("The Resurrection of the Sign") 253–66.

[139] Pseudo-Denys, *De Divinis Nominibus*, 4, 4 (PG 3: 697–700).

[140] See Ezek 1, 4–26.

5 THE HENAD IN TIBET: RDZOGS CHEN AND ORIGINAL SELF-AWARENESS

In the second half of the 8th century CE, the Indian Yogin Padmasambhava (Tib. Gu rub rin po che) accepted the invitation of King Khri srong lDe brtsan to move permanently to Tibet and to spread the Buddhist *dharma* (Tib. *chos*) in the Himalayan kingdom. The events surrounding the so-called Early Transmission of Buddhism to Tibet are shrouded in legend, and many Tibetan folk tales present Padmasambhava as a legendary hero endowed with supernatural powers, set on "taming" Tibet's local deities and enlisting their allegiance to the new religion.[1] While historical events surrounding the establishment of the first academy at bSam yas may be difficult to reconstruct, scholars agree that, for a brief period at least, the Buddhist *dharma* was able to make deep inroads into Tibetan culture, both in its Mahāyāna version and in its more esoteric tantric forms. This ensured that Buddhist teachings would survive the end of royal patronage in the mid 9th century, going underground when supporters of the earlier, shamanistic tradition regained the upper hand. When the so-called Later Transmission returned Buddhism to Tibet in the 11th century, the lineages originating from this earlier phase in the country's history became known as the Ancient School (rNying ma), whose teachings were consciously set in opposition to the versions of the *dharma* popularized by bKa rgyud or bKa' gdams *yogis*.[2] While of course undergoing profound changes, both the "ancient" and the "modern" schools have survived to the present day.

Our focus here is on a particular current of rNying ma teaching, namely the tradition known as rDzogs chen (Tib. for "great perfection"). The Ancient School shared this tradition with the followers of the pre-

---

[1] Geoffrey Samuel, *Civilized Shamans: Buddhism in Tibetan Societies* (Smithsonian Series in Ethnographic Inquiry. Washington DC: Smithsonian Books, 1993), 464. Many pre-Buddhist deities would later be invoked as *dharma* protectors, in an exemplary application of the Mahāyāna principle of *upayakauśalya*.

[2] Reginald A. Ray, *Secrets of the Vajra World: The Tantric Buddhism of Tibet* (Boston, Mass. & London: Shambala, 2002), 34–36. Ray notes how the very notion of a unitary rNying ma school effectively emerged as a reaction to the later lineages.

Buddhist Bon tradition, which itself was a reason why representatives of later lineages such as the rSa skya and the dGe lugs regarded rDzogs chen as an "inferior" form of teaching;[3] rNying ma practitioners, on the other hand, regarded rDzogs chen as the highest form of tantric practice, surpassing any of the practices of the modern schools. The tendency of rival Buddhist schools to demote their opponents' beliefs to "preparatory" status is an ancient one, itself rooted in the self-conscious distancing of early Mahāyāna from the early Hīnayāna tradition; a distinction was customarily made between "indirect" (*neyārtha*) and "direct" (*nītārtha*) texts, where the former, though valuable for individuals of lower spiritual attainment, were subordinated to the latter, which expressed the "true mind" of the Buddha. This strategy, which ensured a certain *modus vivendi* among different schools, rested on complex philosophical assumptions about the nature of ultimate reality, which, as we will see, strongly differed from the position of the Christian authors that we have explored so far.

The goal of rDzogs chen's practitioners was no different from the goal of those who embraced the practices of later schools of thought. Both wanted to attain Buddhahood, and both, in proper Mahāyāna fashion, envisaged the latter as a reality that was active within the samsaric world. Beyond that, however, important disagreements existed as to the nature of Buddhahood and its cosmological role; and these disagreements led to further differences as to the manner whereby Buddhahood could be attained by individual practitioners, as well as to the relation between spiritual practice and the goal it sought. Does spiritual practice have a transformative effect, as affirmed by the members of the dGe lugs school? Or are rDzogs chen practitioners right in thinking that practice merely retrieves a dimension of reality which in fact is always present, but which is now defiled by ignorance and attachment? In simpler words, does *what we do* have any actual impact on the tenor of our spiritual attainment? We have seen by now that the debate between Maximos' theology of deification and Origenist spirituality reflected similar preoccupations,

In the course of this chapter, we will explore a number of classic texts so as retrace rDzogs chen's beliefs concerning the nature of practice and the cosmic scope of Buddha nature. The anonymous treatise *Kun byed rgyal po* ("The All-creating Sovereign") shall introduce us to rDzogs chen's un-

---

[3] In the 13th century, the Sa sKya teacher Sa sKya Pandita attacked rDzogs chen teachings as "invalid." See Roger Jackson "Sa sKya Pandita's account of the bSam yas debate: history as polemic," *JIABS* 5 (1982): 89–99.

derstanding of Buddhahood, which is construed along the lines of an *exitus-reditus* myth; 'Jam dpal bshes gnyen's (Snsk. Mañjuśrīmitra) *rDo la gser zhun* ("Gold Refined From the Ore") and a few extracts from 'Jigs med gLing pa's *kLong chen sNying tig* ("kLong chen pa's seminal heart") shall then help us to get acquainted with the actual practice of rDzogs chen, whose goal is the retrieval of an indestructible condition of awareness. These texts will highlight a number of contacts between rDzogs chen and the practice of Evagrian spirituality, in particular between the rDzogs chen doctrine of the universal mind and Evagrios' belief in the undifferentiated *nous* that preceded the creation of our cosmos. The idea of a primordial henad might have abandoned our Christian shores by the late 7th century, but on the plateau of Tibet it would play an important part until the present day.

THE PRIMORDIAL BUDDHA AND THE RETRIEVAL OF ONENESS

A contemporary rNying ma teacher, Chos rgyal nam khas nor bu, remarks that rDzogs chen writings can be classified into three categories according to their primary scope.[4] The *men ngag* (Snsk. *upadeśa*) are teachings written out of the experience of an individual practitioner, whose purpose is largely didactic and parenetic, in the hope that future generations might be able to benefit from their insights. The *rgyud* (Snsk. *tantra*) set out the ontological assumptions underpinning the *men ngag*, thereby outlining rDzogs chen's beliefs as to Buddha nature and its cosmological role. The third group of texts, known as *lung* (close to Snsk. *āgama*), are effectively commentaries upon particular passages of the *rgyud*, sometimes inserted within the original *rgyud* text, sometimes existing as independent works. To this classification, one may add a fourth set of texts known as the "essential heart" writings. The latter bring together the teachings of the other three groups and show their inner coherence, while also including instructions as to how not to forego the insight that one gains when putting these teachings into practice.[5]

The Tibetan noun *rgyud* is etymologically related to the term "thread," thereby stressing an underlying continuity between the ontological presup-

---

[4] See Chos rgyal nam kha nor bu, Preface to *The Supreme Source: The Fundamental Tantra of the Dzogchen Semde 'Kunjed Gyalpo'* (trans. and comm. Chos rgyal nam kha nor bu and A. Clemente; Ithaca, N.Y.: Snow Lion Pub., 1999), 13–15. The author of the text (hence, *Kun byed rgyal po*) is unknown. In the commentary (56), this threefold division is ascribed to Mañjuśrīmitra, the bodhisattva of wisdom.

[5] See Reginald A. Ray, *Secrets of the Vajra World*, 301.

positions of practice, practice itself, and its ultimate fruit.[6] The term *Pha-lāyāna*, or vehicle of the fruit, which is sometimes used to indicate the tantric tradition within Mahāyāna, similarly highlights the intrinsic relation between spiritual practice and its fruit, to the point that effectively the fruit is itself the path. In the doctrinal system of the rDzogs chen tantras, this continuity between the various aspects of practice is undergirded by the assertion of the existence of a primordial "condition of purity" (*gdod ma'i gzhi*), which constitutes the foundation of the samsaric world in which we live and of the experience of enlightenment whereby this world can be transcended. rDzogs chen doctrine is thus fully in line with the Mahāyāna reinterpretation of the third noble truth, but the belief in the ultimate identity of *samsara* and *nirvāna* is read as reflecting a deeper truth concerning the nature of the universe, which is said to flow in its entirety from an ineffable "base of primordial purity" (*ye thog ka dag gi gzhi*).[7] A considerable proportion of rDzogs chen texts is thus taken up with reflections as to the nature of this ontological foundation of reality, which is effectively assimilated to the all-encompassing Buddha nature of other Mahāyāna traditions.

While Dol po pa's characterization of Buddhahood as plenitude in open polemic with Madhyamaka philosophy immediately comes to mind, rDzogs chen texts even surpass their (much later) *gzhan stong* counterparts in developing a positive conceptualization of Buddhahood. The anonymous text *Kun byed rgyal po* goes as far as personifying the underlying basis of Buddhahood, postulating the existence of a primordial Buddha ("the all-performing king"), who is called Samantabhadra or Kun tu bzang po ("the all-good"), after the chief deity of the pre-Buddhist Bon religion. Within this reality, we are said "to live, move and have our being"; the primordial Buddha is the basis of our practice, as well as its ultimate goal.

Faced by this surfeit of theistic language, which is virtually unparalleled in Buddhist literature, various scholars have set out to trace the origins of this notion in the *prakrti* notion of the Sāmkhya school of philosophy, or in

---

[6] The term *rgyud* also indicates "lineage" and in fact, in the collection of Tibetan texts known as *bKa' 'gyur*, different Tantric tradition are defined by continuity of practice across time. At a deeper level, *rgyud* may indicate karmic continuity within one's consciousness (Sans. *samtāna*). See Geoffrey Samuel, *Civilized Shamans*, 225–226. It is not difficult to trace all three meanings of *rgyud* in the Evagrian tradition.

[7] See Chos rgyal nam kha nor bu and Adriano Clemente, Commentary to *Kun byed rgyal po*, 20.

Kashmirian Shaivite speculation on the nature of the supreme deity.[8] rDzogs chen tantras such as the *Kun byed rgyal po*, however, are better read against the Tibetan developments in the Mahāyāna speculation on Buddha bodies (*kāyas, sku*), which seek to articulate the relation between the Buddha's salvific activity and his cosmic role. The *Astasāhasrikā Prajñāpāramitā* sūtras already distinguished the physical body of the Buddha (*rūpakāya*) from his so-called *dharmakāya*, claiming that the former was in fact subordinate to, and a manifestation of, the Buddha's ultimate insight into the empty nature of reality.[9] This move was motivated by the desire to safeguard the Mahāyāna expansion of the canon from the remonstrances of the Hinayana, but it effectively opened the way to a gradual conflation of Buddhahood with the whole of existing reality (*tattva*).

Throughout the *Perfection of Wisdom*, *dharmakāya* indicates the pure collection of the Buddha's teaching (including any that might yet be revealed in the future), but also the Buddha's excellent attributes (whereby he cognizes the ultimate truth of *śūnyatā*) *and* the very nature of things as empty. The *dharmakāya* is effectively "what is set forth or exemplified in the Buddha's very being";[10] in fact, if it is truly the case that all beings are empty of inherent existence, the *dharmakāya* is the true being of everything that exists, and everything that exists has the potential to become truly enlightened Buddhas. In general, the *dharmakāya*, which is permanent and unchangeable, provides the basis for all other *dharmas*, as emptiness is the ultimate foundation of phenomenal illusion; at the same time, the *dharmakāya* serves as the basis for the Buddha's physical manifestations, which are an expression of the Buddha's compassion for sentient beings.

The conceptual ancestry of texts such as *Kun byed rgyal po* is thus a blend of pre- or extra-Buddhist traditions and of Buddhist philosophical speculation, where the former provides a metaphorical framework for the latter. The development of the *dharmakāya* doctrine was made possible by an effective conflation of the notion of *dharmās* (the teaching of the Buddha) and the notion of *dharmatā* (the underlying structure of reality, Tib. *chos*

---

[8] Samten G. Karmay, "A discussion on the doctrinal position of rDzogs chen from the 10th to the 13th century," *JA* 263 (1975): 147–155; also Eva K. Neumaier-Dargyay, "The concept of a 'Creator God' in Tantric Buddhism," *JIABS* 8.1 (1985): 31–47.

[9] Edward Conze, *The perfection of wisdom. In eight thousand lines and its verse summary* (San Francisco: City Lights Pub., 1973), 291.

[10] Paul Williams, *Mahāyāna Buddhism: the doctrinal foundations* (New York: Routledge, 1989), 176.

nyid). In the Chinese traditions inspired by the *Avatamsaka sūtra*, the Buddha's body of *dharmās* was explicitly identified with the *dharmadhātu* (Tib. *chos nyid dbyings*), the totality of the cosmos seen in its empty aspect; similarly, the particular form of Madhyamaka philosophy that was to gain the upper hand in Tibet, the *dharmakāya* doctrine entails that all beings in a way exemplify the Buddha.[11] A contemporary rNying ma interpreter, Chos rgyal nam khas nor bu, explicitly views the "primordial purity" of the rDzogs chen *rgyud* as identical with the *dharmakāya*, so that the "all-performing king" Samantabhadra is also the source of the bodies of form whereby the Buddha's teachings are transmitted.[12]

Earlier, we saw how Maximos' theological synthesis sought to present the difference and variety of the cosmos as an ordered manifestation of the divine Wisdom. The notion that the *logoi* of creation and those of Scripture are grounded in the divine Wisdom which then becomes manifest in the flesh clearly echoes the speculations on Buddhahood of the *Prajñāpāramitā* sūtras; we shall return again to this issue when reading Tsong kha pa. The Christian belief in the purposeful nature of creation, however, is something that does not begin with Maximos, and indeed the whole polemic with Classical natural theology rested on the conviction that classical cosmologies (as well as their Origenist counterparts) could not accommodate the Christian notion of a divine Wisdom that led the universe and that simultaneously offered guidance to those able to discern its cues.

By the late 4th century, the development of Christian theology was able to integrate Hellenist speculation on the *logos* into the orthodox consensus by locating the source of this divine guidance within the Godhead, and postulating a virtual identity between divine *sophia* and the eternal Son. For Maximos, *pronoia* and *paideusis* were regarded as expressing the involvement of the Christian deity with creation; but the terms of his solution were the result of a long and protracted struggle. At an earlier time, Evagrios had effectively *identified* God with an all-encompassing *nous*; while Maximos' *Ambigua* had privileged the language of agency, so as to underscore the irreducible *otherness* of the deity in relation to the cosmos, the *Kephalaia Gnostika*

---

[11] Daisetz T. Suzuki, *On Indian Mahāyāna Buddhism* (New York: Harper & Row, 1968), 149–152.

[12] See Chos rgyal nam kha nor bu and Adriano Clemente, Commentary to *Kun bjed rgyal po*, in *The Supreme Source*, 21. The commentators note that this claim is also made by the great rNying ma master kLong chen pa in a 14th century colophon to the *Kun bjed rgyal po*, though he himself admits that its ascription to kLong chen pa is contested.

showed no hesitation in postulating an undifferentiated mind as the foundation of the whole universe. The very same notion of the all-encompassing
mind, which cognizes and simultaneously constitutes reality's ultimate nature, is what we find in the *Kun byed rgyal po*' notion of the primordial Buddha.

In her reading of this rDzogs chen text, which in other respects is not
unproblematic,[13] Eva Neumaier-Dargyay reminds us that Buddhist thought
resorted to metaphors so as to accommodate a more intuitive construal of
Buddhist epistemological insights into the philosophical casting gradually
acquired by the *dharma*.[14] In this respect, a tension necessarily existed in Tibet between those who privileged the ineffable insights disclosed in the
course of meditational experience, and those who emphasized the ultimate
normativity of philosophical speculation. It is not difficult to imagine how
the latter position was favored by the supporters of a more institutionalized
form of practice, whereas the former was embraced all the more eagerly by
yogins who had had little exposure to the more philosophical currents of the
Buddhist tradition. As pointed out by Samuel, the very same *yogins* were also
more likely to be in touch with the "shamanistic" currents of Tibetan religion, and thus had the resources to elaborate a synthesis that appealed to
wider sensitivities than just those of the monastic élites.

Before the *dharma*'s transmission to Tibet, and in fact even the before
the rise of Mahāyāna, those schools that posited the superiority of non-
conceptual insight such as the Sarvāstivada ("all exists") had postulated the
existence of a non-substantial ground that carried the flow of momentary
mental entities, and that was itself described as an eternal and immutable
mind (*paramartha citta*). While other Hināyāna schools had rejected this notion, the belief in a sort of all-encompassing mental substratum had been
taken up again within Mahāyāna, giving rise to the belief in a "foundational
consciousness" (*ālayavijñāna*), providing an element of continuity beyond an

---

[13] See Eva K. Neumaier-Dargyay, *The sovereign all-creating mind: The motherly Buddha, A Translation of the Kun byed rgyal po'i mdo* (Albany, N.Y.: SUNY Press, 1992), 2.
Her edition of the *Kun byed rgyal po* contains a translation where she insists that this
text's construal of the unity of samsāra and nirvāna hints at a "divine reality of a
feminine dimension." This might echo Rosemary Radford-Ruether's musings on
gaja (see her *Integrating Ecofeminism, Globalization, and World Religions*, Lanham, Md.:
Rowman & Littlefield Publishers, 2005), but one might then argue along the same
lines that Evagrios' primordial *nous* is "feminine."

[14] Eva K. Neumaier-Dargyay, *The sovereign all-creating mind*, 11–12.

individual's mental phenomena,[15] or in the presence of a "Buddhahood matrix" (*tathāgatagarbha*), securing that the experience of enlightenment was within the reach of every sentient being.[16]

   Within the Yogācāra school, the *ālayavijñāna* purified of all adventitious defilements was often identified with the *tathāgatagarbha*; by postulating a link between either concept and the *dharmakāya*, individual practice would acquire a cosmic dimension, whereby the individual sought to retrieve an inner undefiled condition which was also a part of a "pure" primordial reality. Yogācāra authors would disagree as to whether the *tathāgatagarbha* could be identified with full-blown Buddhahood or it was only its "germ," but rDzogs chen tantras were unequivocal in their claim that the condition of pure awareness which was the ultimate ontological foundation of our being was no different from the primordial Buddha itself. In the esoteric writings of the bKa rgyud tradition, which belonged to the Later Transmission, the final degree of realization transcending the separation between *saṃsāra* and *nirvāna* was called *mahāmudrā*, or "great symbol"; the tantric deities visualized by the practitioner served as the symbol of the ultimate unity (*zhung byug*) of all aspects of reality. In the *Kun byed rgyal po*, the notion of the primordial Buddha served the same function as the *yidam* (Sans. *istadevata*) of the later, but within the tradition of rDzogs chen the emphasis was not on reconstructing a union between opposites, but rather on retrieving the never forsaken unity of the primordial state where the opposition between dual and non-dual consciousness never arises. While a number of Tibetan masters have attempted a synthesis of *mahāmudrā* and rDzogs chen methods, the goal of the former is largely to transform our habitual impure vision into a symbolic mandala of reality by means of a visualization, whereas the latter dismisses all the preliminary stages associated with tantra such as initiation, mantras, or visualization, on the ground that there is nothing we need to purify or "construct." In rDzogs chen, all you need to do is to ac-

---

   [15] Lambert Schmithausen, *Ālayavijñāna. On the origin and the early development of a central concept of Yogācāra philosophy* (SPB IV. Tokyo: The International Institute of Buddhist Studies, 1987), 197–204.
   [16] See Jikido Takasaki, *A study on the Ratnagotravibhāga (Uttaratantra), being a treatise on the tathāgatagarbha theory of Mahāyāna Buddhism* (SOR 33. Roma: Istituto Italiano per il Medio ed Estremo Oriente, 1966), i-xiii. As Eva Dargyay also confirms, the Ratnagotravibhāga's conception of *tathāgatagarbha* comes remarkably close to the notion of *ka dag* in the *Kun byed rgyal po*. See Eva K. Neumaier-Dargyay, *The Sovereign All-Creating Mind*, 12–13.

cess the primordial condition of awareness; any practice that sees itself as *transformative* would be misguided.

The *Kun byed rgyal po*'s first section is devoted to the so-called teachings on "manifestation" (*mngon du phyung ba*), which come close to a compendium of rDzogs chen cosmology. In the opening of the text, we contemplate the primordial Buddha surrounded by his retinue; Samantabhadra personifies the *dharmakāya*, whereas his vast audience is composed of innumerable instances of his form bodies. Both the Buddhas and bodhisattvas who have attained enlightenment (*sāmbhogikakāya*) and the sentient beings who dwell in the world of desire (*nairmānikakāya*) are ultimately inseparable from his essence; even Sattvavajra, who is Samantabhadra's interlocutor throughout the text and who is customarily associated with the transmission of tantric teaching, is presented as an emanation of the "all-powerful king." The vision of the sphere (*thig le*) whence Sattvavajra issues symbolically underscores that the primordial consciousness underpinning all of reality has no beginning and no end. In fact, "the teachings, the disciples, the epochs and the places" all arise from this sphere and remain in it forever.[17]

The notion of *thigle* echoes the Evagrian understanding of the henad as the noetic substratum of reality, whence everything flows and whither everything returns; indeed, Evagrios' reluctance in the *Kephalaia Gnostika* to countenance an ontologically unique role for the eternal Logos (which is then also reflected by the dearth of Trinitarian references in his corpus) might be said to mirror the *Kun byed rgyal po*'s demotion of Sattvavajra (who functions as a sort of emissary of the primordial Buddha) to a condition ultimately undistinguishable from that of all other sentient beings. The accusation of isochristism leveled against the Evagrian monks of northern Egypt—which, as Clark reminds us, played a crucial role in the earlier wave of the Origenist controversy—actually describes quite properly the cosmological vision of this rDzogs chen text, where each sentient being is posited as enjoying the same dignity as Sattvavajra. Origen's use of the sphere as metaphor for the resurrected body and Plato's resort to the same symbol to indicate the integrity of spiritual being before the fall are symptomatic of a distaste for the world of form in which fallen beings dwell; and the first verses of the *Kun byed rgyal po* are equally adamant in positing the subordi-

---

[17] *Kun byed rgyal po*, 1.1–2.1, in Chos rgyal nam kha nor bu and Adriano Clemente, *The Supreme Source*, 135–136.

nate position of the plurality of phenomena, contrasted to the "oneness of the fundamental condition" that Samantabhadra embodies.[18]

Origen's *De Principiis* did not go into detail as to the reason for the fragmentation of the henad, but the dialectic of unity and plurality that underpins his cosmology and that is taken up by the Evagrian school implies that an undue love of self (*philautia*) is the fault which ultimately led to the primordial fall; our attachments set us in opposition to each other, engendering tensions and divisions and delaying the restoration of the primordial harmony. In the *Kun byed rgyal po*, *philautia* finds an echo in the dual consciousness of those who mistakenly believe in the separation of self from other, and therefore inhabit an existential horizon characterized by illusion. In Ch. 3, Sattvavajra is told that those who meditate on the "natural perfection" of the supreme source are bound to advert to the oneness of reality, whereas heeding individual thoughts engenders a stance of mental dualism leading to fragmentation; in Ch. 6, the chain of karmic action is traced back to the tendency to heed the suggestions of the five aggregates, whereas authentic practice ought to overcome any form of dualist thought.[19] Evagrios' more explicitly parenetic writings are equally keen on emphasizing the possibility to retrieve an inner noetic dimension beyond the reach of discursive thought. Origenist spirituality privileged the practice of imageless prayer over other forms of devotion as it enabled the primordial nature of the *nous* to shine undefiled.[20]

In the texts of the *Philokalia* attributed to Evagrios and his disciples, the virtues that replace our passions and gradually lead us to the ultimate insight are regarded as a providential gift from God. For Maximos, the virtues lead to the renewed incarnation of the Logos in each practitioner, but inasmuch as they are tied to the world of matter, Evagrios claims that they are destined to be shed at the end of time, together with the "garments of

---

[18] *Kun byed rgyal po*, 8.2–8.7, in Chos rgyal nam kha nor bu and Adriano Clemente, *The Supreme Source*, 137.

[19] *Kun byed rgyal po*, 22.5–22.7, in Chos rgyal nam kha nor bu and Adriano Clemente, *The Supreme Source*, 141.

[20] One should be careful, however, lest one superimposes too much of Origen's "distaste" for the phenomenal onto rDzogs chen, since many passages of the *Kun byed rgyal po* rather tend to emphasize the aesthetic appreciation of diverse phenomena as "one taste" in light of the rDzogs chen recognition. Phenomena are like reflections that beautifully ornament a mirror, and you do not need to erase them; problems arise when you do not realize they are reflections, you reify them and grasp at them.

skin" which we received at birth. As the henad was purely noetic, it could not encompass virtues and passions which necessarily belong to the differentiated world of form; together with matter, they entered the world only after the fall. The *Kun byed rgyal po*, on the other hand, takes a fundamentally different line: the pure consciousness at the basis of the universe is the foundation of the five passions (attachment, anger, pride, ignorance and jealousy), as well as of the five wisdoms which are the true nature of the former.[21] In the primordial Buddha is the root of all that we see in the world of form; nothing was added later from another source, since everything was in him already. The Mahāyāna doctrine of *apratishtitā nirvāna* enables the rDzogs chen tantras to explode the dichotomy between Buddhahood's abiding in an utterly unconditioned state and its involvement in conditioned reality, ascribing both to the same primordial reality; the Origenist dialectic of unity and diversity, on the other hand, was too suspicious of difference to tolerate the presence even of the germs of virtue in the henad.

This distinction is crucial for how rDzogs chen construes spiritual practice in contrast with Evagrios; the latter's concept of primordial unity had no place for *agapē*, whereas the *Kun byed rgyal po*'s readiness to see all forms of wisdom as flowing from *ka dag* is complemented by the assertion that the original condition of self-awareness is also identical with all forms of practice (as noted in Ch. 4). The essence of the primordial Buddha is the source of all teachings that enable the retrieval of the pure basis of reality (*men ngag*), as well as of the inferior teachings based on dual consciousness.[22] The author of the text, however, leaves no doubt as to his conviction that the erroneous beliefs which underpin the lower tantras are actually a hindrance for their practitioners; those who focus on "the sense faculties and their objects" and practice elaborate deity visualizations fail to understand that we already dwell in the unaltered pure state.[23] A similar criticism is leveled against those (such as the practitioners of *mahāmudrā*), who regard the

---

[21] *Kun byed rgyal po*, 10.7–12.5, in Chos rgyal nam kha nor bu and Adriano Clemente, *The Supreme Source*, 138.

[22] *Kun byed rgyal po*, 15.3–17.6, in Chos rgyal nam kha nor bu and Adriano Clemente, *The Supreme Source*, 139.

[23] This type of tantra is unable to transcend dual consciousness, as practitioners visualize themselves as the deity of the *samaya* vow (*samayasattva, dam tshig sems dpa*), whereas the deity of wisdom (*jñānasattva, ye shes sems dpa*) is visualized outside oneself. In the rDzogs chen tantras, the primordial awareness already encompasses both.

relation between the empty nature of reality and wisdom as causal.[24] Tantras
from the Later Transmission agree with rDzogs chen that one should not
practice for the sake of a particular result, and that active striving to obtain
something is a deviation from authentic spirituality; the *Kun byed rgyal po*,
however, lays a greater emphasis on the ontological rationale of this belief,
noting that Samantabhadra transcends all wisdom and practice, since, as the
text has him say, "there is no path that can lead to me."[25]

The second part of the *Kun byed rgyal po*, which is devoted to the "definitive teaching" (*nges par bstan pa*) about the mind, continues the discussion
of the "pure basis," emphasizing how there is no distinction between retrieving *ka dag* and experiencing enlightenment. The primordial Buddha is
associated with *bodhicitta*, which in Mahāyāna Buddhism represents the principle of compassion informing the *bodhisattva* path, but which the rDzogs
chen tradition effectively equates with original self-awareness. This move is
eased by the fact that while the Sanskrit term *bodhicitta* indicates the awakened mind, its Tibetan counterpart *byang chub sems* can be translated as "clear
and perfected mind," thereby reaffirming the *Kun byed rgyal po*'s understanding of the ultimate nature of reality.[26] The very fact that the form bodies
whereby the *dharma* is communicated to sentient beings are themselves
manifestations of the primordial Buddha itself indicates that there is no duality between original self awareness and the compassion that flows from
it.[27] The Madhyamaka doctrine of the two truths which underpins much
philosophical speculation in Tibet is condemned in Ch. 11 precisely because

---

[24] In ch. 15–17 of her *Start where you are: a Guide to Compassionate Living* (Boston,
Mass.: Shambala, 2001), 92–108, the contemporary American master Pema
Chödrön (herself coming from a bKa rgyud background) argues for a distinction
between absolute *bodhicitta* (emptiness) and relative *bodhicitta* (the ability to act wisely
according to circumstance) along the terms of cause and effect. This is essentially
the approach that the *Kun byed rgyal po* condemns.
[25] *Kun byed rgyal po*, 32.5–36.4, in Chos rgyal nam kha nor bu and Adriano
Clemente, *The Supreme Source*, 146. Jerome, with his intense preoccupation with a
hierarchy of merit—a major factor behind his vehement attack on Origenist spirituality—would have balked at statements of this section of the *Kun byed rgyal po*,
such as "there are no levels of realization to cultivate and to tread."
[26] Chos rgyal nam kha nor bu, Commentary to the *Kun byed rgyal po*, in Chos
rgyal nam kha nor bu and Adriano Clemente, *The Supreme Source*, 92.
[27] *Kun byed rgyal po*, 81.2–81.7, in Chos rgyal nam kha nor bu and Adriano
Clemente, *The Supreme Source*, 156–157.

it draws an unnecessary distinction within the empty ground of reality.[28] The nature of the "all-powerful king" is such that it explodes any dichotomy between a "real" or "inexpressible" ground and its conventional counterpart, locating both in the pure basis.[29] In this respect, the "return to the One" postulated in the *Kephalaia Gnostika* is less comprehensive than the view presented in the *Kun byed rgyal po*, where even the "garments of skin" that drive our passions and sustain our practice are ultimately no different from the basis. rDzogs chen masters were of course totally unacquainted with any form of Western thought; had they been exposed to the Evagrian construal of the divine nature, however, they might have critiqued it in much the same way as they critiqued Dol po pa's dualistic opposition between the unconditioned basis of the universe and phenomenal reality—the latter being, in a *gzhan tong* perspective, nothing but a web of adventitious defilements.[30]

Evagrios' radical apophaticism construed the goal of practice as an epistemological insight into the divine, which was the source of our individuality and the goal of our striving, but could not follow the road of the *Kun byed rgyal po* and regard belief in the very *existence* of separate realities as a delusion. If Origenist spirituality favored imageless prayer over other forms of devotion, the purpose of this conceptual iconoclasm was to underscore God's irreducible *otherness* in relation to creation, but not to deny the reality of creation as such. According to *De Principiis*, the fragmentation of the henad was an actual event belonging to the realm of time, and so shall be the eschatological restoration of this unity; the attainment of *gnōsis* merely ensures that the individual practitioner anticipates the eschaton in his own experience and momentarily transcends the world of difference. From a rDzogs chen perspective, even such a belief would be categorized as marred by dual consciousness and by a belief in the dialectic of cause and

---

[28] *Kun byed rgyal po*, 55.1–55.6, in Chos rgyal nam kha nor bu and Adriano Clemente, *The Supreme Source*, 151.

[29] *Kun byed rgyal po*, 66.2–66.6, in Chos rgyal nam kha nor bu and Adriano Clemente, *The Supreme Source*, 153–4.

[30] Kennard Lipman, discussing Mañjuśrīmitra's *rDo la gser zhun*, claims that one might apply the term *isotropic* (=the same in all directions) to *thig le chen po*. See Kennard Lipman, Intro. to Mañjuśrīmitra, *Primordial experience- an Introduction to rDzogs chen meditation* (trans. Namkhai Norbu and K. Lipman; Boston, Mass.: Shambala 2001), page ix, note 1. The same of course could be said of the primordial *nous* in Evagrios.

effect, which is precisely the flaw of the forms of tantra based on visualization.

The third part of the *Kun byed rgyal po*, in fact, presents the teaching of rDzogs chen as "beyond cause and effect" (*nges par bstan pa*) and stresses how in the fundamental basis of reality "there is no marvelous object to see," as the pure nature "cannot be seen or heard and transcends all definitions."[31] Sentient beings draw their intellectual points of reference from the samsaric world in which they live, but discursive reasoning cannot even approach the pure basis of reality, about which nothing can be said. This radical opposition between discursive reasoning and mystical insight entails the demotion of philosophical discourse to a subordinate role, unable to *say* anything meaningful about ultimate reality; a contention that would be crucial in the polemics between the rNying ma and the dGe lugs school, but also reminiscent of Evagrios' conviction in the *Kephalaia Gnostika* that discursive reasoning (*dianoia*) has to be transcended to enable the true nature of the *nous* to emerge. In this respect, the Tibetan term *rig pa*, which can be translated as intelligence or naked awareness, comes close to the notion of *nous*; the fact that in the rDzogs chen tradition *rig pa* is assimilated to the *dharmakāya* again mirrors the Evagrian identification of our *nous* with the foundation of reality that defies all conceptualization.[32] In Ch. 21, Samantabhadra dismisses even the possibility of analogical description of the pure basis, claiming that *ka dag* is not an object to conceptualize, and that "as soon as one conceptualizes the condition 'as it is', meditation becomes conceptual."[33] In this way, one comes to understand the paradoxical assertion that "dharma" and "non-dharma" are always joined, since one cannot even *describe* the path to enlightenment without falling into delusion. This is the rationale of paradoxical assertions, such as "it is an error [to assume] that the teacher carried the name 'Buddha'," or that "there is not the slightest trace of teaching that all things are formless."[34] In this way, the authors of the *Kun byed rgyal po* are implicitly dismissing Tsong kha pa's whole philosophical enterprise as misguided, since the goal of the dGe lugs master, as we

---

[31] *Kun byed rgyal po*, 84–6–86.5, in Chos rgyal nam kha nor bu and Adriano Clemente, *The Supreme Source*, 159.

[32] Reginald A. Ray, *Secrets of the Vajra World- The Tantric Buddhism of Tibet*, 298.

[33] *Kun byed rgyal po*, 84–6–86.5, in Chos rgyal nam kha nor bu and Adriano Clemente, *The Supreme Source*, 159.

[34] *Kun byed rgyal po*, Ch. 22, in Eva K. Neumaier-Dargyay, *The Sovereign All-Creating Mind*, 107.

shall see later, was to systematize the various stages of practice which lead to ultimate insight.

While the rNying ma tradition did establish a number of monastic centers so as to perpetuate its teachings, its overall attitude towards philosophical reflection is closer to the Chinese Zen tradition than to the more speculative Indian schools. In his work *Dzogchen: the Self-Perfected State*, Nam khas nor bu notes that in his tradition the goal of the masters is to transmit a *state* of knowledge, so that "no importance at all is attached to philosophical opinions and convictions."[35] In practice, of course, the *Kun byed rgyal po*'s rejection of "views" is accompanied by considerably detailed descriptions of how these "views" are to be overcome. While Evagrios' spiritual writings effectively offered little instruction as to the effacement of *dianoia*, the third part of the *Kun byed rgyal po* outlines how discursive reasoning can be overcome by the practice of *khregs gcod* ("cutting through"), which ensures that nothing remains but the pure basis; in addition, ch. 23 and especially 29 outline how one is to *rest* in the condition beyond the views, which is known as the practice of *thod rgal* ("leap-over"). Reginald Ray notes that the teaching of *thod gal* is usually taken up in the "essential heart" writings, whereas other rDzogs chen texts are mainly preoccupied with *khregs gcod*.[36] The discussion of *thod rgal* in the *Kun byed rgyal po* (which is traditionally considered a tantra) reminds us that in any case, from a rDzogs chen perspective, one can never draw an ontological distinction between the result of practice and practice itself.

The chapters in part three devoted to resting in *ka dag* also argue how there is no ontological distinction between the individual practitioner and Samantabhadra. Ch. 24 echoes the opening section in emphasizing how the primordial wisdom of total consciousness communicates its true nature directly, but the rejection of all dual reasoning is provocatively accompanied by the assertion, "as all of you are created by me, you beings of three world are my children."[37] By now, we should have realized that theistic language of this kind is a mere metaphor, but if we still entertained any doubt, the text reminds us that sentient beings are also "equal" to the source, and are "inseparable" from what many, in their deluded state, strive to attain. The

---

[35] Nam khas nor bu, *Dzogchen: the Self-Perfected State* (Ithaca, N.Y.: Snow Lion Publication, 1996), 28–29.

[36] Reginald A. Ray, *Secrets of the Vajra World- The Tantric Buddhism of Tibet*, 301.

[37] *Kun byed rgyal po*, 92.6–93.6, in Chos rgyal nam kha nor bu and Adriano Clemente, *The Supreme Source*, 163.

assertion in Ch. 25 that one's mind is effectively the true teacher of the *dharma*[38] could of course make sense also in light of strong *gzhan tong* readings of the *tathāgatagarbha* theory, but in the context of the *Kun byed rgyal po* the vehicle of enlightenment is the mind with all the qualities that arise from it. As such, rDzogs chen's path of "no path" goes beyond a mere retrieval of original self-awareness, since *ka dag* is also "the basis of morality and of all the infinite behaviors that lead to the path of liberation."[39]

rDzogs chen's forceful assertion of our equality with the source parallels Evagrios' "non-dialogical" approach to practice, which von Balthasar regarded as essentially Pelagian and incompatible with Christianity's incarnational thrust.[40] At the same time, the *Kun byed rgyal po*'s readiness to envisage the primordial Buddha as the source of all wisdom ensured that rDzogs chen, to use the terminology of Maximos the Confessor, could accommodate both *theōria* and *praxis*.[41] According to Evagrios, the virtues are merely tools paving the way to *gnōsis*, but the ultimate insight is devoid of any agapic dimension, since the basis of all virtues is located in phenomenal reality, and the latter is destined to disappear. This approach comes closer to the Theravada notion of practice, but in rDzogs chen the insight into the nature of reality transforms the phenomenal into a theatre of compassionate activity.

The latter assertion might appear inconsistent with the emphasis on "non practice" that characterizes Ch. 26–28. The original audience of the *Kun byed rgyal po* would have been composed almost exclusively of monastic practitioners, who had undertaken to follow the rules of the code known as Vinaya, and as such would often devote time and energy to discuss its correct implementation. On one level, the practice of *khregs gcod* would do away with these superstructures, but on another level, it would be erroneous to infer that the *Kun byed rgyal po* enjoins ethical indifference. At this point, a Christian theologian may be reminded of how the Reformed doctrine of justification construes the relationship between grace and good works; the latter cannot procure the former, though it discloses it whenever God has

---

[38] *Kun byed rgyal po*, 92.6–93.6, in Chos rgyal nam kha nor bu and Adriano Clemente, *The Supreme Source*, 163.

[39] *Kun byed rgyal po*, 93.7–96.3, in Chos rgyal nam kha nor bu and Adriano Clemente, *The Supreme Source*, 163.

[40] Raymond Gawronski, S.J., *Word and Silence: Hans Urs von Balthasar and the Spiritual Encounter between East and West*, 5–40.

[41] *Kun byed rgyal po* Ch. 2, 53–55, in Eva K. Neumaier-Dargyay, *The Sovereign All-Creating Mind*, 107.

thought fitting to bestow it.[42] Yet, the roots of this argument are already present in the *Philokalia*: in vol. 1, one finds a short treatise by Mark the Ascetic entitled *On those who think that they are made righteous by works*, where the practice of the virtues is not disparaged, but is presented as an outward sign that the individual has already attained the highest form of *gnōsis*.[43] Similarly, the *Kun byed rgyal po*'s discussion of "morality" (*tshul khrims*) in Ch. 26 draws a clear line between deeds that help one to "ascend" and deeds (such as murdering one's parents, or even a Buddha) that cause rebirth in a lower realm.[44] At the same time, authentic realization is not tied to external actions, but to one's knowledge of the true condition of our consciousness; thus, in no way it reflects "one's age, intelligence and education."[45] For this reason, the *Kun byed rgyal po* affirms that "the perfection beyond action" is not merely beyond "effort or intention,"[46] or "lowering and elevating,"[47] but it is not even an object of meditation, since, once we retrieve our original self-awareness, we simply let it be, entering the stage of "non-meditation" (*gom med*).[48]

In part four, the *Kun byed rgyal po* continues to stress how the principle of enlightenment *is* the vehicle of practice and is no different from the ulti-

---

[42] Admittedly, the "good works" targeted by Luther's original polemic were chiefly those undertaken in obedience to monastic vows—something that for Luther reduced religious practice to a commercial transaction. Luther's argument, however, was retrieving an older polemic against excessive trust on devotional superstructures.

[43] Mark the Ascetic, *On those who think that they are made righteous by works*, in *Philokalia*, Vol. 1, 125–147; in Migne, Mark the Monk, *Opuscula 2—De his qui putant se ex operibus justificari* (PG 65: 929–966). For a similar argument, see also Symeon the New Theologian, *On Faith*, in *Philokalia*, Vol. 4, 16–25 (PG 120: 693–702).

[44] Chos rgyal nam kha nor bu and Adriano Clemente, Intro. to the *Kun byed rgyal po*, in *The Supreme Source*, 103–5.

[45] Chos rgyal nam kha nor bu and Adriano Clemente, Intro. to the *Kun byed rgyal po*, in *The Supreme Source*, 105; also *Kun byed rgyal po*, 96.5–98.6, in Chos rgyal nam kha nor bu and Adriano Clemente, *The Supreme Source*, 165.

[46] In her translation of Ch. 22 of the *Kun byed rgyal po* (*The Sovereign All-Creating Mind*, 105), Eva K. Neumaier-Dargyay calls *ka dag* "deedless" (*bya med*), and yet "purposeful" (*don nyid*).

[47] Eva K. Neumaier-Dargyay, *The Sovereign All-Creating Mind*, 106.

[48] *Kun byed rgyal po*, 96.5–98.6, in Chos rgyal nam kha nor bu and Adriano Clemente, *The Supreme Source*, 165. Those who think otherwise are compared to "monkeys."

mate perfection beyond action (*bya med rdzogs pa*). The ontological identity
of Sattvavajra and Samantabhadra is underscored so as to stress that the
form bodies of the primordial Buddha might mediate the teaching of
rDzogs chen, but the ultimate object of non-meditation is the emptiness of
the *dharmakāya* (Tib. *chos sku*).[49] The relation between the mind (*sems*) and
wisdom (*ye she*) reflects the relation between absolute and relative *bodhicitta*
in the tantras of the Later Transmission, but the recurrent use of the mirror
metaphor reminds us that rDzogs chen views them as inextricably one. In
this perspective, the *dharmakāya* is the reflecting surface, whereas the *sāmbhogikakāya* and the *nairmānikakāya* are the reflections that appear on it only
to vanish again.[50] In this way Samantabhadra's nature as compassion and its
expression form a unity beyond all dualism; to borrow a Christian expression on the nature of the Godhead, one could almost say that *bodhicitta diffu-
sivum sui*. Any view that separates "view" and "behavior" in our individual
practice is ultimately a hindrance, as it entails a failure to grasp the unity of
self-awareness and of compassionate acts.[51] In this respect, rather than to
Evagrios, the *Kun byed rgyal po* comes closer to the position of Maximos the
Confessor in the *Ascetic life*, where *praxis* is not subordinate to *theōria*, but the
two aspects of practice are inextricably linked and are both instrumental to
the individual's deification.

The last section of the *Kun byed rgyal po* is devoted to "the teaching establishing knowledge" (*gtan la 'bebs pa*), where the authors provoke their
readers by constantly referring to the "non-existence" of enlightenment;
and the same theme is then taken up in the closing chapters of the tantra
where we are reminded that there is no path to tread.[52] The role of the
teacher is thus not to impart knowledge, but rather to help his disciples re-
awaken and rediscover the truth—a truth which transcends the limits of
verbal expression. Wittgenstein's habit to warn his students that the study
of philosophy led away from the truth would have resonated with this ap-

---

[49] *Kun byed rgyal po*, 116.6–117.5, in Chos rgyal nam kha nor bu and Adriano
Clemente, *The Supreme Source*, 175.

[50] Chos rgyal nam kha nor bu and Adriano Clemente, Intro to *Kun byed rgyal po*,
in *The Supreme Source*, 109. In other words, one could say that there cannot be a
dharmakāya without a *sāmbhogikakāya* and a *nairmānikakāya*.

[51] *Kun byed rgyal po*, 129.3–133.2, in Chos rgyal nam kha nor bu and Adriano
Clemente, *The Supreme Source*, 181.

[52] *Kun byed rgyal po*, 172.2–174.3, in Chos rgyal nam kha nor bu and Adriano
Clemente, *The Supreme Source*, 195.

proach where "views" actually obstruct one's self-awareness.[53] In the context of Origenist spirituality, the elder's function is equally not to transmit a particular technique, but to help restore one's inner equilibrium so as to retrieve one's original noetic condition.

Ch. 43's claim that teacher and disciple are fundamentally the same, since they are an expression of *ka dag*, has an obvious relevance for the rDzogs chen understanding of the *dam tshig* (Sans. *samaya*) vow. Taking the *dam tshig* vow is the tantric counterpart of undertaking the bodhisattva path; its implication is that the disciple chooses to remain beholden to his master's teaching, inasmuch as the latter's realization enables him to retrieve the seed of Buddhahood which all sentient beings possess.[54] In rDzogs chen, the notion of *dam tshig* presupposes that the teacher himself reveals all the phenomena of the universe *in his own form*, so that, by maintaining their allegiance to their teacher, they come to realize that they themselves are an expression of the same pure basis. Evagrios might view the *pathētikon* as the matrix for the virtues, but he still would not view it as part of humanity's noetic foundation; the *Kun byed rgyal po*'s approach is that, as our self-awareness cannot be defiled, "there is no need to block the senses tied to the interdependence of ignorance."[55] Only in rDzogs chen's a-temporal perspective can we understand the *Kun byed rgyal po*'s notion of *dam tshig*-less *dam tshig*, whereas the Origenist Weltanschauung, while committed to a cyclical understanding of the universe, does not deny the reality of ontological change in oneself or the cosmos. The henad may recurrently reconstitute itself, but is not "immovable" as the primordial Buddha of rDzogs chen.[56]

The text of the *Kun byed rgyal po* lays down the ontological foundation for rDzogs chen practice and thus enables us to start discerning the points of contact and the differences with the Origenist tradition. Nam khas nor

---

[53] Ray Monk, *Wittgenstein: the Duty of Genius* (London: Penguin Books, 1990), 424, 490, 502–3. In Edgar L. Doctorow's *City of God* (New York: Random House, 2000), 153–155, a fictional Wittgenstein puzzles his students by telling them that, in order to understand what he really means, they should read what he never wrote.

[54] Chagdud Tulku, *Gates of Buddhist Practice: Essential Teachings of a Tibetan Master* (rev. ed. Junction City, Calif: Padma Publ., 2001), 229–247.

[55] *Kun byed rgyal po*, 145.7–146.7, in Chos rgyal nam kha nor bu and Adriano Clemente, *The Supreme Source*, 187. Using a more Christian terminology, trying to purify one's passions to turn them into virtues falls short of the ideal of rDzogs chen, as it still reveals a dualist frame of mind.

[56] *Kun byed rgyal po*, 179.2–179.6, in Chos rgyal nam kha nor bu and Adriano Clemente, *The Supreme Source*, 198.

bu's remark that the primordial Buddha cannot be regarded as a creator God, since that notion still reveals a dualist frame of mind, may also lead us to question the theistic credentials of the undifferentiated *nous* in the *Kephalaia Gnostika*. The question remains, of course, whether the non-dialogical nature of the highest mystical insight is at all compatible with the Christian notion of the Godhead.

RDZOGS CHEN AND INDIVIDUAL COGNITION: THE COMPASSIONATE NATURE OF PRIMORDIAL REALITY

According to Nam khas nor bu's classification, 'Jam dpal bshes gnyen's *rDo la gser zhun* can be classified as a *men ngag* text, which outlines how the teachings of the rDzogs chen tantras are to be put into practice.[57] Legendary accounts tell of 'Jam dpal bshes gnyen's readiness to perform extraordinary feats of asceticism and self-denial, whose ultimate inability to bring about enlightenment he came to realize after his encounter with the rDzogs chen master dGa'rab rdo rje. While the exact time of its composition cannot be determined beyond doubt, Kennard Lipman notes how the text reveals the author's mastery of Yogācāra and Madhyamaka thought, which are then deployed so as to underscore rDzogs chen's superiority over all philosophical systems.[58]

The chief purpose of the *rDo la gser zhun* text is to outline rDzogs chen's method of "non-action" (*bya ba med pa*), while also indicating how its outlook is no less tenable than other systems of Buddhist thought. In particular, its author is particularly interested in exploring rDzogs chen's views on human cognition, which he carefully distinguishes from their Yogācāra counterparts, and which are presented as inextricably linked with rDzogs chen's beliefs on the salvific value of reality as a whole. The text thus emphasizes the ultimate coherence between rDzogs chen's epistemology and

---

[57] The text includes a set of verses and a longer prose commentary "under twelve headings." The actual title of the work is *Byang chub sems bsgom pa* ("Cultivating the Primordial State of Pure and Total Presence"), though the name *rDo la gser zhun* ("Gold refined from the Ore") is more commonly used. 'Jam dpal bshes gnyen is the Tibetan name of Mañjuśrīmitra, a semi-legendary scholar from Sri Lanka who was resident at Nalanda when the first rDzogs chen master dGa' rab rdo rje was there. There was also a second 'Jam dpal bshes gnyen, who was regarded as a teacher of Guru Rinpoche about a century later and thus as directly influencing the Early Transmission; some sources tend to confuse the two figures. See Kennard Lipman, Intro. to Mañjuśrīmitra, *Primordial experience*, 5–6; 136 (notes).

[58] Kennard Lipman, Intro. to Mañjuśrīmitra, *Primordial experience*, 10–11.

the Mahāyāna vision of the cosmos as a stage for compassionate activity, developing an all-encompassing vision which differs significantly from the solutions favored for instance by the followers of Tsong kha pa. Similarly, while rNying ma and dGe lugs masters agree that the way sentient beings experience reality is what ultimately causes them to suffer, the two schools would considerably disagree on the nature of the correct therapy, or indeed, as one may easily guess, on whether a therapy is what is actually needed.

The Yogācāra critique of the belief in the existence of objects endowed with inherent properties is well known. In the *rDo la gser zhun*, heading 5 of the commentary retrieves Vasubandhu's analysis of how lack of insight necessarily conditions our experiencing process, so that our basic structure of perception (*ālayavijñāna, kun gzhi rnam par shes pa*) becomes increasingly hardened into a subject-object dichotomy at the source of samsaric discomfort.[59] In this perspective, "mind" is effectively the *potentiality* of experience, whereas what we usually regard as our "self" is merely a flow of perceptions where habitual tendencies (*vāsanā*) build up, eventuate in particular patterns of action, or slowly fade away. Yogācāra thinkers would distinguish five sense perceptions from a basic thought process, an ego-centered consciousness and an eighth level where karmic seeds are stored determining our behavior over time; thus, whatever is construed as our personality is in fact the result of a pre-personal process which is already in place.[60] The ontological primacy of this impersonal dimension is reinforced by the claim that there is nothing objective existing apart from our experiencing; indeed, this experiencing is not grounded in a subject.

A first reaction to such a claim could be to think that Descartes' "malicious demon," telling us that there is such a thing as the external world, was more than a rhetorical trope, the only proviso being that the demon is in fact our own mind. In fact Yogācāra does not postulate a Berkeleyan form of idealism; Vasubandhu's critique did not question the existence of the flux of material reality, but merely that of "objects" with permanent qualities. Indeed, as Kennard Lipman points out, the Yogācāra notion of "mind" (*citta, sems*) indicates an embodied perceptive process, as opposed to merely intellective apperception.[61] In this perspective, the realization of

---

[59] Mañjuśrīmitra, *Primordial Experience* (Commentary, 26–33), 77–79.

[60] For the eight levels of consciousness, see Paul Williams, *Mahāyāna Buddhism*, 90–93; also Dan Lusthaus, *Buddhist Phenomenology: A Philosophical Investigation of Yogacara Buddhism and the Ch'eng Wei-shih Lun* (New York: RoutledgeCurzon, 2003), 4–6, 127–129, 193–200, 264–273.

[61] Kennard Lipman's Introduction to Mañjuśrīmitra, *Primordial Experience*, 16.

enlightenment enables us to overturn the karmic conditioning of the *ālayavi-jñāna* and thus break out of the deluded habits which bring us to view reality as a close set of objects coming under the evaluative gaze of an unchanging self. The author of the *rDo la gser zhun* clearly finds Yogācāra's epistemology helpful, though rDzogs chen's iconoclastic attitude towards "views" which we know from the *Kun byed rgyal po* ensures that the very framework of Vasubandhu's critique is presented as reflecting the dichotomizing tendency of the deluded mind. The standard Madhyamaka critique to Yogācāra is here retrieved and brought into line with the rNying ma belief that analyzing reality in terms of cause and effect is the purview of the lower tantras, whereas rDzogs chen goes beyond the strictures of dual consciousness. The "viewless view" developed by this school should not be regarded as yet another philosophical system, but merely as an antidote to the distorted perception of those who live under delusion.[62]

Had 'Jam dpal bshes gnyen been acquainted with Evagrian epistemology as outlined in the *153 Texts on Prayer* or in the writings of Mark the Ascetic and Isaiah the Solitary, he would have found much that was familiar and also much to critique. In their analysis of human behavior, the authors of Vol. 1 of the *Philokalia* ascribed a great role to the acquisition of spiritual *diakrisis*, or insight, which Latin writers would call *discretio spirituum*. The spirituality of the Desert Fathers elaborated a sophisticated hierarchy of the states of mind leading one to sin, ranging from the first inner stirrings through a deliberate "consideration" of the temptation to the actual decision (*sygkatathesis*) to commit the sinful act; in their perspective, the actual sin does not reside in the sinful action, but in the decision to commit it, which reflects "ignorance" as to the true nature of reality.[63] The notion of "imprints" left on our psyche by past actions and effectively determining our future behavior, while challenging the belief in the unchanging nature of our virtues or passions, quite clearly echoes the *vāsanās* postulated by the followers of Vasubandhu. In the same way, Evagrios understands spiritual

---

[62] Mañjuśrīmitra, *Primordial Experience* (Verses, 68–73), 61. In his introduction (18), Kennard Lipman notes how this argument reflects Nāgārjuna's critique of "views"; the verses, on the other hand, reflect a very different ontological framework from that of the Madhyamaka master, where even the existence of saṃsāra and nirvāna are postulated as projections of the dualist mind.

[63] See Mark the Ascetic, *On the Spiritual Law*, 25–28, 48, 61–62 ("hell" is "ignorance of heart," while "perdition" is "forgetfulness"), 89–91, 139 (on the presence of former sins in one's memory), in *Philokalia* (Vol. 1), 112, 113, 114, 116, 119; in Migne, Mark the Monk, *Opuscula 1– De Lege Spirituali* (PG 65: 906–929).

progress as the gradual acquisition of *diakrisis*; the highest mystical insight, which upends all previous epistemological categories, reflects the Yogācāra notion of *asrayaparavrti*, where the *ālayavijñāna* sheds all traces of delusion and contemplates reality with the same perspective as the Buddha.

Evagrios would of course posit divine providence as regulating the mechanism of our actions' imprints, in the same way as "the Hindus" view the "maturation of (previously accumulated) tendencies" as something "done by Śiva."[64] At this point, 'Jam dpal bshes gnyen would part ways from Evagrios, and construe this process as an intrinsic feature of the ground of reality, whose true nature must be grasped if one is not to be "caught up in experience" and postulate the existence of intrinsic objects. By providing a closer analysis of human cognition than is for instance developed in the *Kun byed rgyal po*, the *rDo la gser zhun* positions rDzogs chen as a critical partner in Tibetan philosophical discourse, but it also lays down more explicit guidelines for its followers, showing the implications of its ontology for everyday practice. Critique of theistic views is also an important theme, and *bhakti* devotional practices are clearly dismissed as reflecting a dualistic frame of mind; in the perspective of 'Jam dpal bshes gnyen, Maximos' preoccupation with ontological boundaries would also have been assimilated to the Indian philosophical views, seeking to objectify the "continuing stream of accumulating tendencies."[65]

While the focus on the inner dynamics of the person's intellect ensures that practice is construed in a Yogācāra fashion as a self-conscious attempt to retrieve clarity, there is, however, no attempt at denying the objective nature of external reality. This attitude, from a rDzogs chen perspective, indicates the persistence of a dualist mindset. As we noted before, while Origenist spirituality seeks the retrieval of an original condition, it actually asserts a cyclical *exitus-reditus* process taking place in time; on the other hand, according to rDzogs chen, discernment (*prajñā*, *shes rab*) would disclose the ultimate non-existence of any such process.[66] The metaphor of the "eye of discernment" which the *rDo la gser zhun* deploys to indicate the "non-conceptual fresh awareness" of "the victorious ones" (who have no need of the "six forms of apprehension") would resonate with the escha-

---

[64] Mañjuśrīmitra, *Primordial Experience* (Verses, 38–45; 46–55), 58–59.

[65] Mañjuśrīmitra, *Primordial Experience* (Verses, 46–55), 58–59.

[66] Kennard Lipman, Intro. to Mañjuśrīmitra, *Primordial Experience*, 19.

tology of the *Kephalaia Gnostika* where all *logoi* are left behind.[67] Evagrios' ultimate *nous*, however, is wholly without attributes; rDzogs chen's pure reality, on the other hand, is endowed with the most excellent qualities that manifest spontaneously, as soon as the original self-awareness is retrieved.

Both Vasubandhu and 'Jam dpal bshes gnyen would have been critical of Evagrios' disembodied notion of the *nous*, but 'Jam dpal bshes gnyen would also have leveled a joint criticism to Evagrios and his Yogācāra counterparts, as being guilty of construing the mind as a reality that interprets experience, but not as the pure basis of reality as a whole. The *rDo la gser zhun* accomplishes an effective Copernican revolution, where *citta* no longer arises from the co-dependent flux of reality, but is itself the ontological foundation of all phenomena, the medium, as well as the content and the source of every experience.[68] In that sense, we are moving beyond a mere analysis of the cognitive process to an analysis of the ground of being, which in itself contains the ground of compassion. rDzogs chen notion of *byang chub kyi sems* which is identified with the "pure basis" is different from mere *sems*, but it also differs from the standard Mahāyāna notion of *bodhicitta*, which, according to Śāntideva for instance, must be "activated" so as to enter the *bodhisattva* path.[69] As Lipman remarks, this entails a radical critique of Yogācāra ontology, which envisaged "reality" as "how things appear to *us*," whereas for 'Jam dpal bshes gnyen, "reality," whether it is interpreted as *saṃsāra* or as *nirvāṇa*, is nothing but the spontaneous compassionate manifestation (*rol pa*) of the ground of being. In this way, the possibility of a Berkeleyan idealism is even more definitively undercut; the *rDo la gser zhun* agrees that the existence of material objects cannot be accounted for by their intrinsic atomic structure, but its assertion of an unchanging basis

---

[67] Mañjuśrīmitra, *Primordial Experience* (Verses, 9–13; 27–37), 56–57; see also Evagrios, *On Discrimination* 18, in *Philokalia*, Vol. 1, 49, where the wholly nonconceptual vision is compared to the "realm of God" disclosed to Israel's elders on Mount Sinai.

[68] Mañjuśrīmitra, *Primordial Experience* (Verses, 74–78), 61, where it is affirmed that "an objective support or site" for the "fundamental structuring of all experience" (the *ālayavijñāna*) does not exist, but that all that exists is the state of total presence.

[69] See Batchelor's translation of Śāntideva, *Bodhicaryāvatāra*, 8, 94–5, in Stephen Bachelor, *A guide to the Bodhisattva's way of life* (2nd ed. Ithaca, N.Y.: Snow Lion Publ., 1999).

simultaneously challenges those who view experience as something entirely non-physical.[70]

Now, if we accept that reality can be characterized as intrinsically compassionate and pure, and that *bodhicitta* does not need to be activated, the question is how the notion of "non-practice" is to be applied to our everyday life. Evagrios saw the cosmos as an expression of the divine condescension towards our weakness, but the fact that it was *created* as a consequence of sin and was destined to disappear entailed that its purpose was merely to sustain man's search for his original condition; once everyone attains the final epistemological insight, the prop of creation can fade away. The *rDo la gser zhun*, on the other hand, does not construe the manifestations of the "pure basis" as a response to our wrong-doing, but rather as a dimension that is wholly independent of our attitude to it and where compassionate action is not a mere step on the ladder to insight, but flows from it as soon as we retrieve our awareness of our pure basis. In Ch. 1, we mentioned how even Christian theologians of the stature of von Balthasar or Staniloae held the belief that Buddhism encouraged an attitude of utter indifference to the suffering of others. Here, we see clearly that this is a misconception: the rDzogs chen notion of "non acting" (or, with all due distinctions, its Zen counterpart)[71] in no way encourages indifference, but rather the awareness that any good deed that we might perform is not building up an individual store of merit, but rather flows from our shared and unchanging Buddhahood. In this perspective, the practice of "non acting" entails that each individual must rediscover her freedom not to act in either a compulsive or a calculated manner; the former would mean that she is influenced by passionate *vāsanās*, the latter that she mistakenly believes that her intrinsic nature can change. As Lipman notes, the instructions appended to the *rDo la gser zhun* teach us that freedom is "something insepa-

---

[70] In this sense, one could say that reality does not resemble Berkeley's tree in the quad that ceases to exist when it is not perceived, but is instead closer to the mysterious all-encompassing mind of Tarkovsky's *Solaris*; see Berkeley's *Principles*, 4–5, in George Berkeley, *A Treatise Concerning the Principles of Human Knowledge* (Whitefish, Mont.: Kessinger Publ., 2004), 17, and Vida T. Johnson and Graham Petrie, *The Films of Andrei Tarkovsky: A Visual Fugue* (Bloomington and Indianapolis, Ind.: Indiana University Press, 1994), 98–110.

[71] Thich Thien-An, *Zen Philosophy Zen Practice* (Berkeley, Calif.: Dharma Publishing, 1975), 64–73, about "Zen as the way of action." Of course the ontology behind Zen is radically different from the ontology behind rDzogs chen.

rable from our being" and as such it cannot be created;[72] the 9th heading of the commentary notes that "without fully taking hold of the primordial state of pure and total presence, freedom will not be obtained, and positive qualities will come to an end."[73]

The "spontaneous" quality of the good actions committed by a person who has reached the highest mystical insight is not a theme in Evagrios, for whom any involvement with material reality can turn into a hindrance.[74] Paradoxically, it is in Maximos the Confessor's contribution to the monothelite dispute that we find something coming closer to the rDzogs chen notion of "non action"; in the *Disputation with Pyrrhus*, where Maximos asserts the presence of a human will in Christ, he notes that such will is wholly untainted by sin, and as such it naturally acts in a manner fully consonant with God's plan.[75] Maximos' purpose in this argument was to show that the incarnate Son of God willed our salvation with a human will, but in emphasizing that Christ's human will was not gnomic (i.e., reaching its conclusions by a deliberative process liable to error), Maximos was presenting a picture of the functioning of the human will freed from the influence of the passions.[76] In this perspective, if we get rid of sin, we retrieve the freedom belonging to us inasmuch as we are created in the image of God, and we can spontaneously behave under all circumstances in a way fully in line with the divine will. The "non reflective" quality of sinless deliberation would also be echoed by Aquinas' construal of God's cognition, which we come to share in the beatific vision.[77]

Where Maximos differs from rDzogs chen is in Maximos' conviction that the inner equilibrium enabling "spontaneous" action eventuates in a practice of natural contemplation—a practice that is gradual no less than analytical, seeking to discern the contours of divine wisdom in the *logoi*. In the rDzogs chen texts known as *man ngag*, of which the *rDo la gser zhun* is an

---

[72] Kennard Lipman, Intro. to Mañjuśrīmitra, *Primordial Experience*, 32.

[73] Mañjuśrīmitra, *Primordial Experience* (Commentary, 54; 128–132), 85; 107–9. In the perspective, Hindu deity such as Śiva personifies the obstructions that prevent one from reaching the "pure state," and hence the good qualities of "non acting."

[74] Evagrios, *On Prayer: 153 Texts*, 71, 150, 152, in *Philokalia*, Vol. 1, 63–64, 71; in Migne, as Nilus of Sinai, *De Oratione*, 62–63; 70 (PG 79: 1177–1178; 1181–1182).

[75] Maximos the Confessor, *Disputation with Pyrrhus* (PG 91: 287–361).

[76] See also René-Antoine Gauthier, "Saint Maxime le Confesseur et la psychologie de l'acte humain," *RecTh* 21 (1954): 51–55.

[77] Thomas Aquinas, *Summa Theologiae*, I, Q.14.

example, the analogous "state of calm" is known as *zhi gnas* (Sans. *samatha*).[78] In the tradition of the dGe lugs pas, however, the ensuing experience of insight (*vipaśyanā, lhag mthong*) is construed analytically and gradually much as in Maximos; and over the next chapters, we will show a number of points of contact between the *Ambigua* and Tsong kha pa's *Lam rim chen mo*. For 'Jam dpal bshes gnyen, on the other hand, practice is immediate, not gradual, and insight attained in meditation is not analytical, but all-encompassing and non-discursive, ensuring that one can "rest" in one's natural condition.

Only those with some experience of this type of meditation can then respond *naturally* to all circumstances, in the same way as the primordial Buddha's *dharmakāya* eventuates in different form bodies according to the different needs of the moment.[79] In fact, if one tries too hard, the desired result shall not come about; the success of a truly "relaxed" approach, on the other hand, is marked by the emergence of particular traits (*nyams*), such as one's renewed awareness of the pure basis, as well as the fact that all practices "are unerringly cultivated."[80] The spontaneous quality of enlightened behavior and its relationship to insight is presented by 'Jam dpal bshes gnyen with the tantric image of the union of Samantabhadra and his consort Samantabhadrī.[81] The latter is identified with the wisdom, whereas the former represents compassionate activity; where any such activity is carried out without the concourse of true wisdom, it shall merely reflect one's worldly desires and "be ultimately non existent."[82] As 'Jam dpal bshes gnyen notes in the last verses of the text and explains more extensively in the commentary, *praxis* pursued with the purpose of accumulating merit is

---

[78] Mañjuśrīmitra, *Primordial Experience* (Commentary, 96–103; 118–123), 98–9 and 104–5 under the 7th heading of the commentary.

[79] Mañjuśrīmitra, *Primordial Experience* (Commentary, 10–16), 73–74. In the 2nd heading of the commentary, the author outlines the relationship between the "eye of discernment" and the "freedom" of the "victorious Ones," which one can also attain through meditation.

[80] Mañjuśrīmitra, *Primordial Experience* (Commentary, 118–123), 104–5. The author is here listing various "signs of proper cultivation," such as perfect intellectual insight or the fact one does not have to "avoid anything" to retrain it.

[81] Tulku Thondup, in his introduction to an anthology of kLong chen pa's writings, calls the pure basis "the union of the primordial mother and father." See Longchen Rabjam, *The Practice of Dzogchen* (trans. Namkhai Norbu and Tulku Thondup; 2d ed; Ithaca, N.Y.: Snow Lion Pub., 1996), xiii.

[82] Mañjuśrīmitra, *Primordial Experience* (Verses, 129–131), 66.

sterile and the work of "the Lord of limitations," because, instead of favoring self-liberation, it effectively thwarts it, introducing a dualist frame of mind as well as judgments on what is skillful and unskillful when this very dialectic is transcended by *ka dag*.[83]

The fact that the *rDo la gser zhun*, unlike other Mahāyāna works such as the *Bodhicaryāvatāra*, has no explicit discussion of the *paramitās*, is indicative of the radical difference between the ontology of rDzogs chen and that of other tantric practices, which see *bodhicitta* as an aspect of reality that needs to be activated, or at least (as in bKa gyud tradition) draw a distinction between absolute *bodhicitta* as the ground of reality and its relative expression taking different forms according to the circumstance. The *rDo la gser zhun*, on the other hand, insists on the inextricable unity of meditation (*sgom pa*) and behavior (*spyod pa*). As such, while approximating the Evagrian emphasis on insight and its effective elision of the divine otherness, it also echoes Maximos' union of *theōria* and *praxis*; and while it stops short of construing primordial awareness as an analytical insight, it is able to view the whole cosmos as an expression of fundamental compassion. An Origenist double creation demotes the material to an afterthought, but the rDzogs chen notion of pure basis encompasses the whole of reality, constituting the goal as well as the vehicle of our practice.

GNOSIS AND GROUND: IMMANENCE AND GRADUALISM IN THE THOUGHT OF 'JIGS MED GLING PA

While the authors of the Kun byed rgyal po are unknown and the life of 'Jam dpal bshes gnyen is shrouded in legend, the life of later rDzogs chen masters has been handed down to us by numerous chronicles and hagiographies. In the 14th century, the life and writings of kLong chen pa (1308–1363)—who lived in the same period as the great master of gzhan stong Dol po pa (1291–1362), and a few decades before the reformer Tsong kha pa (1357–1419)—played a crucial role in transforming rDzogs chen into a coherent philosophy, at a time when the Later Transmission had come to an end and the doctrinal divisions that would divide Tibetan Buddhism into different schools were assuming their long-lasting configura-

---

[83] Mañjuśrīmitra, *Primordial Experience* (vv. 101, 109–110), 63–64; also Kennard Lipman's Intro. to Mañjuśrīmitra, *Primordial Experience* 38–9.

tion.[84] His great work Tshig don rin po che'i mDzod ("Treasury of words and meanings") defends the compatibility of rDzogs chen practice with an understanding of Buddhahood as an all-encompassing intelligence. His writings develop the earlier tantric tradition stretching back to Padmasambhava, but they also seek a more coherent synthesis, which on one hand views syllogistic methodologies as ultimately "foreign" to the "poetic" nature of the Old Tantras, but on the other hand is ready to accommodate a measure of philosophic reasoning as an auxiliary prop.[85]

As noted by David Germano in his partial translation of the *Treasury*, however, kLong chen pa's chief preoccupations were neither hermeneutical nor philosophical, focusing rather on rDzogs chen's "extra-textual" dimension where individual practitioners seek to "contemplatively take into their own experience" (*nyams su len pa*) the teachings of the great perfection.[86] Again, a comparison with the Evagrian School suggests itself. While the *Kephalaia Gnostika* outlines the coherence of Origenist ontology and spirituality, the primary concern of the texts in the *Philokalia* is to outline their application to the spiritual practice of the individual. And while Evagrios' *Praktikos* stresses the crucial role of the spiritual father in fostering the disciples' spiritual growth, kLong chen pa is similarly concerned with the role

---

[84] In *The practice of Dzogchen*, we find a section (145–188) where the life of kLong chen pa is recounted in great detail (though of course in markedly hagiographic style), and where the intellectual ancestry of his work is retraced.

[85] It might be worth observing that Schelling's *Wiederbezauberung* strategy was after all developed in a similar manner. Schelling was eager to defend the "poetic" revolution of German Romantic Idealism (embodied by authors such as Novalis) from the inroads of a Kantian philosophy all too eager to privilege "analysis" over "vision." Like the authors of the *Kun byed rgyal po*, Schelling emphasized that the division between subject and object had to be transcended into a unique vision of the universe as an all-encompassing Mind, an intelligence that was operative at all levels in the cosmos and of which everything was a fleeting manifestation. See Friedrich W. J. von Schelling, *Bruno, or On the Natural and the Divine Principle of Things* (trans. M. Vater; Albany, N.Y.: SUNY Press, 1984).

[86] David Germano, "Poetic thought, the intelligent universe, and the mystery of self: the Tantric synthesis of rDzogs chen in 14th century Tibet," (PhD diss., Univ. of Wisconsin-Madison, 1992), 114, in his summary of the eighth *vajra* topic. On page 6, Germano sketches a comparison between Dzogchen practice and Heidegger's call for the contemplation of "Being" in opposition to the "ontic" concerns of much Western philosophy. For Germano, this desire to set guidelines for the practical application of a philosophical system is analogous to Heidegger's use of Husserl's phenomenology.

played by the master in helping the practitioner to retrieve original self-awareness.

The eighth and ninth sections of the *Treasury* is particularly relevant inasmuch as they outline how the master helps us recover our inner wisdom, but also how the path of rDzogs chen rests on a constant dialectic between the immediacy of the insight and the gradual unfolding of its realization.[87] The counterintuitive implications of this theme would be developed by rNying ma authors for centuries and in the 18th century they would be analyzed in great detail by the master 'Jigs med gLing pa, whose clan claimed to descend from kLong chen pa and who in many ways saw himself as the continuator of his work.[88] The very fact that 'Jigs med gLing pa's main work is entitled *kLong chen sNying tig* ("kLong chen pa's seminal heart") indicates how no one writing within the rNying tradition could ignore the thought of the great 14th century systematizer; on the other hand, it demonstrated the virtually inexhaustible potential of a tradition whose textual corpus was constantly expanding through the production of commentaries or the so-called "discovery" of *terma* texts.[89] The *Seminal Heart* was itself regarded as Padmasambhava's own teaching to King Khri srong lDe brtsan, later concealed and "discovered" in 'Jigs med gLing pa's mind about one thousand years later. 'Jigs med gLing pa would also add a number of commentaries "in his own hand," but, as van Schaik notes, this purported tie with the beginnings of the tradition was simply meant to ensure that his writings would be given the same authority as the work of the earlier rDzogs chen masters.[90]

---

[87] See again David Germano, "Poetic Thought," 114–128. This dissertation contains only the translated text of the first five *vajra* topics (out of eleven), so here I only refer to Germano's summary of the relevant sections.

[88] 'Jigs med gLing pa (1730–1798) lived at a time when the rNying ma tradition was re-establishing its presence by means of a number of monastic centers. See Sam van Schaik, *Approaching the Great Perfection- Simultaneous and gradual methods of Dzogchen practice in the Longchen Nyingtig* (Somerville, Mass.: Wisdom Publication, 2004), ch. 2, 21–29.

[89] In his work *Trol thig wang chog*, the same 'Jigs med gLing pa would explain that rNying ma *terma* teachings were concealed by Padmasambhava so as to make sure that his tradition would not die out. See Tulku Thondup, *Hidden teachings of Tibet: An Explanation of the terma tradition of Tibetan Buddhism* (Boston, Mass.: Wisdom Publications, 1997), 62–64.

[90] Sam van Schaik, *Approaching the Great Perfection*, xi.

The *Seminal Heart*, which in its final version contains eleven different texts, parallels the *Kun byed rgyal po*'s emphasis on non-duality, reasserting how the enlightened condition is immanent in the samsaric state. At the same time, it also emphasizes the experiential distinction between the original self-awareness and the conditioned state; in this way, it is able to assert that the "pure basis" subsists at all times beneath our deluded condition, while also acknowledging that the retrieval of this condition may not be immediate and in fact, due to different levels of karmic conditioning, might actually be accomplished differently by different individuals.[91] The gradualism of the dGe lugs pa, which we shall analyze later and which rNying ma masters believed radically misunderstood the non-constructed nature of the ultimate insight, differs radically from the gradualism of 'Jigs med gLing pa, which underscores how the extent to which the *same* basis is manifested reflects the different level of spiritual maturity of the practitioner. In this way, there is a remarkable parallelism with the Evagrian notion that the purity of our noetic ground is retrieved in different manners, since not all advance on the path of prayer in the same way.[92] If one follows the *Kephalaia Gnostika* in identifying our noetic basis with the divine, the similarity with the *Seminal Heart* emerges clearly; according to John Cassian, who was responsible for making the spirituality of the Desert Fathers known in the West, the intellect of those who have attained the final insight "is always with God," but at the same time "there are many similar ways of seeing and apprehending God, which grow in us according to our labor and to the degree of our purification."[93]

'Jigs med gLing pa's construal of gnosis conflates an epistemological and an ontological dimension, so that the enlightened form of awareness is also the basis for all phenomena. On the other hand, however, a measure of distinction is drawn between the static aspect of the ground and its dynamic manifestation; in this case, the latter is more directly associated with gnosis, as well as with the *dharmakāya*, and is characterized as a dynamism (*rtsal*) or luminosity (*'od gsal*).[94] It is almost too easy to discern here an echo of the Palamite distinction between the divine essence and the divine energies (which, in the *Triads*, are presented as both dynamic and luminous), but, as

---

[91] Sam van Schaik, *Approaching the Great Perfection*, 51.

[92] Evagrios, *On Discrimination*, 20–23, in *Philokalia*, Vol. 1, 49–52.

[93] See John Cassian, *On the Holy Fathers of Sketis*, in *Philokalia*, Vol. 1, 96–97.

[94] Sam van Schaik, *Approaching the Great Perfection*, 53–54, as well as his reference to 'Jigs med gLing pa, *Vajra Verses on the Natural State* (a text of the *Seminal Heart*), 517.

we shall see, other Tibetan traditions had adopted a similar strategy and viewed the *dharmakāya* as itself flowing from a higher aspect of the enlightened state which was epistemically exclusive to the Buddha. 'Jigs med gLing pa is clearly aware of the scholarly discussion that surrounded the discussion of the Buddha bodies in the *Abhisamayālamkara*, and in *The White Lotus* he accepts the distinction between *dharmakāya* and the *svabhāvikakāya*, identifying the latter with the pure basis whence the former flows.[95] His commitment to non-dualism, however, ensures that in his understanding the *dharmakāya* does not derive from the ground of the *svabhāvikakāya* as an effect flows from its cause; this dGe lugs teaching is challenged by another *Seminal Heart* text noting that this "unfabricated" gnosis is "not constructed by excellent buddhas," and is identical with "the Primordial Lord himself."[96]

The tension between re-iterated assertions of non-duality (in this case especially liable to a theistic interpretation) and the occasional distinction between the immanent ground and its manifestation is solved by showing how gnosis is the manner, whereby we might come to apprehend the foundation, though it is the latter that grounds this knowledge. The fact that gnosis is associated with a nirvanic *dharmakāya* should not let us lose sight of the fact that the same basis can be turned into the samsaric *ālaya* described by the *rDo la gser zhun*; indeed, 'Jigs med gLing pa echoes kLong chen pa's belief that "it is uncertain" whether "the gnosis that shoots out from the ground" shall experience liberation or delusion.[97] In the *Seminal Heart*, "unripened gnosis" can eventuate in "self-recognition" (*rang ngo sprod*), or fail to do so (*rang ngo ma shes pa*); the former engenders a condition that is wholly "free from elaboration (*spros bral*)" and "non-conceptual (*rtog med*),"[98] whereas the latter entails a movement "away from the ground" resulting in a dualistic understanding of reality. The ground, however, remains always there, and Jigs med gLing pa repeatedly echoes the *Kun byed rgyal po* in noting that the switch from one condition to the other is triggered by the recognition of something that is always immanent; in a text of the *Seminal*

---

[95] See 'Jigs med gLing pa, *The White Lotus*, v. 476, in Sam van Schaik, *Approaching the Great Perfection*, 180–1.

[96] See Sam van Schaik, *Approaching the Great Perfection*, 55, as well as his reference to 'Jigs med gLing pa, *Subsequent Tantra of Great Perfection Instruction*, 100–101.

[97] kLong chen pa, *Tsig don Dzos*, 116, in Sam van Schaik, *Approaching the Great Perfection*, 56.

[98] See Sam van Schaik, *Approaching the Great Perfection*, 54.

Heart, he notes that this recognition is a "self-sufficient method," like "a knot in a horse's tail coming undone by itself."[99]

Readers of the *Philokalia* will discern an echo of the contrast between *dianoia* and *nous*; the former, unlike the latter, is discursive and conceptual, but it is ultimately identical with the noetic ground; it is impossible to predict whether the intellect of an individual shall rest content with *dianoia* or transcend it into *nous*, but what is certain is that the latter is there at all times. Evagrios' treatise *On Discrimination* notes that when the intellect "has shed its fallen state and acquired the state of grace," it shall "see its own nature like a sapphire or the color of heaven." The fact that this noetic dimension has an ontological, and effectively a spatial connotation, is underscored by the claim that in Scripture "this is called the realm of God," "seen by the elders on Mount Sinai (Ex 24:10)."[100] If we turn to the *Seminal Heart*, we find 'Jigs med gLing pa telling us that gnosis, which is "without support and all pervasive" opens up in its emptiness "as a space-like expanse," which, "in its luminosity, is non-conceptual and radiant like a polished crystal."[101] The fact that the *Seminal Heart* associates *dharmakāya* with emptiness, and then equates the latter with gnosis (*rig stong*), while possibly echoing *rang stong* concerns,[102] points to the fact that even a nirvanic form of dual cognition (such as Yogācāra's *parinispannasvabhāva*)[103] is subordinate to the transcendent awareness of the pure basis, where the dynamic luminosity of the *dharmatā* is understood to be undivided from the empty ground of reality. Evagrios' *On Prayer* similarly notes how there are two levels of *theōria*, and how the dispassionate contemplation of the *logoi* of creation actually dis-

---

[99] Sam van Schaik, *Approaching the Great Perfection*, 56, as well as his reference to 'Jigs med gLing pa, *The Wisdom Guru: Practice Instructions*, 333.

[100] Evagrios, *On discrimination*, 18, in *Philokalia*, Vol. 1, 49.

[101] 'Jigs med gLing pa, *Distinguishing the Three Essential Points of the Great Perfection* (Verse 118). An English translation of this work is included in Sam van Schaik, *Approaching the Great Perfection*, 162–165.

[102] The passage just quoted is consistent with *rang stong* preoccupations, but other texts in the *Seminal Heart* (such as *Experiencing the Enlightened Mind of Samantabhadra*, 111, quoted in Sam van Schaik, *Approaching the Great Perfection*, 55) balance this off by echoing the passages of the *Kun byed rgyal po* that are more consistent with *gzhan tong*.

[103] Dan Lusthaus, "What is and what is not Yogācāra," online: http://www.human. toyogakuen-u.ac.jp/ ~acmuller/ yogacara/ intro-asc.htm, 6–8.

tracts from the contemplation of the immaterial and formless deity.[104] On the other hand, the fact that this immanent dimension is also the basis of the *dharmatā* is closer to *gzhan stong* notions of Buddhahood than to the Origenist understanding of matter as fallen.

From these considerations, we see how the *Seminal Heart* echoes the *rDo la gser zhun*'s condemnation of (specifically dGe lugs) methods of practice based on intellectual analysis. The intrinsic inferiority of analytic reasoning (*blo*), which mirrors the Evagrian *dianoia*, is implied in the *Seminal Heart* by the assertion that the ground "is free from imputation"; for 'Jigs med gLing pa, even "the tongues of the conquerors" are incapable of expressing this truth, which cannot be sought as an "object of knowledge" (*shes bya*).[105] In fact, as noted by van Schaik, throughout his writings the very terms "philosopher" (*rtog ge pa*) or "scholar" (*mkhas pa*) are used to indicate individuals who are blinded by their pride. In another *Seminal Heart* text, rDzogs chen practitioners are explicitly warned from imitating the "falsity" of the "clever thinkers" who "analyze endlessly"; in fact, "here" (in the rNying ma tradition) those who merely "follow words" are "not considered sages."[106] The purpose of the *Seminal Heart* text known as *Seeing Nakedly the Natural State of the Great Perfection* is to underscore the immanent nature of the pure basis; we are told that "by not forgetting the nature of one's own awareness [...] at some points the unelaborated ultimate truth, transcending terms and example, will appear."[107]

'Jigs med gLing pa's language is markedly Evagrian in its contention that the "accumulation of adventitious thoughts and emotions" obscures the pure basis, but if we look more closely, we see that the writings of the *Philokalia* emphasize the need to discriminate between good and evil thoughts, whereas the *Seminal Heart* argues that "whatever thoughts and emotions arise" ought to be considered "nakedly" (*gcer mthong*) and "they

---

[104] Evagrios, *On Prayer: 153 Texts*, 57, 67–68, in *Philokalia*, Vol. 1, 62–63; in Migne, as Nilus of Sinai, *De Oratione* 56, 66–67 (PG 79: 1177–1180; 1181–1182).

[105] See Sam van Schaik, *Approaching the Great Perfection*, 74, and his reference to 'Jigs med gLing pa, *An Aspirational Prayer for the Ground, Path and Result*, 445.

[106] Sam van Schaik, *Approaching the Great Perfection*, 75, and his reference to 'Jigs med gLing pa, *The Words of the Omniscient One*, 521–522; 536.

[107] See 'Jigs med gLing pa, *Seeing nakedly the Natural State of the Great Perfection: Necessary Instructions for Beginners*, v. 568, in Sam van Schaik, *Approaching the Great Perfection*, 235.

should never be analyzed and examined."[108] Non rDzogs chen forms of practice are characterized as inferior (*dman pa*), but also as relying on philosophical (and thus non-experiential) views (*yid dpyod*), which are based on texts and not on direct gnosis.[109] The elder of the *Praktikos* and the master of the *Seminal Heart* are both instrumental in helping to retrieve one's noetic basis, but the former is supposed to guide his disciples in the acquisition of *diakrisis*, whereas the latter must lead practitioners to do virtually the opposite, until "the thoughts and emotions that arise in meditation" are "liberated into the sameness of stillness and movement."[110] On the other hand, the claim that "thoughts and emotions are liberated into the *dharmakāya* without benefit or harm," indicating that our final condition is independent of our ethical effort, is again consonant with the Evagrian belief in the final dissolution of the *logoi* at the apokatastasis.

The text known as the *White Lotus* continues the polemic against the belief that the ultimate condition might be constructed gradually, but also sets out to show how this view may be "combined with the way progress is counted" in the *Perfection of Wisdom* literature.[111] The tantric path of liberation is here likened to a wide field adorned with the jewels of wisdom and the sprouts of compassion, all of which are endowed with the "sublime qualities" of original awareness. The Vajrayāna that the *Kun byed rgyal po* personified in Sattvavajra[112] is effectively presented as a *nītārtha* practice, ensuring that path and stages are completed all at once; on the other hand, causal vehicles such as Madhyamaka teaching, moving from relative to ultimate truth, are demoted to *neyārtha* status. While the *rDo la gser zhun*, especially in the prose commentary, tended to regard gradual practices as intrinsically misleading, the *White Lotus* prefers to resort to a common Mahāyāna strat-

---

[108] See 'Jigs med gLing pa, *Seeing nakedly the Natural State of the Great Perfection*, v. 569, in Sam van Schaik, *Approaching the Great Perfection*, 236.

[109] *Yid dpyod* is of course a crucial component of Tsong kha pa's (and dGe lugs) epistemology. See also Jeffrey Hopkins, *Meditation on Emptiness* (Boston: Wisdom Publications, 1983), 701–705.

[110] See again 'Jigs med gLing pa, *Seeing nakedly the Natural State of the Great Perfection*, v. 569, in Sam van Schaik, *Approaching the Great Perfection*, 236.

[111] The full title of this *Seminal Heart* text is *The White Lotus: Supporting Instructions Following on From the Graduated Path of Ripening and Liberating in the Vajrayāna*. See the English translation in Sam van Schaik, *Approaching the Great Perfection*, 173–207. 'Jigs med gLing pa notes the tension with *Prajñāpāramitā* literature in v. 466 (in van Schaik, 174).

[112] In the *White Lotus* (187), the same role is played by Vajradhāra.

egy that poses one's understanding of the path as the "most advanced" form of practice; in this way, practices such as Mahāmudrā can be seen as "the skillful means and compassionate activity of the buddhas and bodhisattvas" for those of "middling and inferior faculties."[113] This device ensures that the "path of application" of the *Perfection of Wisdom* is not presented as *contradicting* the teaching of the Great Perfection. Here, one clearly sees the radical difference between the Buddhist and the Christian position: a Christian theologian such as Maximos the Confessor, faced by the challenge of Origenist spirituality, could not opt for a latitudinarian conclusion, and *would have to assert* the incompatibility of the two systems.

One might object that in the *Wisdom Guru* the critique of Yogācāra doctrine which we already encountered in *rDo la gser zhun* remains particularly pointed. 'Jigs med gLing pa was well aware that rDzogs chen could be misinterpreted read as a mind-only teaching; thus he emphasizes how appearances, unlike dreams, do not cease together with perceptual activity, since they arise from the flux of co-dependent origination.[114] The focus of the *White Lotus*, however, is to explain how different schools of thought enable practitioners to come close to the perfection of rDzogs chen; thus, the strategy followed by the author is to present the different philosophical views as effectively preparatory steps towards the great perfection. In this way, 'Jigs med gLing pa is able to argue that it is possible to integrate one's intensifying awareness of the already existent basis with the graduated practices of the other *yānas*. On one hand, the *White Lotus* affirms that retrieval of self-awareness requires "no view and meditation" and "no maintaining of vows" while engendering "a continuous bliss" that is free from "the weariness of being caught in the cage of the paths and stages";[115] on the other hand, another text of the *Seminal Heart* points out that teachers introducing these views on the immanence of the ground to unprepared disciples are effectively "thieves" who use the great perfection for their own purposes,

---

[113] 'Jigs med gLing pa, *The White Lotus*, v. 486, in Sam van Schaik, *Approaching the Great Perfection*, 187.

[114] See Sam van Schaik, *Approaching the Great Perfection*, 80, and his reference to 'Jigs med gLing pa, *The Wise Guru*, 323–324.

[115] 'Jigs med gLing pa, *The White Lotus*, 513, in Sam van Schaik, *Approaching the Great Perfection*, 92. The passage itself is an echo of the *Kun byed rgyal po*, in Eva K. Neumaier-Dargyay, *The Sovereign All-creating mind*, 71.

but fail to consider the different abilities of their disciples.[116] In particular, 'Jigs med gLing pa is eager to show that Mahāmudrā practices virtually correspond to what rNying ma tradition calls *khregs gcod*, while preserving the exclusive rDzogs chen character of the highest practice of *thod rgal*.

In the *Seminal Heart*, the stages of the Mahāmudrā path are effectively interpreted as levels in the realization of the pure basis. The Sanskrit term *mudrā*—which can be translated as "symbol" or "seal," but here also as "form"—indicates that in the realized state the whole of reality becomes expressive of the underlying emptiness as well as of the compassionate activity of the Buddha. While *mahā* normally means "great," in this context it indicates that the emptiness to which reality points surpasses all terms of comparison. The use of the term "symbol" might be misleading, since it could be construed as pointing to an extrinsic reality, but in Mahāmudrā all phenomena point back to themselves, underscoring how there is no fixed reference point but the underlying *śūnyata*.[117] Of course, differences would arise between those viewing this *śūnyata* in terms of Tsong kha pa's doctrine of emptiness, and those who, following Dol po pa, would rather emphasize its identity with a fully-realized Buddha nature. 'Jigs med gLing pa's reading, however, prefers to underscore how Mahāmudrā teaches you to retrieve your condition of original self-awareness; in the *White Lotus*, the goal of Mahāmudrā practice is called "one-pointedness," the unveiling of the mind's true nature.[118] Practitioners following gradualist methods ought to begin by establishing through meditation that notions of existence and non-existence do not apply to the nature of mind, so that, after some practice, some "very strong experiences of emptiness" ought to arise; by intensifying one's practice, one ought to attain a greater steadiness of insight, until one is able to abide uninterruptedly in this awareness.[119] The *Perfection of Wisdom* associates these three stages with a gradual transformation of the five sense organs, which are "empowered in a pure land" and eventually "arise as the

---

[116] 'Jigs med gLing pa, *The Words of the Omniscient One*, 523, in Sam van Schaik, *Approaching the Great Perfection*, 93, who notes that the passage is itself based on quotes from kLong chen pa.

[117] Reginald A. Ray, *Secret of the Vajra World*, 261–265.

[118] 'Jigs med gLing pa, *The White Lotus*, vv. 488–492, in Sam van Schaik, *Approaching the Great Perfection*, 187–191.

[119] 'Jigs med gLing pa describes these three stages as "lesser," "medium," and "great worldly yoga," which can be compared to "lesser," "medium," and "great one-pointedness" in Mahāmudrā. See 'Jigs med gLing pa, *The White Lotus*, vv. 488–489, in Sam van Schaik, *Approaching the Great Perfection*, 187–189.

all encompassing wisdom." 'Jigs med gLing pa, however, notes that "this is not actually true"; the rDzogs chen notion of "not-progressing" underscores how the pure basis does not necessitate transformation. While the discussion of these practices in the *White Lotus* admits that "great one-pointedness (*rste gcig*)" is equivalent to the highest insight of the Great Perfection, 'Jigs med gLing pa expresses concern that the Mahāmudrā reading might engender "complacency of thinking," when in fact this experience is independent of our efforts.[120]

Following a similar strategy, the *Seminal Heart* outlines the consistency between rDzogs chen and Mahāmudrā use of emotions in practice. In the tradition of the *Kun byed rgyal po*, emotions are regarded as dualist reactions to the undifferentiated expanse of the basis, of which they are a part; these emotions must then be integrated into one's practice until their true nature as manifestations of the primordial wisdom is revealed. Urgyen Rinpoche notes that negative emotions such as "great despair," "fear," and "intense worry" are actually an opportunity to recognize "the true state of non-dual mind"—opportunities which those trained in artificially tranquil conditions effectively lack.[121] In this way emotions can be the ground of confusion as well as the source of liberation. Within Mahāmudrā, the mind that has become "fully pointed" is naturally led to consider how all emotions are thoughts and emotions are ultimately indistinguishable from the basis; while at an earlier stage it might be necessary to use the notion of emptiness as *antidote* to disturbing conditions such as "suffocating fear and terror," intensifying practice makes this approach unnecessary, until no more "grasping at emptiness" takes place. In *The White Lotus* this practice of simplicity, or "non elaboration" (*spros bral*), is associated with the so called "path of seeing," which indicates the individual's ability to rest in the union of emptiness and form. If the *Prajñāpāramitā* sūtras contend that this form of yoga grants "freedom from illusory phenomena," this is again a concession to the dualist frame of mind which in theory accepts the undivided nature of *nirvāna* and *samsāra*, but which in practice fails to grasp its implications,[122] whereas according to the Great Perfection, the Buddha nature exists forever free in the hearts of all beings.

---

[120] 'Jigs med gLing pa, *The White Lotus*, vv. 491, in Sam van Schaik, *Approaching the Great Perfection*, 187.

[121] See Tulku Urgyen Rinpoche, *Rainbow painting* (Hong Kong: Rangjung Yeshe Publications, 1995), 25.

[122] 'Jigs med gLing pa, *The White Lotus*, vv. 497, in Sam van Schaik, *Approaching the Great Perfection*, 194.

'Jigs med gLing pa resorts to the notion of *upayakauśalya* also to accommodate the two remaining forms of Mahāmudrā practice, known as
"one taste" (*ro gcig*) and "non-meditation" (*sgom med*) yoga. The former flows
from the recognition of the emptiness of all thoughts and emotions; in the
wake of "non elaboration," the energy used to distinguish pleasant from
unpleasant experiences is no longer necessary, since the individual abiding
in the realized state is indifferent to any such distinction. At this stage, the
practice of Mahāmudrā begins to overflow into our relationship with other
sentient beings; after the tendency to seek pleasure for ourselves is undercut, our potential for compassionate behavior is released.[123] In the *Seminal
Heart*, the condition of "great one taste" where practitioners go beyond
meditation and can cultivate the six *paramitās* is then equivalent to the highest form of the "path of meditation," where the whole of reality becomes
the stage for our compassionate activity.[124] The logical conclusion of this
progression is a condition where the distinction between meditation and
non-meditation is utterly meaningless, as every thought or action is understood to rest in the unalterable basis. What New Transmission tantras call
the practice of "non-meditation," the Old Transmission name "path of no
more learning"; the former emphasize how at this stage the practitioner
abides in the realm of the undivided Buddha bodies, whereas the latter underscore the "crossing over" into a condition of spontaneous presence.
Both positions emphasize the unity of the practitioner with the *dharmakāya*
and its compassionate manifestations, but the latter is adamant that the resulting "play of emanations" does not flow from our intensified practice.[125]

The *Seminal Heart* is thus characterized by a tension between the ac-
knowledged necessity to resort to gradual methods and the reiterated assertion that such methods must ultimately be transcended. In the *Words of the
Omniscient One*, a text echoing many of the concerns of *The White Lotus*, 'Jigs
med gLing pa develops yet another hierarchy of practices to free one's
thoughts and emotions, moving from dualism through non-dualism to the
acknowledgment that there is nothing to liberate; after all, he seems to say,
even Old Transmission masters such as Vimalamitra saw it as their concern
to introduce the Great Perfection to individuals of lesser levels of attain-

[123] Reginald A. Ray, *Secret of the Vajra World*, 280–281.
[124] 'Jigs med gLing pa, *The White Lotus*, vv. 501–502, in Sam van Schaik, *Approaching the Great Perfection*, 197–8.
[125] 'Jigs med gLing pa, *The White Lotus*, vv. 509, in Sam van Schaik, *Approaching
the Great Perfection*, 202–203.

ment.[126] 'Jigs med gLing pa, however, also resorts to gradualist language when he discusses the unfolding of the excellent qualities of the basis, which practitioners discern as they reconnect to the ground. In *The White Lotus*, he preempts his opponents' question as to why the wondrous qualities of Buddhahood are not all visible as soon as original self-awareness is retrieved.[127] His answer resorts to a *motif* of Hindu mythology, the divine bird Garuda that emerged fully formed from its egg and whose victory over the serpents symbolizes the defeat of ignorance by Vedic knowledge.

'Jigs med gLing pa notes that this bird (known as *Khyung* in Tibetan) may reach perfection before hatching, but after hatching might take some time to get rid of the bindings of the egg; in the same way all perfected qualities are sealed inside the body of the practitioner, and cannot unfold until this shell is deposed.[128] We might detect here an echo of the notion of *prarabda karma*, the "seeds" of past actions that must take their course even after enlightenment is attained; but while this argument might appease a few, it seems to re-introduce a dualism between a pure and an impure dimension that is ultimately foreign to rDzogs chen. The Evagrian School effectively resorted to a similar argument, viewing the experience of mystical insight as anticipating an eschaton that could only be realized after the realm of matter had disappeared. These passages in the *Seminal Heart* appear to reintroduce time into the discourse of the Great Perfection—something that the *Kun byed rgyal po* had dismissed as a dualist delusion.

A similar remark can be made if we turn to 'Jigs med gLing pa's analysis of the so-called "four visions" (*snang ba bzhi*), whereby enlightened practitioners come to experience the excellent qualities inscribed in the basis. The *Seminal Heart* is ready to acknowledge the points of contact between Mahāmudrā and *khregs gcod*, but the supreme practices known as *thod rgal* (leap-over), whereby one sustains the highest insight, are posited as unique to the Great Perfection; and while we noted earlier that part two of the *Kun byed rgyal po* devoted a few chapters to practice after the retrieval of the basis, the text known as *The Great Perfection Tantra of the Expanse of Samantab-*

---

[126] 'Jigs med gLing pa, *The Words of the Omniscient One*, 524, quoted in Sam van Schaik, *Approaching the Great Perfection*, 109.
[127] 'Jigs med gLing pa, *The White Lotus*, vv. 498, in Sam van Schaik, *Approaching the Great Perfection*, 124.
[128] 'Jigs med gLing pa, *The White Lotus*, vv. 498–9, in Sam van Schaik, *Approaching the Great Perfection*, 124–5.

hadra's Wisdom furnishes a much more systematic presentation of the pro-
gressive manifestation of the consequences of this insight.[129]

Origenist spirituality would have had little use for a practice such as
thod rgal; in the *Kephalaia Gnostika*, it appears that before the eschaton the
highest noetic insight can only be glimpsed, whereas, after the restoration of
the henad, the multiplicity of different *nooi* is permanently eliminated. In
rDzogs chen, on the other hand, the risk of a come-back of dualist thought
is always present; as such it becomes necessary to elaborate a teaching (*sems
ma chos*, "do not correct your mind"),[130] whereby one can continue to explore the spontaneous self-perfection of the cosmos without falling into
error. This is why, in the *Seminal Heart*, the primordial Buddha tells Sattvavajra that all phenomena might be perfect in their own essence, but also
warns that it takes time before this perfection is fully perceived, even by
enlightened eyes. In this text, four different "lamps" (centers of wisdom
within our body) support the move from the "vision" of the "manifest true
condition" to an "experience" of the latter; the latter is then replaced by the
"full extent of gnosis" which in its turn is eventually superseded by "an ex-
haustion of the true condition." In fact, it is only after one has reached the
"limit" of these four visions that "the characteristics of full enlightenment"
are truly present.[131]

The fact that for 'Jigs med gLing pa one might discern levels of realization even within *thod rgal* is indicative of the extent to which by the 18th century even those masters who viewed full-fledged enlightenment as an innate
feature of all sentient beings had come to assimilate some of the practices
from the more recent gradualist schools. Van Schaik notes that other *Seminal Heart* texts not included among his translations describe the "four visions" of *thod rgal* as "developing" the primordial experience and as enabling
one to "arrive" at "the full extent of gnosis";[132] in this perspective, the dis-

---

[129] It might not be accidental that the title of this *Seminal Heart* text explicitly
mentions the primordial Buddha, thereby enabling 'Jigs med gLing pa to present
his reflections as a sort of explanation of the earlier text. Both texts are written as
dialogues between Samantabhadra and Vajrasattva.

[130] See Chos rgyal nam kha nor bu and Adriano Clemente, Intro. *Kun byed rgyal
po*, in *The Supreme Source*, 107.

[131] 'Jigs med gLing pa, *The Great Perfection tantra of the expanse of Samantabhadra's
Wisdom*, vv. 87–88, in Sam van Schaik, *Approaching the Great Perfection*, 111 and again
143.

[132] 'Jigs med gLing pa, *The Subsequent Tantra of Great Perfection Instruction*, 104, in
Sam van Schaik, *Approaching the Great Perfection*, 111.

tinction between rDzogs chen and bKa rgyud or bKa' gdams practices centers on the time it takes to reach the goal, rather than immediacy vs. gradualism. This might be the speculative counterpart of the metaphor of the bird, shedding the remnants of its egg; the principle of skillful means can always be invoked to justify these strategic appropriations of dualist procedures, but one gets the impression that 'Jigs med gLing pa may be going beyond the boundaries of his own rNying ma tradition.

CONSTANTINOPLE II AND THE *RIS MED* MOVEMENT: DIFFERENT STRATEGIES FOR SIMILAR IMPASSES

In the course of the 19th century, 'Jigs med gLing pa's work would become paradigmatic of a wider tendency among Tibetan masters to transcend sectarian boundaries and seek some form of synthesis between the teachings of the different schools. The concentration of political power in the hands of the Dalai Lamas from the mid 17th century had resulted in the ascendancy of the dGe lugs pa order, whose emphasis on philosophical analysis and monastic discipline contrasted with what Geoffrey Samuel called the "shamanic" tendencies of other traditions. The *Seminal Heart* had little to say about the external discipline enforced in monastic establishments, and it viewed the relationship between master and disciple as effectively symbolic of the need to sustain our awareness of the pure basis; at the same time, it was ready to incorporate different tantric as well as sutric teachings within its understanding of practice. Following this example, masters such as 'Jam dbyangs mKhyen brtse (1820–1892) and 'Jam mgon Kong sprul (1813–1899), both considered emanations of Mañjuśrī, were instrumental in favoring an eclectic approach to practice that blended insights from the Old and the New Transmission while it also envisaged an auxiliary role for philosophic speculation.

Scholars agree that most non-dGe lugs masters of the past two centuries have followed this trend and have developed some form of synthesis between the existing tantric traditions, thereby ensuring that the dGe lugs political ascendancy did not result in the disappearance of the more "shamanic" practices.[133] The so-called "eclectic" (*ris med*) movement never developed into a full-blown school such as the rNying ma or the bKa rgyud,

---

[133] See Reginald A. Ray, *Secret of the Vajra World*, 59–64; David S. Ruegg, "A Tibetan's Odyssey: A Review Article," *JRAS* 2 (1989): 304–311; Geoffrey Samuel, *Civilized Shamans*, 536–537 (on 537, he claims that "Tibetan Buddhism today outside the dGe lugs pa order is largely a product of the Rimed movement").

but it certainly fostered a revival of the intellectual tradition of these schools, while simultaneously securing a measure of popular support through the publication of numerous expositions of the *dharma* for lay people.[134] In fact, it should not be surprising that the 'Jigs med gLing pa, the figure whom *ris med* masters revered as their chief inspiration, came from a rNying ma background. As Samuel notes in *Civilized Shamans*, rDzogs chen's notion of *ka dag* as a condition of all-embracing enlightenment that could accommodate and transcend all "lower" or "conceptual" teachings served well as a philosophical tool asserting the unsurpassable ultimacy of the great perfection.[135] The fact that the Dalai Lamas, despite holding the highest political office in the land, were not expected to exercise any control on the speculative development of competing schools, ensured that the *ris med* could thrive alongside dGe lugs.

If one looks carefully, one sees quite a few similarities with the situation in 6th century Byzantium. In her discussion of the earlier controversies opposing ecclesiastical authorities in Alexandria and the monastic settlements of the desert, Elizabeth Clark notes how the dispute on mental images was symptomatic of a deeper tension between an urban, institutional Christianity, and the more "anarchic" world of the anchorites who were fleeing the strictures of the post-Constantinian church.[136] The very fact that the spirituality of the Evagrian school has little to say about liturgical practice or the sacraments—after all, *theōria* is quite sufficient to procure salvation—is an implicit declaration of independence from the clerical establishment, whereas Maximos' emphasis on liturgy as the culmination of *praxis* is indicative of a very different theological vision, which views the celebration of the Eucharist as the culmination of spiritual practice.

The parallelisms do not stop here. In the same way as Maximos' qualified retrieval of classical natural theology grew into a Christocentric rendition of cosmological speculation, we will now see how in 14th century Tibet, the dGe lugs master Tsong kha pa accomplished a similar synthesis, bringing together an earlier philosophical tradition and the on-going speculation on the Buddha bodies. In both contexts, an educated elite was at work trying to elaborate a speculative vision that would bring together an earlier

[134] Geoffrey Samuel, *Civilized Shamans*, 539.

[135] Geoffrey Samuel, *Civilized Shamans*, 538.

[136] See again Elizabeth A. Clarke, *The Origenist Controversy: The Cultural Construction of an Early Christian Debate* (Princeton, N.J.: Princeton University press, 1992), 100–1.

philosophical tradition with the insights of on-going practice; but again, in both cases, an alternative spirituality (and its attendant theology) continued to flourish, and continued in its attempts to critique or subvert the increasingly "established" position.

In the early Christian period, this cultural dichotomy was a likely factor behind the Monophysite schism of 451, but it could also be taken as an explanation for the century-long survival and recurrent reemergence of Origenist spirituality, long after Trinitarian and Christological orthodoxy had embraced positions that were very distant from *Kephalaia Gnostika*. In Tibet, the dynamics favored the survival of the Old Tantra tradition and the birth of *ris med* even after the establishment of the dGe lugs ascendancy. The critical attitude of rDzogs chen towards monasticism as well as the practice of philosophy, and the reluctance of later Origenists to accept the orthodox theological establishment, were different manifestations of a similar skepticism towards "institutionalized" religion and its "official" doctrinal positions. Of course, neither Evagrios and his followers, nor 'Jigs med gLing pa and 'Jam dpal bshes gnyen could be characterized as "unlearned";[137] yet, in both cases, they were seen as representatives of an alternative mode of discourse, whose open dismissal of formal philosophical training had a certain appeal to a populace, who had little or no access to "official" learning.[138]

As the dichotomy between "immediacy" and "gradualism" corresponds largely (albeit imperfectly) to the dichotomy between "shamanistic" and "clerical" approaches, a sociological (as opposed to theological) explanation of the resilience of Old Tantra might nonetheless argue that despite their increased political power, the dGe lugs élites of pre-modern Tibet never sought to impose ideological conformity, while the representatives of minority traditions were ready to come to terms with the establishment. The Samye debates following the Early Transmission of the *dharma* appear to have asserted the superiority of the gradual path of enlightenment (championed by Shantarakshita) over the assertion of the immanent pres-

---

[137] We should not forget that, before retreating to the desert of Egypt, Evagrios had studied in Constantinople and had known Gregory of Nazianzos; see the biographical note on Evagrios, in *Philokalia*, Vol. 1, 28. Similarly, as we noted earlier in this chapter, 'Jam dpal bshes gnyen had probably studied at Nalanda in India before moving to Tibet.

[138] While Evagrian spirituality was born and then thrived in areas where the hold of orthodox Christianity on the population was weaker, scholars also agree that the teaching of rDzogs chen owes much to the pre-Buddhist Bon religion of Tibet.

ence of Buddhahood (championed by Hua Shang),[139] but in a Buddhist context no such decision could ever be considered normative or final. In fact, the authorities' trust that monastic institutions could be instrumental in supporting the social *status quo* was balanced by their eagerness to retain the support of those favoring alternative forms of practice. The *ris med* movement in the 19th century and the current Dalai Lama's openness to the rNying ma tradition thus reflects a long tradition of tolerance.

This conscious compromise ensured that the *Kun byed rgyal po* would never go the way of the Evagrian corpus; and here is where the two traditions part company. The anathemas cast against Origenism in 543, and again, ten years later, at Constantinople II, condemned the type of spirituality and cosmology which underpin the *Kephalaia Gnostika*, and underscored their incompatibility with the Christology that had developed over the 5th and 6th centuries.[140] Maximos' reflections in the *Ambigua* and the *Two Hundred Texts on Theology and the Incarnation of the Son of God* were developed in the context of a post-conciliar consensus opposed to both apokatastasis and isochristism. The concern of Emperor Justinian and of Saint Saba that the "subversive" nature of Origenism spirituality might pose a threat to the institutional church, coupled with Maximos' later speculations on *theōsis*, ensured that the cosmic Christocentrism of Chalcedon would become the normative theological paradigm.

We will now turn to Tsong kha pa's own theology of the Buddhahood, and explore his understanding of embodiment, whose points of contact with Maximos' position will become increasingly evident. By the end of this discussion, we will be able to appreciate the extent to which the Christian and the Mahāyāna Buddhist tradition have developed analogous, and yet divergent positions on the salvific value of the natural order.

---

[139] Reginald A. Ray, *Indestructible Truth: The Living Spirituality of Tibetan Buddhism* (Boston, Mass.: Shambala, 2002), 98–99. Ray's discussion concurs with David L. Snellgrove and Hugh E. Richardson's claim in *A Cultural History of Tibet* (Bangkok, Thailand: Orchid Press, 2004), 79, that such decision "argued in favor of the conventional intellectual and moral training which had guaranteed the stability of Buddhist monasticism since the days of its founder." At the same time, Ray notes that according to older sources, it was Hua Shang (also known as Mahāyāna) who actually won the debate.

[140] Antoine Guillaumont, *Les 'Kephalaia Gnostica' d'Évagre le Pontique et l'histoire de l'Origénisme chez les Grecs et chez les Syriens*, 169–170.

6 THE GIFT OF *DHARMAKĀYA*: CONTEMPLATION AND PHILOSOPHY IN TSONG KHA PA'S UNDERSTANDING OF PRACTICE

In the preface and again in the third volume of his *Theodrama*, Hans Urs von Balthasar insists that an authentically Christian conception of reality cannot reduce creation to a self-enclosed system, but must show how reality as a whole is *an event*, which engages my freedom and which demands a response. Creation is the sacrament of God's love; it is the locus of God's self-disclosure; it is the stage where the *drama* of the human condition unfolds. Each one of us is given the choice to enter into the Trinitarian dialogue of love, or to seek an autonomous self-realization that can only frustrate our deepest aspirations.[1] Von Balthasar's rendition of *analogia entis* is deeply personalist, involving the response of the individual to the God who calls him or her across the ontological chasm; it is effectively an *analogia libertatis*, which demands nothing less than the gift of our life.[2]

This dialectic of contemplation and response actually reflects Balthasar's indebtedness to Maximos, who articulates it in the terms, by now familiar, of *theōria* and *praxis*. For both Maximos and Balthasar, the object of *theōria* is not merely the earthly life of Christ, but the whole of the created order. The qualified retrieval of classical cosmological speculation discussed in Ch. 3 reflected the perceived need to give an articulate theological account of the relationship between the divine pedagogy (paideusis) in its twofold expression as creation and incarnation. Gawronski's characterization of Christianity as "dialogical" in opposition to the "monological"

---

[1] Hans Urs von Balthasar, *Theo-Drama: Theological Dramatic Theory*, Vol. 1: *Prolegomena* (San Francisco: Ignatius Press, 1988), 15–24, 79–87.

[2] Angelo Scola notes that Balthasar's *analogia libertatis* must be understood as a "perfect correspondence (*Entsprechung*) between God's historic self-manifestation in Jesus Christ and a human freedom that is truly free." See Angelo Scola, "A style of thought," in Elisa Buzzi, ed., *A generative thought-an introduction to the works of Luigi Giussani* (Montreal: McGill-Queen's Univ. Press, 2003), 3–33.

nature of Buddhism that was mentioned in Ch. 1 rested largely on
Balthasar's reading of the cosmos as a *gift*, which demands a personal commitment on the part of the individual.[3] Such a construal of "Christianity"
and "Buddhism," however, fails to consider the fundamental teachings of
Mahāyāna on the nature of enlightenment and the purpose of practice. In
the early twentieth century, some scholars interpreted the shift from Theravada to Mahāyāna as yet another instance of the "Indian" tendency to deify
major historical figures; yet, as we will see in this chapter, this characterization would be profoundly flawed.[4] In Mahāyāna Buddhism, no less than in
its Tibetan rendition known as Vajrayāna, the Buddha was seen as a supremely insightful religious teacher, as well as the embodiment of the true
nature of things. The body of the historical Buddha, in this perspective, is
the ultimate example of salvific contingency, the manifestation of *dharma*,
the interpretive key of the cosmos.

Yet, in Mahāyāna, the body of Gautama is only one of the Buddha's
embodied manifestations, whose reach encompasses the cosmos, and
whose purpose is to manifest Buddhahood's salvific power. The *Perfection of
Wisdom* text known as the *Astasāhasrikā* draws a clear distinction between
the historical body of the Buddha and the corpus of his teachings (*dharmakāya*),[5] which also indicates the "perfect qualities" ascribed to the Buddha
by Abhidharma literature, as well as the emptiness (*śūnyatā*), which is the
ultimate nature of reality. The Buddha's teaching and the emptiness of all
that exists are thus effectively identified with each other and with the Buddha's historical manifestation, much as in *Amb. 10* the *logoi* of Scripture and
the *logoi* of creation are encompassed and transcended by the transfigured
Christ. While Maximos stresses how *praxis* flows from contemplation of the
logoi in *theōria*, the Mahāyāna tradition of Buddhism insists that familiarity
with the *dharmāh* which sustain the cosmos lead to wisdom and eventually
to the practice of compassion.

Our goal in this chapter is to present Tsong kha pa's understanding of
contemplation in the context of his understanding of Buddhahood, showing that this type of "contemplation" invests the natural order, no less than

---

[3] See Raymond Gawronski SJ, *Word and Silence*, 21–24, 48–51; Mark A.
McIntosh, *Mystical Theology*, 6–7, who in his turn refers to John Zizioulas.

[4] Julius Evola, *The Doctrine of Awakening : The Attainment of Self-Mastery According
to the Earliest Buddhist Texts* (trans. H. E. Musson; Rochester, Vt.: Inner Traditions:
1996), 22–25.

[5] Paul Williams, *Mahāyāna Buddhism*, 171–172.

the writings of the Buddhist tradition, with a sort of sacramental power.[6] This approach will show that Gawronski's and Staniloae's treatment of Buddhist practice is deeply flawed; yet, it would be equally misleading to conclude that Tsong kha pa's understanding of the Buddha's salvific embodiment is identical to what one finds in Maximos' *Ambigua*. Ultimately, the Christian image of creation is one of overflowing plenitude. The ordering wisdom of the *dharmakāya*, on the other hand, is a gift that leads one towards emptiness.

THREE BODIES OR FOUR? NON-ABIDING *NIRVĀNA* AND THE BUDDHA'S ACTIVITY IN THE CONDITIONED WORLD

By the time Mahāyāna came to regard itself as distinct from the earlier Hinayāna schools, its innovative interpretation of the third noble truth had had important repercussions on the way the Buddha's activity in the cosmos was conceived. The purpose of the teaching of "non-abiding" (*apratisthitā*) *nirvāna* was to affirm that the Buddha could attain full awakening, move beyond conditioning, and yet remain active within *samsāra*, so as to bring all sentient beings to enlightenment.[7] Śāntideva's *Bodhicaryāvatāra*, which posits *bodhicitta* as the chief engine of practice, is paradigmatic of the Indian as well as of the Tibetan Mahāyāna traditions, which invariably see the Buddhas as forever acting in the universe, guiding others to awakening.[8] As a result of this doctrinal shift, it became necessary to articulate more precisely what forms the Buddhas' activity would take. The doctrine of the different Buddha bodies which undergirds Tsong kha pa's vision provided an apposite template for this purpose.

In Mahāyāna texts, the *rūpakāya* (body of form) indicates the body of the historical Buddha, but also includes other "embodiments" in different historical contexts or even different dimensions. In the last chapter, we saw how rDzogs chen authors, sometimes retrieving elements from pre-Buddhist cosmologies, viewed the whole of the cosmos as flowing from the

---

[6] As mentioned in Ch. 1, an overview of the life and work of Tsong kha pa may be found in *The Central Philosophy of Tibet: A Study and Translation of Jey Tsong khapa's 'Essence of True Eloquence'* (Princeton, N.J.: Princeton University Press, 1984), 63–89. A brief account will be given here on p. 213.

[7] John Makransky, *Buddhahood Embodied: Sources of Controversy in India and Tibet* (SUNY Series in Buddhist Studies. Albany, N.Y.: SUNY Press, 1997), 11.

[8] Śāntideva, *Bodhicaryāvatāra* 8, 94–5, in Stephen Batchelor, *A guide to the Bodhisattva's way of life* (2d ed. Ithaca, NY: Snow Lion Publ., 1999).

Buddha's insight and compassion. In this perspective, the very purpose of conventional reality is to furnish sentient beings with ethical guidelines and to provide the context for their implementation. The earliest traditions of Buddhist epistemology had characterized *dharma* as "the smallest unit of experience that human beings can have."[9] According to Scholastic Abhidharma, samsaric *dharmāḥ* come into being and disappear as a result of karmic causes, whereas nirvanic *dharmāḥ* were unchanging and existed beyond the realm of causality.[10] Madhyamaka philosophers preferred to view the perfect attributes of the Buddhas as co-extensive with his cognition of emptiness—a cognition which of course transcended the boundaries of verbal expression. In the text known as *Ratnāvalī*, Nāgārjuna notes that the *dharmakāya* (body of *dharma*) reflects the Buddha's insight into *śūnyatā*, whereas the physical body (*rūpakāya*) of Śākyamuni is the expression of his compassion and the fruit of the merits accumulated in past lives.[11] This dichotomy of emptiness and form offers a paradigm for the simultaneous pursuit of wisdom and compassion that defines the Mahāyāna path. The fact that reality is empty of inherent existence entails that all sentient beings rest in the *dharmakāya* and can become an expression of the compassion of the Buddha.

Yet what is crucial is that sentient beings *understand* the empty nature of reality; and to this purpose, they have to undergo an extensive program of epistemic purification. In the *Madhyamakakārikā*, Nāgārjuna writes that "the doctrine of the Buddha is taught with reference to two truths," or levels of reality, which are "ultimate truth" (*paramārthasatya*) and "conventional truth" (*lokasaṃvṛtisatya*). This distinction is so crucial that those who fail to grasp it are unable to understand "the profound essence" (*tattva*) of the teaching on liberation.[12] According to Nāgārjuna, enlightenment is attained when the tendency to conceptualize is undercut, thereby drawing a sharp distinction between samsaric and nirvanic modalities of cognition. Conceptualizing reason as such is *not* an invalid epistemic tool; on the contrary, it is the instrument enabling us to deal with our everyday conventional world. One must distinguish instead between ordinary reason and the reason

[9] Reginald A. Ray, *Indestructible Truth*, 369–370.
[10] Reginald A. Ray, *Indestructible Truth*, 372.
[11] See Nāgārjuna, *Ratnāvalī* 3, 10–13, in Paul Williams, *Mahāyāna Buddhism*, 173. Analogously, in the writings of the Desert Fathers, *dianoia* cannot deliver the ultimate mystical insight.
[12] See Nāgārjuna, *Madhyamakakārikā* 24, 8–10, in Paul Williams, *Mahāyāna Buddhism*, 69.

which discloses ultimate truth; the latter is equivalent to the experience of awakening and thus to full-fledged Buddhahood. Nāgārjuna's claim that the two levels of reality imply each other and, like *samsāra* and *nirvāna*, are ultimately undivided, serves him to rebuke the accusations of nihilism leveled against Mādhyamaka. Conventional reality *does* exist, after all. At the same time, while this approach emphasizes the intrinsic (one is tempted to say perichoretic) relation between the *dharmakāya* and the *rūpakāya*, the latter is presented as the phenomenal manifestation of the former, or in other words as a pointer towards ultimate emptiness.

At a later stage, Yogācāra philosophy deepened the Mādhyamaka reflection on how the *dharmakāya* becomes manifest in phenomenal reality, postulating a plurality of *rūpakāyāh* and explaining them as "natural outflows" (*nisyandāh*) of the *dharmakāya*. Through them the Buddha can choose to teach the *dharma* to different sentient beings in line with their different level of attainment.[13] In the *Mahāyānasamgraha*, a further body is described that is known as *sāmbhogikakāya* (body of bliss). This body is physical, is not tainted by the imperfections of our earthly bodies, and it also possesses the marks of perfection earlier associated with the *dharmakāya*. This supreme body dwells in a supernatural realm (known as Pure Land) and teaches the *dharma* to higher bodhisattvas and supernatural beings.[14] Belief in the *sāmbhogikakāya* would serve as a support for the growing corpus of Mahāyāna literature, which was attributed to the Buddha despite its much later date of composition; new texts and *sūtras* were ascribed to the *sāmbhogikakāya* dwelling in the Pure Lands, while the *nairmānikakāya* (body of transformation) became an emanation of the body of bliss for beings unworthy of this higher state of being. The historical Buddha was one such emanation, but so are all who practice and teach the *dharma*, as well as those who strive to live an ethical life consistent with their conscience and beliefs.

The fact that the Buddha is now said to have effectively three bodies perfectly dovetails Yogācāra epistemological reflection.[15] In the Samdhinirmocana Sūtra, the Buddha is asked to illustrate how the flow of our thoughts and perceptions is related to the outside world. Is there anything but our minds? How is it that some people believe in the existence of in-

---

[13] John Makransky, *Buddhahood Embodied*, 96.

[14] Asanga, *Mahāyānasamgraha* 10, 35, in Etienne Lamotte, *La somme du Grand Vehicule d'Asanga*, Tome 2 (Louvain, Belgium: Museon, 1938).

[15] See Gadjin M. Nagao, "On the theory of Buddha-Body (*Buddha-kāya*)," *Eastern Buddhist* 4.1 (1973): 25–53.

herent objects? How are we to relate to conventional reality once we realize its ultimate emptiness? This text answers these questions by developing the so-called doctrine of the three aspects of reality. According to this doctrine, language wrongly tends to ascribe inherent existence to material objects; such distorting activity of speech, itself rooted in a misleading subject-object dichotomy, gives rise to the so-called "constructed reality" (*parikal-pitasvabhāva*). The underlying substratum which is systematically misinterpreted by language and which is the result of co-dependent origination (*pratītyasamutpāda*) is then characterized as "dependent reality" (*paratantras-vabhāva*).[16] Through meditation, one may undergo a radical cognitive transformation known as "overturning of the basis" (*āśrayaparāvrtti*), which enables one to discern the "true nature of things." This "true nature of things" is termed "suchness" (*tathatā*), or, more generally, "perfected reality" (*pariniṣpannasvabhāva*). Much as each "body of form" flows from the "body of dharma," this "perfected reality" and its "constructed" counterpart can be regarded as flowing from the *paratantrasvabhāva*. The former is the exclusive preserve of awakened practitioners; the latter is how reality is experienced by deluded individuals.

These different Mādhyamaka and Yogācāra teachings provided the background of Tsong kha pa's reflections on spiritual practice. By the time the *dharma* was transmitted to Tibet, the Mādhyamaka school was already divided into opposed branches, known as Prāsaṅgika (Tib. *thal gyur ba*) or Svātantrika (Tib. *rang rgyud pa*).[17] For the former, the best way to proceed in the context of a philosophical debate is to show to one's opponents the undesirable consequences of their positions; for the latter, it is necessary to

<hr>

[16] Robert A. F. Thurman, *Tsong Kha Pa's Speech of Gold in the Essence of True Eloquence* (Princeton, N.J.: Princeton University Press, 1984), 212–214.
[17] It is important to remember that the distinction was drawn *a posteriori* by various Tibetan scholars, and that the main actors in the debate would not have recognized these labels. Tsong kha pa was adamant that the distinction rested on a real philosophical difference, but some Tibetan as well as Western scholars have tended to play down the distinction. The author Bu ston rin chen grub (1290–1364), for instance, claimed that the distinction was an artificial conceptual creation (*bod kyi rtog bzo*) devised by Tibetan masters for their own purposes. See David S. Ruegg, *The Literature of the Madhyamaka School of Philosophy in India* (Wiesbaden: Otto Harassowitz Publ., 1981), 58, in Jan Gonda, ed., *History of Indian Literature*, Vol. VII, Fasc. 1.

develop ones' own independent arguments (*svātantra*).[18] The oppositions between these two schools hinged on how they interpreted Nāgārjuna's notion of the two truths; Svātantrika and Prāsangika shared the belief that reality was ultimately empty, but the former was ready to countenance inherent existence conventionally, whereas the latter regarded this belief as a return to pre-Mahāyāna tradition.[19]

The Svātantrika eagerness to assert the validity of autonomous proofs could more easily be accommodated with a belief in the validity of conventional cognition, which after careful discernment may procure an insight into the true nature of reality.[20] As a consequence, the Svātantrika position could appropriate the insights of earlier philosophical traditions if they appeared useful, while simultaneously asserting the inexpressible character of ultimate truth. 'Jam dpal bshes gnyen's attack in the *rDo la gser zhun* on those who resort to "views," while coming from a tradition rejecting all forms of Mādhyamaka dualism, is an effective indictment of those scholastic traditions "reifying" philosophical procedures and thereby affirming that the *dharma* could be given logical expression.

To counter accusations of essentialism, some Svātantrika thinkers were induced to co-opt Yogācāra speculation as an auxiliary teaching.[21] This synthesis, which Tibetan scholars would call Yogācāra-Svātantrika Madhyamaka, continues to assert the inherent existence of conventional reality, but contends that this inherent existence is located in the mind. In this way,

---

[18] The thinkers Buddhāpalita (late 5th-early 6th century) and Candrakīrti (early 7th century) are regarded as the major Prāsangika thinkers, whereas Bhāvaviveka is considered the beginner of Svātantrika. The former tradition can be regarded as favoring a more apophatic approach to practice, and in fact they accused the Svātantrikas of having imprisoned the dharma within the cage of Indian logic. In late 4th century Byzantium, Gregory of Nazianzos and Eunomios exchanged similar accusations. See the articles by William L. Ames, "Bhāvaviveka's own view of his differences with Buddhapālita," and C. W. (Sandy) Huntington Jr., "Was Candrakīrti a Prāsangika?," in Sara McClintock and Georges Dreyfus, eds., *The Prāsangika-Svātantrika distinction: What Difference does a Difference make?* (Boston: Wisdom Publications, 2003), 41–66 and 67–91.

[19] See Tsong kha pa, *Legs bshad snying po*, Ch. 4, in Robert A. F. Thurman, *The Central Philosophy of Tibet- A Study and Translation of Jey Tsong Khapa's 'Essence of True Eloquence'* (Princeton, N.J.: Princeton University Press, 1984), 265–273.

[20] Donald S. Lopez, *A Study of Svātantrika* (Ithaca, N.Y.: Snow Lion Press, 1987), 356–371.

[21] The main text of the Yogācāra-Svātantrika Madhyamaka school is Śāntarakṣita's *Madyhamakālamkāra*. See Paul Williams, *Mahāyāna Buddhism*, 59.

philosophical arguments may be deployed without retracting the Mahāyāna notion of *śūnyatā*.[22] In this way, speculation on the nature of conventional reality continues to have a therapeutic value, but it also makes legitimate meaningful assertions on how conventional reality is structured. Tsong kha pa's own position, however, followed Prāsangika Mādhyamaka; he denied inherently established existence, even if his understanding of the Buddha bodies blended Mādhyamaka and Yogācāra views. How did Tsong kha pa come to develop this remarkably eclectic position?

In the academic curriculum of Tibetan monastic institutions, such as the great university of Samye, pride of place was given to the study of *Perfection of Wisdom* literature, and a text often used as a compendium was the exegetical work known as *Abhisamayālamkāra*. This text, which had reached its final form by the early sixth century, gives a systematic presentation of various practices, concluding with a description of the Buddha bodies which emphasizes the compassionate activity of the Buddha throughout the universe.[23] While the *Abhisamayālamkāra* as a whole gave rise to a vast commentarial tradition, the final chapter devoted to the Buddha*kāyas* was especially controversial, as members of different schools read it in line with their previous commitments to contrasting doctrinal positions. The author of the *Abhisamayālamkāra* rehearsed the customary distinction between the different "bodies of form," while resorting to the terms *dharmakāya* and *svābhāvikakāya* to refer to the transcendent foundation which gives rise to the *rūpakāyāḥ*. Before Buddhism was transmitted to Tibet at all, Indian commentators were already divided on whether the terms *dharmakāya* and *svābhāvikakāya* were synonymous or whether they referred to two different realities. As John Makransky explains in his work *Buddhahood embodied*, the controversy centered on the number of the Buddha bodies, but it also reflected far deeper disagreements on the nature of the Buddha's on-going activity in a conditioned world.[24]

While the Madhyamaka position associated *dharmakāya* with the ultimate and the *rūpakāya* with the phenomenal, Yogācāra thinkers construed the *dharmakāya* as effectively straddling the divide between the two levels of reality. On one hand, in line with Chinese cosmological speculations, the

---

[22] Bhāvaviveka's version of Svātantrika would then be labeled Sautrantika-Svātantrika Madhyamaka, pointing to its philosophical closeness to the Sautrantika school of Hinayāna. See again Paul Williams, *Mahāyāna Buddhism*, 59–60.

[23] John Makransky, *Buddhahood Embodied*, 3.

[24] John Makransky, *Buddhahood Embodied*, 6, and *passim*.

dharmakāya was posited as identical with the *dharmadhātu*, the total expanse of reality. On the other hand, the *dharmakāya* was referred to as the *svābhāvikakāya*, the "body of essence," indicating the flow of non-conceptual consciousness that characterizes Buddhahood.[25] How the same reality could encompass these two ostensibly opposed aspects clearly escaped logical expression, but Yogācāra thinkers argued that Buddhahood was "primarily an object of yogic realization, not of philosophical speculation."[26] The epistemological insight of awakening discloses how *dharmakāya* and *svābhāvikakāya* are ultimately identical.[27] This was the position developed by the sixth century Indian commentator Ārya Vimuktisena, for whom the *Abhisamayālamkāra* asserted the existence of three Buddha bodies.

In his reading of the text, Ārya Vimuktisena was heavily influenced by Yogācāra epistemology and in particular by the notion of *āśrayaparāvrtti*. As a result, he tended to view non-conceptual gnosis as the very essence of Buddhahood (*svābhāvikakāya*). The object of this gnosis was "reality as it is" (*parinispannasvabhāva, or tathatā-viśuddhi*), where impure aggregates are effaced by the purified *dharma*-realm (*dharmakāya*). In the state of enlightenment, the dichotomy between subject and object is transcended, so that *svābhāvikakāya* and *dharmakāya* are identical.[28]

Ārya Vimuktisena's hermeneutical approach viewed established meditational practice as normative. A radically different approach was taken by the eighth century commentator Haribhadra, who read the *Abhisamayālamkāra* as a philosophical exercise, seeking to present the doctrine of the Buddha bodies as a coherent system of thought. Haribhadra's thought reflected the development of Yogācāra-Svātantrika Madhyamaka thought, and followed Śāntaraksita in interpreting Yogācāra thought as a conceptual introduction to the "higher insights" of the Mādhyamikas.[29] His approach, however, was also characterized by a heavy reliance on logic, which in his opinion could unravel *conceptually* the paradox of "active nirvāna." His dissatisfaction with Yogācāra's apophatic approach led him to the conclusion that

---

[25] Asanga, *Mahāyānasamgraha*, 10, 1, in Etienne Lamotte, *La somme du Grand Vehicule d'Asanga*.

[26] John Makransky, *Buddhahood Embodied*, 12.

[27] John Makransky, *Buddhahood Embodied*, 60–62.

[28] This discussion, which for reasons of space is very sketchy, is based on John Makransky, *Buddhahood Embodied*, Ch. 4 (62–64), Ch. 9 (188–191), Ch. 13 (362–367).

[29] In fact the later Tibetan tradition would contend that Haribhadra was Śāntaraksita's own disciple. See David S. Ruegg, *The Literature of the Madhyamaka School of Philosophy in India*, 88–104.

the reluctance of earlier scholars to give a philosophical account of the experience of enlightenment was only symptomatic of the deficiency of their intellectual tools. What Haribhadra accomplishes in his work is to re-read the *Abhisamayālamkāra* in line with a Madhyamaka understanding of Buddha nature. In the *Ambigua*, Maximos had accomplished an analogous result, re-reading passages from earlier Fathers in line with Chalcedonian Christology.

Haribhadra's central contention was that the Yogācāra identification of *svābhāvikakāya* and *dharmakāya* is ontologically untenable, as it brings together the conditioned reality of the latter and the unconditioned (and ultimately empty) reality of the former.[30] Rigorous philosophical reflection, as opposed to meditation practice, shows that *apratiṣṭhitā nirvāna* is no paradox. All we need to do is to understand that the Buddha's own realization includes two aspects: an unconditioned thusness that fully transcends the world (the *svābhāvikakāya*), and a "pure form of conditioned consciousness" which encompasses the totality of "dharma gnoses" (*jñāna-dharmakāya*).[31] In this way the dichotomy between ultimate and conventional is established within *nirvāna* itself; but the consequence is that we now have four Buddha bodies. The *svābhāvikakāya* is the ultimate emptiness of all aspects of Buddhahood; it is entirely set apart from the "dharma gnoses" through which the Buddha engages the world and which produce the different *rūpakāyāh*.[32]

It is important to remember that the term *kāya* means "body," but it can also be read as "collection" or as "support"; in the first case, Buddhahood is ultimately co-extensive with the *dharmas*, while in the second it is their ultimate source and origin.[33] While the Abhidharma positions mentioned above viewed the enlightened state as the acquisition of certain excellent qualities (*dharmāḥ*), the *Perfection of Wisdom* tradition viewed it instead as an insight into the emptiness of reality as a whole (*dharmatā*). Haribhadra's understanding of the Buddha bodies adopted this second interpretation, while also reading *kāya* as "support." As a result, the four bodies of the Buddha are mapped onto the Madhyamaka doctrine of the two truths; the *svābhāvikakāya* is identified with the ultimate emptiness of the *dharmatā*, and as such it alone can be identified with the Buddha's essence. The other

---

[30] John Makransky, *Buddhahood Embodied*, 214–215.
[31] John Makransky, *Buddhahood Embodied*, 216.
[32] See John Makransky's translation of Haribhadra's commentary to Ch. 8 of the *Abhisamayālamkāra* in *Buddhahood Embodied*, 218–225.
[33] John Makransky, *Buddhahood Embodied*, 5.

three bodies are associated with conventional reality. While the *jñāna-dharmakāya* is logically prior to its own manifestations as *rūpakāyāh*, they are all an expression of the Buddha's pure awareness.[34] What is most striking about this theory is that a dimension of conventional gnosis is re-introduced into the Buddha's own realization. Much as Maximos viewed *theōria* as disclosing God's plan, contemplation of the cosmos becomes a first step towards awakening. By applying the tools of logical and philosophical analysis to the *jñāna-dharmakāya* (which is here the *support* of the *dharmatā*), we can *begin* to share in the Buddha's own epistemological insight, though it is only *after* enlightenment is experienced that we can fully share the Buddha's understanding of emptiness. While Yogācāra masters viewed meditation practice as disclosing the highest insight while regarding philosophical speculation as potentially misleading, Haribhadra affirms the ability of natural contemplation to introduce us *gradually* to the dimension of Buddhahood. In Phil 2:5, the Apostle Paul invited his audience to acquire the "mind of Christ," coming to see creation as Christ himself had seen it; for Haribhadra, and for Tsong kha pa after him, the Buddha's wisdom is what enables us to know the inner structure of the cosmos.

The scholarly consensus is that Ārya Vimuktisena's reading of the *Abhisamayālamkāra* in line with Yogācāra thought was closer to the intentions of its author,[35] but what matters to our overall argument is that Haribhadra's understanding of Buddha nature would come to be accepted as authoritative by Tsong kha pa, whose reading of the whole Mahāyāna tradition was profoundly influenced by Haribhadra's blend of Yogācāra and Madhyamaka thought.

THE DEFEAT OF "PRIVATE REASON": TSONG KHA PA'S CRITIQUE OF SVĀTANTRIKA

The life and work of Tsong kha pa (1357–1419) can only be understood against the background of late Medieval Tibet,[36] where, in the wake of the

---

[34] John Makransky, *Buddhahood Embodied*, 233–242.

[35] John Makransky, *Buddhahood Embodied*, Ch. 8 ("Internal evidence that *Abhisamayālamkāra* Chapter 8 teaches the three Yogācāra *kāyas*"), 159–185.

[36] I am of course using the term "Medieval" on the ground of expediency, conscious that its meaning presupposes a Western set of references. Throughout *Civilized Shamans*, Geoffrey Samuel uses the term "pre-modern" Tibet to refer to the period prior to the Chinese invasion of 1950.

New Transmission, the country's spiritual landscape was characterized by an extraordinary variety of practices and traditions, and where each monastic lineage effectively taught different understandings of the *dharma*.[37] Geoffrey Samuel points out how the "shamanic" tradition represented by rNying ma chose to welcome these different teachings as "fragments" of their own tradition, ultimately leading to the same realization.[38] Tsong kha pa similarly intended to systematize all traditions into a balanced and unified whole, but his conviction was that monastic discipline could only be restored if pride of place were given to the study of Buddhist philosophy and epistemology. As a result, after attaining enlightenment in 1398 at the age of forty-one, Tsong kha pa devised a monastic curriculum centered on the study of Prāsangika-Madhyamaka philosophy.[39] The very fact that his awakening was believed to have followed a vision of Buddhapalita, the Indian founder of the Prāsangika-Madhyamaka tradition, would ensure that the dGe lugs order, to the present day, would regard this philosophy as normative.

According to another tradition, Tsong kha pa's inner conviction as to the centrality of philosophical speculation for practice derived from yet another visionary experience—his repeated encounters with Mañjuśri, the bodhisattva of wisdom, whom Tibetans traditionally honor as the protector of scholarly pursuits. Mañjuśri is said to have encouraged him to write his massive *Great Treatise on the Stages of the Path to Enlightenment* (*Lam rim chen mo*), as well as his later *Essence of True Eloquence* (*Legs bshad snying po*).[40] In complete contrast to rDzogs chen, with its frequent condemnation of "views," the short version of the *Legs bshad snying po* exclaims: "of all deeds, the deeds of speech are supreme; hence it is for them that the wise commemorate a Buddha."[41]

---

[37] See Matthew Kapstein, "Religious syncretism in 13th century Tibet: The *Limitless Ocean* Cycle," in Barbara N. Aziz and Matthew Kapstein, eds., *Soundings in Tibetan civilization* (New Dehli: South Asia Books, 1985), 358–371.

[38] See Geoffrey Samuel, *Civilized shamans*, 503–504; on 504, the quotation from *Rig pa ngon trod* is paradigmatic of this radical apophaticism that effectively views all different teachings as "pointers" towards the truth.

[39] Reginald A. Ray, *Indestructible Truth*, 194–195.

[40] Robert A. F. Thurman, *The Central Philosophy of Tibet*, 3–5. Mañjuśri is pictured raising the sword of wisdom so as to free all beings through the path of philosophy.

[41] See Tsong kha pa, short version of the *Legs bshad snying po*, 183, in Robert A. F. Thurman, *The Central Philosophy of Tibet*, quoted also on 3.

These claims by Tsong kha pa may surprise contemporary Westerners, who profess some interest for Buddhism, but think that the latter demands a virtual silencing of intellectual reasoning. As Thurman points out, however, such radical anti-intellectualism is deeply mistaken. In fact, it is bound to leave one all the more vulnerable to the dictates of the dominant culture; merely to ponder on the abyss of our ignorance and its distance from the insight of the Buddha is not going to help us attain enlightenment or overcome suffering.[42] Tsong kha pa, on the contrary, was profoundly convinced that the human intellect has the power to understand reality; or even that there was nothing in the Buddha's insight, which is forever beyond our reach. In this way, Tsong kha pa's position is a challenge both to religious traditions that view enlightenment as an exclusive prerogative of the deity, and to philosophical systems for which ultimate questions can never be answered adequately. As in Nāgārjuna's introduction to the *Mūlamadhya-makakārikā*, the Buddha is saluted as the "supreme philosopher" who embodies the truth of his teaching in his very self.[43] The Buddha's insight brings "perfect bliss" to sentient beings, who are thus introduced to the truth of their condition; the transcendental nature of Buddhahood that was manifest in Śākyamuni constantly strives to dispel the ignorance at the root of our suffering. For Tsong kha pa, Buddhist practice demands no *sacrificium intellectus*;[44] the very notion of active *nirvāna*—upon which we ought to pattern our own practice of compassion—is inconceivable unless it rests on "a sustained and penetrating contemplation" of reality.[45]

We can now see how Maximos' position on divine embodiment reflects Tsong kha pa's. Nāgārjuna's invocation of the Buddha as the embodiment of wisdom and the dGe lugs master's reprise of this theme throughout his works echo the notion of the incarnate cosmic order which is a chief concern of the *Ambigua*. Maximos' critique of the Origenist system retained Origen's conviction that the Christian faith was the worthy heir

---

[42] See Robert A. F. Thurman, *The Central Philosophy of Tibet*, 9.

[43] See Nāgārjuna, *Mūlamadhyamakakārikā* 1, 1, in Robert A. F. Thurman, *The Central Philosophy of Tibet*, 10. On 12, the same Thurman quotes Dignaga's *Pramāna-samuccaya*, where the Buddha is said to be "reason personified" (*pramānabhūta*).

[44] See Jeffrey Hopkins, *Emptiness in the Mind-Only School of Buddhism: Dynamic Responses to Dzong-ka-ba's 'The Essence of True Eloquence'* (Berkeley, Calif.: University of California Press, 2003), 15–16. Hopkins uses "Mind-Only" as a translation to Cittamātra, which (with various provisos) can be regarded as synonymous with Yogācāra.

[45] See Robert A. F. Thurman, *The Central Philosophy of Tibet*, 13.

and continuator of classical cosmological speculation, which was now supplemented with the cues offered by the incarnate life of the Word. Maximos' notion of *nature* as setting the terms of human morality parallels the
belief in the *jñāna-dharmakāya* embraced by Haribhadra, for whom the conventional reality framing the Buddha's compassionate activity is fully susceptible to logical analysis. If there is a difference, it is one of emphasis;
Maximos' approach is essentially contemplative, whereas Tsong kha pa's
position privileges the speculative. Yet, even Tsong kha pa's therapeutic
understanding of speculation echoes the notion of *diakrisis* developed by
the Desert Fathers.[46] In both cases, the ultimate effacement of all misap-
prehensions about reality leads to a mystical insight that entails the ontological transformation of the individual.

While Evagrios' affirmation of the salvific value of the cosmos was not
as uncompromising as Maximos', the overwhelming consensus in his
school was that created reality possessed a soteriological potential. For both
Evagrios and Maximos, however, this potential was obscured by the tendency to view *our own needs* as setting the *terms* for the use of nature. In this
perspective, a purification of our cognitive mode was necessary to attain the
condition of *apatheia*, which in turn leads to *theōria*.[47] Where the early Christian Fathers differed from Tsong kha pa's position was in the extent to
which they only gave scant indications as to the *techniques*, whereby this goal
could be achieved. In this respect, the Indo-Tibetan tradition of Mahāyāna
is striking for the subtlety and complexity of its introspective analysis,
whose goal is to attain and to sustain the Buddha's insight.

Indeed, in Tsong kha pa we find a conviction that an adequate understanding of contingent, conventional reality is a necessary preparatory stage
for the experience of enlightenment.[48] The greatest danger is here "private

---

[46] I am thinking here of the movement away from *dianoia* (a sort of private reason) to *nous* (which is shared by all). See Martin Laird, "The 'open country whose
name is prayer': apophasis, deconstruction, and contemplative practice," *Mod
Theol* 21 (1): 141–155.

[47] Evagrios, *On Discrimination*, 1–2, 5, in *Philokalia*, Vol. 1, 38–39 and 40–41.

[48] M. David Eckel compares Tsong kha pa's attitude to Nāgārjuna, who in *Mūlamadhyamakakārikā* notes "It is impossible to teach the ultimate without being
based on the conventional, and without understanding the ultimate, it is impossible
to attain *nirvāna*." M. David Eckel, "The Satisfaction of No-Analysis," 176–190, in
Sara McClintock and Georges Dreyfus, eds., *The Prāsangika-Svātantrika distinction*,
173–203.

reasoning," which is nothing but a speculative counterpart of *philautia*.[49] As long as we fail to understand the truth about the ordinary reality we inhabit, we are also unable to practice compassion and help other sentient beings. For this reason, the dGe lugs founder lays the foundations of a philosophy, which integrates into spiritual practice our engagement of the conventional, but which simultaneously clarifies to what extent phenomenal reality can be revelatory of ultimate truth.

In the introductory section of the *Legs bshad snying po*, Tsong kha pa portrays the Buddha as triumphing over the traditions of Indian philosophy that favor and sustain "self-centered" interpretations of reality. In his interpretation of this passage, Thurman associates the yogin Shambu with Shiva, the destructive deity that is the patron of the Nyaya school of logic and the Vaiśeśika school of metaphysics.[50] In seeking to construe an all-encompassing understanding of reality, both traditions never question reason's capacity to grasp the true essence of the various components of the cosmos, and as such can easily incur a variety of mistakes. Equally dangerous is the belief of the Mimamsa—here represented by Indra "who rides upon the clouds"—in the possibility to *manipulate* reality for our purposes; this might favor the development of human civilization, but it possesses a self-destructive potential.[51] Along these lines, the reference to Brahma's creativity—symbolized by the primordial egg Hiranyagarbha—hints at the danger of clinging to our separate, individual nature. The followers of Anangapati, who view the pursuit of pleasure as the highest goal in life, bring this tendency to its extreme consequences; they trust merely their own senses and dismiss as senseless philosophical speculation and the very notion of spiritual discipline. In Tsong kha pa's view, even embracing theism in search of personal salvation—which is the strategy adopted by the followers of Viṣṇu—is no solution at all, as theism rests on a dualist perspec-

---

[49] See again Jeffrey Hopkins, *Emptiness in the Mind-Only School of Buddhism*, 15–16. Hopkins uses "Mind-Only" as a translation to Cittamātra, which (with various provisos) can be regarded as synonymous with Yogācāra.

[50] See Robert A. F. Thurman, *The Central Philosophy of Tibet*, 14.

[51] *Mimamsa* of course focused on exact performance of Vedic ritual, which was believed to have certain effects even in the absence of all-seeing deities. Thurman envisages the modern technological spirit as sharing the same faith in blind mechanical processes.

tive perpetuating the subordination of the individual soul to the deity.[52] The
poetic passage (almost a verbal mandala) which Tsong kha pa places at the
beginning of this work signifies the defeat of self-centered philosophy at the
hands of the Buddha's authentic insight.[53]

This same theme is treated extensively throughout the whole work. In
Ch. 4 and 5, Tsong kha pa critiques the philosophical position of different
Madhyamaka sub-schools, resorting to Bhāvaviveka's interpretation of Nāgārjuna to buttress a critique of Yogācāra-influenced Madhyamaka episte-
mologies.[54] According to Tsong kha pa, the inability to deepen one's practice is caused by the belief that a proper understanding of the two Madhyamaka truths (*bden pa gnyis*) can be attained on the basis of independent logical arguments (*svātantra*). As in Nāgārjuna, the dGe lugs master associates
conventional reality with phenomenal appearances and ultimate reality with
their underlying emptiness. Objects may be said to possess a conventional
identity established by the power of mental labeling. This is true even if this
identity does not arise from any characteristic found in the objects themselves; rather, the deepest truth about these objects is that they have no
such identity at all. On one hand, the Sautrantika's belief in the ability of
bare cognition to known independently existing entities is fully rejected. On
the other hand, it asserts that inferential cognition, by postulating so-called
"metaphysical entities" (*spyi mtshan*), enables us to engage conventional
truth, even if these entities do not exist.[55] It is thus possible to know the
ultimate and the conventional truth about a particular aspect of reality *simultaneously*, by the concurrent use of bare and inferential cognition. The error
of Svātantrika Mādhyamikas is to believe that the metaphysical entities postulated by inferential knowledge have a real, as opposed to a mental, conventional existence. This clinging to mental concepts effectively obfuscates
our understanding of ultimate truth; Tsong kha pa's conclusion is that reali-

---

[52] Tsong kha pa, *Legs bshad snying po*, Prologue, in Robert A. F. Thurman, *The
Central Philosophy of Tibet*, 187; also Thurman's commentary to it, *ibid.*, 3–15. All references to the *Legs bshad snying po* rely on Thurman's translation.

[53] Robert A. F. Thurman, *The Central Philosophy of Tibet*, 17.

[54] As opposed to a critique of Yogācāra *per se*.

[55] Alexander Barzin, *The Validity and Accuracy of Cognition of the Two Truths in Gelug-Prasangika and Non-Gelug Madhyamaka* (http://www.berzinarchives.com/sutra/
sutra_level_5/validity_prasanghika_madhyamaka.html, in *The Berzin Archive*, 2002),
2–4

zation cannot be attained if one fails to cultivate a proper (pure, selfless) understanding of conventional reality.[56]

The strategy employed to make this point in the *Legs bshad snying po* is to dissect Bhāvaviveka's take on the Yogācāra three natures, so as to show that Bhāvaviveka has fallen out of the "pure" tradition of the Mādhyamikas and has come to believe that it is possible to attain realization "even without realizing the lack of intrinsically identifiable reality in persons and things."[57] At the outset of Ch. 4, Tsong kha pa quotes Bhāvaviveka's assertion in the *Prajñāpradīpa* (*Lamp of Wisdom*), according to which the repudiation of the reality of the constructed nature by certain Yogācāra philosophers does not merely "repudiate verbal and mental expressions," but it extends to a "repudiation (*apavāda*) of the *facts* (*vastu, dngos po*)."[58] If this were a repudiation of the *ultimate* reality of dependent and absolute nature, Bhāvaviveka would have no objection (after all, this is what Mādhyamikas have been saying all along), but Yogācāra philosophers actually deny the *conventional* reality of these natures! And this is something that might have some unpleasant consequences. When we mistake a rope for a snake, it is certainly appropriate to realize that no snake is there, but snakes *in general* are not a fiction of our imagination; as D. Eckel puts it, they might even threaten our conventional foot with their conventional teeth.[59] As a result, Bhāvaviveka concludes, it is necessary to admit that snakes are endowed with conventional existence; to deny this would contradict "something that is generally accepted (*prasiddha*)."[60]

According to Tsong kha pa, this claim by Bhāvaviveka is also implicit in the contention by the *Samdhinirmocana sūtra* (*The Elucidation of Intention*) that unless something is established with its own identity, it is empty of identity at all—thus indicating that the Yogācāra dependent nature has "an

---

[56] Alexander Barzin, *The Validity and Accuracy of Cognition of the Two Truths*, 10.

[57] Tsong kha pa, *Legs bshad snying po*, Ch. 4, in Thurman, 265–269. M. David Eckel, in the article "The Satisfaction of No-Analysis" quoted above, quotes the same passage but he translates "real things" as opposed to "facts," which possibly fits better the following example about snakes.

[58] Bhāvaviveka, *Prajñāpradīpa*, Ch. 25, 243, quoted in Tsong kha pa, *Legs bshad snying po*, Ch. 4, in Thurman, 266. The *Prajñāpradīpa* is a commentary of Nāgārjuna's *Mūlamadhyamakakārikā*.

[59] M. David Eckel, "The Satisfaction of no analysis," 178.

[60] Tsong kha pa, *Legs bshad snying po*, Ch. 4, in Thurman, 268.

intrinsically identifiable reality."[61] Tsong kha pa wants his readers to come to the conclusion that Bhāvaviveka was arguing for the superiority of Madhyamaka over Yogācāra thought, but in using the doctrine of the three natures as a stepping stone, the same Bhāvaviveka overstepped the boundaries of his own tradition and committed himself to views (such as the existence of conventional realities) that Madhyamaka masters such as Nāgārjuna would have rejected.[62] As a result, Tsong kha pa implies, those who follow the teaching of Sautrantika-Svātantrika are unable to reach enlightenment. David Eckel notes that Bhāvaviveka might have resisted Tsong kha pa's interpretation of his position,[63] though the dGe lugs master would have probably defended his position by saying that he was merely drawing out the implications of Bhāvaviveka's argument. Be that as it may, Tsong kha pa's reading of Bhāvaviveka serves him as a first rhetorical foil to foreground the superiority of the Prāsangika interpretation of Madhyamaka thought.

The opinions of Śāntarakṣita and Kamalaśīla discussed in the rest of Ch. 4 are then said to "accord" with Bhāvaviveka's interpretation, inasmuch as they both believe "in a conventional reality established (in things) by their intrinsic identity."[64] When presenting Kamalaśīla's views, Tsong kha pa emphasizes how the latter accepts the early Madhyamaka "notion of utter non-existence of production and cessation," but qualifies it by claiming that one should not "insist upon the literalness" of such statement, since Mādhyamikas are quite ready to accept "production" (i.e., postulation of metaphysical entities) in the conventional sense.[65] The Tibetan tradition of

---

[61] Tsong kha pa, *Legs bshad snying po*, Ch. 4, in Thurman, 266; also M. David Eckel, "The Satisfaction of No-Analysis," 180. A few lines down Tsong kha pa points out that this passage in the *Samdhinirmocana sūtra* is "the clearest source (for the demonstration) of this master's (Bhāvaviveka's) belief in the conventional intrinsic identifiability of things."

[62] It is interesting to observe that, while Bhāvaviveka is regarded as the chief representative of the Sautrantika-Svātantrika (as opposed to the Yogācāra-Svātantrika) Madhyamaka school, Tsong kha pa finds that the root of his deviation from Prāsangika is (paradoxically) his acceptance of some Yogācāra theories.

[63] In "The Satisfaction of no analysis," 183–187, M. David Eckel points out that in other passages of the *Prajñāpradīpa*, Bhāvaviveka gives a more sophisticated understanding of conventional reality as "emptiness of whatever is dissimilar," which does not exactly dovetail with how Tsong kha pa reads him.

[64] Tsong kha pa, *Legs bshad snying po*, Ch. 4, in Thurman, 278.

[65] Tsong kha pa, *Legs bshad snying po*, Ch. 4, in Thurman, 279.

textual hermeneutics had developed the notions of *trang don* (Sansk. *neyartha*) and *nge don* (Sansk. *nītartha*) to distinguish texts whose meaning is not immediately evident (and thus necessitate interpretation) and texts that can be read at face value. Tsong kha pa critiques Kamalaśila's "creative" reading of Madhyamaka philosophy by pointing out that Kamalaśila is effectively setting a precedent for the re-interpretation of other works "belonging to the middle wheel of the *dharma*," such as the *Transcendent Wisdom Heart*. In this way, every time a negation of intrinsic existence is not accompanied by the term "ultimate," the text can be construed as implicitly affirming the reality of conventional existence.[66]

Again, Tsong kha pa might be reading more in Kamalaśila than the latter actually intended, though in this case Kamalaśila's way of reasoning follows the Mahāyāna tradition of re-interpreting earlier texts in line with later doctrinal developments. Unlike Bhāvaviveka's version of Madhyamaka thought, Kamalaśila and Haribhadra's reputed master, Śantarakṣita, are ready to resort to a different philosophical system (Yogācāra) as a concession to those "unable to realize all at once the 'realitylessness' of all things."[67] Śantarakṣita, for instance, points out explicitly that an analysis of the mind according to "mind-only" principles helps one "understand" the truth of "the central way [of the Mādhyamikas] that abandons all extremes."[68]

This second version of Svātantrika might be more nuanced than Bhāvaviveka's own approach, but in the course of Ch. 5 of the *Legs bshad snying po*, Tsong kha pa sets out to argue that all belief in the intrinsic existence of conventional reality is ultimately incompatible with the teaching of the Mādhyamikas. After observing that Candrakīrti explicitly attacks the Svātantrika position of Bhāvaviveka,[69] Tsong kha pa begins the presentation of his position by asking what "mental habit," or repeated cognitive move, has led so many Buddhist scholars (including many pre-Mahāyāna masters) to believe in the "intrinsic identifiability" (*svalakṣaṇasiddha*) of things. The answer goes back to the puzzlement many feel when they are confronted by sentences such as "this *person* performed this action and experienced this result." Who is the subject of this sentence? Is she the same as the aggregates

---

[66] Tsong kha pa, *Legs bshad snying po*, Ch. 4, in Thurman, 280.

[67] Tsong kha pa, *Legs bshad snying po*, Ch. 4, in Thurman, 281, quoting Kamalaśila.

[68] Tsong kha pa, *Legs bshad snying po*, Ch. 4, in Thurman, 275.

[69] Tsong kha pa, *Legs bshad snying po*, Ch. 5, in Thurman, 288–291.

that make up her body, or is she something different from them? Also, does she change over time or is she always the same? If they pose an effective referent for this term, the result is "the establishment of person as having intrinsically identifiable status."[70] These people commit the fundamental mistake of not being "content" with the mere conventional term. Tsong kha pa's point is that the Svātantrika ought to be satisfied with conventional reality as such, since attempting to ground it further would be a misunderstanding of the whole Madhyamaka enterprise.

The long suffering reader may ask at this point whether Tsong kha pa's purpose is not ultimately self-defeating, since he questions the very possibility of philosophical argumentation. Tsong kha pa's overall purpose, however, is not to advocate a radical epistemological apophaticism concerning conventional truth, since a proper understanding of conventional truth is the first step to advance on the spiritual path. According to R. Thurman, the subtext of Ch. 5 of the *Legs bshad snying po* points to the *ethical* superiority of Prasangika, as it helps practitioners purify the way in which they engage their world.[71] The reason for this is that the "non-acceptance" of the "logical privacy" of the Svātantrika has a "distinctive specialty":[72] it forces the practitioner to abandon the presumption that she can explain conventional reality *on her own terms*. Every individual is asked to undergo a sort of Copernican revolution, and realize that one's "privately established objective basis" are mere distortions of reality. The term *svatantra* (Tib. *rang gyud*) comes to indicate independently established reasoning as a sort of "unethical," *self-centered* reasoning (*Eigensprache*).[73]

---

[70] Tsong kha pa, *Legs bshad snying po*, Ch. 5, in Thurman, 291.

[71] Robert A. F. Thurman, *The Central Philosophy of Tibet*, notes 99–100, 321–323.

[72] Robert A. F. Thurman, *The Central Philosophy of Tibet*, notes 99, 321.

[73] Thurman is quite ready to compare Candrakīrti's dialectical approach to the strategy deployed by Wittgenstein in the *Philosophical Investigations*, where the Austrian thinker views the task of the philosopher as akin to that of a skilled therapist, eager to help his patients to let go of their own mistaken views. In this perspective, Tsong kha pa would agree with Wittgenstein's understanding of dialectic as an essential *public* enterprise, whose purpose is not to promote one's own opinions, but to unmask the untenable nature of those of our opponent. See Richard McDonough, "Wittgenstein's Reversal on the 'Language of Thought' Doctrine," *The Philosophical Quarterly* 44, 177 (1994): 482–94. See Ludwig Wittgenstein, *Philosophical Investigations* (trans. G. E. M. Anscombe; 3d ed; London: Blackwell, 2002), Aphorisms 1–10; also Garry Hagberg, "Philosophy as Therapy: Wittgenstein, Cavell, and Autobiographical Writing," PHIL-LIT 27.1 (2003): 196–210.

It should thus be clear that Tsong kha pa's analysis is not *primarily* concerned with language and logic. Tsong kha pa shared Wittgenstein's faith in the *propedeutic* value of cognitive transformation; what truly matters, in other words, is the maieutic process of rediscovery of the truth.[74] For this purpose, Tsong kha pa relies on the traditional distinction between scriptures teaching "the emptiness of things," "non-production," and "creationlessness" (classified as *nītartha*, or "already interpreted"), and those teachings using expressions such as "self," "person," and "humanity" (classified as *neyartha.*, yet to be interpreted).[75] The latter are still entangled in "desires" and "cravings," and have to be carefully unpacked to find their deeper, authentic meaning.[76]

Even this approach to textual hermeneutics resonates with the position of the early Christian writers. The Alexandrian exegetical tradition postulated a correspondence between the level of one's spiritual attainment and one's understanding of Scripture. In Part 4 of *De Principiis*, for instance, Origen distinguished the literal meaning from the spiritual meaning, even if these two levels were inextricably linked. The whole sweep of Scriptural narrative was meant to lead the reader to a deeper appreciation of the mystery of Christ; contradictions in the text were explained as "pedagogical tools" of the Holy Spirit.[77] Tsong kha pa would have talked of skillful means, much as the *Bodhicittavivarana* Nāgārjuna views all sūtric statements on intrinsic existence as a concession to "the fear of emptiness of the naive."[78] The similarities, indeed, run quite deep. Seeking to oppose philosophical determinism, the Origenist universe classified individuals into different categories who were more or less responsive to the divine message as a consequence of their past actions; as a result, Scripture contains a variety of books for their spiritual nourishment. Tsong kha pa' karmically regulated cosmos similarly includes people more or less receptive to the *dharma*, and it is for this reason that "the Buddha teaches the *dharma* according to the tolerance of the disciple."[79]

---

[74] Chizuko Yoshimizu, "Tsong kha pa's Reevaluation of Candrakīrti's Criticism of Autonomous Inference," 260.

[75] See the quote from the *Akshayamatisūtra* in Tsong kha pa, *Legs bshad snying po*, Ch. 3, in Thurman, 253.

[76] Tsong kha pa, *Legs bshad snying po*, Ch. 3, in Thurman, 254.

[77] Origen, *De Principiis*, 4, 2 (PG 11: 345–7).

[78] See Tsong kha pa, *Legs bshad snying po*, Ch. 3, in Thurman, 258.

[79] See Nāgārjuna, *Rājaparikathāratnāvalī*, quoted in Tsong kha pa, *Legs bshad snying po*, Ch. 3, in Thurman, 258.

Let us go back to Maximos' *Ambigua*. If Tsong kha pa had read Maximos' analysis of the Transfiguration scene, he might have concluded that Christ was the key to the Christian *dharmāh*, or even that eternal Word was the Christian counterpart of *dharmakāya*. In Christ, one may discern the inescapable interdependence of the whole cosmos; the *logoi* of creation and the *logoi* of scripture gesture towards the Wisdom that underpins creation, and yet this Wisdom eternally transcends them. And why is it so important to think that the eternal Logos encompasses, and yet *transcends* all the *logoi*? For Maximos, this countered the tendency to view the world as a self-enclosed reality, which could be explained *in its own terms*; he was opposing the Evagrian temptation of a *svātantrika* Christianity. For Tsong kha pa, only a *prāsangika* understanding of the cosmic body of the Buddha can sustain the practice of compassion. For Maximos, the *kenōsis* of the self is needed so as to read the cosmos "correctly," as a sacrament of God's love.

MEDITATION AND INSIGHT: THE *LAM RIM CHEN MO* AND THE INTEGRATION OF PHILOSOPHY INTO PRACTICE

It should be clear by now that Tsong kha pa's vision is more explicitly "philosophical" than any of the different Nying ma schools that were discussed in the last chapter. Tsong kha pa understood his philosophical work as operating within a tradition with clear boundaries; the conviction that the ultimate nature of reality had been revealed once and for all in the teachings of the Buddha constitutes for him a *datum*, against which all deliverances of rational speculation are to be assessed.[80] To use yet another set of Christian theological categories, the concurrent beliefs that the Buddha's teaching offer a definitive insight into reality, and that the Buddha lived in full accordance with this insight, constitute a sort of a *norma normans non normata*; similarly, for Madhyamaka Buddhists, authors like Nāgārjuna are regarded as the source of the apostolic *traditio*. If the role of the theologian is to confirm and encourage the faith of her community in the "reasonableness" of its beliefs and practices, few works may be said to be as "theological" as Tsong kha pa's *Lam rim chen mo* (*The Great Treatise*), whose chief goal is to outline the relationship between Mahāyāna practice and the philosophy of Madhyamaka.

In the third part of this work, Tsong kha pa argues that inner calm, or "meditative serenity," is characterized by the absence of conceptual discur-

---

[80] See Elizabeth Napper, *Dependent-Arising and Emptiness*, 78, quoting from Tsong kha pa, *Legs bshad snying po*, Ch. 3, in Thurman, 264.

siveness, lack of obfuscation, and a concomitant sensation of bliss. At the same time, practitioners should not rest satisfied in this condition, but continue cultivating the special insight that flows from having ascertained the meaning of reality.[81] A Christian theologians reading Tsong kha pa is reminded that apophaticism and kataphaticism are not incompatible; the former stresses the ultimate transcendence of the mystery, while the latter helps us not to lose sight of the specific content of revelation.[82] Tsong kha pa's acceptance of Haribhadra's notion of the Buddha bodies, and his concomitant belief that the Buddha's attainment encompasses a conventional component, ensures that philosophical speculation is seen as integral to the path to enlightenment.

If we turn to Vol. 3 of the *Lam rim chen mo*, we find an extensive discussion of the deep congruence between meditative practice and its philosophical articulation.[83] While Tsong kha pa concedes that inner stabilization can also be attained by followers of non-Buddhist schools (*tīrthika, mu stegs pa*), he quotes Kamalaśila to reassert that their reluctance to cultivate insight left them mired in suffering.[84] In Madhyamaka, only the realization of selflessness ensures that "afflictions" do not return "to disturb the

---

[81] See Tsong kha pa, *Lam rim chen mo*, 564 (Elizabeth Napper, *Dependent-Arising and Emptiness*, 153; *Great Treatise*, Vol. 3, 107). This of course connects with Thurman's critique earlier of those who think "Buddhism" and "speculation" as incompatible.

[82] An excessively "apophatic" approach to dogma views analogical statements as metaphors, thereby assuming that they cannot describe the transcendent. This reflects a general rejection of *analogia entis* (see Thomas Aquinas, *Summa Theologiae*, I, Q. 12), as well as a more general flight from ontological reasoning.

[83] This particular section has been translated by Elizabeth Napper in her work *Dependent-Arising and Emptiness*, 153–215, but another version can also be found in Vol. 3 of the translation of the whole of the *Lam rim chen mo* published by Snow Lion in 2002; see Tsong kha pa, *The Great Treatise on the Stages of the Path to Enlightenment—Lam rim chen mo* (trans. The Lamrim Chenmo Translation Committee; Joshua W. C. Cutler, ed. in chief, Guy Newland, ed.; Ithaca, N.Y.: Snow Lion Publications, 2002). In the next pages I shall refer to both translations of this work, which is a virtual summa of Tsong kha pa's own thought. As the divisions into chapters followed by the two translations are not identical, I shall instead quote the number of the *folium* indicated in the 2002 translation.

[84] See Kamalaśila, *King of concentration sūtra*, quoted in Tsong kha pa, *Lam rim chen mo*, 564–5 (Elizabeth Napper, *Dependent-Arising and Emptiness*, 153–154; *Great Treatise*, Vol. 3, 107–8).

mind."[85] The theme of "pride," which reflects a failure to realize selflessness and thus wipes away years of practice, echoes episodes from the lives
of the Desert Fathers, where we find anchorites who seemingly attain high
levels of holiness, but then come to a sad end because of their enduring
philautia.[86]

Tsong kha pa stresses the importance of finding a suitable spiritual
master, since awareness of selflessness is not "generated naturally," but
rather comes from an "external holy guide."[87] At the same time, practitioners must develop an intellectual understanding of emptiness, since
"through mere calm abiding there is no pure exalted wisdom," and without
this insight, no master or bodhisattva can be of help.[88] In comparison with
rDzogs chen's belief in an immediate enlightenment, Tsong kha pa's approach is more guarded; if one fails to use Madhyamaka philosophy, he argues, the true nature of reality will remain hidden, and even practitioners of
Madhyamaka may only hope for a gradual disclosure of this insight.

At this point, Tsong kha pa takes up again the discussion of "interpretable" and "definitive" texts already broached in the *Legs bshad snying po*,
noting how textual analysis predisposes one to gain special insight. In order
to fulfill the "prerequisites" for this insight, one must rely on the texts of
the sutric tradition, but interpret them in the light of Nāgārjuna's commentaries; if there is a reference to "conventionalities," this means that these
texts are *sūtras* of interpretable meaning.[89] The *Lam rim chen mo* follows

---

[85] The "Udraka" mentioned by Kamalaśila might have been a non-Buddhist
practitioner, who for a time managed to emulate the powers of accomplished Buddhist meditators, but was later punished for his lack of insight, and was reborn in a
lower realm. See Elizabeth Napper, *Dependent-Arising and Emptiness*, 729–730 (note
294).

[86] See for instance John Cassian, *On the Holy Fathers of Sketis and on discrimination*,
in *Philokalia*, Vol. 1, 94–108. Here, we encounter various monks, who fall prey to
various temptations because they pursued the spiritual life, but failed to practice
diakrisis. The Russian Orthodox tradition would lay great emphasis on the dangers
of practice without discrimination, which invariably leads to pride (*prelest'*).

[87] See Tsong kha pa, *Lam rim chen mo*, 566 (Elizabeth Napper, *Dependent-Arising
and Emptiness*, 155; *Great Treatise*, Vol. 3, 108–109).

[88] See Kamalaśila, *Stages of Meditation*, Book 2, f.5311, quoted in Tsong kha pa,
Lam rim chen mo, 566 (Elizabeth Napper, *Dependent-Arising and Emptiness*, 156; *Great
Treatise*, Vol. 3, 108–109).

[89] As in the Catholic tradition, "Scripture" may not be interpreted outside
"tradition." See also the passage (probably by Kamalaśila) cited by Tsong kha pa in

Tsong kha pa's other writings in applying the distinction between two textual categories to the various teachings attributed to the Buddha. It also applies them to the distinctions internal to the Madhyamaka movement, such as that between the Mādhyamaka "of the model texts" (*gzhung phyi mo'i*) and "partisan" Madhyamaka (*phyogs 'dzin pa'i*),[90] or that between Prāsaṅgika and Svātantrika that was discussed in the previous chapter.

While Tsong kha pa views Nāgārjuna as the normative interpreter of Mahāyāna thought, he also stresses how his thought is in strict continuity with the "glorious" Candrakīrti and the "master" Buddhapālita, whose thought does not necessitate further interpretation, but already expresses the fullness of truth.[91] This strategy enables Tsong kha pa to affirm the ultimate unity of the Mahāyāna corpus, and to claim that even apparently contradictory texts present the same view on emptiness, which an authoritative interpretive community can bring out on the basis of texts of "definitive meaning." On one hand, Tsong kha pa's hermeneutics functions very much like Origen's, for whom the Christian Church can extract the hidden Christological meaning of the Old Testament on the basis of the New.[92] On the other hand, Tsong kha pa's conviction that the secrets of the Mahāyāna corpus emerge in proportion to the spiritual level of the recipient is analogous to Maximos' discussion in the *Quaestiones ad Thalassium* of the semantic polyvalence of the Christian Scriptures.[93] The manifestation of the Buddha in history offers the ultimate key for the texts of the tradition, much as the incarnation of the Word is the only hermeneutic lens that may "open up" the two testaments.[94]

Lam rim chen mo, 568 (Elizabeth Napper, *Dependent-Arising and Emptiness*, 160; *Great Treatise*, Vol. 3, 110–111).

[90] According to Elizabeth Napper (*Dependent-Arising and Emptiness*, 739, note 313), the term *phyi mo* refers to the models of the alphabet (Sansk. *mātṛkā*) used to teach how to read and write. Of course the use of this term underscores how the first group alone gives a faithful interpretation of the Madhyamaka tradition.

[91] See Tsong kha pa, *Lam rim chen mo*, 571–573 (Elizabeth Napper, *Dependent-Arising and Emptiness*, 164–167; *Great Treatise*, Vol. 3, 114–117).

[92] See Origen, *De Principiis* 4, 2–4 (PG 11: 345–350), and Aquinas, *Summa Theologiae*, I, Q.1, Art. 9. Aquinas notes that there is no truth accessible through the "spiritual sense" that is not taught by the "literal sense" at some point in Scripture.

[93] See for instance Paul Blowers, *Exegesis and Spiritual Pedagogy in Maximus the Confessor*, 166–172.

[94] See again *Amb. 10*'s reference to the garments of Christ as symbolizing Scripture (PG 91: 1125d-1128d). Pushing the comparison further, one could say

In the Evagrian corpus, the ultimate mystical insight appeared to know no different degrees, or levels; the practitioner would be fully one with Christ, as in rDzogs chen one is united with the "pure basis." Tsong kha pa, on the other hand, postulates the existence of different stages of "entry into suchness," which are followed by the actual "settling" of suchness.[95] "Suchness," or *nirvāna*, is a condition where all concepts related to the self are eliminated; when we attain it, our predisposition to believe in the existence of appearances is fully superseded. As such, the gaining of liberation necessitates continuous practice, and it might be obtained only after numerous lives; while spiritual progress may be slowed down by unskillful actions, it becomes impossible to fall back into *samsāra* once insight into reality is "settled." In the *Lam rim chen mo*, even the final "settling" of one's awareness is attained by growing familiarity with the philosophical tradition. On one hand, the foundation of spiritual progress is a wish to "cast cyclic existence aside," and this wish is only possible if one discerns the root of what cyclic existence is.[96] On the other hand, "entry into suchness" is only complete when we generate a second, related wish to abandon the mistaken views that cause suffering. What practice has to achieve, then, is to engender a condition where the acceptance of a mistaken view is no longer possible (a sort of *egchōresis gnomikê*).[97]

The first step in this procedure is to identify the object that philosophical discourse must then negate.[98] Tsong kha pa quotes Śāntideva's assertion that "without contacting the entity (*dngos po, bhāva*) which is imputed,

---

that *theōria*, when directed at the *logoi* hidden in Scripture, fulfils the same function as the reading of text searching for their ultimate meaning (which is itself an expression of the Buddha's *dharmakāya*). See also HH the Dalai Lama, *The Good Heart: A Buddhist Perspective on the Teaching of Jesus* (Somerville, Mass.: Wisdom Publications, 1996), 89–95 (where the Dalai Lama discusses Luke's Transfiguration narrative).

[95] See Tsong kha pa, *Lam rim chen mo*, 574 (Elizabeth Napper, *Dependent-Arising and Emptiness*, 168; *Great Treatise*, Vol. 3, 119–120).

[96] See Candrakīrti, *Clear Words*, in Tsong kha pa, *Lam rim chen mo*, 575, (Elizabeth Napper, *Dependent-Arising and Emptiness*, 170; *Great Treatise*, Vol. 3, 120–121). Napper uses the expression "view of the transitory collection." Tsong kha pa mentions Candrakīrti's *Clear Words* to note that this root can be found in the so-called "reifying view of the perishing aggregates."

[97] See Maximos the Confessor, *Disputatio cum Phyrro* (PG 91: 287–304).

[98] See Tsong kha pa, *Lam rim chen mo*, 578 (Elizabeth Napper, *Dependent-Arising and Emptiness*, 176–77; *Great Treatise*, Vol. 3, 123).

one will not apprehend the absence of that entity."[99] Restricting the object of negation may lead to a so called "eternalist" view, but the opposing danger may also ensue, if the existence of co-dependent origination is also questioned. The "enemies" of co-dependent origination claim that the latter "cannot exist on its own," and as such valid cognition "cannot establish it"; in this perspective, Candrakīrti's claim that "the world is not valid in any way" would entail that the Madhyamaka master rejected ultimate as well as conventional production.[100] For Tsong kha pa, this is a mistaken position, since Madhyamaka philosophy does not challenge conventional existence; on the contrary, any form of spiritual progress rests on the dialectic of conventional cause and effect (which is exactly what rDzogs chen denies). The accumulation of wisdom and merit result in the acquisition of the "two excellences," the *dharmakāya* and the *rūpakāya*;[101] if the mechanism of cause and effect is denied, Tsong kha pa implies, one may no longer be assimilated to the Buddha.

Tsong kha pa's underlying conviction is that the fruit of insight is the "body of truth," the ordered disposition of the cosmos that the Buddha most fully embodies. The *dharmakāya* is therefore the truth about the universe, which in the historical Buddhas becomes a manifest truth; language as such is meaningful because Buddhahood is the very essence of reality. According to Nāgārjuna, if words had no meaning, it would be impossible to assert even the validity of the four noble truths.[102] For Tsong kha pa, the "distinguishing feature" of Madhyamaka is that the conventional truth of language grounds assertions about reality even in a context where intrinsic emptiness is asserted. This position dovetails with the Madhyamaka understanding of the Buddha bodies that was mentioned earlier in the chapter. The belief that in the *dharmakāya* there is a conventional component, and as such it is possible to have a detached, non-dual insight (something strongly

---

[99] The source is again Śāntideva's *Bodhicaryāvatāra* 9, 140ab, in Stephen Batchelor, *A guide to the Bodhisattva's way of life.*

[100] See Candrakīrti's *Commentary* on Nāgārjuna's *Mūlamadhyamakakārikā*, VI, 31a, quoted in Tsong kha pa, *Lam rim chen mo*, 581 (Elizabeth Napper, *Dependent-Arising and Emptiness*, 179; *Great Treatise*, Vol. 3, 127–128).

[101] See Nāgārjuna, *Sixty Stanzas of Reasoning*, 60, quoted in Tsong kha pa, *Lam rim chen mo*, 582 (Elizabeth Napper, *Dependent-Arising and Emptiness*, 181; *Great Treatise*, Vol. 3, 128–130).

[102] See Nāgārjuna's *Mūlamadhyamakakārikā* 24, 14–19, quoted in Tsong kha pa, *Lam rim chen mo*, 583 (Elizabeth Napper, *Dependent-Arising and Emptiness*, 184–185; *Great Treatise*, Vol. 3, 130–131).

opposed by rDzogs chen) is analogous to the notion that the eternal Logos scatters his *logoi spermatikoi* across the universe, so that one may be led to an intuition of its unity in God. Without creation or the world of forms, there may be no spiritual progress; contingency and *saṃsāra* are themselves sacramental gifts.

For Tsong kha pa, a lack of intrinsic existence does not entail the lack of an ability to perform "functions," such as giving rise to phenomena or offering spiritual guidance.[103] Many who deny the conventional existence of a creator or of a primal substance feel compelled to deny the conventional existence of forms, and in the same way many who assert the latter also feel bound to assert the former.[104] Such misunderstandings reflect a mistaken view of conventional reason. The latter operates in the context of how "a given phenomenon appears to it," but it can be characterized as "non-analytical" because it does not seek to understand the deeper structure of reality. On one hand, the presence of conventional reasons in the mind-stream of all individuals ensures that practitioners continue to operate and interact with others in a way that seemingly contradicts the *dharma*. On the other hand, this *epochē* of absolute truth does not mean that mistaken beliefs should be tolerated; reifying views such as "I" or "mine" should still be challenged and exposed.

For Tsong kha pa, practitioners act as a sort of "leaven" among sentient beings, helping them modify their conceptual understanding of reality. Faith without intellectual conviction is a form of "bondage" that undercuts inner serenity; compassion without "analytical discrimination" will eventually die out.[105] The practice of compassion is impossible, unless one is

[103] Tsong kha pa, *Lam rim chen mo*, 595–97 (Elizabeth Napper, *Dependent-Arising and Emptiness*, 200–203; *Great Treatise*, Vol. 3, 143–145). Candrakīrti is once more the favored authority; his use of the term "thing" does not justify an essentialist reading of his argument, since his intention is to refer to entities which "perform functions," producing causes and effects "like a magician's illusions." See Candrakīrti, *Commentary on the Four Hundred Stanzas*, quoted in Tsong kha pa, *Lam rim chen mo*, 597 (Elizabeth Napper, *Dependent-Arising and Emptiness*, 202–3; *Great Treatise*, Vol. 3, 144–145).

[104] See Tsong kha pa, *Lam rim chen mo*, 626 (*Great Treatise*, Vol. 3, 175–178).

[105] Tsong kha pa quotes with approval Kamalaśila's negative remarks about those who "do not think about anything when they meditate," and as a result "perform no virtuous deeds, such as deeds of generosity," thinking the latter fit only for "foolish beings." See Kamalaśila, *Stages of meditation* 3, 13–14, quoted in Tsong kha pa, *Lam rim chen mo*, 775 (*Great Treatise*, Vol. 3, 332–333).

grounded in the "correct" view; even holding the "correct views" mechani-
cally, or out of deference to an instructor, is "unskillful." What is needed is
"consideration, evaluation, examination," and "thorough searching";[106] if
liberation could be attained just by holding one's mind in check, Tsong kha
pa quips, falling asleep would free one of all subject-object duality better
than any type of meditation.[107] In the words of Asanga, the achievement of
"equipoise" is what guarantees one's ability to "enter the path of differenti-
ating phenomena."[108]

For Tsong kha pa, the culmination of practice is a condition of
enlightenment that does not prevent, but actually enjoins a detached use of
conventional reality. It is this particular understanding of active *nirvāna* that
determines Tsong kha pa's acceptance of the teaching of the four Buddha
bodies; the Buddha's insight is partly non-discursive (*svābhāvikakāya*), and
partly co-extensive with a pure, dual insight (*jñāna-dharmakāya*).[109] To echo
Maximos' metaphor in *Amb. 10*, the *jñāna-dharmakāya* are like the garments
of the Buddha, which cloth his inner being; yet now this being has no transfigured countenance, and possesses no substance or form.

THE ORDER OF NATURE: A CLOSER LOOK AT TWO SIMILAR ARGUMENTS

Tsong kha pa's intricate philosophical argumentation supports a vision of
practice that clearly has many points of contact with Maximos' understanding of *theōria* and *praxis*. An awareness of how the two systems rest on dif-

---

[106] See Asanga, *Śrāvaka Levels* 101, 2, 3–6, quoted in Tsong kha pa, *Lam rim chen mo*, 771 (*Great Treatise*, Vol. 3, 328–329).

[107] See Tsong kha pa, *Lam rim chen mo*, 777, 780 (*Great Treatise*, Vol. 3, 333–334; 336–337). This might strike as a fundamentally elitist approach, given that only a fraction of people have the time and ability to study Madhyamaka. Tsong kha pa, however, tempers his position claiming that the insight leading to compassion does not require extensive study, and is in fact available to all "ordinary beings," who sometimes even surpass monks with extensive philosophical training. "Ordinary people," of course, may even be helped in their practice by "erroneous concepts," which advanced practitioners would have to reject.

[108] See Asanga, *Śrāvaka levels*, 107.5, 206, in Tsong kha pa, *Lam rim chen mo*, 802 (*Great Treatise*, Vol. 3, 357–358).

[109] Christian readers schooled in Byzantine theology may compare the distinction between *jñāna-dharmakāya* and *svābhāvikakāya* to the distinction between essence and energies in the Godhead.

ferent foundations is however necessary if the Christian theologian is to draw any lesson from reading the works of the Tibetan master.

Both Maximos and Tsong kha pa take what in modern epistemological parlance would be considered a foundationalist line of argument, claiming that the correct use of *reason* is bound to lead one to embrace their respective ontology. The hymn introducing the *Legs bshad snying po* shows that for Tsong kha pa, the Buddha's teaching's claims to truth—and their implications for the life of the individual—are radically distinct from the claims to truth (and the cultic demands) of the traditional religions in whose midst Buddhism emerged. The Buddha is the embodiment of reason; he is the one who discloses the meaning of reality, and as such all those who are diligent scholars of reality will acknowledge the validity of these claims. The *dharmāh* flow from the Buddha's insight and as such, they serve as a sort of *preparatio Buddhae*, leading one slowly towards enlightenment. We have seen how this perspective, where the acquisition of Buddha nature takes place gradually, is opposed to the *Kun byed rgyal po*'s radical hostility to "views," according to which Buddhahood is already present in all sentient beings, and all that is needed is the ability to see it.[110] Tsong kha pa's approach had a greater appeal to the practitioners operating within the confines of monastic institutions, whereas rDzogs chen's roots in the shamanic tradition made the practice of Buddhism more accessible to individuals who lacked the necessary philosophical training.

Maximos' understanding of *theōria* presupposes the long tradition of speculation on the *logoi* which derived from Stoic philosophy and which accompanied Patristic theology from its very inception. Maximos' writings do not engage non-Christians philosophical worldviews; his polemic with Origenism rested on the conviction that the latter, while claiming that the Word was the hermeneutic key of all reality, failed to do justice to the full impact of the incarnation. Maximos' Christocentric natural theology grows from the claim in the Letter to the Romans that the order of nature is a testimony to the existence and the glory of God, and that all those that fail to acknowledge His providence and might shall be considered guilty. In this perspective, Christianity is not only one of many manifestations of the truth, but the only correct interpretation of reality.

---

[110] Of course the *Ris med* scholars mentioned in the last chapter attempted to develop an uneasy *via media* between the two extreme positions; see Ringu Tulku, "The Rime movement of Jamgon Kongtrul the Great," in PIATS 7, Vol. 2 (Vienna: Verlag der Österreichischen Akademie der Wissenschaften, 1995).

When in the early 20th century Ernst Troeltsch challenged Christianity's claim to universality, he was setting an important precedent for all those theologians who, increasingly skeptical of any claim to absolute truth, would come to regard Christianity as a mere expression of Western culture, a set of beliefs that were no more "rational," for instance, than their Hindu or Buddhist counterparts.[111] This approach, which admittedly had deep roots in the Protestant distrust of Scholasticism, was the direct opposite of the apologetic argument developed by Church Fathers. For Augustine, for instance, "Christianity is not based on mythical images and vague notions that are ultimately justified by their political usefulness," but rather, "it relates to that divine presence which can be perceived by the *rational analysis of reality*," so that "Christianity's precedents and its inner groundwork lie in philosophical enlightenment, and not in religions."[112] In contemporary religious discourse, this Augustinian view[113] has been replaced by its virtual opposite, according to which "Eastern" religions are considered worthier of respect for the very fact that they acknowledge their culturally bound character and—allegedly—have no use for such appeals to reason.

Of course, this characterization of "Eastern" religions fails to capture Tsong kha pa's position. His presentation of Prāsangika philosophy as the correct heir of the Madhyamaka tradition, and as the *correct interpretation* of reality, fully rests on the conviction that only this particular form of Mahāyāna can provide its followers with a *rational* explanation of their world. Tsong kha pa and Maximos act as apologists for their beliefs, because they are convinced that reality is ultimately *reasonable*, and that the human intellect has the means to understand its ultimate meaning. In both cases, "revelation" —the teaching of the Buddha, or of the Christian Scriptures—set the guidelines for this intellectual search, but the latter has to be carried out by the individual in person, until one assimilated this truth and made it his own. I do not wish to claim that Christian apologetics ought to jettison its claim to the rationality of the Christian faith; what I am arguing is that Christianity's claim to be the only *religio vera* must acknowledge and engage analogous claims in other traditions.

[111] Ernst Troeltsch, *Die Absolutheit des Christentums und die Religionsgeschichte* (München: Siebenstern Taschenbuch-Verlag, 1969), 79–81.
[112] Joseph Ratzinger, *Truth and Tolerance—Christian Belief and World Religions* (San Francisco: Ignatius Press, 2004), 169.
[113] See for instance Augustine, *De Civitate Dei*, VI, 2, and its discussion of Marcus Terentius Varro, also discussed by Ratzinger, *Truth and Tolerance*, 165–169.

How do the visions of Maximos and the visions of Tsong kha pa ultimately differ? On one hand, Tsong kha pa's Buddhological vision comes close to a theistic position by viewing the wisdom of the Buddha as the ultimate structure of the cosmos, even if it does not follow the rNying ma position in viewing the universe as a gift to sentient beings. On the other hand, the eternal Logos is the interpretive lens as well as the ontological source of the universe—a universe, whose chief characteristics are variety and plenitude. In a Christian perspective, the *logoi* set the terms for the unfolding of a cosmos that is not destined to revert to nothingness, but will endure eternally in God's love. The *jñāna-dharmakāya*, on the contrary, delineates a universe where the kaleidoscope of appearances masks an underlying emptiness, and where the variety of the *dharmāh* will be reabsorbed into the undifferentiated depths of *śunyatā*. The conclusion is that the *Lam rim chen mo* seems to put forth a framework of practice that radically challenges the vision of rDzogs chen, but Tsong kha pa's vision comes closer to Evagrios than to Maximos in postulating the effacing of all difference in the Buddha's ultimate insight.[114] This remains the case even if the cosmic sacramentalism of the *Kun byed rgyal po* mirrors Maximos' assertion of the Logos as the ultimate source of creation more closely than Tsong kha pa's Buddhological speculation.

What about the extent of the highest mystical insight? Maximos' belief that the practice of *theōria* leads one gradually to acquire the mind of God must be read in line with the Cappadocian tradition that emphasized the ultimate, utter unknowability of the divine nature. The Trinitarian orations by Gregory of Nazianzos lambasted the Eunomian pretension to "comprehend" the divine essence, and Gregory of Nyssa's notion of *epektasis* in *De Vita Moysis* reminded those wishing to understand the divine mystery that the latter remained forever inaccessible to the human mind.[115] Maximos' "mountain of the Lord" is Tabor, not Sinai, but on Tabor, like on Sinai, the divine mystery is only partially disclosed; the transfigured Christ might be the cornerstone of the divine project for the cosmos, but the divine wisdom remains forever *other*, inaccessible even to our deified intellect.

---

[114] In this perspective, the often quoted eschatology of Book 4 of the *Kephalaia Gnostika*, where everything is reabsorbed by an undifferentiated *nous*, comes closer to the position stressing the ontological ultimacy of the non-discursive *svābhāvikakāya* than its counterpart in Maximos which sees the *logoi* as eternally enduring.

[115] See Gregory of Nyssa, *De Vita Moysis* (PG 44: 404ad).

On the contrary, when Tsong kha pa credits the insight of the Buddha with the ability to disclose the structure and purpose of the universe, he does not construe this insight as something epistemologically exclusive to the historical Śākyamuni. Rather, the tendency to magnify the extraordinary nature of the Buddha's achievement, which set him apart from that of ordinary sentient beings, co-exists with the conviction that every practitioner—at least in theory—can reach the same insight through commitment and perseverance. Here, Tsong kha pa comes closer to Evagrios' isochristism, where any ontological distinction between the individual soul and that of Christ is effectively erased. Much as in the horizon of Buddhist cosmology every enlightened individual can create a new world, the *Kephalaia Gnostika* mentions the possibility of multiple creations by souls that have reached the highest level of attainment.[116]

At the beginning of this chapter, we recalled the notion of creation as gift and sacrament developed by von Balthasar in the *Theodrama*, and the concurrent notion of spiritual practice as co-extensive with the gradual shedding of self-centeredness. While Tsong kha pa does not posit the Buddha as "creating" conventional reality, by reading the *Lam rim chen mo* we realize that an understanding of contingency as carrying a fundamental soteriological potential is not exclusive to Catholic or Orthodox Christianity, even if the salvific goals of the different traditions remain substantially different.

---

[116] The popularity of such heterodox beliefs among 6th century Origenists is attested also by other sources. See for instance the exchange between Cyril and Abba Cyriacus of the Laura of Souka, where the latter condemns the claims of the Origenists ("they say that our resurrection bodies pass to total destruction, and Christ's first of all. They say that that the Holy Trinity did not create the world and that at the restoration (*apokatastasis*) all rational beings, even demons, *will be able to create aeons*... they say that we shall be *equal to Christ* at the resurrection..."), in Cyril of Scythopolis, *The Lives of the Monks of Palestine* (trans. J. Binns and R. M. Price; Cistercian Studies Series, No. 114. Collegeville, Minn.: Cistercian Publ., 1991) 252–254. See also Adam G. Cooper, *The Body in St. Maximus the Confessor*, 69–70.

7 *IMITATIO BUDDHAE* AND DEIFICATION: PERFECTIONS AND VIRTUES IN TSONG KHA PA AND MAXIMOS THE CONFESSOR

In the second volume of the *Lam rim chen mo*, Tsong kha pa argues that the desire to attain Buddhahood will remain unfulfilled if practitioners focus on "wisdom" and forget the importance of "method," or their grasp of "method" remains inadequate or partial.[1] Method, in this context, indicates the application to ordinary life of the insights that are obtained in contemplation, according to guidelines that focus on the process of cause and effect. Before discussing the importance of the six perfections (*paramitā*s), Tsong kha pa stresses that "quietist" approaches to practice that ignore method (such as those taught in rDzogs chen) cannot possibly lead to enlightenment. Once more, Tsong kha pa appeals to Kamalaśīla, who had similarly emphasized the necessity of "method," and whose authority enables the dGe lugs master to position himself with regard to the doctrinal disputes between different Tibetan schools.[2]

One more time, the purpose of this section of the *Lam rim chen mo* is to show that non-gradual (quietist) methods cause the decline of the *dharma* by failing to appreciate the role that contingent, conventional reality has in the context of practice. While the *Legs bshad snying po* stressed the importance of contemplation and speculation, in the *Lam rim chen mo* conventional reality is presented as the context of compassionate activity, without which the goal of Buddhahood remains beyond reach. Again, this claim reflects the conviction that the *dharmakāya* encompasses a detached, dual aspect, and that it is possible to meditate and reflect about contingent, limited reality in an enlightened manner that is spiritually helpful. Tsong kha pa's understanding of the Buddha bodies challenges the belief that *any* thought inevitably ties us to *saṃsāra*, and that ethical discipline should only be taught to practitioners unable to meditate on emptiness. In the *Lam rin chen mo*, on the other hand, the difference between virtuous and ordinary thoughts resembles the

---

[1] Tsong kha pa, *Lam rim chen mo*, 342 (*Great Treatise*, Vol. 2, 87).
[2] Tsong kha pa, *Lam rim chen mo*, 343 (*Great Treatise*, Vol. 2, 87).

difference between a golden and an ordinary rope. For Tsong kha pa and Kamalaśīla, stabilizing the mind in a non-conceptual state is an important aspect of spiritual practice, but those who intuit the reality of emptiness should not rest in this insight; rather, they should cultivate "conventional states of mind" pertaining to virtuous deeds.[3] For the dGe lugs master, upholding such "pure duality" is at the core of practice, and any other understanding of *nirvāna* would fall short of its non-abiding (*apratishtita*) quality that is the crucial characteristic of Mahāyāna.

In the *Lam rim chen mo*, the theology of the six perfections is declined in accordance with Haribhadra's notion of Buddhahood, furnishing Tsong kha pa with an ontological framework where the practice of the virtues is envisaged as gradually assimilating one to the compassionate activity of the Buddha. In the context of *imitatio Buddhae*, meditation is then complemented by an active engagement with the conventional world, even if this practice effectively rests on the "categories of dichotomous conceptualizations" usually associated with the unenlightened state.[4] For the dGe lugs master, different approaches fundamentally reflect a pre-Mahāyāna sensitivity which radically separates *nirvāna* from *samsāra*, but in so doing disregards the pedagogical role of ordinary reality, as well as its ability to channel the realization of ultimate truth.

In this way, the doctrine of the four bodies adopted by Tsong kha pa and the dGe lugs school turns conventional reality into the foundation of moral discipline.[5] If we compare this approach with the vision of Maximos the Confessor, his grounding of *praxis* in a sweeping vision of the Logos who encompasses the whole universe attempts an analogous strategy, inasmuch as it views the effort of the individual practitioner as a part no less than a continuation of Christ's own work. Maximos' development of this theme rests on the retrieval of a theurgic version of Neo-Platonism, for which every action can bring the universe closer, or further away from its eschatological goal. Tsong kha pa' polemic with "quietist" approaches to practice mirrors Maximos' impatience with the eschatological vision characterizing the Evagrian school, for which human activity had no ultimate impact on the destiny of the universe. In the course of this chapter, we will

---

[3] Tsong kha pa, *Lam rim chen mo*, 344 (*Great Treatise*, Vol. 2, 88).
[4] John Makransky, *Buddhahood Embodied*, 303.
[5] John Makransky, *Buddhahood Embodied*, 304–305. This mattered deeply to the dGe lugs master, who championed the reform of social as well as of monastic institutions.

elucidate how these two authors construe individual *praxis* as an endeavor of cosmic resonance, but also attempt to show how their two visions rest on distinct ontological presuppositions.

THE OPERATIVE TRANSCENDENT: *APRATISHTITĀ NIRVĀNA* AND DIVINE SELF-DISCLOSURE AS MATRICES FOR VIRTUOUS ACTIVITY

The problem that both Tsong kha pa and Maximos have to face is the question of the modality, whereby ultimate reality or the transcendent deity may at the same time be present in our conditional or created dimension. By now, we should start to see how the different articulations of Buddhahood or divine embodiment developed by the two authors are merely different solutions to the fundamental problem of the salvific value of ordinary circumstances. We will now see how Tsong kha pa and Maximos both react to a vision of practice that would restrict the spiritual path to a limited number of individuals, leaving enlightenment or deification beyond the reach of the majority of the practitioners.

In the early centuries after the spread of Buddhism to the Indian subcontinent, Buddhist practice was the virtual reserve of the monastic *sanghas*, who embraced strict celibacy and led itinerant lives. This approach drew a sharp line between the pursuit of the "noble path" and those who chose to remain in the world. For the followers of so-called Nikāya Buddhism, the attainment of *nirvāna* followed a rigorous course of ascetic discipline and world renunciation, without which it was impossible to curb the cravings (*trsnā*) at the root of suffering.[6] While monastic communities would provide ethical guidance to their lay supporters, it was understood that the latter could at most hope for a better rebirth in their next life. The scholastic philosophy of this period, known as Abhidharma, painted a horrific picture of the conditioned existence of sentient beings, emphasizing on the other hand the unconditioned (*asamskrta*) and undefiled nature of the nirvanic state.[7]

While different texts employed different philosophical terminology, *nirvāna* was invariably associated with the extinction (*nirodhasatya*) of the passions causing the cycle of rebirths. As the Buddha, as well as many of his

---

[6] Richard F. Gombrich, *Theravāda Buddhism: A Social History from Ancient Benares to Modern Colombo* (London and New York: Routledge and Kegan Paul, 1988), 18–20, 87–114.

[7] John Makransky, *Buddhahood Embodied*, 27.

disciples, had attained enlightenment when still in their body, it was said that their *nirvāna*, for the duration of their earthly life, retained a margin of conditioning, but even such conditioning would evaporate at the time of death. Having reached *parinirvāna*, the Buddha was no longer troubled by this world, and in fact no longer took notice of the suffering of those left behind in *samsāra*. The historical Gautama is now "the One who Went Forth" (*Tathāgata*); all that is left of him is his *dharma* and the community of his disciples.[8]

This earlier notion of *nirvāna* as a permanent reality which is totally "other" from the ordinary world reflects a belief that everything in the mundane world is merely a reflection of a more powerful archetype in the celestial sphere.[9] This perspective, which echoes Plato's myth of the cave in the *Republic*, affirms that our imperfect condition in this world must have a positive celestial counterpart, and that a few elected spirits can catch a glimpse of this higher reality. This is a highly aristocratic approach, where access to the celestial sphere requires an almost superhuman effort; it may challenge the aristocracy of cast, where the priestly class exerts a monopoly on religious rights, but it replaces it with an aristocracy of the spirit, whose members set themselves apart from the masses and their superstitious rituals.[10]

The gradual emergence of Mahāyāna radically challenged this position, as the pursuit of compassion came to acquire a greater role in the overall understanding of practice. Pressure from the laity resulted in the development of a more inclusive approach; the individualist approach to practice of the earlier period, where the primary concern was one's own awakening, was displaced by a greater emphasis on the *bodhisattva* ideal, where enlightenment is pursued for the sake of all sentient beings. Practice becomes a fundamentally altruistic pursuit; some texts even talk of *bodhisattva*s choosing to postpone their entry into *nirvāna* until every sentient being reaches salvation. As mentioned already in the last chapters, what happens is an effective transformation of the notion of *nirvāna*; liberation from *samsāra* no longer entails a flight from ordinary reality, but ordinary reality becomes

[8] Richard F. Gombrich, *Theravāda Buddhism*, 72–8.
[9] In her biography of the Buddha, the British scholar Karen Armstrong claims that this reflects a commitment to "perennial philosophy," though she says little as to what the latter term truly indicates. See Karen Armstrong, *Buddha* (London: Penguin, 2004), 186–187.
[10] See also Joseph Campbell, *The Masks of God: Oriental Mythology* (London: Penguin, 1991), 211–18.

itself the channel of one's compassionate activity. This conceptual shift is variously defined by talking of the identity of *samsāra* and *nirvāna*, or by introducing the concept of non-abiding (*apratishtitā*) *nirvāna*.[11]

In this way, practice may be construed as a communitarian endeavor, where individuals may choose to transfer merit to other sentient beings, and where, most importantly, the Buddha's engagement of the world of matter does not cease with his death. The Buddha continues to act until the consummation of the age, turning the entire universe into a manifestation of his compassion. This doctrinal shift had important implications for how ordinary believers understood their practice. Complex rituals (such as the so called three-fold service, or *triskandhaka*) started to emerge surrounding the individual's formal expression of compassion for other sentient beings; the effort necessary to learn the traditional meditation techniques started to be undertaken for the sake of fostering the salvation of all.[12] Even more importantly than the outward changes in practice, Buddhism experienced the doctrinal developments needed to accommodate the assertion of reality's fundamental emptiness with the growing belief in a transcendent dimension that is active on behalf of suffering sentient beings. Clearly, a balance was needed to ease the tension between apophatic and kataphatic approaches to the mystery. If we turn to the debates on the relationship between Christ's humanity and divinity which tore apart the Christian community in the early centuries of its existence, we see that doctrinal development in Christology reflected a similar dynamic.

How could the resources of philosophy and language be used to articulate the reality of a mystery that remained ultimately unknowable, but chose to reveal itself fully in human form?[13] It was clear that if the Logos had agreed to take human flesh and to dwell among us, the natural order had become invested with a soteriological value and could exert a pedagogical function in leading us towards God. In their different declinations, Maximos' rendition of the Chalcedonian dogma and the doctrine of the

---

[11] See Akira Hirakawa, *A History of Indian Buddhism from Śākyamuni to Early Mahāyāna* (trans. P. Groner; Honolulu, Hawaii: University of Hawaii Press, 1990), 26–56, *passim.*

[12] See Kelsang Gyatso, *Meaningful to Behold: The Bodhisattva's Way of Life* (4th ed.; Boston, Mass.: Wisdom Publications, 1994), 9–43, 79–103.

[13] This is the tension at the core of the Chalcedonian statement. The reluctance on the part of certain followers of Cyril to countenance two natures in Christ mirrors the reluctance on the part of Theravada Buddhists to admit that the ultimate mystery might inhabit the ordinary and the conventional.

Buddha bodies outlined in the last chapter are different articulations of the presence of the ultimate within the contingent, the created, and the conventional. On one hand, the incarnate body of Christ and his glorified body in heaven are manifestations of the eternal Logos, who inhabits the whole cosmos while he ultimately transcends it. On the other hand, the three *kāyah* of the Buddha are not separate ontological realities, but different manifestations of the Buddha's realization. Christ's different bodies are not static realities, but dynamic invitations to a greater familiarity with the Godhead. In the same way, as noted by John Makransky, the Yogācāra textual tradition tends to avoid the nominal terms *svābhāvikakāya*, *sāmbhogikakāya* and *nairmānikakāya*, preferring verbal counterparts that cannot refer to separate, discrete entities.[14] Not a few Westerners that embrace Buddhism do so in reaction to the theist character of Christianity, which they no longer view as tenable or even compatible with contemporary scientific understanding. The Mahāyāna notion of non-abiding *nirvāna*, however, presents us with an understanding of Buddhahood as a reality turned towards us, a Buddha who is always *pro nobis*.[15] In both traditions, the source and benchmark of doctrinal development is the way in which ultimate reality is experienced differently at different times. If the term *apratishtitā nirvāna* indicates an "attainment that is somehow both unconditioned and operative within conditions," the same could be said with reference to the incarnate Christ.[16]

The question that follows, of course, is *how* this break of the ultimate into the conditional is experienced by ordinary practitioners. Buddha's iden-

---

[14] John Makransky, *Buddhahood Embodied*, 57.

[15] As Karl Barth would say of the Christian God. Reticence to accept this belief might explain the relatively greater popularity of conservative Theravada Buddhism among individuals, who were brought up in strict Christian or Jewish backgrounds. This comment was offered by Larry Rosenberg during a meditation session in spring 2003 at the Insight Meditation Center, Cambridge, Mass.

[16] Catherine La Cugna points out in her 1993 *God for us* that the Trinitarian narrative did not emerge in the Christian Church as a philosophical experiment, but rather as an attempt to articulate the experience of the divine as a reality that was fully transcendent and yet had become fully accessible in Christ. The perichoretic exchange of love between the three persons of the Trinity is indicative of how human relationships flourish if they are similarly informed by mutuality and love; at the same time, the event of the incarnation signifies God's definitive embrace of created reality, which becomes the sacramental vehicle of the divine *agapē*. See Catherine M. La Cugna, *God for us: the Trinity and Christian life* (San Francisco: Harper, 1993), 251.

tification with an ultimate insight that includes different facets establishes a hierarchy of access that is based on one's own spiritual level, but that does not discriminate on the basis of intellectual knowledge or caste. Those who have attained enlightenment perceive it as knowledge of reality's ultimate emptiness (*svābhāvika*); the great bodhisattvas who are about to attain liberation enjoy it as the knowledge shared by the Buddha in the supernal realms (*sāmbhogika*). Those who are on yet a lower level experience it as the knowledge imparted by the Buddha during his different manifestations (*nairmāṇika*). The reality that is operational here, however, is always the same, much as Trinitarian theology is not postulating the existence of three distinct deities, but rather the three different manifestations of a single, undivided reality.[17]

We can now look back to an earlier point in our discussion, when we examined Maximos' reflections (in *Amb.* 7) on the controversial expression *moira theou*.[18] In Chapter 4, we saw how Maximos used this phrase by Gregory of Nazianzos to develop a distinctive Christocentric cosmology, taking good care to absolve this Cappadocian Father from all accusations of Origenism.[19] For Maximos, the expression *moira theou* signals the existence of a profound ontological bond between contingent reality and the divine realm, which at the same time does not, however, entail the erasure of the fundamental difference between creation and creator. While the ultimate source for this vision is the Neo-Platonism of Iamblichus and the Pseudo-Denys, this is now revisited Christologically in such a way that created reality is an expression of the divine wisdom manifested in Jesus.[20] In this way, the Platonic notion of participation (*metexis*), which is often lambasted for devaluing material reality, comes to serve the opposite purpose, indicating the ultimate dignity of the particular and its role in the divine plan.

While the Yogācāra tradition equated Buddhahood with an epistemological insight, the Madhyamaka reading of the Buddha bodies favored by Tsong kha pa comes closer to Maximos' vision, inasmuch Tsong kha pa retrieves the Abhidharmic construal of Buddhahood which views the latter

---

[17] In the same way as one could say that *omnis Trinitatis operatio indivisa est.*

[18] Maximos the Confessor, *Amb.* 7 (PG 91: 1068c-1069a).

[19] See Polycarp Sherwood, *The Early Ambigua by Maximos the Confessor*, 1–32.

[20] One could say that, rather than *moira theou*, we are here *moira Christou*. This shift would have been impossible to make in an Evagrian context, characterized, as we saw in Ch.2, by a tendency to eliminate the ontological distinction between the individual and Christ (for Evagrios' isochristism, see *Kephalaia Gnostika*, 4, 8, in *Les Six Centuries des 'Kephalaia Gnostica'*, 138–139).

as encompassing the ontological foundations (*dharmatā*) of every aspect of reality. Thus, perhaps to the dismay of some Western practitioners, the reading of Buddhahood that underpins the *Lam rim chen mo* acquires undeniable theistic overtones. The *dharmakāya* of conditioned gnosis, connecting the Buddha with the conditioned world, is analogous to the *logoi spermatikoi* that are rooted in the eternal Logos, in the same way as the Buddha's detached, dual insight is rooted in the higher *svābhāvikakāya* (or essence body).[21] The lower "body of knowledge" frames the Buddha's interventions on behalf of sentient beings, much as the *logoi spermatikoi* sustain God's providential manifestations in history. As they advance on the spiritual path, sentient beings come closer and closer to intuit the higher aspect of the *dharmakāya*, even if it is only fully enlightened Buddhas that have direct access to it.[22] The tension between conditioned and unconditioned gnosis within Buddhahood mirrors the tension captured by Maximos in his account of the Transfiguration, where Scripture and nature point to the eternal Word, though the depths of the mystery remains forever inaccessible.[23] The apostles on Tabor, like bodhisattvas in a pure land, are vouchsafed a higher insight than ordinary mortals: yet the bodhisattvas may hope one day to attain the fullness of the mystery, whereas the disciples must rest content to contemplate what their humanity is able to bear.

Tsong kha pa's reflections on the practice of the virtues presuppose also the Mahāyāna teaching on the body of manifestation (*nairmāṇikakāya*), in the same way as Maximos' vision rests ultimately on the earthly life of Christ depicted in the *Liber Asceticus*.[24] The term *nairmāṇikakāya* was initially used to indicate the figure of the historical Buddha, but it came also to refer to the Buddha's different manifestations throughout history, which will continue until no sentient beings are left in *samsāra*. The shift away from the early understanding of the Buddha as radically separate from our world provided a rationale for an intensified devotional life centered on the relics of Gautama, as well as his increasingly popular pictorial representations.[25] Both relics and images were regarded as an extension of the Buddha's pas-

---

[21] John Makransky, *Buddhahood Embodied*, 227.

[22] See Haribhadra's *Commentary* to *Abhisamayālamkāra* vv. 8.2–8.6, quoted in John Makransky, *Buddhahood Embodied*, 233.

[23] Maximos the Confessor, *Amb.* 10 (PG 91: 1125d-1128d).

[24] See *Abhisamayālamkāra* vv. 8.33, quoted in John Makransky, *Buddhahood Embodied*, 253.

[25] See David Germano and Kevin Trainor, eds., *Embodying the Dharma: Buddhist Relic Veneration in Asia* (Albany, NY: SUNY, 2003), 14–26.

sage on earth and thus came to be regarded as part of the *nairmāṇikakāya*. Clearly, a similar dynamic can be traced in the early Christian period, as the early church came to accept and reflect theologically on the role of relics and icons in one's spiritual life.

It is against these expanded notions of Buddhahood and divine embodiment that one may understand Maximos and Tsong kha pa's preoccupations with the imitation of Christ, on one hand, and the imitation of the Buddha, on the other. The incarnate Logos is the pattern for our conduct, and the historical Buddha provides the unsurpassed model of spiritual practice, since in both cases they are the foundations of the reality where we live. For Maximos, our eschatological destiny is foreshadowed in the mystery of the hypostatic union; the deified individual continues Christ's mediating work and becomes a revelation of the divine *agapē*.[26] For Tsong kha pa, all those, who "through forms such as Śākyamuni's, carries out the desired benefit of beings in all realms of the universe equally for as long as cyclic existence lasts,"[27] are themselves the *nairmāṇikakāya*. In this way, the teaching of *apratiṣhtitā nirvāṇa* and the doctrine of incarnation provide the ontological foundation for the human engagement of conditioned reality, affirming our role as potential channels of a transcendent benevolence that does not cease with the Buddha's demise or the Ascension of Christ.

THE NECESSITY OF FORM: VIRTUES AND PERFECTIONS IN THE *LAM RIM CHEN MO*

If we now turn to the second volume of the *Lam rim chen mo*, we find many of the themes already discussed in the *Legs bshad snying po*, but the emphasis is here on the practical application of insight. The text opens with a brief outline of the stages towards enlightenment, accompanied by the proviso that these stages are only meant for the person of great capacity. Advanced practitioners are advised to leave behind any hope of higher status within the round of births and deaths, aiming rather at liberation from this cycle; they are also warned that vehicles lower than the Mahayana do not measure up to the dignity of the human condition, since caring merely for one's own welfare is a trait shared also by animals.[28] Tsong kha pa cites various authorities for whom to be "consumed" with whatever "brings happiness and

---

[26] Maximos the Confessor, *Amb.* 41 (PG 91: 1304d-1316a).

[27] See Haribhadra's *Commentary* to *Abhisamayālamkāra* v. 8.33, quoted in John Makransky, *Buddhahood Embodied*, 253.

[28] Tsong kha pa, *Lam rim chen mo*, 281–282 (*Great Treatise*, Vol. 2, 13–14).

benefit to the world" is the distinctive trait of a great personality,[29] and notes that to be engaged in other people's welfare indirectly achieves one's own. Once more, Tsong kha pa argues for the ultimate *reasonableness* of the Buddhist vision of reality, appealing to the neutral authority of reason and experience to affirm the superiority of Mahāyāna.[30]

Tsong kha pa repeatedly stresses that practice has a profound *transformative* quality. He concedes that developing the wish of enlightenment (*bodhicitta*) is a sufficient condition to be regarded as a Mahāyāna practitioner, but such wish cannot bring about the qualities of a true bodhisattvas, lest it is accompanied by the wisdom of selflessness and the practice of the virtues. Bodhicitta and wisdom come together to accomplish the transformation of the individual, much like father and mother come together to conceive a child.[31] Without this union one risks falling into "the extreme of *nirvāna*,"[32] which indicates the inactive quiescence pursued by Theravada practitioners. Yet, even after this union is achieved, one's transformation hinges on developing "certainty" that the various "personal instructions" of the path are intrinsically related to compassion. Unless one is "rooted" in compassion, one's resolve may be frustrated by the sheer amount of suffering that plagues the world, leading back to self-centeredness out of despair. The authority of Kamalaśila is invoked to remind the reader that even if they have attained the perfection of the path, bodhisattvas persevere in the samsaric world because of their compassion.[33]

According to Tsong kha pa, therefore, one may not assert that compassion is unnecessary after emptiness has been fully mastered. The *Lam rim chen mo* mentions a sūtric passage, where the Buddhas who inhabit the higher realms invite the bodhisattvas to continue in the practice of the virtues even after leaving behind all forms of conceptual deliberation. The "children of good lineage" (*rigs kyi bu*), by which are meant those who are well advanced on the spiritual path, are in fact called to contemplate the extra-ordinary powers of the bodies of the Buddha and to produce some-

---

[29] See Candragomin, *Śisya-lekha*, 100–101, in Tsong kha pa, *Lam rim chen mo*, 282 (*Great Treatise*, Vol. 2, 14–15).

[30] Tsong kha pa, *Lam rim chen mo*, 283 (*Great Treatise*, Vol. 2, 16).

[31] Tsong kha pa, *Lam rim chen mo*, 287 (*Great Treatise*, Vol. 2, 18). Of course for Tsong kha pa the father takes priority in determining the identity of the child.

[32] Tsong kha pa, *Lam rim chen mo*, 288 (*Great Treatise*, Vol. 2, 20).

[33] Kamalaśila, *Stages of Meditation*, II, D3916, in Tsong kha pa, *Lam rim chen mo*, 295 (*Great Treatise*, Vol. 2, 30).

thing similar in themselves.[34] While blurring the distinction between *sāmb-hogikakāya* and *nairmāṇikakāya*, this invitation affirms the virtues of "form" as part and parcel of the Buddha's achievement. Another common mistake is the belief that every virtue and each and every quality accompanying their realization are implicitly present in the state of meditative equipoise, and thus there is no need to put them to practice. Such stance would entail that followers of the lower vehicles possess all the virtues without knowing it, and thus are "anonymous Mahāyānists." It is still true, however, that emptiness pervades all the virtues at all times even if one is unaware of it, much like the grief of a mother who lost her child pervades every one of her actions without being identical with them.[35]

Tsong kha pa concedes that some passages in the *sūtras* appear to support "quietist" positions. The *Sūtra-samuccaya*, for instance, cites a passage according to which adhering to the six perfections is "demonic activity"; the *Tri-skandhaka-sūtra* states that observing "ethical discipline" because of a belief in the "supremacy" of ethics is a fault to be confessed.[36] Tsong kha pa claims that the contradiction is only apparent, and goes on to classify these texts as *neyārtha*, extracting a deeper meaning in accordance with his stance. The first passage is read as stigmatizing a practice of the virtues motivated by a "mistaken adherence" to the self of persons and the self of objects; and this is the type of practice that the second passage urges to confess. The error of "the quietists," which is the same as the error of rDzogs chen, is to view these texts as *nītārtha*; more fundamentally, they do not fully appreciate the Madhyamaka distinction between conventional and ultimate truth. If every virtuous deed presupposed the apprehension of ultimately existing entities, practitioners ought to stay away from the six perfections "just as they reject hostility and pride."[37] The doctrine of the two truths as declined by Tsong kha pa shows, however, that the Buddha's embodiment of truth (*jñāna-dharmakāya*) is an "attainment" caused by his merits no less than his embodiment of form (*rūpakāya*); the cognition of ultimate emptiness and the cognition of conventional causes and effects are both neces-

---

[34] *Sūtra of the Ten Levels*, D44, in Tsong kha pa, *Lam rim chen mo*, 349 (*Great Treatise*, Vol. 2, 92–93).

[35] Tsong kha pa, *Lam rim chen mo*, 351 (*Great Treatise*, Vol. 2, 93–94).

[36] The first passage is quoted in *Sūtra-samuccaya*, D3934; the second is from *Tri-skandhaka-sūtra*, D284. Both are in Tsong kha pa, *Lam rim chen mo*, 352 (*Great Treatise*, Vol. 2, 94–95).

[37] Tsong kha pa, *Lam rim chen mo*, 352 (*Great Treatise*, Vol. 2, 95).

sary for enlightenment.[38] In his defense of the conventional, Tsong kha pa's final line of argument is that it was by engaging the conventional and plunging into the immeasurable see of "establishing causes" that the Buddhas attained their exalted status. Even Nāgārjuna, who is otherwise famous for his deconstruction of causality, reverts to causal language when noting that no measure can be given of the causes of *rupakāya* and *dharmakāya*.[39]

In terms of his actual discussion of the virtues, Tsong kha pa conforms to the traditional Mahāyāna view that posits all virtuous activity as subsumed under the heading of the six *paramitās*, even though the expressions that the unconditioned can take in the world of forms are effectively limitless. The dialectic of ultimate and conventional reality constantly resurfaces in the presentation of the various perfections, and so is the mechanism of causes and effects underpinning our conventional existence. On the one hand, the very fact that one engages in these practices is the result of virtuous conduct in one's past lives, so that one should at all times strive to "increase their causes."[40] On the other hand, we are warned that followers of Mahāyāna that cultivate "non-discursive yoga" should not "delight" in the resources at their disposal for the practice of the virtues, since otherwise they might fall into a habit of grasping. The material possessions that you give away, as well as your body and the companions that support you on the path, are the result of your practice of the perfections in an earlier life. If you lose sight of their proper purpose and regard them as opportunities for your own enjoyment, you shall be condemned to future suffering.

As mentioned above, the discussion of the six perfections invariably stresses how these practices result in an ontological transformation that brings us closer to the Buddha's condition. In fact, the qualities of the bodhisattvas are exalted to such an extent, that the distinction between bodhisattvas and Buddhas is blurred; the bodhisattvas are effectively subsumed

---

[38] Tsong kha pa sees therefore no need even to comment upon Nāgārjuna's words when the latter states that "discerning even the non-composite" (i.e., emptiness) "and still being disillusioned with composite virtue" is truly "a demonic activity." See *Sūtra-samuccaya*, D3934, in Tsong kha pa, *Lam rim chen mo*, 353 (*Great Treatise*, Vol. 2, 97).

[39] Nāgārjuna, *Precious garland*, 3.10, in Tsong kha pa, *Lam rim chen mo*, 356 (*Great Treatise*, Vol. 2, 98). In the same passage, Tsong kha pa quotes Nāgārjuna's follower Vimalakīrti, when the latter notes that the bodies of the *tathagatas* are "produced" from "immeasurable virtuous paths."

[40] Tsong kha pa, *Lam rim chen mo*, 358–359 and 361 (*Great Treatise*, Vol. 2, 104–105 and 107–108).

into the Buddha's bodies of form.[41] A distinction is retained, however, between the four perfections whereby the conventional world is mastered, and the two perfections (meditative stabilization and wisdom) whereby the ultimate insight is attained. The existence of a hierarchy within the six perfections indicates again that the results of practice are not reaped immediately, but follow an order that reflects the nature of reality. While all perfections are to be pursued simultaneously, the last two build upon the merits reaped by the others and accompany practitioners to the threshold of enlightenment.

This systematic approach structures Tsong kha pa's exposition, and echoes his claim in the *Legs bshad snying po* that even speculative practice must follow a certain order to deliver any result. The perfection of generosity, for instance, lays the foundation for all other perfections, as it undercuts the attachments that condition our mind.[42] In the *Jātaka-mālā* stories, which recount the past lives of the Buddha, we see that the Buddha was always ready to give away his body ("suffering, ungrateful and continuously impure"), if this alleviated the suffering of others.[43] Generosity is closely tied to awareness of impermanence, inasmuch as the realization that body and mind "move on moment by moment" encourages us to seek what is truly "permanent and pure."[44]

What truly matters, however, is the purification of one's intention, which may totally change the character of one's actions even if they are outwardly identical. The *use* of one's own body or our own resources without giving them away is acceptable, if it is done to benefit suffering beings; different circumstances and conditions in life may call for different responses.[45] When giving things away, one should recall that the goal is "unexcelled enlightenment," but should also perform an act of intellectual humility and acknowledge that the recipients of one's gifts are effectively one's

---

[41] For this tendency to exalt the bodhisattvas and grant them an ever increasing role in devotional life, see Alfred Bloom, *Shinran's Gospel of Pure Grace* (Tucson, Ariz.: University of Arizona Press, 1965), 70–96; Leslie Kawamura, ed., *The Bodhisattva doctrine in Buddhism* (Waterloo, Ontario: Wilfred Laurier University Press, 1981).

[42] Tsong kha pa, *Lam rim chen mo*, 366 (*Great Treatise*, Vol. 2, 115).

[43] *Jātaka-mālā*, 22, in Tsong kha pa, *Lam rim chen mo*, 367 (*Great Treatise*, Vol. 2, 116).

[44] *Śikṣā-samuccaya*, D3940, in Tsong kha pa, *Lam rim chen mo*, 367 (*Great Treatise*, Vol. 2, 116).

[45] Tsong kha pa, *Lam rim chen mo*, 371 (*Great Treatise*, Vol. 2, 120).

teachers.[46] At the same time, one should take care, lest one starts to despise those that do not practice generosity, thus falling into pride, or to pursue generosity in a utilitarian spirit, in order to reap merits for the future. Tsong kha pa is inviting practitioners to tread a difficult balance: on one hand, they must bear in mind that the goal of practice is to attain liberation; on the other hand, any motivation that "expects fruition" must be systematically uprooted.[47] The *Lam rim chen mo* contains a section devoted to these inappropriate forms of giving, which might be accompanied by karmic results, but cannot produce any merit.[48] The primacy of correct intention is so crucial that "purely mental generosity" can "increase merit immeasurably with little difficulty"; indeed, the mental construction of innumerable gifts that are offered symbolically to all beings is a practice favored by advanced bodhisattvas.[49]

The same principle applies to the practice of the second perfection, ethical discipline; even if one is utterly unable to make any difference to the suffering that one encounters, the mere intent to refrain from harming others is sufficient to produce merit on their behalf.[50] Ethical discipline leads to the "pure wisdom" that "eliminates all the seeds of wrongdoing"; our mindstream is gradually assimilated to that of the most compassionate bodhisattvas.[51] This perfection entails a constant engagement in fostering other people's welfare, but it does not exempt practitioners from exercising self-restraint or seeking individual liberation. Those who have taken the bodhisattva vows are not only bound to refrain from deeds that are wrong "by nature," but must respect the stricter codes of monastic observance. Again, this discipline is said to lay the foundations for greater spiritual progress in

---

[46] Tsong kha pa, *Lam rim chen mo*, 374 (*Great Treatise*, Vol. 2, 123).
[47] Tsong kha pa, *Lam rim chen mo*, 376 (*Great Treatise*, Vol. 2, 126).
[48] As an example of "inappropriate" generosity, Tsong kha pa mentions the case of a ruler who gives away someone else's child or spouse after having them kidnapped. Tsong kha pa, *Lam rim chen mo*, 377 (*Great Treatise*, Vol. 2, 128).
[49] Tsong kha pa, *Lam rim chen mo*, 389–390 (*Great Treatise*, Vol. 2, 140–141).
[50] Tsong kha pa, *Lam rim chen mo*, 391 (*Great Treatise*, Vol. 2, 144). Tsong kha pa refers to the text *Engaging in the Bodhisattva deeds*, which admits that we cannot make sure that no fish ever comes to harm, but already by "attaining an attitude of abstention" from harm, we can "perfect ethical discipline."
[51] Tsong kha pa, *Lam rim chen mo*, 394 (*Great Treatise*, Vol. 2, 146); Alex Wayman, "A Defense of Yogācāra Buddhism," *Philosophy East and West* 46 (1996): 447–477.

the other perfections in this life and to attain liberation in the next, "as a *causally concordant* behavioral effect."[52]

The third and fourth perfection similarly concern the world of form, and enable the practitioner to reach the heights of tranquility and insight. The perfection of patience does not merely entail disregarding the harm that is done to us; it also means that we should endure the sufferings caused by the mental traces of earlier misdeeds, as well as retain faith in the teachings despite occasional disappointments. This perfection is attained by gradually disciplining one's mind, but its cultivation also brings benefit at the level of practice, securing that we are not conditioned by anger when dealing with the suffering of others.[53] Tsong kha pa emphasizes the connection between patience and happiness, inasmuch as patience prevents rebirth in lower realms. In fact, the dGe lugs master invites practitioners to ponder "the cause and effect relationship" wherein "benefits such as these" arise from patience.[54]

Such causal relationship, unfortunately, also applies when we are overwhelmed by anger; a momentary angry thought is sufficient to erase the merit accumulated in eons of patient behavior. Anger is never justified, neither from the point of view of the object, nor from that of the subject. On one hand, those who inflict harm do not have full control over themselves; the imprints of their earlier actions turn them into "slaves" of their own afflictions.[55] On the other hand, if your anger is determined by inability to bear suffering, you should know that suffering exhausts your negative karma and thus it should actually be welcomed. The perfection of patience enables one to atone for one's past errors, much as painful treatment is sometimes necessary to eliminate diseases. In this perspective, one ought to

---

[52] Tsong kha pa, *Lam rim chen mo*, 398 (*Great Treatise*, Vol. 2, 150).

[53] Tsong kha pa, *Lam rim chen mo*, 399 (*Great Treatise*, Vol. 2, 153). Tsong kha pa references a text known as the *Compendium of Perfections*, which claims that "patience is the best approach for dealing with the inclination to disregard others' welfare."

[54] Tsong kha pa, *Lam rim chen mo*, 400 (*Great Treatise*, Vol. 2, 154).

[55] Again, this does not happen from "discordant," but rather from "concordant" causes. See Tsong kha pa, *Lam rim chen mo*, 409 (*Great Treatise*, Vol. 2, 163). To be angry at the imprints of earlier actions is as rational as being angry at a stick impelled by a hostile person.

rejoice when people show contempt for you, or prevent you from attaining
honor, since in this way they cut the bonds of your attachment.[56]
    Of course, the perfection of patience needs to be cultivated over time,
and Tsong kha pa invites practitioners to begin by growing accustomed to
small suffering and then to increase steadily one's capacity to accept it. If
one perseveres, the very sight of great suffering shall embolden us, "much
like the sight of blood encourages warriors in battle."[57] In fact, perseverance
is a perfection in its own right, which the *Bodhisattva levels* characterize as "a
flawless state of mind that is enthusiastic about accumulating virtue and
working for the welfare of living beings."[58] When one becomes "conditioned" in such a state of mind, one is bound to attain enlightenment; thus
it is in our best interest to cultivate it. Tsong kha pa acknowledges that
some people might fall victim to procrastination, or simply be overwhelmed
by their attachment to "inferior activities," but again such attitude might be
turned into its positive counterpart, and thereby help eliminate the discour-
agement that is detrimental to practice.[59] For Tsong kha pa, it is always
helpful to recall the words of the Buddha ("the authoritative person who
speaks what is true and correct"), who claimed that even flies can attain
enlightenment.
    In his discussion of perseverance, Tsong kha pa cites an interesting
passage from the *Cloud of Jewels Sūtra*, which claims that enlightenment is not
a reality that has been achieved by *one* supernatural being once and for all,
but rather a dimension that different practitioners have to attain *individually*
in their own time.[60] Quoting from a variety of sources, Tsong kha pa emphasizes how liberation may be sought in different manners, in line with the
inclinations and karmic predispositions of different individuals. The various
perfections *change* your ontological make up, and the nature of this change
reflects the type of practice that you follow. If the *Legs bshad snying po* and
Vol. 3 of the *Lam rim chen mo* argue that the theoretical analysis of the conventional is a necessary component of practice, Vol. 2 of the *Lam rim chen
mo* develops an analogous argument for the practical engagement. Tsong
kha pa's treatment of "meditative stabilization" and "wisdom" at the end of

---

[56] Tsong kha pa, *Lam rim chen mo*, 413 (*Great Treatise*, Vol. 2, 167–168); of
course this is virtually identical to the attitude in the Sermon of the Mount, Matt 5,
1–10; also HH the Dalai Lama, *The Good Heart*, 53–66.
[57] Tsong kha pa, *Lam rim chen mo*, 421 (*Great Treatise*, Vol. 2, 176).
[58] Tsong kha pa, *Lam rim chen mo*, 425 (*Great Treatise*, Vol. 2, 182).
[59] Tsong kha pa, *Lam rim chen mo*, 429 (*Great Treatise*, Vol. 2, 187).
[60] Tsong kha pa, *Lam rim chen mo*, 431 (*Great Treatise*, Vol. 2, 189).

his outline of the six perfections indicates that even the higher stages of practice integrate contemplation with compassionate outreach, or, to use Maximos' terminology, require the simultaneous pursuit of *theōria* and *praxis*.

In Chapter 4 we saw how for Maximos the highest form of *praxis* is the liturgy, whose structure is reflected in the architectural form of the Christian temple. There, the contemplation of created reality passes over into the contemplation of the ultimate mystery, and the Eucharist antici-pates the eschatological transformation of the cosmos.[61] For Maximos, our participation in the divine nature does not cease with the last judgment, but continues for all eternity as we grow in the knowledge of God and partici-pate in the love of the celestial Jerusalem.[62] Inner equilibrium (*apatheia*) is a precondition for higher forms of *praxis*,[63] much as in the *Lam rim chen mo* insight is the springboard for ever higher forms of compassion. *Theōria* leads to "volitional supersession" (*egchorēsis gnomikē*), after which it is impos-sible to deviate from *praxis*; meditative stabilization brings about a "one pointed state of mind" that is "stabilized on virtue"; after focusing on inner peace, one can generate the "good qualities" or virtues that sustain compas-sionate activity.[64]

ACTIVE *APATHEIA* AND *AGAPĒ*: A COMPARISON

In the *Capita de Charitate* and the *Liber Asceticus*, Maximos argues that hu-manity's fundamental orientation to the divine is fulfilled as men and women overcome *philautia* and become capable of channeling God's own *agapē*. As noted by Polycarp Sherwood, Maximos understands ethical disci-pline as overcoming the tensions between the demands of passions and the deliverances of the *nous*; if our desire is turned to the pleasures of the flesh, we condemn ourselves to a life of suffering.[65] The ascetic struggle is geared to the acquisition of self-mastery (*egkrateia*), which restores all human facul-

---

[61] Maximos the Confessor, *Mystagogia*, 4 (PG 91: 671–672).

[62] According to Joseph P. Farrell, Maximos' approach to the question of Christ's will only makes sense in light of this eschatological "concordance" of our human wills with God's own will; see Joseph P. Farrell, *Free choice in St. Maximus the Confessor* (South Canaan, Pa.: Saint Tikhon's Seminary Press, 1989), 165–167. Far-rell's strictly Palamite reading of Maximos, however, appears forced.

[63] Walther Völker, *Maximus Confessor als Meister des geistlichen Lebens*, 410–432.

[64] Tsong kha pa, *Lam rim chen mo*, 449 (*Great Treatise*, Vol. 2, 210).

[65] Polycarp Sherwood, Introduction to *The Ascetic Life and the Four Centuries on Charity*, 84–87.

ties to their original purpose through the imitation of Christ. While the relationship of *theōria* and *praxis* has already been explored in the earlier part of this work, I wish to turn to Maximos' construal of the virtues as a manifestation of God's own "active *apatheia*."

In *Amb. 10*, before the account of the Transfiguration, Maximos discusses the significance of the figure of Melchisedec, whom he presents as a paradigm of the transformation which is accomplished by the pursuit of virtues. Melchisedec was said to have "neither beginning nor end of days," because his contemplation transcended spatial and temporal limitations, while his being "without father and mother" signaled that in him the divine attributes had superseded the ordinary qualities of nature.[66] The eternal priesthood that is ascribed to him in the Letter to the Hebrews is read by Maximos as a hint that Melchisedec, "firm in virtue in a manner most closely resembling the divine," always kept the eye of his *nous* in steadfast contemplation of God.[67] The priest-king of Salem was assimilated to God in terms of knowledge and virtue, attaining a condition of *apatheia* beyond the laws of nature; his intellect penetrated into God and he received the divine imprint in his very being. For Maximos, whoever is holy performs "what is beautiful" (i.e., the virtues) in an extraordinary manner, deserving to be called a "type" of God. Since Christ the eternal high priest is the model and cause of the good that is manifested in all the saints, Melchisedec could imitate the incarnate Word even before the manifestation of the latter in the flesh.[68] *Amb. 10* likens to "most transparent mirrors" (*eidōla*) those individuals, who have conformed their life to the example of Christ, and who now possess the very "pattern" (*morphē*) of the divine Logos.[69]

The passions, then, are the very tool that enables us to advance on the spiritual path, since without the passions we could not acquire the virtues and imitate the earthly life of Christ.[70] Admittedly, one may point at passages that seem to say the opposite: in *Ep. 33*, Maximos compares the *nous*

---

[66] In this description, Maximos is drawing both upon Gen 14:18–20 and from Heb 7:3.

[67] Maximos the Confessor, *Amb.* 10 (PG 91: 1140a).

[68] Maximos the Confessor, *Amb.* 10 (PG 91: 1141c).

[69] Maximos the Confessor, *Amb.* 10 (PG 91: 1137c). The use of the image of the mirrors term probably comes from the Pseudo-Denys, *De Divinis Nominibus* 4, 22 (PG 3: 724–725).

[70] Curiously, Walther Völker argues in *Maximus Confessor als Meister des geistlichen Lebens*, 410: "the passions *always* draw us down" ("Deren Wirkung ist *immer* eine niederziehende"). This assertion does not seem to be borne by Maximos' writings.

under the influence of the passions to a bird, whose feet are tied and who thus cannot fly to the heavens; in *Amb. 38*, he mentions the need to "withdraw" and "utterly slaughter" the *pathē*.[71] These passages, however, refer to the situation before the beginning of spiritual practice, whereas the *Capita de Charitate* clearly do not associate *apatheia* with an extirpation of the passions, but rather with the soul's ability to purify them and put them to good use.[72] Maximos' anti-Origenist assertion of the soteriological value of *kinēsis* ensures that *apatheia* is not incompatible with a continued "movement" of the passions, but actually presupposes it. The same passage on the *pathē* in *Amb. 38*, referring to an apocryphal account of the flight into Egypt, continues to tell us that the divine Logos "tramples" upon "the motions and passions of the flesh" and grants us *apatheia* as a reward for "fleeing with him." Later on, after this initial struggle is over, the practice of the virtues will guide us back from Egypt to Judea, introducing us to the depths of Christ's mystery.[73]

For Maximos, if the passions "lay hidden in the soul," and therefore we fail to acknowledge our flaws, suffering is going to be inevitable.[74] At the same time, Tsong kha pa noted with respect to the perfection of patience that the sublimation of the passions "towards a spiritual manner" (*pros pneumatikēn hexin*) is accomplished primarily through "suffering" (*ponos*); without the latter, the intellect cannot be purified. While Evagrios presents the spiritual struggle as a real battle with demons, Maximos does not emphasize the role of preternatural agents, and views their role as merely one among many factors shaping our inner life.[75] What is crucial, however, is that for Tsong kha pa inner peace is attained largely because of our efforts, whereas for Maximos, dispassion is a gift from God. Indeed, the notion that *apatheia* is bestowed on us as a reward is reflected in Maximos' frequent use of the expression "the grace of dispassion" (*hē tēs apatheias cha-*

---

[71] Maximos the Confessor, *Ep.* 33 (PG 91: 627); also, *Amb.* 38 (PG 91: 1300b), which mentions "the transformation and ultimate suppression of the passions" (*tēn tōn pathōn hypochōrēsin kai teleian nekrōsin*).

[72] Maximos the Confessor, *Capita de Charitate* 1, 35–36, in *Philokalia*, Vol. 2, 56 (PG 90: 967–968).

[73] Maximos the Confessor, *Amb.* 38 (PG 91: 1300bc).

[74] Maximos the Confessor, *Capita de Charitate* 2, 44, in *Philokalia*, Vol. 2, 73 (PG 90: 999–1000).

[75] Maximos the Confessor, *Capita de Charitate*, 1, 91–92, in *Philokalia*, Vol. 2, 63 (PG 90: 981–982); apart from the demons, the other factors are "angels, wind and diet."

ris).⁷⁶ Since the angelic passions are now acting in accordance with their *logos*, *apatheia* allows us to lead the angelic life here on earth, fully absorbed in the contemplation of the divine.⁷⁷

The link between *apatheia* and *agapē* is also stressed in the *Capita Theologiae et Oeconomiae*, where Maximos tells us that the incarnate Logos bestowed *apatheia* on his disciples in the upper room, through the words "Peace be with you."⁷⁸ *Apatheia*, however, is not merely bestowed "for the sake of peace" (*dia tēs eirenēs*),⁷⁹ but first and foremost "for the sake of love" (*dia tēs agapēs*); this is the Leitmotif of the *Capita de Charitate*. True detachment is accompanied by the love "which expels the fear of judgment" (1 John 4:18), and this enables us to overlook other people's faults;⁸⁰ those who are "perfect in love" show the same disposition to all, no longer discriminating between "Greek or Jew, male or female, bond or free."⁸¹ In this way, the redeemed individual becomes like the sun, which lets his light shine upon the good and the bad. On one hand, we come to resemble Christ, who suffered and gave the hope of final resurrection to all members of the human race;⁸² on the other hand, we come to resemble God Himself, who loves all with equanimity and detachment.⁸³

In the *Capita de Charitate* and *Quaestiones ad Thalassium*, Maximos presents human *apatheia* as an image of its divine counterpart.⁸⁴ The former

---

⁷⁶ See for instance Maximos the Confessor, *Amb.* 45 (PG 91: 1353a-1356a). This text, much like other passages in the *Quaestiones ad Thalassium*, claims that *apatheia* restores us to the condition of the first parents before the fall.

⁷⁷ See also Gregory of Nyssa, *De Vita S. Macrinae* (PG 46: 969–970): "the life of Macrina and her mother was given its rhythm by the imitation of the angels" (*pros mimēsin tēs tōn aggelōn zōēs errhythmizeto*).

⁷⁸ Maximos the Confessor, *Capita Theologiae et Oeconomiae*, 2, 46, in *Philokalia*, Vol. 2, 73 (PG 90: 1145–1146).

⁷⁹ Walther Völker, *Maximus Confessor als Meister des geistlichen Lebens*, 417.

⁸⁰ Maximos the Confessor, *Capita de Charitate*, 4, 92, in *Philokalia*, Vol. 2, 112 (PG 90: 1069–1072).

⁸¹ Maximos the Confessor, *Capita de Charitate*, 2, 30, in *Philokalia*, Vol. 2, 70 (PG 90: 993–994).

⁸² Maximos the Confessor, *Capita de Charitate*, 1, 25, in *Philokalia*, Vol. 2, 55, (PG 90: 965–966).

⁸³ Maximos the Confessor, *Capita de Charitate*, 1, 25, in *Philokalia*, Vol. 2, 55, (PG 90: 965–966).

⁸⁴ See again Maximos the Confessor, *Capita de Charitate*, 1, 36, in *Philokalia*, Vol. 2, 56 (PG 90: 967–968); also *Q.Th.* 47 (CCSG 7: 321–325), where the roads "made straight" for the Lord refer here to the passions returned to their virtuous state.

differs from the latter inasmuch as it is the outcome of the synergy between humanity's efforts and God's own *agapē*, which nurtures us and sustains us in this life and the next. Gregory of Nyssa, in his *Commentarium in Canticum*, actually uses the term *erōs* to indicate what elevates the soul towards God;[85] and Maximos follows this tradition when claiming that the gift of *apatheia* transforms the passion of concupiscence (*epithymia*) into "passionate love for God" (*pros ton theon erōta*).[86] The *Capita de Charitate* present an explicit correspondence between the two lower levels of the soul and the two forms of love: *epithymia* is associated with *erōs* and the passion of anger (*thymos*) with *agapē*.[87] Yet, despite the occasional reference, the theme of divine *erōs* surfaces only rarely in Maximos' works; for instance the *Liber Asceticus*, which is a crucial text of Maximos' spiritual theology, never mentions it all. *Agapē* is the antidote to the spiritual conceit which accompanies the first stages of spiritual knowledge; while Evagrios thinks that the "true" gnostic is no longer threatened by the *pathē*, Maximos believes that knowledge must always be accompanied by love, in the same way as the two are forever united in the Godhead.[88] In this way, the individual comes to resemble God, who like the sun lets his light shine upon good and bad alike, as well as Christ, who suffered for all men and gave us the hope of final resurrection.[89]

In Ch. 4, we noted how Maximos' Christology reflects an underlying preoccupation with ontological boundaries, so that the incarnation becomes the guarantee of their enduring quality. In this perspective, what is accom-

---

[85] Gregory of Nyssa, *Commentarius in Canticum Canticorum* 1; 6 (PG 44: 763–788; 883–906).

[86] Walther Völker, *Maximus Confessor als Meister des geistlichen Lebens*, 426; see also Maximos the Confessor, *Q.Th.* 49 (CCSG 7: 354–355), where the passions turned into virtues aid our battle against "Sennacherib" (the devil) who wants to take over our soul.

[87] Maximos the Confessor, *Capita de Charitate*, 2, 48, in *Philokalia*, Vol. 2, 73 (PG 90: 969–970).

[88] Maximos the Confessor, *Capita de Charitate*, 4, 62 in *Philokalia*, Vol. 2, 108 (PG 90: 1061–1064); Evagrios, *Praktikos* 21 (PG 40: 1227–1228), also in Evagrius Ponticus, *The Praktikos and Chapters on Prayer*, 21–22. It is true however that Evagrios is not entirely consistent on the matter. See Walther Völker, *Maximus Confessor als Meister des geistlichen Lebens*, 429.

[89] See Maximos the Confessor, *Capita de Charitate*, 1, 71, in *Philokalia*, Vol. 2, 60 (PG 90: 975–976). Maximos notes here, however, that we have "equal hope of resurrection," but "each man determines his own fitness for glory or punishment."

plished by *agapē* and the practice of the virtues is the reintegration and the development of the soul that was shattered and fragmented by *philautia*. Here we find a significant divergence from Tsong kha pa's vision. The *Lam rim chen mo* presented compassion as the source of the six perfections, but Tsong kha pa's understanding of spiritual practice, resting on the interplay of ultimate and conventional, could not regard the development of the conventional self as a *goal* of practice. Rather, since the self belongs to the conventional world, it only possesses an instrumental value, and eventually dissolves into the empty ground of *dharmakāya*. While the practice of the perfections is construed as *imitatio Buddhae*, their purpose is not to reconstruct a shattered conventional self, but to turn it into a pointer towards the ultimate, where differences of identity are fully erased. The *mimēsis Christou* at the core of the *Capita de Charitate* underscores on the contrary the intrinsic value of the virtues as bringing Christ anew into the flesh, in a way that does not cancel individual difference, but exalts and preserves personal identity.

Dalmais and Thunberg note that Maximos' classification of virtues and vices corresponds closely to Evagrios' treatment of the same topic, which in its turn rested on a trichotomous division of the soul.[90] The Evagrian School tended to construe *apatheia* in more negative terms, as a reality that would help us move beyond the "kingdom of the *logoi*" into the "kingdom of God." The *Kephalaia Gnostika* makes it clear that the *nous* reaching unity with God "on the wings of *apatheia*" has shed its bodily frame.[91] While Evagrios' *Praktikos* does link *agapē* with detachment, the purpose of *agapē* is primarily to undercut the passions at their root, rather than develop their positive counterpart.[92] In fact, in saying that *agapē* "possesses" nothing but God (for it is itself God), Evagrios seems to suggest that at the highest level, *apatheia* may no longer eventuate in *praxis*.[93] According to the *Prak-*

---

[90] See Lars Thunberg, *Microcosm and Mediator*, 290–299; Irénée-Henry Dalmais, "L'anthropologie spirituelle de Saint Maxime le Confesseur," *Recherches et Débats* 36 (1961): 202–211; also his "La fonction unificatrice du Verbe Incarné dans les oeuvres spirituelles de Saint Maxime le Confesseur," *ScEccl* 14 (1962): 445–459.

[91] See Evagrios, *Kephalaia Gnostika* 2, 6, in *Les Six Centuries des 'Kephalaia Gnostica'*, 62–63.

[92] Evagrios, *Praktikos*, 53 (PG 40: 1233–1234), also in Evagrius Ponticus, *The Praktikos and Chapters on Prayer*, 30–31.

[93] Or at least this is how Thurnberg (*Microcosm and Mediator*, 404) reads Evagrios' *Tractatus ad Eulogium Monachum* 23 (PG 79: 1124c). As with the treatise *De Oratione*, Migne attributes this work to Nilus of Sinai.

tikos, those who truly possess dispassion have left behind the virtues of patience and self-mastery as something no longer necessary.[94] In Maximos' *Epistula 2*, on the contrary, *agapē* encompasses all the virtues; the claim that charity includes, or so to speak *possesses* all the virtues recalls Tsong kha pa's assertion that all perfections flow from compassion.[95]

The different relationship between contingency and *agapē* in Evagrios and in Maximos emerges clearly if we look back at what Evagrios had to say about the use of mental images in prayer. For the Origenist school, using mental supports for one's prayer bordered on the idolatrous, since the *nous* cluttered with the images of created reality remained scattered and fragmented, and fails to acknowledge its identity with the kingdom of God. Evagrios insists that the only way towards the pre-conceptual purity of the mind (which is clearly analogous to rDzogs chen's "pure basis") is the elimination of the imprints of material reality. Maximos' commitment to the Chalcedonian vision, on the contrary, makes him appreciate more fully the salvific power of created difference; the incarnation reveals that the natural order is the cosmic vesture of Christ. In this perspective, dispassion heals our disordered mental processes and enables us to relate to mental images in a sinless manner. In the *Capita de Charitate*, the highest stage of *apatheia* is not a condition when mental images no longer arise, but one where dispassion is not unsettled by their manifestation.[96]

The allegory of *Amb. 38*, where Christ "tramples" the passions and then leads us back to the "Judea of the virtues," is actually developed further in the *Capita Theologiae et Oeconomiae*. Taking up the theme of "the last days of creation," Maximos reads the sixth day as symbolizing the cultivation of the virtues which lead to *apatheia*; the seventh day then represents the desert of detachment, when the intellect is no longer troubled by mental images. This condition, however, is followed by yet another higher reality, when the soul crosses the Jordan and again "enters into possession of the virtues." It is this higher form of activity that turns us into the "dwelling

---

[94] See again Evagrios, *Praktikos*, 36–40 (PG 40: 1231–1232), also in Evagrius Ponticus, *The Praktikos and Chapters on Prayer*, 25–27. Evagrios' construal of *apatheia* might be said to come closer to a pre-Mahāyāna understanding of *nirvāṇa*.

[95] See Maximos the Confessor, *Ep. 2* (PG 91: 393c-395c). See also Lars Thurnberg, *Microcosm and Mediator*, 311.

[96] Maximos the Confessor, *Capita de Charitate* 1, 91–93, in *Philokalia*, Vol. 2, 63–64 (PG 90: 981–982).

place of God."[97] While Maximos does not say so explicitly, it would have been fully in line with his use of Scripture to point out that it was Joshua who led the Israelites into the Promised Land; and who was Joshua, if not the type of Christ who leads humanity to deification?

At this point, the dialectic of unity and multiplicity underpinning Maximos' "Christocentric turn" is revealed in its full practical import. *Agapē* constitutes the unifying factor that orders, but does not suppress the different human faculties; similarly, *agapē* is the power that makes the same human nature, undefiled by sin, shine in every person, and enables their manifold individualities to shine. Through "the blessed passion" of charity, both humanity in general, and the individual in particular, come to reflect God's Trinitarian love, and mirror the cosmic perichoresis of the eternal Logos and the created *logoi*.[98] The unification of man in his ascent towards God, and the fragmentation of the Logos in his descent towards man, represent one more perfect symmetry. The more human beings acquire *apatheia*, the more the one *apathēs* Logos turns them into a channel of his activity. In *Amb. 10*, God and man are said to be examples (*paradeigmata*) of each other: out of condescension for humanity, God becomes man to the extent that man deifies himself by means of *agapē*. Similarly, out of love for God, man becomes divine, and is drawn into the depths of the divine mystery, inasmuch as he discloses the invisible God by means of the visible virtues.[99]

This positive view of the virtues is linked with the anti-Origenist thrust of Maximos' anthropology, which consistently stresses the salvific potential of *all* components of humanity. At the same time, Maximos is here developing Origen's notion of Christ's "repeated incarnations" in the virtues of the believer.[100] The genealogy of this position in the writings of the Confessor goes back to *De Principiis*, but also reflects the mediation of the Cappadocians. In line with his general subordinationism, Origen associated the Father with unity, and the Son with multiplicity, and argues that men could participate in the latter (though not in the former) by means of the vir-

---

[97] Maximos the Confessor, *Capita Theologiae et Oeconomiae* 1, 52–54, in *Philokalia*, Vol. 2, 58 (PG 90: 1101–1104).

[98] Maximos the Confessor, *Capita de Charitate* 3, 67, in *Philokalia*, Vol. 2, 93 (PG 90: 1037–1038); Lars Thunberg, *Microcosm and Mediator*, 312, 317.

[99] Maximos the Confessor, *Capita Quinquies Centena*, 4, 79–80, in *Philokalia*, Vol. 2, 255 (PG 90: 1339–1340).

[100] See Paul in Gal 4:19: "my little children, of whom I travail in birth again until Christ be formed in you…" (*tekna mou, ous palin ōdinō mechris ou morphōthē Christos en hymin*).

tues.[101] Evagrios follows Origen in associating the virtues with Christ's own flesh, but again the virtues are an instrument to attain *apatheia*, and do not entail a continued positive engagement of reality.[102] In the *Contra Eunomium*, Gregory of Nyssa claims that the Son, rather than *possessing* the virtues, actually *is* the virtues.[103] In line with the move from subordinationist to *homoousios* Christology, Gregory tells us that one can participate in Christ, who is the "ruler of *apatheia*," but this relationship is always a partial one, and does not cancel our personal identity. According to Daniélou, Gregory's mention of the virtues as the "colors" of the divine image hint at the manifold manner of Christ's presence; and this is exactly the position that Maximos chooses to develop in light of the later development of Christological doctrine.[104] Once more, a conceptual paradigm is lifted from its Origenist sources and revisits it in line with his Chalcedonian commitments; in the *Capita Theologiae et Oeconomiae* the opposition of unity and multiplicity of *De Principiis* grows into the integrated plurality of the incarnate Logos.

When does this integration take place? Full deification seems only to be attained in the next life, but Maximos' statement that "God forever wishes to become incarnate in those deemed worthy"[105] indicates that Christ's indwelling in the believer begins already in this life. In *Amb.* 33, Maximos notes that the Logos is born in the soul of man and then grows through the *tropoi* of the different virtues;[106] much as the same created *logos* may be manifested in different individual *tropoi*, the eternal Logos "thickens" in different ways in the different individuals where he is incarnate

---

[101] Origen, *De Principiis* 1, 2, 2 (PG 11: 130–131).

[102] See for instance Evagrios, *Monastic mirror*, 118–120 (*Texte und Untersuchungen*, xxxix 4b. Leipzig: Gressman ed., 1913), 160–163. One is led to wonder whether this tendency of Origenist spirituality to relegate love at the margin of practice (after all, one is only saved by *gnōsis*) is not a distant ancestor of Luther's *sola fide* stance, which resulted effectively in the "secularization" of charity. See Paul Hacker, *Das Ich im Glauben bei Martin Luther: Der Ursprung der anthropozentrischen Religion* (Bonn: Verlag "Nova et Vetera," 1966), especially the section "Säkularisierung der Liebe," 166–174.

[103] Gregory of Nyssa, *Contra Eunomium* 3, 7 (PG 45: 611–615).

[104] See Jean Daniélou, *Platonisme et théologie mystique*, 101–103.

[105] Maximos the Confessor, *Q.Th.* 22 (CCSG 7: 143): *ho theos aei thelōn en tois axiois anthrōpos ginetai*.

[106] Maximos the Confessor, *Amb.* 33 (PG 91: 1285cd), based on Gregory of Nazianzos, *Orationes* 38, 2 (PG 36: 313–314).

again.[107] A variety of metaphors is used to express this point: Christ's in-habitation in our hearts discloses manifold "treasures of wisdom and knowledge";[108] faith gives birth to the Logos, but the Logos gives birth to a variety of virtues;[109] the presence of the Logos in the variety of our virtues mirrors the extent to which the one Logos is present in the variety of the commandments.[110] All the same, an unresolved tension remains as to the ultimate ontological nature of these virtues: on one hand, they are mere *types* of the divine qualities; on the other hand, they already partake of the divine energies that will be fully enjoyed after death. This is a major difference from Tsong kha pa's *Imitatio Buddhae*: in Tsong kha pa's horizon, the six perfections turning practitioners into the "body of form" are no different in kind (if perhaps different in degree) from the Buddha's own qualities.

In the *Lam rim chen mo*, Tsong kha pa explores the relation between undifferentiated emptiness and the multiplicity of the *rupakāya*; in *Amb.* 10, and in other passages of the *Ambigua*, Maximos uses the language of unity and plurality to assert that the "most unique (*moniotatos*) Logos" is refracted in a most varied spectrum of virtues, in line with the capacity of the indi-vidual.[111] While Theravada Buddhism and the Evagrian school emphasized equilibrium or *apatheia* as the goal of the path, for Maximos and Tsong kha pa detachment, or dispassion, is functional to *praxis*. In this latter dialectic the virtues of individual practitioners make manifest God's agapic love for creation, or Buddhahood's compassionate outreach towards sentient beings. Those who are ontologically transformed by the divine energies leave be-hind their ordinary faculties, much as the bodhisattvas acquire the Buddha's own supernatural qualities.[112] At the same time, for Maximos these virtues

---

[107] Maximos the Confessor, *Capita Theologiae et Oeconomiae*, 2, 37, in *Philokalia*, Vol. 2, 146–147 (PG 90: 1141–1142).

[108] Maximos the Confessor, *Capita de Charitate*, 4, 70, in *Philokalia*, Vol. 2, 109 (PG 90: 1065–1066).

[109] Maximos the Confessor, *Capita de Charitate*, 4, 73, in *Philokalia*, Vol. 2, 109 (PG 90: 1065–1066).

[110] Lars Thunberg, *Microcosm and Mediator*, 328; also Maximos the Confessor, *Quaestiones et dubia* 142 (CCSG 10: 101).

[111] In the Latin version of the *Ambigua*, Eriugena talks here of a *verbum singu-larissimum*, or "unparalleled." See the comments by Claudio Moreschini in his anno-tated version of *Ambigua*, 654.

[112] In a similar way, Chalcedonian Christology tells us that the eternal Son of God assumed human attributes which he retained for all eternity: Christ reigns in

are invested with enduring plenitude, whereas for Tsong kha pa the highest insight does not result in a reification of the six perfections, but in the realization of their emptiness.

DGE LUGS GRADUALISM AND RDZOGS CHEN'S "RETRIEVAL OF THE PURE BASIS": A FALSE CONTRADICTION?

At the end of the fifth chapter, I mentioned the emergence of the *ris med* synthesis as having fostered, against the background of the dGe lugs ascendancy, a more eclectic approach to religious practice. I also reflected on the significance of *ris med*, which accommodated a plurality of voices, in comparison with the denouement of the Origenist crisis in the mid 6th century. In this section, I wish to look again at the distinct outcome of these two disputes, and suggest that the gradualism of Tsong kha pa's *Lam rim chen mo* could coexist with the immediacy of 'Jam dpal bShes gnyen's *rDo la gser zhun* due to a shared understanding of Buddhahood as a reality that is active within the conditioned world. The teaching of active *nirvāṇa* that undergirds both dGe lugs and rDzogs chen can thus tolerate a variety of approaches to spiritual practice, in a way that Maximos' Chalcedonian position is unable to sustain.

The rDzogs chen belief that the goal of practice is the retrieval of a pure, primordial experience preceding verbal conceptualization clearly entails a conviction that the linguistic act can never capture the inner structure of reality.[113] When Yogācāra philosophy stresses the distinction between appearance and reality, it effectively says that appearance of things is indistinguishable from our own experience, and that material reality lacks inherent properties. rDzogs chens' critique of mind-body dualism goes even further, and echoing Western deconstructions of Cartesian dualism it even argues that no objective reality may be legitimately posited outside the reach of our sensory perceptions. For 'Jam dpal bShes gnyen, to think that the experiencing process is the *cause* of our errors is itself a misguided notion,

---

heaven with a human body. Such assertion would make no sense in a Buddhist context.

[113] When Merleau-Ponty warns that one's views of reality are little more than "ready-made meanings" as long as we fail to find "the primordial silence" beneath the "chatter of words," he is telling us that the hermeneutics of experience in which we are constantly engaged, and which Descartes sees as the hallmark of human subjectivity, is itself the source of suffering and delusion. See Marcel Merleau-Ponty, *The Phenomenology of Perception*, 179.

since the mechanism of cause and effect is a mere mental projection. The diatribes of the *rDo la gser zhun* against "views" seem directly to criticize the painstaking arguments of the *Lam rim chen mo* in favor of ethical practice, as well as the claim that it is "the mechanism of concordant causes" which regulates the practice of the six perfections. If the *rDo la gser zhun* is correct, Tsong kha pa's belief that patience or perseverance sustain the development of "good qualities" can only ensnare us in the web of duality and conceptualization.

Does this mean that 'Jam dpal bShes gnyen and the other rDzogs chen masters advocated ethical indifferentism or anarchy? Clearly, this is not the case. The purpose of rDzogs chen's analysis of experience is to show that ultimately all experience is *one*, and cannot be sliced into "parts, colors and qualities you can get a hold on."[114] While the way things appear in the world of forms gives rise to different sensations, ultimately they cannot be divided from the unique reality of awareness, which is uncaused and untouched by external circumstances. Contingent events cannot be labeled as positive or negative, they just *are*; even the notion of suffering loses meaning. Instead of seeking to ascend an ontological ladder towards higher states of being, practitioners are invited to grasp that "there is no defect in whatever thought or awareness arises," and to attain equanimity towards favorable or unfavorable circumstances.[115] In this perspective, the entire universe is the creative self-expression of a fundamental, primordial purity beyond unity and plurality, which is identical with *bodhicitta* and is fundamentally well-disposed towards sentient beings. While Tsong kha pa calls practitioners to "*awaken*" *bodhicitta*, and identifies it with the "mind of enlightenment," the *Kun byed rgyal po* insists that compassion is the very structure of the universe to which we need to become attuned.[116] What is emphasized is not the inner logic and decipherability of the cosmos (the key themes of the *Legs bshad snying po* and Vol. 3 of the *Lam rim chen mo*), but rather its intrinsic purity and responsiveness to human needs.

The notion of the mind as creative power is an important theme in Vedic and post-Vedic literature, and it also plays an important role in Taoist cosmological speculation. Both these strands deeply influenced the devel-

---

[114] See Klong chen pa, *Grub mtha' rin po che'I mdzod*, 333–334, quoted in Namkhai Norbu and Kennard Lipman, Intro. to Mañjuśrīmitra's *Primordial experience*, 22.

[115] See Mañjuśrīmitra, *Primordial Experience* (Commentary, 116), 103.

[116] See Eva K. Neumaier-Dargyay, Intro. to *The Sovereign All-Creating Mind*, 28–30.

opment of Tibetan Buddhism, and, as noted in Ch. 5, it is likely that these different strands merged with the earlier Bon tradition to give rise to the rDzogs chen synthesis. In this context, the term "mind" is to be interpreted metaphorically as indicating a pristine, self-originated awareness (*rang bzhin*) that has no object, but also no underpinning subject. This awareness encompasses an actuating potency (*ngo bo*), which unfolds in the multiplicity of reality and is motivated by the desire to share the joy and beauty of existence. In light of the discussion in the last two chapters, it is easy to draw a correlation between the rDzogs chen pure ground and the *jñāna-dharmakāya*, and also to associate the emanatory process of the actuating potency with the *rupakāya*. As mentioned in Ch. 6, Tsong kha pa's postulation of four Buddha bodies complicates the discussion, introducing a distinction between the emptiness of the ultimate epistemological insight and the "detached duality" of the *jñāna-dharmakāya*.[117] Instead of being a self-originated reality, the latter body of *dharmāh* flows from the accumulated merits of the Buddha, and then branches out in the different manifestations of the *rupakāyāh*. This reading of Buddhahood echoes the teaching of rDzogs chen: an ordering intelligence overflows into a differentiated phenomenal reality for the sake of sentient beings.

One might argue that the rDzogs chen notion of primordial Buddha also comes close to a theistic position, inasmuch as it explicitly posits a creative intelligence which sustains the universe. This intelligence, however, is said to be ultimately impersonal; the emergence of the universe is not the result of a creative act, but the sort of on-going emanation that we encounter in Neo-Platonic literature. In addition, while for Tsong kha pa the phenomenal world tends to be a gift coming from the Buddha's highest insight,[118] for rDzogs chen the emergence of contingency is the result of passions.[119] Once more, this reflects the tension between Maximos' more positive reading of creation and Origen's own understanding of the fragmenta-

---

[117] The author(s) of the *Kun byed rgyal po* have a much stronger sense of phenomena as the expression of the *dharmakāya*. The *Lam rim chen mo*, on the other hand, tends to foreground more strongly the opposition of ultimate and conventional in line with Madhyamaka ontology.

[118] *Kun byed rgyal po*, Ch. 2, in Eva K. Neumaier-Dargyay, *The Sovereign All-Creating Mind*, 53.

[119] This is clear in the myths about the descent of the primordial Buddha into the world of "plurality." See Stephen Hodge's translation of *The Maha-Vairocana-Abhisambodhi Tantra* (Routledge Curzon, London: Routlegde Curzon, 2003), 451–465.

tion of the henad. At the same time, Tsong kha pa's model is far from identical with Maximos'. On one hand, by driving a wedge between the highest dimension of Buddhahood and phenomenal reality, the dGe lugs master may be seen as developing a model where the *jnana-dharmakaya* effectively grounds practice in ultimate reality, while affirming the inherent dignity of the conventional. On the other hand, before drawing quick parallels with von Balthasar's notion of *analogia libertatis*, one should consider that Tsong kha pa's *svābhāvikakāya* is not a necessarily existent reality (or a personal power), *choosing* to create a world out of compassion. Similarly, the *jñāna-dharmakāya* is not a gift from a higher power, but something that is co-dependently originated and may never aspire to transcend *śūnyatā*. In this perspective, Tsong kha pa's vision is more suggestive of the succession of creations and falls in *De Principiis*, since no created order can escape from its destiny of emptiness.

Both the rNying ma and the dGe lugs construals of Buddhahood are concerned with the dialectic of unity and plurality, of emptiness and form. The opposition between *svābhāvikakāya* and *jñāna-dharmakāya* might appear to locate unity in the former and plurality in the latter, but the distinction is only apparent, since the doctrine of the two truths reminds us that *svābhāvikakāya* is the true nature of the body of *dharmāh*, and thus contingent reality is only conventionally plural. In a rDzogs chen perspective, the dialectical relationship of *rang bzhin* and *ngo bo* serves a similar function, even in a work such as the *Kun byed rgyal po* where the illusory nature of the world of forms is more heavily emphasized than in Tsong kha pa's *Lam rim chen mo*. In both traditions, contingent reality is envisaged as a support for our spiritual path; the dGe lugs master is far more preoccupied than his rNying ma counterparts with the inner coherence and the logic of conventional reality, but both approaches intimate that spiritual progress hinges on our forging a relationship with this reality in a way that is consonant with our nature. rDzogs chen literature is keener to note that compassion *is* the very ground of being, but the *Kun rhyed rgyal po* and the *Lam rim chen mo* share the fundamental Mahāyāna belief in *apratishtitā nirvāna*. As such, both Tsong kha pa's injunction to awaken the mind of enlightenment and the rDzogs chen invitation to retrieve the pure basis rest on the conviction that contingent plurality is fundamentally sacramental.

At this point, one could object that this fundamental congruence of ontological vision does not erase the opposition between immediacy and gradualism. Yet even here, the two systems are more latitudinarian then it may appear at first. On one hand, the rDzogs chen belief in the emptiness of ultimate reality allows the accommodation of gradualist practices, if these are of help to individual practitioners. On the other hand, Tsong kha pa's insistence in the *Legs bshad snying po* that conventional reality lacks substantial existence—implying that at the ultimate level no ontological change may be accomplished—entails that gradual practices as such are only a form of skillful means (*upayakauśalya*). Once you leave conventionality behind, there is no fundamental contradiction between the insistence on "concordant causes" of the *Lam rim chen mo*, and the radical critique of causal mechanisms of the *rDo la gser zhun*. For Tsong kha pa, gradualism should actually be condemned if it claimed that it could permanently (ultimately) transform the conventional; but this, not surprisingly, is also the concern of the *Kun rhyed rgyal po*'s polemic against "the vehicle of cause and result."[120] At the same time, we saw how later rDzogs chen authors could remain critical of the notion of "gradual method," and yet accommodate a "hierarchy of spiritual *realization*" through which practitioners would "progress one level at a time."[121] This is not substantially different from the view expressed in the *Lam rim chen mo*, where the goal of practice is a gradual intensification of one's understanding of the ultimate nature of reality, culminating in the acquisition of the Buddha's own epistemological insight.

By combining gradualism and immediacy in a unique synthesis, the texts of the *Seminal Heart* mentioned in Ch. 5 are doing nothing but develop, or explicitly affirm, the "irenic" tendencies that are implicit in the doctrine of the two truths when combined with a belief in the active nature of *nirvāna*. Thus, the co-existence of the rNying ma and the dGe lugs tradition reflects a shared conviction that the cosmos as a whole is the embodiment of the Buddha, as well as the stage for the Buddha's outreach towards sentient beings. This is clearly very different from the position of the Origenist school. Evagrios' henad in the *Kephalaia Gnostika* was not bursting with desire to share its purity and joy with humanity; rather, it envisaged all the passions as a blemish and a flaw. This is a universe where *agapē* is *not* the ground of all being; this function is served by a totally undifferentiated (and ultimately indifferent) cosmic *nous*. The "operative transcendent" we encounter in Tibet functions like an all-encompassing active *apatheia*, a Buddha nature that is always, forever, turned towards us.

We are now left with a number of fundamental questions. There is little doubt that the more irenic nature of Buddhist doctrinal discourse, as

---

[120] *Kun byed rgyal po*, Ch. 9, in Eva K. Neumaier-Dargyay, *The Sovereign All-Creating Mind*, 71–72.

[121] Sam van Schaik, Intro to *Approaching the Great Perfection*, 129.

well as its in-built readiness to self-criticism, is at first more attractive to the contemporary West, fatigued by different traditions' conflicting claims to truth. In this perspective, Maximos' reluctance to accommodate Origenist spirituality in a comprehensive synthesis—despite his qualified appropriation of many of its elements—might appear to be just one more instance of dogmatism and intolerance. But *could* Maximos have opted for such an overarching synthesis? Or rather, was it not the case that the fundamental tenets of the Christology of Chalcedon were *forcing* him to such a solution? And even more fundamentally, could it be the case, perhaps, that Maximos' approach provides us with theological resources able to value and redeem the contingency and particularity of created reality that the Tibetan notion of Buddhahood seems to lack? Is Mahāyāna thought truly able to assert the value of this contingency and particularity? And if not, why is it that the Mahāyāna approach seems more attuned to current philosophical reflection, even as we grow ever more sensitive to the claims of "diversity" and "plurality"? These are the questions we will discuss in the final chapter.

8 THE VIRTUES OF PARTICIPATION: MAXIMOS' THEOLOGY OF DIVINE EMBODIMENT AFTER THE ENCOUNTER WITH BUDDHISM

In the introduction, I mentioned how systematic theology suffers if it relegates spirituality to the realm of the subjective, and no longer views it as a resource for speculative reflection. On one hand, if mystical experience is dismissed as irrelevant for speculative reflection, academic discourse about God can set up its own agenda, but this quickly loses relevance for the broader Christian community. On the other hand, if theologians follow William James and stop looking at individual religious experience for cues about God or our relationship with the divine, theology quickly succumbs to the claim of Kantian epistemology that ultimate reality cannot be known.[1] Finally, an individual, who chooses to engage in "spirituality" apart from the tradition of faith or the wider needs of her community, is a far cry from Paul's portrayal of the *anēr pneumatikos*, whose standard is Jesus' own ministry among the poor, sick, and hungry. What is left is a theology that betrays its calling so as to gain the approval of the academic community; and a spirituality that degenerates into a form of therapy concerned only with one's inner states.

Maximos' critique of the Evagrian School reflected a profound dissatisfaction with the spiritualizing flight from human experience that characterized the Origenist movement. The tendency to view spiritual progress in terms of one's *identification* with the divine demoted the embodied dimension of practice to the realm of the provisional, while also making it virtually independent of the communitarian aspect of ecclesial life that finds its culmination in the liturgy. Evagrian spirituality may actually resonate with contemporary seekers since it is a spirituality for isolated individuals, who at the same time are eager to leave behind the burden of their own identity. It is also a spirituality that anticipates William James' aversion to metaphysical statements, inasmuch as the highest noetic insight of the *Kephalaia Gnostika*

---

[1] See William James, *The Varieties of Religious Experience* (Cambridge, Mass.: Harvard University Press, 1985), 34, 36, 37.

surpasses the reach of human reason and it is not a source for doctrinal statements about God.

Maximos the Confessor, on the contrary, envisages spiritual practice as an embodied reality for individuals who are members of the ecclesial community, and whose identity is ultimately shaped by their relation with their surrounding reality and their neighbor. He also challenges the separation between spirituality and speculative reflection, the former being far more than a "technology of the self," but rather an itinerary introducing us into the divine reality and its relationship with the world, finally enabling us to co-operate with God's on-going work in creation. Does this mean that we come to *know* God's inner being? Yes, and no. According to Maximos, the fullness of God's mystery is never *comprehended*; even as we attain an insight into the very life of God, our identity is never lost. At the same time, through spiritual practice, we may begin to *understand* the divine reality, which sustains the created order and is disclosed in the incarnate Word.

Tsong kha pa's concern with grounding ethical practice in conventional reality mirrors Maximos' critique to the extent that he brings contingency and difference back to the core of spirituality. This is made possible by his conviction that the created order flows from the Buddha's ultimate insight, and that an engagement of the conventional brings us closer to the experience of enlightenment. At the same time, given that the Mahāyāna doctrine of *apratishtitā nirvāna* underpins the teaching of Tsong kha pa as well as the vision of rDzogs chen, neither approach envisages spirituality as a self-serving pursuit indifferent to the needs of other sentient beings. This fundamental agreement is then compounded by their characterization of conventional reality as ultimately empty and therefore as devoid of intrinsic value. As a result, Tsong kha pa's critique of "immediate" or "quietist" approaches amounts to a discussion of which skilful means are better suited to lead one to enlightenment; the *ris med* solution developed by Jigs med ling pa is effectively implicit in Tsong kha pa's vision.

The two Buddhist accounts follow Origenist spirituality in anticipating the Kantian mistrust for epistemic claims about the ultimate, as well as James' call for greater metaphysical restraint in the interpretation of religious experience. Conventional reality might lead us closer to the ultimate, but it is also a ladder that is left behind as we approach our final goal. Thus, even Tsong kha pa's construal of the sacramentality of the contingent is considerably weaker than Maximos' corresponding vision, where, in virtue of God's deifying love, creation as a whole is eventually subsumed into the eschatological order. The knowledge of the divine inscribed in the cosmos and in the mystery of Christ never passes away, but provides the foundation for an ever more penetrating insight. In Maximos' synthesis, there is no demarcation of a conventional order, to which is appended a relationship with the ultimate dimension of reality; rather, creation as a whole exists insofar as it *participates* in God, and receives its being from Him. It is this mystery of participation, disclosed in the vision of the transfigured Christ, which enables Maximos to affirm the ultimate value of creation, in a world where there is no distinction between conventional and ultimate, but rather a hierarchy of being within the same order of reality. For Tsong kha pa, statements about conventional reality have no other referent, whereas for Maximos statements about the created order enable us to make analogical claims about the divine mystery. Arguably, the vision of the dGe lugs master, by severing the relation between conventional discourse and the ultimate insight, unwittingly comes closer to the modern notion of nature as an entirely self-enclosed realm that is open to secular manipulation.

In this chapter, I am going to explore how Maximos' and Tsong kha pa's alternative visions of divine embodiment relate to a number of contentious areas within contemporary systematic discourse. These areas include the possibility of a natural theology, the role of language and philosophical reflection in the articulation of the Christian faith, the sacramental value of contingency and its relation to the liturgy, and the impact of spiritual practice on the construction of the self. Finally, in my conclusion, I am going to address contemporary Buddhist critiques of the Christian notion of divine embodiment, and will suggest that Maximos' notion of incarnation provides us with the resources to develop a Christian theology of religions—a theology that is respectful of difference but affirms the ultimacy of the Christian revelation. This analysis will highlight the points of contact between Tsong kha pa's vision and postmodern construals of language, personhood, and difference, which at the same time find themselves challenged by Maximos' participatory ontology.

WHO IS AFRAID OF NATURAL THEOLOGY? PARTICIPATION AND THE CHALLENGE OF NIHILISM

In his foreword to James K. A. Smith's volume on Radical Orthodoxy, John Milbank expresses his disagreement with those theologians, who uncritically embrace the structures of a given culture or politico-economic system, and then proceed to view them as normative for speculative theological reflection.[2] Smith himself echoes this critique arguing that "formulating the claims of Christian revelation in terms of given cultural frameworks" gives rise to a theology, where religious experience is articulated in "philosophically derived" categories that are ultimately alien to the modality of God's self-disclosure.[3] According to Smith, Christian thinkers who set out to make sense of revelation in (supposedly) "universally accessible" terms quickly move on to advocate the superiority of one culture over all others, subscribing to "imperialist" or "Constantinian" projects.

The concern underlying this critique of "correlationist" strategies is ultimately the fear that theology, by turning to philosophy for guidance, might not only legitimize the autonomy of philosophy as an autonomous endeavor, but might effectively recognize its own subordination to non-theological forms of discourse. When, for instance, certain theologians subject the notion of God to general ontological concepts, they believe they can control the divine mystery by means of limited and inadequate human categories. In this perspective, the appropriation of Aristotelian philosophy by medieval scholasticism is the most obvious example; more recently, one finds this tendency in Bultmann's adoption of Heideggerian thought as the ultimate benchmark for a demythologized Christianity, and in liberation theology's resort to Marxist sociological analysis.[4] Radical Orthodoxy claims that such strategies reduce the position of theology to just one viewpoint among many, and in fact a viewpoint courting the approval of other, supposedly "neutral" sciences. By abandoning the humanities, the natural sciences, and all other disciplines, to their own devices, theology is merely paving the way for their colonization by secular thought, whose long-term goal is the relegation of theology into the realm of the subjective and the conjectural.

What are the roots of secularity's claim to independence? In *Theology and Social Theory*, Milbank explores the history of Western thought, looking for the crisis that ruptured the pre-modern harmony of a world where all spheres of reality and human life were understood as "suspended' from the

---

[2] John Milbank, foreword to James K. A. Smith, *Introducing Radical Orthodoxy: Mapping a Post-secular Theology*, (Grand Rapids, Mich.: Baker Academic, 2004), 14.

[3] James K. A. Smith, *Introducing Radical Orthodoxy*, 35.

[4] In another work, James K. A. Smith goes back to the issue of Bultmann's indebtedness to Heidegger and his blindness to the radically anti-Christian nature of Heidegger's philosophy. See James K. A. Smith, *The Fall of Interpretation: Philosophical Foundations for a Creational Hermeneutic* (Downers Grove, Ill.: InterVarsity Press: 2000), 4–11.

transcendent.[5] This attitude ensured that all human activities were undertaken within a religious horizon, and therefore were oriented towards a goal situated beyond the boundaries of material reality. One may of course question whether such a harmony ever characterized human society as a whole; perhaps, this equilibrium was only achieved imperfectly for brief periods of time in purposefully established communities. For Milbank, what made this harmony possible was the generalized (though implicit) acceptance of a *participatory* worldview: the world receives its being as an utterly gratuitous *gift* from God. In *After Writing*, Catherine Pickstock develops the same theme arguing that within this worldview *all* space was doxologically oriented towards the divine.[6] What happened, however, was that later Western thought challenged this harmonious vision, and severed the created order from its transcendent origin. Authors of the Radical Orthodoxy school see the roots of this rupture in Duns Scotus' turn from analogy to univocity, which upends the Thomist vision of *analogia entis*.[7] For Aquinas, creation exists to the extent that it participates in the being of the creator; God's own existence can then be understood by analogy with the mode whereby creatures exist. Scotus, for his part, turns being into an autonomous category, which is then indifferently distributed to God and to His creatures.[8]

Once this rupture is consumed, everything is transformed. On the one hand, God becomes utterly unknowable; He is no longer ontologically related to creation and as such it is impossible to draw any analogical inference about His being.[9] On the other hand, the created order comes to possess its own subsistence independently of God; it is now possible to understand creation without any reference to its creator. Milbank characterizes this situation as a form of double idolatry that demeans God while exalting creation beyond its due.[10] Philosophy is now sundered from theology, and it

---

[5] John Milbank, *Theology and Social Theory: Beyond Secular Reason* (Oxford, U.K., and Cambridge, Mass.: Blackwell, 1990), 9.

[6] Catherine Pickstock, *After Writing: On the Liturgical Consummation of Philosophy* (Oxford, U.K., and Cambridge, Mass.: Blackwell, 1997), 40–43.

[7] John Milbank, *The World Made Strange: Theology, Language, Culture* (Oxford, U.K., and Cambridge, Mass.: Blackwell, 1997), 42–45.

[8] See also Jean-Luc Marion, *God without Being: Hors-Texte* (trans. T. A. Carlson; Religion and Postmodernism Series, Chicago: University of Chicago Press, 1991), 80–82.

[9] John Milbank and Catherine Pickstock, *Truth in Aquinas* (New York: Routledge, 2000), 33–35.

[10] John Milbank, *The World Made Strange*, 45–47.

is also divided into various branches, each of which explores one area of being without any unifying (overarching) vision. Admittedly, laying the responsibility for this turn entirely at the feet of Scotus may appear unjustified, and critiques of the Radical Orthodoxy school have conceded that Scotus is merely representative of a wider trend away from participatory ontology.[11] The implication of Radical Orthodoxy's construal of the history of Western thought is nonetheless clear: any intellectual endeavor that fails to acknowledge reality's ultimate grounding in the divine being is necessarily nihilistic, since, without God, created things can only be perceived as the *nothing* which they are in themselves.[12]

Milbank and Pickstock see the Scotist turn as the ultimate ancestor of all attempts to build "natural theologies" that work their way up to God without starting from divine revelation. In the worldview of Radical Orthodoxy, any endeavor to argue back to God from a supposedly independent nature is doomed to failure, since, without *analogia entis*, the link between the two realms has been cut; in fact, one risks to create a notion of deity that is just one item out of many, rather than the very ground of being of the earlier Christian tradition.[13] The Suarezian reading of Aquinas which was targeted by the *nouvelle théologiens* is one more consequence of the divorce between grace and the natural order.[14] In fact, scholars of the Radical Orthodoxy school would go even further and dismiss Rahner's approach to Christology (and soteriology) as yet one more instance of a "correlationist" theology that resorts to a "secular" discourse (in this case, anthropology) to express the truths of the Christian revelation.[15] The proposed antidote to these deviations is a resolutely theological narrative, which would assert a "theological" reading of reality as the only legitimate one.

---

[11] See Olivier Boulnois, "Reading Duns Scotus: From History to Philosophy," *Mod Theol* 21.4 (2005), 603–608.

[12] This line of argument is clearly related to Athanasius' reasoning in *De Incarnatione*, 1, 1–5 (PG 25b: 97–106).

[13] James K. A. Smith, *Introducing Radical Orthodoxy*, 100.

[14] Bellarmino, for instance, envisaged the possibility of a wholly *natural* happiness independent of God. See Fergus Kerr, *After Aquinas: Versions of Thomism* (Oxford, U.K., and Cambridge, Mass.: Blackwells, 2002), 232, note 6.

[15] Apparently, according to John Milbank, this type of theology inhabits "a bizarre academic twilight zone," which is only inhabited "by the intellectually craven and impotent." See John Milbank, foreword to James K. A. Smith, *Introducing Radical Orthodoxy*, 12.

Unfortunately, this solution may not be so easily available. Is it actually possible to develop an account of the Christian faith which is *solely* theological? When Pickstock and Milbank call for a return to Aquinas' model of participation, they also advocate a retrieval of Plato that does away with the spiritualizing interpretations of his dialogues and actually revalues embodiment as an expression of the supreme Beauty ever keen to draw all souls to itself.[16] But one might then say that Aquinas and his Radical Orthodoxy followers are themselves indulging in a "correlationist" strategy. After all, they are choosing one set of philosophical categories among many and presenting it as normative for theological discourse. Is this legitimate? Or is this not one more instance of natural theology? In addition, in overemphasizing the subordination of the created order to its divine origin, is there not a risk of erasing the distinction between nature and grace, ultimately blurring the distinction between creation and redemption? Challenging the autonomy of the secular to replace it with a monist approach—one that absorbs everything in God and that fails to respect what Catholic theologians called "the dignity of secondary causality"—seems hardly an improvement.[17]

At this point, if we turn back to Maximos' critique of Origenist spirituality and its counterpart in Tibet, we might find a way out of this conundrum, and show that a natural theology might be developed, which sees itself neither as independent of Christian revelation, nor as entitled to set its terms. In Chapter 3, we saw how Maximos developed his theological reflection in continuity with the efforts on the part of earlier Christian thinkers to recruit Greek philosophical thought at the service of Christian theology. On one hand, there was no doubt that the Cappadocians held "reason" in high regard: the dying Macrina's appeal to a "shared opinion" (*koinē hypolēpsis*), or Gregory of Nazianzos' use of "humanity's common notions," are just two

---

[16] This is a major theme in the first pages of Catherine Pickstock's *After writing*, 10–22. Whether this reading is actually justified is of course one more problem, given the obvious tendency in, say, *Phaedo*, to present the body as a prison whence one ought to try to escape. See Catherine Pickstock, "The Soul in Plato," in Dean-Peter Baker and Patrick Maxwell, eds., *Exploration in Contemporary Continental Philosophy of Religion* (New York: Rodopi, 2003), 115–126, and the criticism of this interpretation in James K. A. Smith, *Introducing Radical Orthodoxy*, 106–108.

[17] This is a critique that has been moved by a number of Catholic theologians, who point out that Radical Orthodoxy is actually far more "Protestant" than many realize. See for instance Nicholas Lash, "Where does Holy Teaching leave Philosophy? Questions on Milbank's Aquinas," *Mod Theol* 15 (1999): 433–45.

examples of a shared esteem for the deliverances of philosophical reasoning.[18] At the same time, expressions such as these were carefully tempered
by the assertion that the weakness of our reason needed the supplementation of faith to overcome its inner contradictions.[19] As noted by Frederick
Norris, the Cappadocians considered the rational faculties a gift from God;
indeed, they believed that there could be no contradiction between revealed
truths and the insights of a purely "rational" theology.[20] "Rational" theology, however, could not reach these truths *autonomously*; the mystery of the
divine economy, of the incarnation and the redemption, were not abstract
truths, but rather realities that had taken place *in time*. As such, one could
resort to classical philosophy to sustain our reflection on the faith, but in
order to explore the significance of Christ's death and resurrection, one had
to consider their impact on our life, and turn to *spiritual experience* as the
chief source for systematic reflection.[21]

Maximos inherited from the Cappadocians an approach to theological
reflection that did not construe natural theology as a self-enclosed system,
but viewed it as a propedeutic exercise whose insights were supplemented—or rather, *aufgehoben*—by the transformation of our lives by the
event of the incarnation. In the words of Jaroslav Pelikan, "natural theology
as *theology* could deal with eternity," but "the theology of revelation as *economy* had to deal with time";[22] the former could study the order of the cosmos, but the latter had to bow before the manifestation of the Lord in history. Indeed, it is only through the incarnation that natural theology would
acquire its proper orientation and significance. The hypostatic union welded
these two aspects of theology into a wider synthesis; as Gregory of Nyssa
notes in the *Oratio Catechetica*, it was the eternal Son of God, "whose being
extended before all time and before all the aeons," who chose to enter the
world of temporal becoming, and in so doing led humanity—which was

---

[18] See Gregory of Nyssa, *De Anima et Resurrectione* (PG 46: 72); Gregory of Nazianzos, *Orationes* 28, 6 (PG 36: 31–34).

[19] In *Orationes* 29, 21 (PG 36: 101–104), Gregory of Nazianzos claims that
"faith is what gives fullness to our reason" (*hē gar pistis tou kath' hēmas logou plērōsis*).

[20] Frederick Norris, *Faith gives Fullness to Reasoning: The Five Theological Orations of
Gregory Nazianzen* (Supplements to *Vigiliae Christianae*, 13. Leiden: Brill Academic
Publishing, 1997), 122–140, *et passim*.

[21] See for instance Basil of Caesarea, *De Spiritu Sancto* 8, 18 (PG 32: 97–100).

[22] Jaroslav Pelikan, *Christianity and Classical Culture*, 270.

veering towards the nothingness of sin—back to the realm of being.[23] The Council of Chalcedon was effectively an attempt to articulate in more precise terms the belief that, in a particular place and at a particular time in history, the cosmic order that natural theology admires had become manifest in the flesh.

When Maximos develops his critique against Origenist spirituality in *Amb.* 7, he has two more centuries of Christological reflection behind him. Yet, the motive of his polemic is not so different from what drove Gregory of Nyssa to write his tract *Contra Eunomium*. For Eunomius, divine revelation merely confirmed the insights of classical natural theology; there was nothing in the deposit of faith that could not eventually be known by human reason, and in fact, the human intellect could come to the same understanding of created reality enjoyed by God Himself.[24] In this perspective, if our knowledge falls short of the plenitude that is characteristic of God, this is not the natural consequence of our finite condition, perhaps made more burdensome by sin; rather, it is an instance of "noetic malignity," since as a matter of fact not even the divine essence is beyond the reach of the human intellect.[25] The Cappadocians viewed this approach as a form of intellectual pride, and resorted to the language of negation to place careful limits to our knowledge of God, whom we can apprehend indirectly in creation, but never fully comprehend.[26] In the *Hexaemeron*, Basil of Caesarea observes that our intellect cannot even come to a full understanding of created reality; thus, it is even more impossible to come to an understanding of the divine nature, even if the natural order and Scriptural revelation offer us hints that can be developed into articles of faith.[27] In this perspective, theology must learn to tread the difficult balance between an apophaticism underscoring the ontological distinction between God and creation, and a more kataphatic discourse that offers a systematic articulation of the content of faith.

By claiming that the human mind can fully comprehend reality and that our intellect is potentially no more limited than God's, Eunomios' vi-

---

[23] Gregory of Nyssa, *Oratio Catechetica* 25; 35; 37 (PG 45: 65–68; 85–82; 93–98). Of course this is a rendition of an Athanasian theme.

[24] Gregory of Nyssa, *Contra Eunomium*, 2 (PG 45: 483–488).

[25] See for instance Jaroslav Pelikan, *Christianity and Classical Culture*, 51, on the Cappadocians' critique of Eunomios.

[26] See Vladimir Lossky, *In the Image and Likeness of God* (Crestwood, N.Y.: St. Vladimir's Seminary Press, 1985), 31–45.

[27] Basil of Caesarea, *Homiliae in Hexaemeron*, 1, 8–12 (PG29b: 19–28).

sion also poses an implicit, but no less real challenge to the understanding of creation that the Cappadocians had developed to counter the pantheistic tendencies of late Antiquity. Admittedly, Eunomios' own confession of faith did not deny divine transcendence, and stated that, in creating the world, God had not been in need of "matter or parts or natural instruments."[28] The notion, however, that intellectual purification erases what distinguishes us from the divine condition makes one wonder whether the belief that God is "wholly Other" reflects a temporary situation to be eventually effaced, or perhaps our inability to see that we are at all times equal to God. But this ambiguity is very close to what one finds in Evagrios' writings. In the spiritual writings included in the *Philokalia*, Evagrios had contended that the pursuit of *gnōsis* enabled one to retrieve one's identity with the original undifferentiated *nous*. In the *Kephalaia Gnostika*, however, Evagrios takes up Origen's reflections about the pre-existence of Christ's soul and argues that what set Christ apart was his ability to preserve the original noetic insight unobfuscated by concepts and plurality.[29] We saw earlier how the condemnation of 553 that anathematized the isochristism of the Evagrian school effectively opposed a pantheistic sleight of hand which erased the fundamental distinction between creation and the creator. At the same time, it also condemned the tendency to elevate the undifferentiated noetic insight into an ontological category setting the terms for what is and what is not divine.

Maximos' critique of Origenism, much like Gregory's attack on Eunomios, wanted to reassert the analogical relation between the created order and the divine reality, which was then reflected in the analogical nature of our knowledge of God. Maximos and Gregory intuited that a Christian understanding of practice could not reduce spiritual progress to intellectual purification, but had to integrate praxis after the model of Christ. Unlike Gregory, however, Maximos' critique is primarily Christological; it is the Chalcedonian reading of the incarnation that provides him with a matrix to articulate his understanding of the created order, of the potentialities and limits of theology, and of the character and purpose of spiritual practice. The notion of distinct realities subsumed in a union that did not jeopardize,

---

[28] Gregory of Nyssa, *Contra Eunomium* 3 (PG 45: 577–582).

[29] See Origen, *De Principiis*, 2, 6 (PG 11: 209–215); Rowan Williams, "Origen on the Soul of Jesus," in Henri Crouzel and Richard Hanson, eds., *Origeniana Tertia* (Rome: Edizioni dell'Ateneo, 1981), 131–137; Evagrios, *Kephalaia Gnostika*, 1, 77, in *Les Six Centuries des 'Kephalaia Gnostica'*, 52–53.

but actually ratified their difference, enables him to overcome the vision of a purposeless materiality destined to dissolution. The manifestation in the flesh of the incarnate Word, who transcends the boundaries of finitude to fill the heavens, intimates the synthesis of kataphatic and apophatic discourse. Finally, the deification of humanity in the hypostatic union sets the pattern for the eschatological transfiguration of humanity, as well as of the cosmos as a whole. By appropriating and grafting the doctrine of the *logoi spermatikoi* onto Christology, Maximos is following the Cappadocian strategy of integrating natural theology into the horizon of the divine economy; by exploring how the mystery of the redemption impacts the natural order, he ensures that the specificity of Christian dogma is not dissolved into an a-temporal vision, and he shows how the incarnation reorients history towards its authentic goal.[30] In this way, Maximos' theology of divine embodiment invests the contingency of the cosmos with a sacramental value that grounds natural theology in the incarnation, and thereby makes it legitimate, without asserting the autonomy of the natural order.

The question is then whether other (non-Christocentric) participatory models could afford a similar solution. What about Tsong kha pa's own version of participation? In Chapter 6, we surveyed the intricate controversies on the nature of Buddhahood which opposed Yogācāra and Madhyamaka thinkers: some interpreters of the *Abhisamayālamkāra* identified the body of *dharma* with the body of knowledge (*jñāna-dharmakāya*), whereas the followers of Haribhadra, including Tsong kha pa, tended to distinguish between these two realities. Much like Maximos in a very different context, the dGe lugs master was concerned with the relationship of ultimate reality with the conditioned world. He was eager to explore whether the latter gave us hints as to the nature of the former, and whether this totally "other" dimension was accessible to ordinary practitioners. Our contemplation of the *dharmatā* (which function very much like the *logoi spermatikoi*) is meant gradually to disclose the order of the universe, to set the terms for the practice of the six perfections, and eventually, as explained in the *Lam rim chen mo*, to attain Buddhahood itself.

---

[30] It is in this perspective that one must also read Maximos' defense of the doctrine of the human will of Christ. If Christ had had no human will, and thus had been unable to make ethical choices in the course of his life, a fundamental aspect of human experience, which stretches *through time*, would not have been redeemed. Dithelitism is the victory of history over a-temporality. See Felix Heinzer, *Gottes Sohn als Mensch*, Ch. 1.

Again, it seems, spiritual experience becomes a source for philosophical reflection, which then feeds back into practice. Tsong kha pa's vindication of conventional discourse and his incorporation into Buddhist practices of what is effectively a form of natural philosophy is developed in opposition to the attack on "views" typical of the rDzogs chen school. Chapter 5 already touched on the points of contact between the Evagrian worldview and the cosmology of the *Kun byed rgyal po*, but now we can observe that, in the same way as Scotus had elevated the category of being over God, a functionally similar role seems to be played by the all-encompassing "pure basis." Earlier, we saw how Radical Orthodoxy's preference for the Thomist construal of truth reflected the conviction that the totalitarian pretensions of metaphysics could be overcome only by positing the source of being in God.[31] A Christian reader could then argue that Tsong kha pa's approach comes closer to Aquinas than to Scotus, inasmuch as the dGe lugs master distinguishes the "body of conditioned gnoses" from the highest insight, whereas the followers of rDzogs chen seemingly subordinate Buddhahood to a pre-existent ontological category, which encompasses all aspects of reality without distinction. The contention that awareness of *ka dag* unveils our pre-existent Buddha nature echoes the Evagrian search for the pure *nous*.[32] At the same time, Tsong kha pa's understanding of Buddhahood enables him to posit (in the *Legs bShad sNying po*) the contemplation of the natural order (natural theology, or *theōria*) as part and parcel of spiritual practice, and as setting the terms (in the *Lam rim chen mo*) for the development of the six perfections (*praxis*).

Some of the conclusions drawn earlier about natural theology are now cast in a different light. On one hand, a reader of the *Kun byed rgyal po* quickly realizes that denying a participatory ontology in no way entails the autonomy of the secular; in fact, rDzogs chen's vision is emphatic in asserting that *nothing* exists apart from the pure basis, and that thinking otherwise is a delusion. On the other hand, the distinction between *svābhāvikakāya* and

---

[31] This is why Milbank and Pickstock talk of theo-ontology in Aquinas. See their *Truth in Aquinas*, 33–34.

[32] As we saw in Ch. 5, the *Kun byed rgyal po* and the *Kephalaia Gnostika* envisage the plurality of phenomena as emerging from an undifferentiated reality (the primordial Buddha, or the henad). Evagrios' cosmology tends to view the emergence of plurality as first and foremost a negative phenomenon, whereas rDzogs chen is readier to view the whole of phenomenal reality as a gift to sentient beings striving to escape suffering. In this respect, the rNying ma understanding of conventional reality as sacramental is stronger than its dGe lugs counterpart.

jñāna-dharmakāya in Tsong kha pa's understanding of Buddhahood shows how the dGe lugs defense of conventional discourse differs from Maximos' parallel retrieval of classical natural theology. The contemplation of the *logoi* discloses the divine plan for the cosmos, which, "in these last times," has been revealed in Christ; the practice of *theōria* enables one to gaze into the abyss of God's own mystery. Within Tsong kha pa's vision, however, philosophical discourse remains within the boundaries of the conventional; the very possibility to make "claims" of any sort about the *svābhāvikakāya* appears a contradiction in terms, since emptiness is beyond the reach of human discourse. Of course, Christian apophatic theology was also trying to affirm the ultimate incomprehensibility of the divine, but for the Cappadocians and for Maximos the created world could furnish the basis of analogous statements, whereas here conventional and ultimate truth belong to two different epistemological plains. As such, Tsong kha pa's ontological vision can envisage conventional reality as a path to Buddhahood, but this construal of participation entails that philosophical reflection is only an instrumental form of discourse. Contemplation and philosophical speculation may lead one to ultimate reality, but are fully superseded at the moment of awakening.[33]

These considerations invite one to ask a number of further questions. Is it truly the case that a participatory ontology is necessarily more attuned to the Christian deposit of faith than an account which resorts to different ontological categories? Or perhaps some accounts of participation are better than others? If so, can we still learn something from non-participatory accounts? And then, does natural theology *necessarily* presuppose the autonomy of the secular realm? We saw that Maximos offers the foundations for a natural theology that grounds the cosmos within the eternal Logos, but could one develop a natural theology using the insights of a non-Christian system of thought that asserts the dependence of creation upon some other extrinsic source? If this is the case, perhaps Christian theologians can still learn something from Tsong kha pa's defense of conventionality, or from the idiosyncratic ontology of rDzogs chen. And finally, though no less crucially, is it really helpful to follow Radical Orthodoxy in its distinction between "theological" from "non-theological" views? Perhaps what we are

---

[33] Parenthetically, this parallels Origen's conviction that in the end the Wisdom revealed in Christ will be superseded by a higher, totally "spiritual" form of divine wisdom. See Origen, *Hom. Lev*, 4, 6 (PG 12: 440–441); *Comm Jo*. 1, 8 (PG 14: 33–36); also Jean Daniélou, *Origen*, 264–5.

facing are just divergent theological standpoints, which resort to different philosophical resources.

Let us start from the last question. First, reading the debates surrounding Eunomios and the Evagrian school in terms of an opposition between a "theological" vision consistent with the Christian tradition and a dissenting "philosophical" view fails to consider that the positions regarded as representative of the Christian "tradition" themselves emerged out of a struggle between conflicting interpretations of the deposit of faith. If we were to apply Pickstock's categories to Eunomios and Evagrios, their belief in the mind's ability to attain a full knowledge of reality would be no less "idolatrous" than Scotus'; in fact, the two of them are far more explicit than the latter in positing our ability to comprehend the divine essence. What the Radical Orthodoxy school terms the "turn to univocity" can then be considered the retrieval of a strand of the Christian tradition that had been superseded by the emerging Christological orthodoxy. At the same time, one of the factors that distinguish Maximos' account from its Origenist counterpart is the fact that in his vision *theōria* sets the terms for *praxis*. Thus, as we noted in Chapter 7, we come to the paradoxical conclusion that the non-theistic vision of Tsong kha pa as well as the radically non-participatory ontology of the *Kun byed rgyal po*, in virtue of their commitment to *apratishtita nirvāna*, come closer to Maximos' vision than the (Christian) pantheism of the *Kephalaia Gnostika*. If the vocation of the Christian is one of ethical as well as intellectual transformation, is the practice of rDzogs chen not closer to the Gospel message than the solipsistic introversion of Evagrios? Does Tsong kha pa's distinction between *svābhāvikakāya* and *jñāna-dharmakāya* perhaps offer a less reductive understanding of ultimate reality than the one intimated by Scotist univocity? It appears that some Christian theologians might have to look beyond confessional boundaries to be reminded of the dangers of their meta-narratives.

Rather than insisting on the caesura between the proponents of a "Scotist" worldview and the apostles of participation, the contrast that emerges within the Christian tradition is one between a worldview where the purification of the human intellect is sufficient to reach the highest epistemological insight, and one where contemplation must be accompanied by practice to enter more deeply into the divine mystery. As such, instead of distinguishing between a purely "theological" stance and one guilty of accommodation to alien forms of discourse, it might be more helpful to acknowledge that each position tries to combine "theological" and "philosophical" elements. These attempts at synthesis between different schools of thought underpin both Tsong kha pa's participatory meta-narrative and the mythological imagery of rDzogs chen; both of them integrate *theōria* with *praxis* even as their vision of the immanent order constantly hovers on the edge of nothingness. Some degree of familiarity with this non-Christian controversy not only unmasks the pretense to universality of the Radical Orthodoxy meta-narrative; it also shows that spiritual practice can co-exist with a non-participatory worldview, and that even a participatory worldview might be unable to affirm the ultimate value of contingent reality. The abjuration of univocity *alone* is highly unlikely to lead everyone back to the harmonious fold of a Christian worldview.

What do we need then to develop a coherent, and authentically transformative synthesis between theology and natural contemplation? My answer would be that the participatory worldview advocated by Radical Orthodoxy necessitates a vigorous Chalcedonian supplementation. Maximos' debunking of the Evagrian system ultimately hinged on replacing the univocal reading of Gregory of Nazianzos' *moira theou* with a participatory interpretation modeled after the hypostatic union; we will see below how this even guarantees the very possibility of theological discourse. Only in this way can one break out of the impasse concerning the nature and purpose of a natural theology. Milbank's and Smith's account of the ontological turn seems to assume that all natural theology is wedded to a strategy of self-destruction, since it undercuts participation and thereby demeans the created order; but the *Ambigua* clearly show that this is not the case. To use a Christological image, we could say that the Evagrian system fails in the same way that the *homo assumptus* theory failed; philosophy talks on behalf of theology, or rather it has forced theology to seek its approval, as if the assent of Christ's humanity had been necessary for the incarnation. For Maximos, on the other hand, the horizon of the divine economy encompasses the philosophical system; to use yet another Chalcedonian metaphor, the hypostasis of theology assumes an anhypostatic philosophical nature.

For Maximos, the mystery of the incarnation not only makes a natural theology possible and legitimate, but actually turns it into an integral part of spiritual practice. The choice then is not between participation and natural theology, but rather between a natural theology based on a Christocentric view of participation, and a natural theology based on purely philosophical presuppositions. The Origenist worldview, moving from the fragmentation of the henad to its final restoration, is unable to ground a natural theology in God's being, since it envisages material creation as an afterthought ultimately unconnected with the divine reality. If the *Kephalaia Gnostika* are right to believe that Christ's kingdom of plurality shall come to an end, this is because they let the *exitus-reditus* cosmology of the Middle-Platonists set the terms of their understanding of redemption; and the undifferentiated *nous* is no more affirmative of creation than the *svābhāvikakāya*. The *Ambigua*, on the contrary, note that it is only the incarnate Christ who unlocks the mysteries of the book of nature; it is in the eternal Logos that the individual *logoi* move, exist, and have their being.

Why would Tsong kha pa's position fail to offer an adequate alternative? The participatory ontology developed by the dGe lugs master, by divorcing the ultimate from the conventional and seeking an ordering principle for the natural order within the conventional alone, can only support a natural theology whose terms are independent of ultimate reality and which might sustain our spiritual progress. This type of natural theology can tell us nothing of ultimate reality in itself. Even if conventional reality helps us attain enlightenment, no analogical inference is possible from the conventional to the ultimate. In Christ, the dialectic of unity and plurality is eschatologically preserved; in the *svābhāvikakāya*, terms like "unity" and "plurality" lose all meaning. What is needed then is not merely a participatory worldview, but one that, as Maximos intuited in *Amb*. 41, explodes the dichotomy between created and uncreated, conventional and ultimate—finally, one that is based on the hypostatic union.[34]

Maximos shows us that affirming the autonomy of the natural order does not entail affirming its independence from the divine reality. For him, humanity is never fully human until it has been deified; in the same way, the created order will truly come into its own when transfigured in Christ on the last day. If this orientation to a supernatural foundation is lost, humanity is no longer able to relate to the different aspects of creation in line with God's will. Disharmony ensues, and the natural order becomes just a resource that one can use for our own purposes and eventually dismiss. In Heideggerian terms, the Christocentric *theōria* of Maximos is a form of *besinnendes Denken*, seeking for *Sinn* outside its own parameters; its alternative is a form of *rechnendes Denken*, where creation is the object of a soteriological utilitarianism bordering on nihilism. Inasmuch as it affirms an instrumental value for conventional reality, the Buddhist approach comes closer to *rechnendes Denken*. Tsong kha pa's Buddhological speculation does not postulate an external ontological source for the universe; in the *Lam rim chen mo* the ultimate transcendental horizon is the utterly empty insight (the *svābhāvikakāya*) which undergirds the world of phenomena. Perhaps, as

---

[34] Maximos the Confessor, *Amb*. 41 (PG 91: 1304–1309); Lars Thunberg, *Microcosm and Mediator*, 404–427.

Connor Cunningham suggests in *Genealogy of Nihilism*, this acknowledgment of the ontological nothingness of the immanent order can serve as a sort of *preambula fidei* for a participatory and (even more crucially) incarnational ontology.[35]

ILLEGITIMATE WORDS? MAXIMOS, THE *SVĀBHĀVIKAKĀYA*, AND THE FLIGHT FROM THEOLOGY

In his work *Of grammatology*, Jacques Derrida takes up and develops the structuralist approaches to linguistics associated with Ferdinand de Saussure. Saussure had argued that within the study of language one can discern a synchronic axis, which explores the timeless system of language and its fixed laws known as "general grammar," and a diachronic axis, which views language as a series of speech-acts that follow one another, a chain of signifying elements whose meaning may actually change over time.[36] In this perspective, the meaning of a proposition is something that emerges from the interaction of different elements, such as nouns, verbs, and propositions. This emphasis on *difference* would become Derrida's central concern; but Derrida would also critique Saussure's "metaphysical" aspirations—such as his presupposition that there was such a thing as an objective structure of language—as well as the tendency—which was shared with Roman Jacobson[37]—to emphasize the *spoken* over the *written* word.[38] This higher regard for oral over written discourse signaled a hope that the spoken word could give unmediated access to the object signified, but for Derrida any belief in unmediated representation is a delusion. As such, he chooses to concentrate on the theory of writing to oppose what he terms "logocentric repression," and to explore how the belief in the actual presence of reality is constantly being produced through the mediation of language.[39]

It is not difficult to see that Derrida's linguistic critique has important implications for theology. Derrida opposes the ever changing flux of lan-

---

[35] See Connor Cunningham, *Genealogy of Nihilism: Philosophy of Nothing and the Difference of Theology* (London and New York: Routledge, 2002), xiii; also James K. A. Smith, *Introducing Radical Orthodoxy*, 102.

[36] Ferdinand de Saussure, *Course in General Linguistics* (trans. R. Harris; London: Duckworth, 1983), 99–109, 139.

[37] Roman Jakobson and Moris Halle, *Fundamentals of Language* (New York: Walter de Gruyter, 2002), 6–30.

[38] Jacques Derrida, *On Grammatology* (trans. G. C. Spivak; Baltimore, Md.: John Hopkins University Press, 1976), 68–74.

[39] Jacques Derrida, *On Grammatology*, 42–51.

guage to the human desire for the immutable and the unchangeable, which subordinates the written word to a speech "dreaming of plenitude."[40] In the Hellenistic tradition and in the Christian Scriptures, this fully present speech, which underpins language and sustains its meaning, is of course the eternal Logos, which became manifest in the incarnate Christ. For Derrida, this belief has rendered theologians oblivious of the limitations of their language; they have become convinced that theological discourse truly expresses ultimate reality, with the result that they worship their own conceptual creations.[41] In this perspective, even Saussure's belief in the metaphysical foundations of language is fundamentally theological in nature. Derrida insists that "Being" as such is the horizon of significance for which the written word constantly yearns, and which is constantly being created as every element of language refers to something other than itself.[42] Derrida calls this horizon, which theologians identify with God, a "quasi-transcendental," since it is simultaneously that which grounds linguistic difference, and a product of human discourse.

Caputo's project of a "religion without a religion" is then an attempt to transfer Derrida's deconstruction of logocentrism to the terrain of theological discourse.[43] For Caputo, traditional theologians holding on to their belief in the plenitude of meaning appear like unfortunate creatures lost in a Heideggerian forest, mistaking intimations of an external world for authentic hints of a wholly transcendent reality. In this perspective, there might be *Spuren*, but there is no way out of the forest; theology cannot hope to escape the game of difference (or rather, *différance*), since all "objective" systems of reference are historically constructed.[44] It becomes clear then that

[40] Jacques Derrida, *On Grammatology*, 71.

[41] Jacques Derrida, *The Margins of Philosophy* (trans. A. Bass; Chicago: University of Chicago Press, 1981), 266–270. Admittedly, Derrida never discusses individual instances of "logocentric" discourse in Patristic theology, focusing on more modern authors such as Hegel.

[42] See also Graham Ward, *Theology and Contemporary Critical Theory* (London: Palgrave Macmillan, 2000), 11–13.

[43] John D. Caputo, *The Prayers and Tears of Jacques Derrida: Religion without Religion* (Bloomington and Indianapolis, Ind.: Indiana University Press, 1997), 26–41.

[44] John D. Caputo, *The Prayers and Tears of Jacques Derrida*, 1–6 ("God is not différance—An Impossible Situation"). Ontology is now *a passion inutile*; however, since we will forever be "haunted" by the desire for a full parousia of meaning, Caputo coins the term "hauntology" to indicate the foundationalist yearnings that continue to disturb philosophical discourse.

any theological discourse in the traditional sense of the word has become impossible. The space opened by *différance* cannot be filled by a God, because this move could only be justified as a leap of faith; the very possibility of revelation has been eliminated, since discourse on ultimate reality can only be constructed "from below."[45] If we want to talk about the ultimate, the radically other, we cannot commit the fallacy to enclose this "other" within an anticipatory horizon; even negative theology, as long as it seeks a unity with a wholly present transcendent reality, has failed to appreciate fully the extent to which language sets the terms for our imagination.[46]

We might wonder at this point whether a theologian could respond to Derrida's challenge without succumbing to Caputo's post-religious horizon and thereby evacuating theological discourse of all positive content. Instead of assuming a defensive attitude and acquiescing to a theology without a transcendental referent, could one not attempt to contest Derrida's accusations and question his portrayal of theological discourse? It might be that what he is portraying is a straw man of his own invention for the sake of developing his argument. I am going to argue that Maximos the Confessor, in fact, would have agreed with Derrida's critique, but that the incarnational vision of the former shows how theology can break out of the impasse of linguistic determination. Tsong kha pa's approach to transcendence and his critique of Svatantrika philosophy, on the contrary, come closer to Caputo's construal of religion, and at the same time intimate the extent to which the latter's flight from theology is itself linguistically determined.

Maximos' theology of the eternal Logos did not solely mirror his preoccupation with natural theology, but also his concern that Origenist spirituality effectively undermined the normativity and ultimacy of Scriptural revelation. Earlier centuries had witnessed intense disputes concerning the relation of New and Old Testament; for the Marcionites, the belief that God's covenant with Israel had been fully superseded made them question

---

[45] Jacques Derrida, *Speech and Phenomena and Other Essays on Husserl's Theory of Signs* (trans. D. Allison; Evanston, Ill.: Northwestern University Press, 1973), 132–136. This work critiques Husserl's phenomenological theory and its alleged blindness to the impossibility to escape the reach of language.

[46] Emmanuel Levinas accuses Husserl and Heidegger of "violence" because they submit "the other" to anticipatory horizons, and advocates a turn to negative theology, but Derrida argues that Levinas is still guilty of believing in the positive infinity of the infinitely other, and therefore of trying to escape linguistic determination. See Jacques Derrida, *Writing and Difference* (trans. A. Bass; London: Routledge & Kegan Paul, 1978), 83.

whether the Old Testament could still be regarded as sacred scripture, or whether in fact it had been inspired by a deity completely different from the God of love of the New Testament. Book 4 of *De Principiis* explores the issue of Scriptural interpretation in great detail, affirming the superiority of the spiritual sense over the literal sense. Origen is quite ready to admit that the letter of Scripture contains the occasional mistakes, though he argues that even these mistakes are intended by the Holy Spirit so as to encourage us to look for a deeper, spiritual significance.[47] Origen clearly affirms the unity of Old and New Testament, both of which gesture towards the incarnation of the eternal Word in Christ, but he also tends to view the Scriptural narrative as a veil that covers the mysterious reality of God. Even the wisdom of Scripture falls short of the authentic divine wisdom that will be revealed on the last day.[48]

This intimation that Scripture, in virtue of being linguistically determined, inevitably falls short of the reality to which it refers, is of course an important concern for Maximos as well. The crucial difference, however, is that for Maximos what the *logoi* of Scripture reveal about the eternal Wisdom of God possesses an ultimate validity, despite the *logoi*'s inability to give *full* expression to the mystery. This differs from the Evagrian position in *On Prayer*, where human language, with its array of different concepts and constructions, belongs to the realm of *dianoia*, which is eventually superseded by the *nous*.[49] The theological endeavor is thereby linked to the world of plurality which the *apokatastasis* is supposed to overcome; theology cannot endure forever if the kingdom of the Logos is supposed to pass. In this perspective, Evagrios' reflections on "pure prayer" envisage not only material creation, but also language as an afterthought, something that cannot belong to the purity of the undifferentiated *nous*.

In the vision on Tabor, however, it is not only the *logoi* of creation that point to the transfigured Christ, it is also the *logoi* of Scripture; Moses and Elijah are also read as symbolizing the Law and the prophets, both finding their fulfillment in the event of the incarnation.[50] Developing a theme that had played an important role in the exegetical works of John Chrysostom, Maximos asserts that the manifestation in the flesh of the eternal Word of

---

[47] Origen, *De Principiis*, 4, 2–4 (PG 11: 345–350).

[48] Jean Daniélou, *Platonisme et théologie mystique*, 53–59.

[49] Evagrios, *On Prayer: 153 Texts*, 57–58, 62–63, in *Philokalia*, Vol. 1, 62–63; in Migne as Nilus of Sinai, *De Oratione*, 56–57, 61–62 (PG 79: 1177–1180, 1179–1180).

[50] Maximos the Confessor, *Amb.* 10 (PG 91: 1164a-1164d).

God is what gives validity to human language and thereby makes theological discourse possible.[51]

One may object that this is exactly what Derrida condemned: a speech "dreaming of plenitude," the unmediated disclosure of a transcendental presence, a discourse that grants us direct access to a reality which is not determined by language. In this perspective, even if Evagrios continues to believe in the existence of a fully transcendent reality, he is at least sufficiently perceptive to admit that language can grant us no access to it; if theology is to survive, it must comes to terms with its own provisional and self-referential character. But both Evagrios and Derrida seem to assume that, whenever theologians make a statement about God, these statements are necessarily univocal, that they describe God *as He is*, and that they entirely open Him up to the scrutiny of the human intellect. If this were the case, one should come to terms with the eventual demise of language envisaged by Evagrios, or simply flee from theology as suggested by Caputo; and even Maximos would do likewise. Maximos, however, *never* believed that theology could grant us *direct* access to a reality not determined by language; equally, he never affirmed the possibility of an *unmediated* disclosure of the divine. In fact, Maximos is not even overly concerned with *speech*; the *logoi* pointing to the divine Wisdom are the *logoi* of Scripture, because Scripture constitutes the foundation for an endless game of interpretation, whose performance constitutes part of our spiritual *praxis*, and which gradually assimilates us to Christ.

Much like Derrida's *On Grammatology*, Maximos' *Ambigua* expresses a deep-seated conviction that there is no such thing as an unchanging correspondence between words and reality that fully accounts for the meaning of linguistic statements. Both of them, on the contrary, view meaning as *emerging* from the on-going interaction of different linguistic elements, which necessarily point beyond themselves. Maximos and Derrida agree that a univocal understanding of language, which affirms the possibility to attain a comprehensive and final insight into reality, is ultimately untenable. The claim that theology could fully disclose the divine reality was the reason for Eunomios' condemnation by the Cappadocians; and Maximos would be the first to condemn any such form of linguistic idolatry. Unlike Derrida, however, Maximos believes that it is possible to talk of ultimate reality analogically; ultimately, he has more faith in the power of language than his con-

---

[51] John Chrysostom, in *Catechesis Prima* (PG 49: 223–231), notes how Christianity effectively "redeems language." This theme is echoed throughout his writings.

temporary counterpart. The knowledge of God we gain from Scripture is imperfect and partial, a sort of bait thrown by the eternal Logos to entice us into deeper intimacy with him; but without the mediation of Scripture (*écriture*), and without our own engagement with the text, we cannot gain any insight into the mystery of God. Maximos knows very well that his theological constructions fall short of God's ultimate reality, but acknowledging that language sets the terms of theological discourse does not entail that theological discourse is *per se* illegitimate or doomed.[52]

In line with these considerations, Tsong kha pa's construal of the *svābhāvikakāya* is surprisingly reminiscent of Derrida's notion of "quasi-transcendental." The re-evaluation of conventional reality in the *Legs bShad sNying po* is accompanied by a re-evaluation of philosophical reflection, which in its turn is sustained by a constant engagement of the texts of the Buddhist tradition. We know that the *jñāna-dharmakāya* encompasses the *dharmatā* of materiality, but the "body of pure gnoses" also contains the *dharmāḥ* of the texts of the Buddhist tradition, which are also an expression of the Buddha's wisdom. We noted in Chapter 6 that the introduction to the *Legs bShad sNying po* presents the Buddha as an embodiment of reason; as such, the texts of the Buddhist tradition can be said to express the Buddha's wisdom in a way that is functionally similar to the Logos' presence in the Christian Scriptures. The *svābhāvikakāya* is then the emptiness of the Buddha's ultimate insights, qualities and *kāyas*; it is an undifferentiated intellection, much like Evagrios' *nous*.

If the *Kephalaia Gnostika* discussed the dialectical relationship of *dianoia* and *nous*, Haribhadra's exegesis of the *Abhisamayālamkāra* opposes the conventional gnoses of the *jñāna-dharmakāya* and the emptiness of the *svābhāvikakāya*. While Evagrios tends to present *dianoia* with negative overtones, Tsong kha pa is readier to construe the *jñāna-dharmakāya* as the way sentient beings can work their way towards the Buddha's ultimate insight; if the *nous* of the *Philokalia*, or the henad of the *Kephalaia Gnostika*, are not the *result* of using our *dianoia*, the *svābhāvikakāya* emerges out of an earlier engagement with the conventional. In Maximos, a relationship of causality exists between language and its foundation in the eternal Logos, but it is the latter that constitutes the ground of the former; for Tsong kha pa, this relationship goes both ways, as language, so to speak, creates the conditions for the emergence of its ontological source. The *svābhāvikakāya* comes closer to

---

[52] Vittorio Croce, *Tradizione e ricerca. Il metodo teologico di san Massimo il Confessore* (Milan: Vita e Pensiero, 1974), 12, 21–28, *et passim*.

Caputo's "hauntological" categories, a metaphor for the source of *différance*, itself shaped by human discourse.

The surprising concurrence between Tsong kha and Derrida shows us that in the absence of a metaphysics of participation accounting for the emergence of language, its place is taken by an immanentized metaphysics, where a univocal understanding of language is supplemented by an ultimate reality which totally defies description (as in Tsong kha pa) or can at most be expressed metaphorically (as in Caputo). In this perspective, the language used in the *Kun byed rgyal po* to describe primordial awareness is purely metaphorical: the images of the primordial Buddha, of its emissary Vajrasattva, and of their splendid retinues, are not based on actual ontological features of *ka dag*, but on our mental projections upon the pure basis. Similarly Caputo's *Religion after Religion* calls for a metaphorical reading of the fundamental tenets of Christian theology, which are no longer descriptions of a reality, but culturally determined expressions of the humanity's frustrated desire for the ultimate.

What distinguishes Maximos from this approach is that he has no time for metaphors; and in fact, metaphors are not what we need. His vision extricates theology from the strictures of linguistic determinacy by asserting that the created order participates in God's being, and therefore human discourse participates in God's own speech. If the order of nature is regulated by *analogia entis*, the order of speech is regulated by *analogia verbi*. Language is able to describe the world inasmuch as it reflects the divine Wisdom which is epitomized by the Logos, and which has addressed humanity in the words of Scripture. An interesting passage in the *Quaestiones ad Thalassium* describes how the Word of God might "admit of circumscription" as far as the historical events it narrates, but remains "wholly uncircumscribed" in terms of its spiritual import, since "the God who has spoken" is by nature "beyond circumscription."[53] The depth of meaning found in the *logoi* of Scripture ensures that "the meaning of what is written" is disclosed in different manners to every individual—in line with his or her degree of spiritual attainment—and is thereby disclosed through our engagement with the text. Those who think that the language of the Bible cannot have more than one meaning "have neglected the whole mystery of the incarnation," since the manifestation of the Logos in the flesh is an invitation to look for

---

[53] Maximos the Confessor, *Q.Th* 50 (PG 90: 465b-468c).

the spiritual significance of the law. Accordingly, *Amb. 21* claims that "the Gospel too […] is flesh and spirit."[54]

Maximos is convinced that the mystery of the incarnation discloses the perichoretic relationship of multiplicity and unity within the contingent order of nature, but this dynamics can also be applied to the phenomenon of language. Iris Murdoch observes that for Derrida *écriture* plays the role of God, but she does not acknowledge that Derrida's *écriture* is burdened by the inability to transcend its own plurality.[55] Thus, *écriture* might be likened more properly to Tsong kha pa's understanding of *jñāna-dharmakāya*, which sets the terms for the conventional reality we inhabit and is thus bound to multiplicity and conceptuality. Aidan Nichols observes instead that in the context of the Christian Scriptures, "plurality" is represented by the letter (*ta grammata*, or *ta graphenta*), in opposition to the uniqueness of the Logos (*to sēmainomen*).[56] Much as the created order exerts its soteriological potential as the individual discerns the divine wisdom operating in creation; in the same way, Scripture discloses its salvific power as the practice of exegesis trains us to recognize the presence in the text of the eternal Word.

Once more, the theology of divine embodiment developed by Maximos offers a way out of a speculative impasse. In the *Legs bShad sNying po*, therefore, the wisdom of the *jñāna-dharmakāya* is entirely provisional; the Mahāyāna *sūtras* express the Buddha's insight into emptiness, but cannot communicate it directly. Commenting a passage of the *Quaestiones ad Thalassium*, Paul Blowers observes instead that Maximos' use of the verb *diabainein* (to go through, or beyond) underscores both the need to *transcend* contingent reality and the passions it inspires, and a sense of *continuity* between plurality and the underpinning spiritual truth.[57] After Chalcedon, it is not necessary to flee theology to find salvation; words are not traps that ensnare us, but windows that free us to explore the divine.

---

[54] One might suggest that a reliance on historico-critical exegesis that excludes the insights of other hermeneutical approaches is perhaps attempting to "circumscribe" Christ.

[55] Iris Murdoch, *Metaphysics as a Guide to Morals* (London: Penguin Books, 1994), 185–216.

[56] Aidan Nichols OP, *Byzantine Gospel-Maximus the Confessor in Modern Scholarship* (T&T Clark: Edinburgh, 1993), 33–35. It is of course through personal engagement with the text that one may come to the presence of the divine.

[57] Paul M. Blowers, *Exegesis and Spiritual Pedagogy in Maximus the Confessor. An Investigation of the Quaestiones ad Thalassium*, 96–100.

PERFORMING THE SELF: IDENTITY, BOUNDARIES, AND THE UNENDING INCARNATION

In his *History of Sexuality*, Michel Foucault argues the understanding of sexual practice prevalent in ancient Greece differed radically from that which emerged in the early Christian era as a consequence of new prevailing models of selfhood and desire.[58] Foucault's notion of "archeology" emphasizes how "knowledge" does not exist "constantly and essentially in its own right," but rather reflects the rules governing the surrounding "social and intellectual space."[59] This "archeological" approach can then be applied to philosophical concepts, as well as to the human subject. The self is the result of a context of competing discourses that the subject has to negotiate in building his or her own identity. The *Archeology of Knowledge* claims that subjects cannot be defined in terms of their relation with a supposed ground of being, but are rather shaped by the rules that condition their historical appearance.[60]

The notion that the self is a reality which is constantly being performed has played a particularly important role in recent feminist reflection on gender and subjectivity. Judith Butler shares Foucault's conviction that the subject is shaped by social practices underpinning deeper strategies of power, but her emphasis is on embodied subjectivity, and on the crucial role of *desire* in determining our conduct.[61] Butler stops short of arguing that, in the absence of objective norms, a subject may become anything he or she desires; she does however claim that awareness of the performative nature of the self might encourage those oppressed by the *status quo* to challenge the latter's claim to neutrality.[62] Julia Kristeva echoes Butler in viewing human subjectivity as constantly striving to achieve a unity which is known to be impossible; she does, however, qualify Butler's position, by arguing that the construction of the self takes place primarily through the

---

[58] Michel Foucault, *The History of Sexuality: The Use of Pleasure*, 14–25, 53–63.

[59] Graham Ward, *Theology and Contemporary Critical Theory*, 60.

[60] Michel Foucault, *Archeology of Knowledge* (trans. A. M. Sheridan Smith; London: Tavistock, 1972), 48.

[61] Judith Butler, *Bodies that Matter: On the Discursive limits of 'Sex'* (London: Routledge, 1993), 62–67. Butler's work critiques the traditional view that sets the mind in opposition to the body, and thereby overestimates the individual's *freedom* to determine his or her own behavior. In this perspective, "thinking" is only an aspect of a wider reflexivity which is shaped by our behavior over time, and which is inseparable from dominant cultural logics.

[62] Judith Butler, *Bodies that Matter*, 220–226.

dynamics of love. A professed agnostic, Kristeva is profoundly attracted to the notion of ethical subjectivity that she finds in Christian writers such as Bernard of Clairvaux. Quoting the latter's motto—*ego affectus est*—she argues that, without interaction with "the other," the subject-in-process cannot hope to attain an equilibrium between self-centeredness and aspiration to transcendence.[63]

What Foucault, and now Butler and Kristeva attack is fundamentally the Cartesian disembodied subject, a notion that is behind the secular reading of community which we are going to discuss in the next section. But the Cartesian dichotomy between *res cogitans* and *res extensa* has a very complex ancestry, and more than a few points of contact with the devaluation of the material that was typical of gnostic readings of creation. When Merleau-Ponty sets out to critique Sartre's belief in the absolute freedom of the subject, he wishes to draw our attention to the fact that our freedom is essentially an embodied freedom, and therefore our actions reflect a history of ethical choices that determine our reactions to external reality.[64] The notion of *sédimentation* in the *Phenomenology of Perception* is of course functionally similar to the Buddhist notion of *karma*, as well as to the belief common among the Desert Fathers that past actions leave a permanent sign in the soul and incline the individual towards a particular form of conduct. What sets apart the post-modern revolt against Descartes' "ghost in the machine" from earlier visions of the unity of soul and body is the rejection by the former of any notion of objective behavioral norm. Kristeva' dismissal of the aspiration to a fixed identity, much as Sartre's notion of bad faith, reflects a deep seated suspicion towards all forms of ethics which appeal to some concept of natural law and thereby are suspected of forcing individuals to conform to standards that stifle diversity and particularity.

The notion of ethical subjectivity that Kristeva elaborates in *Tales of Love* would of course resonate with the construal of practice in Tsong kha pa's *Lam rim chen mo*. If engaging in acts of compassion towards suffering sentient beings enables us to come closer to the goal of enlightenment, interaction with "the other" is the primary activity that shapes our identity. In the *Kun byed rgyal po*, the rhetoric against "fixed identities" is stronger than in

---

[63] Julia Kristeva, *Tales of Love* (trans. L. Roudiez; New York. Columbia University Press, 1991), 376–378. See also Graham Ward, *Theology and Contemporary Critical Theory*, 93–96.

[64] See Maurice Merleau-Ponty, *Phenomenology of Perception* (trans. P. Kegan; London and New York: Routledge, 2002), 15–30, 60–74.

the writings of the dGe lugs master; indeed, seeking to "construct" one's own self according to certain extrinsic models indicates that we have not retrieved our awareness of the primordial basis. Tsong kha pa's notion of *dharmāh*, while emphatically not the blueprint for a fixed subjectivity, enables instead a more structured dialectic of interaction between different subjects. The six perfections outlined in the *Lam rim chen mo* stop short of setting identical rules of conduct for all practitioners, but suggest a fundamental direction for the proper use of conventional reality. As mentioned in Chapter 7, the pursuit of wisdom and compassion after the example of the Buddha clearly parallels the simultaneous pursuit of *theōria* and *praxis*. Identity is thus construed in imitation of an extrinsic paradigm, which however is understood as bringing forth the potentiality of each individual. Tsong kha pa would, however, agree with Kristeva when the latter, after expressing her admiration for the Christian ethics of alterity, distances herself from Christianity's "fundamental fantasies" of perfected subjectivity.[65]

The *Lam rim chen mo* and the *Tales of Love* rest on the conviction that the purification of desire is the key to a condition of inner equilibrium where the subject can attend to the needs of her neighbor. In both perspectives, the inner energies of the individual are actually released once the exclusive concern for the self is overcome, so that "exchanging self for other" and "transference" (in the psychoanalytic sense) become the primary mode of social interaction. Tsong kha pa and Kristeva share with the early Christian tradition a critique of *philautia* as the primary determinant of disordered subjectivity; for Kristeva, communion with the (non-existent) God enables the mystics to "repair the wound of Narcissus."[66] By redirecting one's impulses, rather than suppressing them, one is able to tap onto a source of inner strength, whose distortion leads one to self-destruction. Yet, what distinguishes Kristeva and Tsong kha pa from the early Christian tradition is the fact that they stop short of employing the ontological language of virtues. It is the latter that ultimately sets Maximos' notion of subjectivity apart from its Buddhist or post-modern counterparts.

Maximos' theology of divine embodiment and the corresponding understanding of the virtues enables his construal of the self to tread the difficult balance between conformity to an extrinsic model and the assertion of individual difference. One might object that Maximos' understanding of the

---

[65] Julia Kristeva, *In the Beginning was Love: Psychoanalysis and Faith* (trans. A. Goldhammer; New York: Columbia University Press, 1988), 52.

[66] Julia Kristeva, *Tales of Love*, 25.

virtues derived largely from the Evagrian model that he was so keen to de-bunk.[67] Evagrios' anthropology, however, viewed the virtues as an *instrumen-tal* tool, which enabled the retrieval of inner equilibrium and of one's ulti-mate identity with the *nous*. In this perspective, the purification of desire enabled one to overcome the fragmentation of the self, but it could not become the ground for a positive assertion of difference. If subjectivity is a provisional reality, the soteriological function of the passible part when turned to the service of "the other" is itself limited in time, and has no im-pact on one's own eschatological condition. From an Evagrian point of view, the notion of "performing" the self would acquire a sort of theatrical connotation, as if the self were a *persona* in its etymological sense: a mask. For Maximos, on the contrary, this "performance" entails an effective shap-ing of one's individuality, whereby the individual participates in Christ's work of mediation.

Underscoring the fundamental unity of the rational and the sub-rational element in the human psyche, Maximos' three-tiered psychology is consistent with his theologically based conviction that the *telos* of spiritual practice is not merely the salvation of the soul, but the deification of the individual as a whole. In Chapter 4 we showed how this holistic vision of the human person rested on Maximos' commitment to the Chalcedonian construal of hypostatic union, which was reflected—albeit imperfectly—in the union of soul and body.[68] Maximos' conviction that personhood is shaped by one's ethical decisions *in time* and is finally ratified for eternity is reflected in his emphasis on Christ's human will, whose absence in a mono-thelite theology would have made the incarnate Word less than fully human. The agony in the garden of Gethsemani represents a supreme instance of an individual setting one's final existential orientation by means of a deter-minant ethical choice.

Maximos is of course aware of the fact that, in our ordinary fallen condition, multiplicity and temporality can easily result in fragmentation and decay. In virtue of our fundamental moral autonomy, however, one chooses the purpose for which one will use the gifts that one has received from God. The fact that this moral autonomy is not absolute, but rather embed-

---

[67] See again Evagrios, *Kephalaia Gnostika*, 1, 84, in *Les Six Centuries des 'Kephalaia Gnostica'*, 56–57. In the *Kephalaia Gnostika*, Evagrios is ready to ascribe a positive function to the passible part of the human soul, but again, this function is only provisional.

[68] This is of course the theme in Lars Thunberg, *Microcosm and Mediator*, 43–49; 95–104.

ded in existent patterns of behavior, brings Maximos closer to Merleau-Ponty's *sédimentation*—and to the Buddhist position—than to a post-modern—and disembodied—notion of freedom. Unlike Merleau-Ponty—and Tsong kha pa—Maximos is ready, however, to countenance an eschatological dimension when we become fully what we have striven to be. Through "eternal good being" (*aei eu einai*), one can *be* what one does without incurring Sartrean *mauvaise foi*.

The key to Maximos' understanding of unity in diversity lies in the distinction between *logos* and *tropos*, which allows for a variety of manifestations of the same human nature in line with the different inclinations of a particular hypostasis. The participation of the *logoi* in the Logos secures the stability of the created order, which unfolds according to God's eternal wisdom, but our participation in the economic manifestation of Christ through the *tropos* is the guarantee that God respects our individual autonomy and the conclusion of history will incorporate the results of our choices. While admittedly Maximos is not entirely consistent on this issue,[69] his earlier readiness to ascribe a passionless *gnome* to Christ indicates that an orientation of human nature towards the good is able to accommodate different expression of man's free will. *Amb.* 10 indicates that a virtuous conduct is the outcome of the synergy between the divine grace and a rightful use of human *gnome*.[70] Indeed, Maximos' notion of habit (*hexis*) as an always changeable condition that is acquired through a succession of human decisions would resonate with Tsong kha pa's understanding of the mechanism of cause and effect in the context of spiritual practice. What Maximos would regard as "bad faith" would be the belief that one has attained a stable condition of virtue through one's merits—much as the dGe lugs master warns against inner pride and constantly mentions the "grace" of the Buddhas and the bodhisattvas.

While Maximos construes *philautia* as an excessive attachment to one's body, which however does have a soteriological role, Tsong kha pa would argue that self-centeredness derives from mistaking conventional reality as ultimate, even if—in the dGe lugs reading of spirituality—engaging conventional reality is a necessary step towards enlightenment. Where they differ is in the relationship between the instrument and the goal; the performance of good deeds cannot in any way shape the final outcome, since deification

[69] Lars Thunberg, *Microcosm and Mediator*, 216; also Larchet, *La Divinisation de l'Homme Selon saint Maxime le Confesseur*, 64–70.
[70] Maximos the Confessor, *Amb.*10 (PG 91: 1116a-1116d).

touches upon body and soul alike, and even the grace of the Buddhas cannot declare conventional reality to be ultimate. Jerome's remonstrance that Origenism undermined hierarchies of merit would of course apply here, even if Tsong kha pa would dismiss it as a basic misunderstanding of the purpose of practice. The construal of the self developed in the *Lam rim chen mo* is then in greater agreement with the post-modern understanding of subjectivity found in Butler or Kristeva than with Maximos' vision, since the latter insists that at the end of time the self does not dissolve into the impersonal.

One might object that Maximos' insistence on the incarnation as the model for a perfected subjectivity is paralleled by the analogous role of the historical Buddha, but Mahāyāna Buddhism does not assert that the actions of the historical Buddha brought about an irreversible change in the ontological texture of reality. The role of that particular instance of *nairmāni-kakāya* was fundamentally propedeutic. Following the Buddha's teaching, practitioners can draw closer to enlightenment and reach the final insight into emptiness. The anhypostatic reading of Christ's humanity favored by Maximos ensures that the hypostatic union is only *sensu lato* called a model for the way we make use of our nature; after all, our humanity rests in a human hypostasis, and thus can never attain the intimacy with the divine that was present in the person of Christ. Yet, in overcoming self-centeredness, we become ourselves more fully, participating in the fruits of Christ's deifying work.

This gradual participation in an event that affects contingent, created order as a whole and prefigures its final destiny is what guarantees that our subjectivity is preserved. On the contrary, in a Mahāyāna perspective (dGe lugs as well as rDzogs chen), the imitation of the Buddha (rather than participation in his work) points to a future, where subjectivity is left behind. If the *dharmāh* of conventional reality are ultimately empty, the merit accumulated through the six perfections is purely instrumental, and practice can only unveil our identity with emptiness. Participation in the already accomplished deification of humanity ensures that our particular *tropos* is eternally ratified, whereas imitation of the Buddha entails a heightened awareness of one's lack of ultimate selfhood. A wholesale post-modern rejection of ontology would thus find it easier to accommodate a Buddhist model of ethical subjectivity, but the result is an effective inability to affirm a more than provisional value of difference.

In Chapter 5 I mentioned that historical and sociological reasons are sometimes put forward for the co-existence of rDzogs chen and dGe lugs readings of practice in Tibet, but later I suggested that there are deeper philosophical reasons for a solution in such blatant contrast with the conclusion of the Origenist dispute. rDzogs chen emphasizes the spontaneous creativity of the pure basis, as opposed to the ordered mechanism of causes emphasized by Tsong kha pa. For the latter, the bodies of form are the actual result of the accumulation of merit and wisdom from long practice. This is why the *ris med* could effectively integrate gradualism and immediacy into an overarching structure; if any form of ethically engaged attitude can bring practitioners closer to the goal of enlightenment, gradualism classifies as an acceptable instance of skillful means. One could venture to say that all forms of Mahāyāna Buddhism are implicitly *ris med*, and that 'Jigs med gLing pa's *Seminal Heart* merely made this fundamental latitudinarianism explicit. The *Ambigua* and the *Lam rim chen mo* are both ready to countenance spiritual practice as a performance, whose fundamental terms (the *logoi* and the *dharmāh*) are set without impinging on our freedom, but for Maximos the personality we acquire in this performance is never deposed, so that a compassionate engagement of the other actually secures the boundaries of the self.

Foucault's polemic against the "invention" of normality as a defensive measure against originality and diversity, and its reprisal by authors concerned with gender, effectively classified the Christian construal of self as oppressive. Foucault's conclusions are fundamentally congruent with the Buddhist understanding of the natural order as conventional and provisional. On the contrary, Maximos' notion of "multiple incarnations" of the Logos is able to assert the ultimacy of personhood and of diversity, while emphasizing their subordination to the service of God in love.[71] Crouzel noted that the idea of Christ's "re-birth" in the believer was present in Origen, even if, as noted by Thurnberg, Evagrian spirituality tends to focus on the virtue of detachment, which alone implies a communication with Christ.[72] For Maximos, deification has the opposite meaning than in Evagrios: for the latter, one moves towards utter simplicity in noetic union with Christ, but for the former, Christ himself "is thickened" through the *tropoi* of the virtues (*tois tōn aretōn tropois pachynomenos*) and is differentiated into the

---

[71] See Lars Thurnberg, *Microcosm and Mediator*, 323; Irénée-Henry Dalmais, "La doctrine ascètique de Saint Maxime le Confesseur d'après le *Liber Asceticus*," *Irén* 26 (1953): 17–39.

[72] Henri Crouzel, *Théologie de l'image de Dieu*, 230; Lars Thurnberg, *Microcosm and Mediator*, 325.

variety of our different selves.[73] In the same way as Chalcedonian Christology transcends unity and plurality, participation in the *logos* of humanity deified in Christ ensures that *aei einai* is bestowed on what we, through practice, have made of ourselves.

WORSHIPPING GOD IN THE FLATTENED CITY: LITURGY, COMMUNITY, AND THE EUCHARISTIC *POLIS*

In *After Writing*, a startling exploration of the liturgical dimension of theology, the British theologian Catherine Pickstock describes the philosopher's journey through life as simultaneously "hermeneutical" and "erotic."[74] In making this claim, Catherine Pickstock might be describing Maximos' understanding of the ascetic life. Spirituality is hermeneutical because it involves the "perpetual discernment" of divine mediation through physicality, and erotic because it strives to be united with the divine source of love that undergirds creation. Ascetic practice moves in the space between divine presence and absence, tracing the route that leads from the created order back to God. In this perspective, Derrida's denial of transcendent supplementation is challenged by an attitude that sees this very supplementation as the inescapable source of all meaning.

Maximos' *Mystagogia* underscored that the erotic movement of the soul, and indeed of the whole natural order, towards its source in God, finds its fulfillment in the liturgy. The liturgy is thus the cement that builds the heavenly Jerusalem, of which the earthly church is the prototype; the economy of harmonious difference, which is the trademark of the redeemed cosmos, is ultimately ordered to the worship of God. One more time, the relationship between the Logos and the *logoi* which culminates in the incarnation is the ontological foundation for the interaction between the different members of the church. As "the center of straight lines that radiate from him," Christ does not allow the "distinctive elements of beings" to generate into hostility and chaos, but rather "circumscribes their extension in a circle," ensuring that "the creations and products of the one God" are

---

[73] Maximos the Confessor, *Capita Theologiae et Oeconomiae*, 2, 37, in *Philokalia*, Vol. 2, 146–147 (PG 90: 1141–1142).

[74] Catherine Pickstock, *After Writing: On the Liturgical Consummation of Philosophy* (Oxford and New York: Blackwells, 1998), 20.

in no way "strangers and enemies of one another."[75] The communication of idioms between the humanity and the divinity of Christ serves as model for the support, which members of the church offer to each other in virtue of their different charisms. The church is then a model of the transfigured cosmos as well as of the deified person, whose *telos* is to glorify God within the boundaries of their own particularity.

Maximos' understanding of community envisages doxology as the foundation of ethics and interpersonal relationships. The *Mystagogia*'s effective suggestion that a society can only flourish if it places *liturgy* at the core of civic life is of course a startling departure from contemporary construals of the body politic. The sacred *polis* that the church prefigures relies on a transcendent source that is beyond its control, whereas the modern *polis* rests on fully immanent, self-given premises and laws that are promulgated and rescinded according to this-worldly concerns for pragmatic justice. Discussing the ontology that undergirds contemporary polities, Pickstock draws our attention to Descartes' *Discourse sur la méthode*, where we are told that, in the planning of a city, "the singular and homogeneous is to be preferred to the multiple and the diverse," and that consistency with pre-established rules and "inner coherence" are preferable to organic development and depth.[76] Descartes is ready to leave behind the subordination of laws to the order of nature; rather cynically, he tells us that Sparta flourished even if its laws were "strange and contrary to morals," because these laws were not questioned by the citizens and strengthened the state in relationship to the outside world. Under these presumptions, the future of the immanent polity is entirely predictable; the sense of a culture's diachronic development in time is entirely replaced by an a-temporal concern for the spread of this "rational" system across space. The fact that militaristic Sparta is taken as an example is not without significance; the immanent polity is necessarily aggressive, intolerant of diversity, especially intolerant, in fact, of those claiming to ground their laws in a source that is "other" than the polity itself.

---

[75] Maximos the Confessor, *Mystagogia* 1, (PG 91: 663–667). This passage echoes Pseudo-Denys, *De Divinis Nominibus*, 11,1 (PG 3: 947–950), where the dialectic of periphery and center is discussed.

[76] René Descartes, *Discourse on Method* (trans. D. Cress; Indianapolis, Ind.: Hackett Publishing Co., 1999), II, 6–13. Descartes' direct influence on political thought is perhaps not that extensive, but his thought is nonetheless emblematic of deep currents in the modern world. See also Catherine Pickstock's discussion in *After Writing*, 57–59.

The liturgical and the modern *polis* are undergirded by two opposing ontologies, which in turn reflect the ways in which the knowing subject relates to the surrounding reality. In the modern *polis*, everything is subordinated to the ordering and categorizing mind, which views all objects as variations of the same *res extensa*, and therefore as equally open to scrutiny. The Cartesian epistemological turn envisages reality as at our full disposal, and effectively eliminates the notion of ontological depth that characterized reality before the triumph of the *cogito*. This supremely solipsistic subject can encompass everything within one's gaze, and admits of no higher authority than one's own perspective.[77] As such, the Cartesian subject is a radically non-liturgical subject; engaging in acts of worship, on the contrary, entails that the order of nature is the product of a higher intelligence, and that there is a depth in being that escapes our comprehension, constantly reminding us that the world is not a self-enclosed reality.

The inherent conflictuality and ultimate nihilism that flow from this approach are evident; if every subject can set the terms for the whole of *res extensa*, every individual shall envisage the others as threats to one's independence and control over reality. Looking back at the Evagrian flight into interiority, one may find not a few points in common with this approach. What is the *nous* in the *Kephalaia Gnostika*, but the most totalizing form of Cartesian *cogito*, brooking no opposition from "the other"? In the *Rules for the directions of the mind*, Descartes forces material reality onto the Procrustean bed of *mathēsis* and *geometria*, and thereby seeks to suppress whatever cannot be reduced to this rationalized plan.[78] The paradoxical result is that, the more reality is forcibly reduced to the material, immanent dimension, the less the abstract categories used to discuss corporeality have anything to do with actual embodied reality. Indeed, the latter is increasingly marginalized; "real" bodies, and "real" matter, are "messy" and unpredictable, and stubbornly resist following the (far more rational!) rules devised for them by the rational subject.[79] In the long run, the purpose of the material order is reduced to lay the foundations for a purely cognitive reality that only exists

---

[77] Alexandre Koyré, *From the Closed World to the Infinite Universe* (Baltimore, Md., and London: John Hopkins University Press, 1968), 117–124. Koyré also emphasizes the Scotist ancestry of Descartes' notion of ego, in line with what was said in an earlier section.

[78] René Descartes, *Rules for the Directions of the Mind* (Indianapolis, Ind.: Bobbs-Merrill Co., 2000), X, 388–404.

[79] See for instance Nancy Cartwright, *How the Laws of Physics Lie* (Oxford: Oxford University Press, 1983), 32–40.

within the mind, turning creation into something that can be manipulated at will. This is the ultimate victory of the *nous*: after reaching the highest insight, it gets rid of material reality all-together, and contemplates its own reflection in the mirror of the mind.[80]

In *Cities of God*, his study of "urban theologies," Graham Ward notes that the fully immanent *polis*, where every subject views himself as the center of cognition, can secure a partial equilibrium by redirecting everyone's energies into the satisfaction of individual desires. Yet, as Hobbes reminds us, this equilibrium is necessarily precarious; at any moment, it can degenerate into a war of all against all.[81] For Maximos our *pathē* played a major role in our gradual assimilation to Christ, but of course Maximos was fully aware that fallen humanity was often unable to order its desires to their proper goal. Ward argues that the contemporary *polis*, whose univocal ontology necessarily leads to social atomism, actually encourages the distorted use of our *pathē*, so as to keep under control the fundamental hostility of all against all. The result is a "city of endless desire," where the ecstatic orientation of desire mentioned by Pickstock is perverted and redirected to exclusively immanent, and largely "econo-sexual" goals.[82] In this new city of endless entertainment, there is no temple, not because the Lamb has chosen to dwell among men, but because the desiring subject has been enthroned in its place. What we have is effectively a parody, or travesty, of the ecclesial community, where *deceit* is employed to convince individuals that the immanent realm is capable of satisfying their aspiration to the transcendent.

According to Ward, since the immanent realm is finite, violence is bound to ensue as every subject tries to secure a greater share of it for himself. Of course, over the past two centuries the world has witnessed a variety of social experiments, seeking a common denominator for a new community, whose members have come to the conclusion that "God is dead," but who want to oppose the degeneration into anarchy. In *The Inoperative Community*, however, Jean-Luc Nancy—an author who makes no mystery of his agnosticism—claims that "the community desired and pined for by Rousseau, Schlegel, Hegel, then Bak-ouine, Marx, Wagner or Mallarmé" reveals in each case a deep-seated nostalgia for the lost Christian commu-

---

[80] This is the implication of Robert Musil's claim in *The man without qualities* that "reality ought to be abolished." See Robert Musil, *L'uomo senza qualitá* (Italian trans. A. Rho; Torino: Einaudi, 1966), 324.

[81] Graham Ward, *Cities of God* (New York: Routledge, 2001), 125.

[82] Graham Ward, *Cities of God*, 170–181, *passim*. The same theme is also discussed in James K. A. Smith, *Introducing Radical Orthodoxy*, 136–139.

nity.[83] Any 'inoperative community' is an attempt to overcome 'technopoli-
tical domination' or to transcend the accompanying tendency to homogenization. But what is it that enables the modern subject to break out of its
solipsist cage? For Nancy, it is love, that love which the Cartesian gaze or
the Evagrian *nous* could not accommodate in their streamlined, disembodied
world. As soon as there is love, an "ontological fissure" emerges that "cuts
across" and "disconnects" the totalizing pretensions of the ego.

The immanent world, therefore, is the world of convenience, whereas
agapē enables us to glimpse the transcendent foundation of our reality. For
Nancy, a truly "post-modern" community can only be based on acts of selfless love which "mime" Christ's kenotic self-emptying. "Joy" emerges from
the acceptance of the other, who is no longer perceived as a threat, but as
an opportunity to engage in an agapic dialogue. Nancy's inoperative community is not an accidental assembly of competitive egos, but a reality that
emerges as one learns how to respond to the need of the other.[84] Unlike
Descartes' urban dream, this new, post-competitive *polis* is not something
that is planned, but something that is *given* to us through the experience of
the infinite that is manifest in different finitudes-in-relation.[85] The term "inoperative" does not indicate passivity or indifference, but rather the subver-
sion of the technoeconomic imperative that has come to dominate the
ethos of the secular city and that has marginalized salvation for the sake of
production.

Nancy tries to offer a way out of the impasse denounced by Ward, but
we are left to wonder whether his solution is truly able to overcome the
nihilistic implications of the Cartesian *cogito*. In a sense, the inoperative
community challenges the evacuation of the corporeal that can be found in
Evagrios, and underscores the dialectic of reciprocity that ought to shape
post-modern communities. For Nancy, however, even when existence is
sacrificed out of love, "it is sacrificed by no one, and it is sacrificed to nothing."[86] Without God, our corporeality is bound to dissolve into nothingness. Commenting upon Nancy's "politics of politics," Ward notes that the
"celebration of difference" in *The Inoperative Community* may be easily over-
turned into its opposite; after all, if "we know that it is all for nothing,"

---

[83] Jean-Luc Nancy, *The Inoperative Community* (trans. P. Connor; Minneapolis,
Minn.: University of Minnesota Press, 1991), 10.

[84] Jean-Luc Nancy, *The Inoperative Community*, 6; 97–100.

[85] Graham Ward, *Theology and Contemporary Critical Theory*, 111–112.

[86] Jean-Luc Nancy, *A Finite Thinking* (trans. S. Sparks; Palo Alto, Calif.: Stanford University Press, 2003), 101.

there is no fundamental reason why difference ought to be cherished and preserved.[87] The weakness of Nancy's approach is that it is still fundamentally monistic; it needs theological supplementation in the shape of an account of analogy that grounds difference in the experience of communion with the transcendent.

At this point, one might observe that the Mahāyāna emphasis on compassion could offer a way out of Descartes' totalizing gaze, without returning to the full panoply of *analogia entis*. It is easy to see, however, that the Mahāyāna alternative shares some of the inherent weaknesses of Nancy's position. If the ultimate aspiration of the Evagrian subject and its later Cartesian manifestation is the suppression of all alternative points of view and the virtual identification of one's gaze with God's, Mañjuśrīmitra's *rDo la gser zhun* shows how the totalitarian aspirations of the ego are ultimately self-defeating. According to the Yogācāra tradition, the way reality appears is not the consequence of an independent state of affairs invested with inherent properties, but reflects our (karmically conditioned) way of seeing. In this way, the centrality of the knowing subject is both affirmed and carefully qualified, and the belief that one may reach a comprehensive understanding of reality is exposed as a form of wishful thinking.[88] Mañjuśrīmitra, writing from a rDzogs chen perspective, goes even further than Yogācāra, and argues that even our experience of "composite objects" is indistinguishable from the basis of fundamental awareness. "Difference" does not arise from the existence of different separate entities, or from the confrontation of different centers of consciousness, but from the various manifestations of the pure basis, which have no external cause apart from themselves. Mañjuśrīmitra's own commentary of the *rDo la gser zhun* mentions nine different types of "division," which reflect one's inability to retrieve fundamental awareness, and which disappear at the moment of enlightenment.[89] Yet, rDzogs chen views the pure basis as itself an inherently compassionate reality, where "commiseration spontaneously arises" in response to the suffering of sentient beings.[90] Reality as a whole acquires a sacramental value even if it cannot point to an ultimate source of goodness which transcends the stream of appearances.

---

[87] Graham Ward, *Theology and Contemporary Critical Theory*, 115.

[88] Namkhai Norbu and Kennard Lipman, Intro. to Mañjuśrīmitra, *Primordial Experience (rDo la gser zhun)*, 21.

[89] Mañjuśrīmitra, *Primordial Experience (rDo la gser zhun)*, 81.

[90] Mañjuśrīmitra, *Primordial Experience (rDo la gser zhun)*, 112.

This approach clearly challenges the social atomism behind Nancy's construal, and, more importantly, the Cartesian belief that this spontaneously creative "reality" can be turned into the streamlined world of *mathēsis*. rDzogs chen does not posit an ultimate ontological source, but the effective immanentism of this *Weltanschauung* is tempered by the belief that reality is not just *graced* (to use a Rahnerian term), but *is* itself grace. The myriads of bodhisattvas and Buddhas mentioned in the *Kun byed rgyal po* are nothing but an expression of the fundamentally compassionate orientation of reality, which we cannot manipulate for our own purposes without ultimately damaging ourselves. As noted in Chapter 5, the "Tibetan henad" is not an indifferent noetic reality, but one that is inherently well-disposed towards sentient beings: a characteristic that can hardly be attributed to Ward's "cities of endless aspiration." At the same time, however, the rDzogs chen construal of difference combines an attitude of awe for the creativity of *ka dag* with the conviction that "divisions" disappear as soon as primordial awareness is retrieved. Like the world of Nancy, the universe of the *rDo la gser zhun* is fundamentally monistic; its various forms and shapes are like ripples on the surface of a pond. The sacramentality of *ka dag* is provisional and wholly self-referential, ensuring that no authentic liturgy is possible in the dwelling of the primordial Buddha.

Tsong kha pa's *Lam rim chen mo*, as we have seen in Chapters 6 and 7, has a stronger reading of ontological difference than the texts from the rDzogs chen tradition. Earlier, we discussed how vol. II of the *Lam rim chen mo* explores the role of conventional reality in the context of practice, emphasizing the mechanism of cause and effect that rDzogs chen is so keen to deny. Difference enables practitioners to engage in the six perfections; difference enables us to accumulate merit for the sake of suffering sentient beings and thereby brings us closer to the goal of enlightenment. By emphasizing compassion over and against its marginalization within schools that preach "immediate" awakening, Tsong kha pa is eager to undercut the tendency towards self-centeredness that he senses for instance in the teaching of the monk Mahayana. While the *Kun byed rgyal po* or the writings of Mañjuśrīmitra emphasize the "spontaneous" nature of *ka dag*'s manifestations, the *Lam rim chen mo* underscores the "order" of conventional reality, which exists so as to support our spiritual practice.[91] Tsong kha pa often

---

[91] Tsong kha pa, *Lam rin chen mo* (Vol 2: 546–549), 88–89, where we are told of the connection between "the wisdom that understands the diversity of phenomena," the so called "factor of method," and "the collection of merit."

mentions the importance of "method," but this is very different from the way this notion is developed in the *Discourse sur la mèthode*. Descartes' ego seeks to subordinate reality to its own purposes, whereas the dGe lugs master views conventional reality as helping us leave behind the totalitarian pretenses of the self. In this perspective, the "other" is no longer a threat, but is invested with a sacramental value that leads us towards the ultimate insight.

We already mentioned how the *imitatio Buddhae* proposed by Tsong kha pa mirrors Maximos' vision of the individual completing Christ's work of mediation. While the points of contact between the cosmological function of the Logos and the role of the *jñāna-dharmakāya* are evident, one should not overlook that the forms of spiritual practice they underpin have radically divergent goals. Maximos' vision is ultimately communitarian, whereas for Tsong kha pa the purpose of practice is an insight into emptiness where difference disappears. One might object of course that the *Lam rim chen mo* espouses the Mahāyāna doctrine of *apratishtitā nirvāna*, and that the practice of compassion continues even after the attainment of enlightenment. Similarly, one might recall that without the *jñāna-dharmakāya* (which encompasses all sentient beings) no-one can attain enlightenment. Difference, however, is only accepted instrumentally, and not as a reality that is unconditionally affirmed as good. The community of the *sangha* and even the bodhisattvas dwelling in the celestial realms have no place in ultimate reality; all that is left is an undifferentiated insight.[92] Trying to hold on to one's embodied nature, through which one may practice compassion at the conventional level, is analogous to the desire deplored in the *Legs bShad sNying po* to make final statements about conventional reality. The flattened city of modernity is of course dismissed as a delusion, but at the end of the path, there is no temple and no city.

On the contrary, the eschatological transfiguration of the cosmos that for Maximos is foreshadowed in the celebration of the liturgy points towards an intensely corporeal reality. The Eucharist which is the core of Christian worship emphasizes the embodied nature of our selves, turning the consumption of food and drink into an action exploding the dichotomy

---

[92] One should be careful lest one construes a Buddhist eschatology as a counterpart of the Christian eschatology. Indeed, Buddhism has no eschatology as such: the "end of *samsāra*," though mentioned in prayers, has little practical meaning, and sentient beings and bodies of form are expected to go on and on. It is only in the (a-temporal) insight of enlightenment that such conventional realities are transcended.

of *theōria* and *praxis*. Maximos notes that the church building can be said to represent man, because the nave suggests the body, the sanctuary symbolizes the soul, and the altar indicates the mind; but it is on the altar that God accomplishes the greatest mystery of the Christian faith and becomes fully present in the bread and the wine. The liturgical culmination of *praxis* in the *Mystagogia* that we discussed in Chapter 4 simultaneously hints at the communitarian nature of our practice, which is embedded in the liturgical life of the church. The Chalcedonian paradigm resurfaces when Maximos tells us that, no matter how different the faithful are "by language, places, and customs," they all are "made one through faith." God realizes this union among natures "without confusing them," but "lessening and bringing together their distinction" in a "relationship and union" with himself.[93] Inasmuch as the church is also a figure of the world, where unity and diversity co-exist, the celebration of the Eucharist foreshadows the eschatological endurance of the cosmic order.[94]

Catherine Pickstock draws our attention to the fact that before the moment of communion, celebrant and congregation beg for the gift of peace, knowing that only Christ is the source of that peace which the world cannot give.[95] Her reading of the repeated invocation of the *Agnus Dei* emphasizes how the Eucharist establishes a redemptive exchange between God's own future and our own present, establishing a sacred community that transcends space and time. The flattened, immanentized reality of the Cartesian subject dwells in a self-enclosed horizon, whereas the worshipping community is open to the constant bestowal of God's peace, which radically transforms the hostile attitude of the self towards the other. While membership in the "city of desire" presupposes acceptance of its rationalist ethos, the gift of the Eucharist indicates that membership of the liturgical *polis* is given by God out of love. As a result, the city of Eucharistic peace shares with Nancy's "inoperative" community a critical attitude towards the solipsism of the modern ego; unlike Nancy, however, Maximos offers the resources to transcend such confrontational attitude, showing that *being a subject* is itself a gift.[96]

---

[93] Maximos the Confessor, *Mystagogia* 1 (PG 91: 663–667).

[94] Maximos the Confessor, *Mystagogia* 2, (PG 91: 667–671).

[95] Catherine Pickstock, *After Writing*, 236–238.

[96] See Catherine Pickstock, *After Writing*, 240; Maximos the Confessor, *Mystagogy*, 4–5 (PG 91: 671–683).

The absence of references to liturgy or the ecclesial community in the literature of the Evagrian School can then be seen to go hand in hand with Evagrios' ultimate dismissal of difference. By privileging one's private point of view, the Evagrian subject anticipates the *hybris* of the modern ego and its strategy of totalitarian *reductio*. Mahāyāna thought, especially in its dGe lugs form, can be a helpful antidote to this danger, by calling for an ethics of radical un-selfing that sees the contingent as conducive to enlightenment. As we noted above, however, even Tsong kha pa's re-evaluation of conventional reality can only ground a weakened or attenuated sacramentality. His vision of ultimate reality does not accommodate the persistence of community, since, in the *svābhāvikakāya*, there is no diversity. In the end, it is only the incarnation that enables Maximos to view difference as life-giving instead of threatening. It is the presence of that incarnation in the Eucharist which guarantees that all reality is ultimately, fully, and eschatologically sacramental. We no longer have to fear the boundaries that divide us from the other; *Amb. 42* and *Q.Th. 53* show us that Christ transcended all differences in a higher synthesis, pointing the way for us to follow. The Origenist ontology foreshadowed a contemporary ontology of self-centered violence; Mahāyāna thought (in its rDzogs chen and dGe lugs renditions) calls for an ontology of selfless instrumentality; Maximos' understanding of the incarnation offers an ontology of communitarian peace.

By calling his study of Maximos *Cosmic Liturgy*, von Balthasar intended to stress the centrality, within Maximos' theology, of the same concern behind Pickstock's reflections on worship: namely, that the mystery of the Eucharist and the significance of creation are intimately related. Maximos' theology of the body turns everything into a sign; in Christ's own saying at the last supper, "This is my body," the sign is fully taken over into the referent, indicating that the created order only "is" to the extent that it tends to an irreversible deification. If the hypostatic union itself exploded the dichotomy of apophatic and kataphatic theology, the Eucharist perpetuates this event in time, and, as Pickstock suggests, makes a continuous claim "which alone makes it possible to trust every sign."[97] Maximos' Chalcedonian reading of the doctrine of *logoi spermatikoi* indicates that every element of the natural order, and not just every member of the human race, is directly united to the eternal Word through its own *logos*; by collaborating in Christ's redemptive plan, humanity ensures that even those components of creation that lack *autexousiotēs* come to partake of the mystery of *theōsis*.

---

[97] Catherine Pickstock, *After Writing*, 262.

THE TEMPTATION OF EMPTINESS: WHAT HAS CHALCEDON TO DO WITH EXPERIENCE?

In their different ways, John Keenan's *The Meaning of Christ* and Joseph S. O'Leary's *Religious Pluralism and Christian Truth* set out to explore how Christian theology can benefit from the Buddhist speculative tradition. Keenan's study starts from the claim that the Christian theological tradition greatly suffers from its neglect of the Christian mystical tradition, which has been allegedly "shunted" to "the periphery of serious theology."[98] Throughout the first part of his work, he contends that the dichotomy between theology and spirituality goes back to the "adoption of Greek patterns of thought" by the early Church. In order to break out of this impasse, Keenan suggests, Christian theology ought to bid farewell to traditional Christology and its talk of two natures in one person, which are totally irrelevant to the spiritual life of individual Christians.

O'Leary's equally iconoclastic critique extends far beyond Christology to address the "totalitarian" tendencies of Christian theological discourse, which in his opinion should accept the dichotomy between conventional discourse and ultimate reality.[99] For O'Leary, when theologians turn their attention to the mystery of Christ, they should not begin from a full-fledged theology of the incarnation (apparently, "blind devotion must be outgrown"),[100] but from an analysis of how "God was at work in Christ." In this perspective, traditional ontological discourse on Christ has been "massive and overwhelming," and this hurdle can only be circumvented if "revelation" is given priority over ontological claims. Theologians should then acknowledge that phenomenology and history have a "concrete" and "empirical" impact upon our lives, whereas "dogmatic claims" concern realities that are "invisible" and "scarcely verifiable."[101] O'Leary's argument is more philosophically sophisticated than Keenan's, but his mistrust of traditional Christology reflects the latter's conviction that the settlement reached at Chalcedon bears no relation to—and effectively suffocates—the salvific impact of Jesus of Nazareth.

---

[98] John P. Keenan, *The Meaning of Christ: A Mahāyāna Theology* (Maryknoll, N.Y.: Orbis Books, 1989), 221.

[99] Joseph Stephen O'Leary, *Religious Pluralism and Christian Truth* (Edinburgh: Edinburgh University Press, 1996), 204.

[100] Joseph Stephen O'Leary, *Religious Pluralism and Christian Truth*, 208.

[101] Joseph Stephen O'Leary, *Religious Pluralism and Christian Truth*, 212–213.

THE VIRTUES OF PARTICIPATION

The solutions offered by these two authors are thus substantially similar: one should revitalize Christological reflection by a vigorous influx of Mahāyāna philosophy, which has the alleged virtue of rejecting the notion of essence (*svabhāva*), and of acknowledging that all ontologies are "the objectification of illusory conceptualization."[102] In the philosophy of Tsong kha pa, heavily influenced by the Mādhyamikas, these notions of emptiness and no-essence attempt to describe the transcendent otherness of ultimate meaning, by mapping its manifestations in the world of dependent co-arising. In this perspective, the goal of the Buddha's *apratishtitā nirvāna* is not to transmit a set of doctrines, but rather to awaken other sentient beings to the co-dependent and empty nature of reality. For Keenan, "Greek" theology focuses on the *content* of the doctrines (*ta noeta*), whereas Mahāyāna thought is interested in effecting a transformation of one's mode of awareness which then affects one's behavior towards other sentient beings. Thus, the notion of emptiness and the dialectic of ultimate and conventional reality of the *Legs bShad sNying po* could furnish a framework to articulate Christ's divinity and humanity in far more "relevant" terms than the concepts of *ousia* and *hypostasis*.

In line with these considerations, could one develop a Christian theology of divine embodiment that retrieves elements of dGe lug pa thought? What would the sacramental value of the contingent, created universe be within such a theological system? Surely, one could object, the term "empty" cannot be used for Christ; but for Keenan and O'Leary, such usage would be countered by the claim that "emptiness," far from negating Christ's ultimate transcendence, is the only tenable way to express it. In his polemic with Svātantrika thought, Tsong kha pa had resorted to Candrakīrti's interpretation of Nāgārjuna, so as to emphasize that the Buddha's ultimate insight was compatible with a variety of conventional expressions, all them empty and defying philosophical expression. If conventional reality has a performative character—and therefore enacts the ultimate which can never be expressed—one might say that Jesus enacted the transcendent and inexpressible reality of God through his ministry and his death. In this perspective, the resurrection, rather than signaling the accomplished reconciliation of humanity with God, would be functionally similar to those instances of *jñāna-dharmakāya* that are especially open to the transcendent and guide

---

[102] Joseph Stephen O'Leary, *Religious Pluralism and Christian Truth*, 222.

other sentient beings to the insight of *svābhāvikakāya*.[103] As Keenan notes in *The Meaning of Christ*, a Mahāyāna Christology would be unable to accommodate models of the atonement that see the crucifixion as marking an irreversible shift in God's relationship with mankind.[104] In line with Tsong kha pa's discussion of *conventional* cause and effect in the *Lam rim chen mo*, one might go further and argue that Jesus, like every bodhisattva engaged in the six perfections, is making use of the historical circumstances where he operates to move closer to the ultimate reality and lessen the suffering of others.

The same Keenan goes on to claim that a Mahāyāna Christology would be rather Antiochean, in the sense that the emphasis would be on a "horizontal" understanding of Jesus as he appears in our historical context.[105] He then argues that the realms of *theologia* and *oikonomia* as they are developed by the Church Fathers can be mapped onto the realms of ultimate and conventional reality. The reason why Jesus was eventually understood as "divine" reflected the cultural conditions of the time for which only "God" could be regarded as fully transcendent. Nowadays, however, to continue asserting that "God" was fully disclosed in the incarnate Christ reflects our culturally conditioned reluctance to let go of "static" conceptions of divinity inherited from Hellenistic philosophy. If the ultimate nature of the *jñāna-dharmakāya* is the emptiness of the *svābhāvikakāya*, a dGe lugs Christology would affirm that the Son was "non-substantial" with the Father.

O' Leary, for his part, is critical of the alleged tendency of traditional Christology to regard Christ as "a substance to be defined," though he is readier than Keenan to enlist Patristic speculation on the incarnation as "skilful means."[106] Echoing Merleau-Ponty, his purpose is to "open up" Christology "without destroying it," but this of course entails a complete rejection of "the Johannine scheme of pre-existence." The latter, of course, sins unforgivably by positing a transcendental signifier that suffocates Christ's historical unfolding. In this perspective, the function of Jesus is to

---

[103] In this sense, we could associate the historical body of Christ with the *nairmānikakāya* and the resurrected body with the *sambhogakāya*; both of them exist within conventional reality and guide humanity to transcendence.

[104] John P. Keenan, *The meaning of Christ*, 230.

[105] John P. Keenan, *The meaning of Christ*, 232. We already noted how this understanding of "Antiochean" Christology has been increasingly questioned, though Keenan continued to use it as a synonym for "low."

[106] Joseph S. O'Leary, *Religious Pluralism and Christian Truth*, 251.

serve as an immanent signifier, whose purpose is to *protect* the signified divine reality from grasp. On one hand, O'Leary seems readier than Keenan to accept that, within Christianity, conventional articulations of the *kerygma* play a greater role than within Mahāyāna. On the other hand, he qualifies his acceptance of such conventional articulations asserting that statements such as "Jesus is God" make sense only in the "networks of relations" where "Jesus unfolds his being."[107] Once the ontological gap between divinity and humanity is dismissed as untenable, theologians eager to express the Christian religious experience theologically must seek a middle path between abstraction and particularity, or, to echo the *Heart Sūtra*, between emptiness and form. Tsong kha pa's doctrine of the Buddha bodies and his emphasis on the compassionate engagement of the conventional could then provide us the resources for a Christology that lets go of a-historical fixations with certain manifestations of the ultimate, and yet does not dissolve Christ in an undifferentiated revelatory process.

What undergirds these arguments is the belief that a Mahāyāna understanding of contingent reality and of divine embodiment can give a better account of the Christian experience than the traditional Chalcedonian formulation. Even more fundamental to this move is the conviction voiced by Keenan that one "cannot go beyond a phenomenology of mystic experience to construct an ontological account."[108] In this perspective, one ought to reject the supposedly "static" discourse of Chalcedon, focus on the transformative power of engaging contingent reality, and, of course, abstain from making any pronouncement about Christ's uniqueness. Anyone who reads Maximos' Christological speculations in the *Ambigua*, but especially in the writings devoted to spiritual direction, will realize however that his commitment to Chalcedonian Christology stems from his conviction that any other account of divine embodiment fails to do justice to the transformative quality of the Christ event. The model of hypostatic union that is affirmed at Chalcedon, as well as the underpinning notion of human nature, can hardly be described as "static." When Maximos underscores the inability of the Origenist system to integrate the incarnational economy into a coherent cosmological vision, he insists that the irreversible transformation of humanity accomplished in the person of Christ provides the paradigm for a *gradual* deification of every individual. Accusing Maximos of marginalizing spiritual experience would be a radical misunderstanding of his posi-

---

[107] Joseph S. O'Leary, *Religious Pluralism and Christian Truth*, 255–256.
[108] John P. Keenan, *The meaning of Christ*, 195.

tion, since it is spiritual experience that provides the ultimate source and benchmark for his Christological analysis.

Along the same lines, one wonders how Keenan can go about overcoming the dichotomy between spirituality and theology, if he assumes that mystical experience offers no legitimate basis for theological accounts of transcendence. Few theologians will be willing to claim that human concepts can articulate mystical experience, but this is no good reason to abandon the theological enterprise. Indeed, Bernard Lonergan warns us that without the addition of reflection, evaluation, and judgment, mystical experience would never be *known* at all.[109] What Keenan is doing, therefore, is to reject one hermeneutical strategy and replace it with another; while Mahāyāna terms take the place of Hellenistic categories, the underlying approach is no different from Maximos', when the latter charts the impact of *theōria* and *praxis* on the individual. In both cases, the goal is to articulate how the Christ event sets the terms for one's spiritual transformation.

The question that needs to be answered is then whether Mahāyāna categories are better at this task than their traditional, "Hellenist" counterparts. Once more, it would seem that a Christology based solely on the dGe lugs understanding of the emptiness could be compatible with the isochristism of Evagrios, or even with a Christology by degrees in the style of Paul of Samosata, but its docetic approach to conventional truth would be unable to articulate the cosmic impact of Christ's incarnation. Once more, what is needed is the participatory approach found in Maximos, which could articulate the cosmic impact of Christ's salvific work. The key word, once more, is participation: participation of the cosmos in the mystery of the Logos, and participation in the event of the redemption, which Christ accomplished once and for all.

Reflecting on whether a 'Christology by degrees' could have any relevance for us today, Geoffrey W. H. Lampe argues that the asymmetry of the Chalcedonian paradigm undermines its attempt to make Christ fully accessible, as well as fully transcendent. For Lampe, even if Christ's full humanity includes a body and a soul, the fact that he becomes "man" as opposed to "a man" shows that the incarnate Logos can never truly be "one of us."[110] Maximos' commitment to the notion that Christ's humanity

---

[109] Bernard Lonergan, *Method in Theology*, 106.

[110] Geoffrey W. H. Lampe, "The Holy Spirit and the Person of Christ," in Stephen Sykes and John P. Clayton, eds., *Christ, Faith and History: Cambridge Studies in*

is anhypostatic, however, reflects his conviction that it is only in virtue of Christ having assumed human nature *in general* that each one of us is directly affected by his redeeming work.[111] The prophet Ezekiel's imaginative vision of the wheels interlocking under God's throne can then be read as intimating the communication of the idioms, the perichoretic relationship of humanity in divinity in the person of Christ. It makes little sense then to talk of these natures as "static," since they have a constant impact on each other; in fact, the transformative impact of Christ's humanity continues throughout the ages, and touches every member of the human race.

In fact, one may even object that a dGe lugs Christology would make ultimate reality even more inaccessible than under the terms of Chalcedon. On one hand, even an "empty" Christology would be based on a fundamental asymmetry: the ultimate reality of Christ's transcendence would be the foundation of his conventional manifestation, while the conventional manifestation (Christ's humanity) could never exist autonomously. On the other hand, a Mahāyāna Christology would be considerably more "docetic" than the anhypostatic construction which Lampe deplores. The historical manifestation of Christ is not taken up to the level of ultimate reality (which would parallel deification), but only assumed as an instrument that *cannot* overcome the division between the two levels of reality. The docetic element is even stronger if one tries to understand the incarnate Christ as functionally equivalent to the figure of Vajrasattva in the *Kun byed rgyal po*; in that case, the emissary of the primordial Buddha led sentient beings back to *ka dag*, but he is himself no different from the all-encompassing primordial basis. A rDzogs chen Christology would be even more static than a dGe lugs version, since it would do away with the mechanism of cause and effect in the conventional realm, eliminating even the conventional illusion of transformation. Maximos' commitment to the notion of *koinōnia idiōmatōn*, therefore, is a guarantee against both docetism and stasis.

Christology (London: Cambridge University Press, 1972), 119–120. Anhypostasy is thus docetism under an assumed name.

[111] Interpreters of Maximos are virtually unanimous on this point, with the exception of Bathrellos, who ridicules Larchet for holding this view, seemingly without realizing the wider theological implications of this position; see Demetrios Bathrellos, *The Byzantine Christ*, 103. One could argue that if Christ had assumed an individual human nature, only this individual nature would have been redeemed and the Trinity would now be a "quaternity" encompassing a human hypostasis, which of course is an untenable position.

If we consider the Evagrian understanding of embodiment, we see remarkable points of contact with the Mahāyāna dialectic of the two truths, inasmuch as the relationship between *dianoia* and *nous* may be said to resemble conventional and ultimate reality. Intellectual purification enables one to rise beyond conceptuality and see the true nature of the mind, which, not unlike emptiness, is always present. This comparison, however, also underscores the inability of this construal to articulate the uniqueness of Christ's work; if the *nous* is functionally similar to the Buddha nature, all those that transcend duality can be equal to Christ. In addition, the tendency of the *Kephalaia Gnostika* to view created reality as a sort of veil of Maya sits uneasily with the Scriptural understanding of creation. The result is a tension between the temporal framework of the *Kephalaia Gnostika*, where the distinction between noetic and material reality disappears at the eschaton, and the effectively a-temporal vision of the *Philokalia*, where at any moment in time spiritual practice may overcome this distinction. In either dGe lugs or rDzogs chen, Christ and the individual practitioner would be different instances of *nairmānikakāya*, pointing to the ultimate reality in which we live, move, and exist.

In light of the Origenist contempt for *kinēsis*, any Mahāyāna approach would arguably be more "static" than Maximos' Chalcedonian synthesis, since the changes taking place in the created order (or conventional reality) have no impact on the noetic (or ultimate) dimension which is necessarily unchangeable. A dGe lugs Christology modeled on Vol. 2 of Tsong kha pa's *Lam rim chen mo* might actually view *praxis* more positively than Evagrios, reading the six perfections as skilful means for the sake of others. At the same time, Maximos' insistence that every *ousia* possesses its own *energeia* suggests a fundamentally dynamic and performative understanding of substance, which results in a dynamic and performative Christology. Christ's human and divine "natures" exist inasmuch as they intervene (and interact) in the historical spheres.

In his study of Maximos' notions of nature and subjectivity, Bernardo De Angelis critiques von Balthasar for mapping the dialectic of *logos* and *tropos* onto the distinction between *ousia* and *hypostasis*, when for De Angelis the *tropos* indicates the mode whereby the hypostasis makes use of a particular substance.[112] One's own identity is then construed in time, within the terms set by the blueprint of the *logos*. Maximos' emphasis on Christ's hu-

---

[112] Bernardo de Angelis, *Natura, persona, libertà*, 88–89. The critique also concerns Polycarp Sherwood's reading of the *Ambigua*.

man will in *Op. 6* indicates that the deification of our nature encompasses and ratifies the way in which Christ's humanity engaged the circumstances where it operated. By participating in his work of mediation, the circumstances of our life, as well as our inner life, will be irreversibly transformed.[113] In light of these considerations, one sees clearly how any claim that a Mahāyāna Christology focuses on inner transformation, whereas Chalcedonian Christology would reduce Christ's work to an extrinsic event, is a radical misunderstanding of the Christian notion of divine embodiment.

In our discussion of language, we noted that that there can be no *diabainein* between conventional discourse and the ultimate reality which it eventually discloses. Keenan hints at this problem when he concedes that there is no continuity between phenomenological statements and the final insight into emptiness: an empty Christology based on Madhyamaka principles could not lay the foundations for a theology of the ultimate. But when he distinguishes *theologia* from *oikonomia*, Maximos the Confessor is not arguing that the latter is the only legitimate object of theological reflection, or that nothing can be said about the former; indeed, the very opposite is the case. It is the hypostatic union which enables us to speak of God's intervention in history; it is God's manifestation in the flesh that enables us to talk of God's own being. In this respect, Maximos' view of created reality as rooting both *theōria* and *praxis* in the Logos indicates that the incarnation is not a mere conventional manifestation of the ultimate, but an event which grounds the deification of the whole cosmos.

---

[113] Maximos the Confessor, *Opuscula theologica et polemica* 6 (PG 91: 245–256); also in Maxime le Confesseur, *Opuscules théologiques et polémiques* (trans. by É. Ponsoye. Paris: Cerf, 1998), 142–144.

9 CONCLUSION

DIVINE EMBODIMENT AND RELIGIOUS DIVERSITY: TOWARDS A CHALCEDONIAN THEOLOGY OF RELIGIOUS DIFFERENCE

In *Models of Revelation*, Avery R. Dulles distinguishes different modalities of divine self-disclosure, which identify revelation with, respectively, a set of doctrines, salvation history, inner experience, God's own dialectical presence in His Word, or a new, transformative awareness of reality.[1] The first two models tend to oppose a "general" or "natural" revelation, which has an introductory character, to the particular or "supernatural" revelation of the Old and the New Testament; at the same time, they are disinclined to acknowledge the revelatory character on other religions. The fourth model, which is exemplified by the work of Karl Barth, radicalizes this position, and affirms explicitly that God's Word revealed in Christ is the only channel of revelation. The third and the fifth model, finally, find it easier to acknowledge the presence of revelation in other religions, though, as Dulles points out, they often do so by relativizing traditional Christian claims.[2] Dupuis' critique of Dulles' approach emphasizes how the exclusivism characterizing more traditional models of revelation stems from their tendency to interpret reality in dichotomous terms: "the natural" is opposed to "the supernatural," the salvific history of Jews and Christians is set apart from other salvation narratives, and an ontological chasm is opened between the content of revelation (Jesus Christ) and its recipients.[3]

The emphasis on "inner experience" and "awareness" in the third and fifth paradigm is of course contested by supporters of more traditional approaches. Karl Rahner, for his part, claimed that God's self-disclosure modifies the way in which we perceive the world, and as such revelation

---

[1] Avery R. Dulles, *Models of revelation* (Maryknoll, N.Y.: Orbis Books, 1992), 121.

[2] Avery R. Dulles, *Models of revelation*, 177–8.

[3] Jacques Dupuis, *Towards a Christian theology of Religious Pluralism* (Maryknoll, N.Y.: Orbis Books, 1999), 238–239.

cannot take place without an experience of inner transformation.[4] The risk, of course, is that we may focus on what goes on in our soul, and forget that revelation puts us in touch with an external reality. At the same time, this approach enables one to break out of traditional exclusivism, and to envisage other religions as bearing *some form* of witness to God's self-disclosure. Any individual or community, to the extent that they are "grounded in the divine," can become "pointers" towards God's "culminating gift" in Jesus Christ.[5] In the history of 20th century Catholicism, this form of qualified inclusivism was given magisterial support with the conciliar declaration *Nostra Aetate.* In this document, Catholicism abandoned the attitude of unqualified suspicion that had long characterized its relation with other religions, and asserted its readiness to welcome "whatever there was of just and right" in other confessions of faith. Great care was taken to reassert the unique salvific value of Christian revelation, but fragments of the truth were said to exist in other traditions as well.[6]

If we turn to Rahner's *Foundations*, we see clearly that Rahner's vision echoes Maximos', as both thinkers regard the hypostatic union as the lynchpin of their theology. Admittedly, Maximos operated centuries after Christianity had become the established religion, and, unlike Athanasius, was never compelled to discuss non-Christian religions. On the other hand, the notion of "anonymous Christian" enables Rahner to view the religious experience of different traditions as something valuable, but as something that derives its ultimate value from the salvation wrought by Christ. In this perspective, the sacred writings of all cultures contain passages that suggest the divine inspiration of their authors, even if it is only in the case of the Old and the New Testament that this inspiration encompassed the entirety of the text.[7] In this way, the dialectic between the Logos and the *logoi* put forth by Maximos is applied to the relationship between Christianity and other religions. On one hand, Rahner seems to say, we can no longer credibly assert that the Wisdom of God is operative only in the Judeo-Christian tradition, but on the other hand, if the soteriological impact of the incarna-

---

[4] Karl Rahner, "Mysticism," *Encyclopedia of theology: The Concise 'Sacramentum mundi'* (New York: Crossroad Publishing, 1975), 1010.

[5] Avery R. Dulles, *Models of revelation*, 182.

[6] *See Declaration on the Relation of the Church to Non-Christian Religions 'Nostra Aetate'* (1965), 2, at www.vatican.va/.../documents/vat-ii_decl_19651028_nostra-aetate_en.html.

[7] See Karl Rahner, *Foundations of Christian Faith* (New York: Crossroads, 1978), Ch. 6, 311–22.

tion is truly universal, everything which *Nostra Aetate* sees as truly valuable in other religions must be somehow related to Christ. Any other solution would amount to admitting a plurality of salvific mediations.

If we reflect for a moment, we see that what Rahner is doing is to re-propose in different terms the notion of *logoi spermatikoi* that informed the theology of Maximos. If the *logoi* of Scripture and the *logoi* of nature are all grounded in Christ, how are we to deny that other religions are also myste-riously tied to the mystery of the incarnation through their *logoi*? If the shin-ing vestments of the transfigured Christ symbolize the *logoi* of inspired Scripture, perhaps, one might find snatches of the *Legs bShad sNying po* among the folds. In this perspective, all religious traditions of humanity find a meaning and a purpose in the event of the incarnation, which transcends them in a way that the resources of these very same traditions are unable to articulate. Our earlier discussion of the ratification of ontological bounda-ries in the Chalcedonian model can then become the foundation of a theol-ogy of religions, where religious pluralism is not a deplorable instance of *diairesis*, but a *diaphora* setting the framework for dialogue between a plurality of traditions. A Christocentric theology of the sacramental value of contin-gency becomes a Christocentric theology of religious difference. Within an Origenist model to inter-religious dialogue, the existing plurality of religious traditions would have to be regarded as a result of the fall, destined to dis-appear in the eschaton as the original noetic unity is restored. Even within a Mahāyāna model, religious difference would only belong to the conven-tional level, a helpful instance of skillful means that dissolves into the *dhar-makāya*. Maximos' Christocentric paradigm, on the other hand, could assert the dignity and the salvific value of each tradition, even as they are all seen as participating in the unique divine Wisdom.

One may object that even this way of engaging different religious iden-tities is not truly respectful of their particularity, and that even this Chal-cedonian reading of "religious contingency" is just one more oppressive metanarrative. Perhaps, some would say, we should simply engage in dia-logue with members of other religions, and see where this dialogue takes us. With inter-religious strife a constant presence on the world stage, indulging in the construction of meta-narratives (which no-one believes anyway) is a luxury we cannot afford; the only way forward is then to go ahead and actually *talk* to each other.[8] For others, on the contrary, inter-religious dialogue is ultimately pointless, given that Christianity possesses the fullness of the truth, and, as such, talking with other traditions ultimately serves no purpose. Can we then just hope for a civilized form of suspicion? Civilized suspicion, however, is not the attitude displayed by Abraham towards his visitors at Mamre; advocates of inter-religious dialogue could do better than just accept the theoretical legitimacy of "inter-religious hospitality," and begin to put this principle in practice.[9]

In response to these considerations, one might perhaps concede that our historical circumstances leave us little time for a theology of religions, but if our dialogue is going to be fruitful, at some stage a theology of religions is going to be necessary. Engaging in a discussion with another tradition saying that the latter, being different, helps us gain a better understanding of our beliefs *because it is different* will not lead us very far; at some point, we will need to discuss *in what way* it is different, and *in what way* this difference illumines our belief. Different religious systems have a different take on the ultimate nature of reality, and if one chooses to be a Christian, one must be able to explain why he or she believes that the Christian take on ultimate reality is better than its counterpart in Mahāyāna Buddhism, or, say, African traditional religions. The question is *how* we can engage the particular claims of the other traditions and how these different claims are ultimately related.

At this point, we find ourselves at a cross-road. Either we decide *a priori* how the non-Christian religions are related to Christianity, and develop a hierarchy of beliefs based on their perceived closeness to the latter; or we set out to engage the different ways in which humanity has come to interpret ultimate reality, weighing their respective claims, and striving to move towards the truth by trial and error. In the latter perspective, we cannot say in advance in what way a particular doctrine is related to, or falls short of, or even makes it easier to understand a particular aspect of Christianity. Maximos' understanding of the divine Wisdom incarnate in Christ as encompassing all expressions of wisdom would then be particularly well suited to provide this endeavor with a theoretical bedrock. The Christological dia-

---

[8] This section reflects a series of discussions held in Spring 2005 with Fr. Scott Steinkerchner OP, and the Rev. John Paul Sydnor. See also Scott Steinkerchner OP, "Painting the Clouds," (PhD diss., Boston College, 2005), Ch.5.

[9] Michael Barnes, S.J., *Theology and the Dialogue of Religions* (London: Cambridge University Press, 2002), 201–210.

lectic between universality and particularity does not submerge the latter into the former, but views the *logoi* in terms of a dynamic which avoids the chaos and the disorder of a purposeless plurality, as well as the forced homogenization of a Christianity that sees other traditions with suspicion, or worse, dread. The philosophical insights of Tsong kha pa, but also the teachings of the Quran, or the traditions of Jewish Cabbalism, can then be regarded as *logoi*. This is the answer to Roquentin's nausea at the superfluity of reality, or to Iris Murdoch's claim that contingent reality forces us to cry for a reason: contingency (even religious contingency) finds its ground in the incarnation.

Some will object of course that the claims made by different traditions are contradictory, and as such they cannot be held in a higher synthesis. Yet, the fact that a variety of claims exists, and that they do contradict each other, could be regarded as providential, inasmuch as we are then forced to engage their contradictions and come to a conclusion. In this perspective, the notion of perichoretic exchange underpinning the doctrine of the incarnation and the Mahāyāna notion of emptiness are both *logoi*, and engaging the two doctrines will lead us to a better understanding of the Logos *because*, after appraising them, we are going to embrace the latter, and reject the former as flawed. Judgments of this sort are ultimately going to be necessary, since one cannot claim that Christianity has a better take on ultimate reality and simultaneously assert that there is more than one ultimate truth.

Maximos' incarnational model envisaged divinity taking over humanity and the variety of created reality without suppressing them, but actually developing their potential to the full. Applied to the problem of religious pluralism, the same model suggests that the eternal Logos does not suppress other religious traditions, but underscores their hidden Christocentric significance. Downplaying the centrality of the incarnation and dissolving the *logoi* in the undifferentiated *nous*, an Evagrian model of religious pluralism would construe different religious views as ultimately unrelated to the transcendent reality that religions seek to reach.

Could one use a non-Chalcedonian model to accomplish the same feat? Instead of a Christological approach, could we not choose to map the different religious traditions onto a Trinitarian template, or perhaps, echoing the calls for a Mahāyāna reading of the incarnation, view them as components of the Buddha's *jñāna-dharmakāya*? Let us begin with the first possibility, which is the central theme of Mark Heim's *The Depth of the Riches*. As mentioned in Chapter 1, the purpose of this work is to develop a Trinitarian theology of "religious ends," on the assumption that different religious practices pursue different religious goals, and that these "goals" are authentic and eschatologically valid.[10] Heim's model classifies religious traditions into three different categories: those enabling practitioners to cultivate a familiarity with God's impersonal dimension (such as Buddhism and Hinduism); those relating the individual to God's personal dimension in an extrinsic manner, so that religious practice consists largely in following divine commands (such as Judaism and Islam); and those enabling religious practitioners to enter into communion with God's personal dimension, which is the ultimate goal of Christianity. At the risk of oversimplification—Hasidic and Sufi traditions, for instance, strive to attain communion with the divine no less than the Christian mystics—this approach establishes a system of correspondences between non-Christian religious traditions and the mystery of the Christian God. The Trinity becomes the locus and source of religious experience in all its aspects, and only a spirituality grounded in the Trinitarian God can embrace and transcend what non-Christian traditions accomplish. In this perspective, for instance, Tsong kha pa's approach to practice would develop our relationship with the divine ousia in its interaction with the natural order, but the agapic dialogue between creator and creation would be beyond its reach.

Heim observes that "if God is Trinity," the various dimensions of the divine life "are a seamless unity in the communion of the three persons"; as such "the various relations with God" outlined above "are themselves irreducible," and none of them "need be or can be eliminated in favor of the other."[11] But is this approach truly respectful of the particularity of the religious other? For Heim, a linear progression from the impersonal to the iconic to the personal appears a logical implication of the system. A theology of religions based on Maximos' Chalcedonian paradigm, on the contrary, would envisage the *logoi* of non-Christian religions as pointers towards the mystery of Christ, but it would stop short of asserting *in which way*, or *which aspects* of the mystery they reveal. Different traditions would be seen as participating in the same Wisdom, without attempting an explicit hierarchy of religious practices. All forms of *theōria* and *praxis* would lead to the mystery of Christ, which sustains and guides them all. We would not try to develop an *a priori* narrative establishing connections between particular *logoi*

---

[10] The following gives a very brief summary of the argument in S. Mark Heim, *The Depth of the Riches: A Trinitarian Theology of Religious Ends* (Grand Rapids, Mich., and Cambridge, Mass.: Wm. B. Eerdmans Publishing Company, 2001), Ch. 5–6, 167–242.

[11] S. Mark Heim, *The Depth of the Riches*, 197.

and particular facets of the eternal Logos. All we could say is that the wisdom of non-Christian traditions is itself disclosive, and effectively participates, in the divine mystery.

In line with what we said in Chapter 8, it is its adoption of a Christocentric ontology of participation that would set a Chalcedonian theology of religions apart from other possible approaches. Of course, the Mahāyāna doctrine of skillful means could seemingly serve as an apposite framework for a theology of the religions. The *dharmāh* of the *jñāna-dharmakāya* could include the four gospels as well as the *Lam rim chen mo*, and in the perspective of the *Legs bShad sNying po*, the statements of non-Christian scriptures could be grouped with the *neyartha* teachings of the Svātantrika Mādhyamikas, paving the way for the higher insights of Prāsaṅgika philosophers. Viewing Christian beliefs as *nītartha* statements would be "unskillful," reflecting an in-built reluctance to face reality's impermanence. At the same time, these beliefs could be viewed as part of the "gift" of conventional reality that the Buddha's compassion has devised to sustain our spiritual practice. In this way, a theology of religions based on Tsong kha pa's understanding of Buddhahood would have a more appreciative view of religious pluralism than an Evagrian approach, as it could establish a positive rationale for religious difference. At the same time, it would stop short of developing an *a priori* narrative connecting different practices to different aspects of ultimate reality, since the very emptiness of ultimate reality would entail that no such connection can be made.

An overarching Buddhist ontology might undercut the natural tendency towards hierarchical categorization of religions, but we might also wonder whether presenting all religious traditions as belonging to the conventional realm is not the most totalizing of all possible meta-narratives. If the *svābhāvikakāya* is an insight into emptiness, engaging the religious other in its own terms shall not increase our understanding of ultimate reality; the moment of awakening necessarily transcends even the most comprehensive understanding of other religious traditions. If *theōria* comes to include the engagement of the *logoi* of different religions, inter-religious dialogue would then become an integral part of religious practice, and hence of spiritual growth; but if the *dharmāh* do not disclose the ultimate insight, merely leading practitioners towards it, their value is again provisional, and engaging them shall not modify our ultimate condition. In this way, Maximos explodes the dichotomy between "extrinsic" and "intrinsic" models of revelation which is implicit in Dulles' account, noting that "revelation" emerges from the personal engagement with the God's self-disclosure in history and in contingent, created reality.

The conclusion drawn in relation to the sacramentality of matter can be repeated here: the dichotomy between conventional and ultimate reality ensures that inter-religious dialogue can at most be regarded as *upayakauśa-lya*, whereas the participation of all *logoi* in the Logos would view it as granting us a glimpse into the divine mystery. Wittgenstein is famous for claiming that the mystery towards which reality is ordered can never be expressed by language. Tsong kha and Maximos would certainly have concurred. Thanks to the incarnation of the Logos, however, contingent reality offers us an insight into the mystery, which will outlast even the passing of this world.

BIBLIOGRAPHY

PRIMARY TEXTS FROM THE CHRISTIAN TRADITION IN THE ORIGINAL LANGUAGE

PG refers to Patrologia graeca. Edited by J.-P. Migne. 162 vols. Paris, 1857–1886.

PL refers to Patrologia Latina. Edited by J.-P. Migne. 217 vols. Paris, 1844–1864.

CCSG refers to *Corpus Christianorum Series Graeca*. Edited by R. Demeulenaere. Leuven: Brepols, 1977–

CSEL refers to *Corpus Scriptorum Ecclesiasticorum Latinorum*. Edited by the Academy of Vienna. Vienna: Tempsky, 1866–1957.

Athanasios. *De Incarnatione*. PG 25b: 95–197.

_____.*Contra Arios*. PG 26: 9–525.

_____. *Contra Gentes*. PG 25b: 3–94.

Augustine. *De Civitate Dei*. CSEL 40.

Barsanuphios. *Doctrina circa Opiniones Origenis, Evagrii et Dydimi* (also known as *Spiritual Letters*). PG 86a: 891–901

Basil of Caesarea. *Adversus Eunomium*. PG 29b: 497–772.

_____. *Hexaemeron*. PG 29b: 3–206.

_____. *De Spiritu Sancto*. PG 32: 67–218.

Clement of Alexandria. *Stromateis*. PG 9: 9–602.

Cyril of Alexandria. *Adversus Nestorium*. PG 76: 9–249.

_____. *In Joannem*. PG 73; PG 74: 9–757.

_____. *Quod Unus sit Christus*. PG 75: 1254–1363.

_____. *Glaphyra in Exodum*. PG 69: 385–539.

Evagrios Pontikos. *Epistula ad Basilium* (also known as *Eighth Epistle*). (in Migne: Basil of Caesarea) PG 32: 243–268.

_____. (In Migne: Nilus of Sinai) *De Diversis Malignis Cogitationibus*. Also PG 79: 1199–1234.

_____. (In Migne: Nilus of Sinai) *De Oratione*. Also PG 79: 1166–1198.

_____. *Praktikos*. PG 40: 1219–1251.

_____. (In Migne: Nilus of Sinai) *Tractatus ad Eulogium Monachum*. PG 79: 1094–1139.

Gregory of Nazianzos. *Epistle CI 'Ad Cledonium'*. PG 37: 175–190.

_____. *Orationes*. PG 35: 387–1252; PG 36: 9–662.

Gregory of Nyssa. *De Anima et Resurrectione*. PG 46: 11–160.

_____. *Oratio Catechetica*. PG 45: 9–106.

_____. *Contra Eunomium*. PG 45: 239–1122.

_____. *De Hominis Opificio*. PG 44: 123–257.

_____. *De Vita Sanctae Macrinae*. PG 46: 949–998.

_____. *De Perfecta Christiani Forma*. PG 46: 251–286.

_____. *Orationes de Beatitudinibus*. PG 44: 1194–1303.

_____. *Commentarius in Canticum Canticorum*. PG 44: 755–1118.

_____. *De Vita Moysis*. PG 44: 298–434.

Gregory Palamas. *Hagioriticus Tomus*. PG 150: 1225–1237.

Ireneus. *Adversus Haereses*. PG 7a: 0433–1118; PG 7b: 1119–1122.

Jerome. *Commentarium in Epistulam ad Ephesinos*. PL 26: 524–528.

John Chrysostom. *Catechesis 1*. PG 49: 223–231.

John Damascene. De Fide Orthodoxa. PG 94: 790–1226.

Justinian. Epistula ad Synodum de Theodoro Mopsuesteno et Aliis. PG 86a : 946–994.

Leontius of Byzantium. *Libri Tres Contra Nestorianos et Eutychianos*. PG 86a: 1267–1394.

Mark the Ascetic. (In Migne, Mark the Monk) *Opuscula 1: De Lege Spirituali*. PG 65: 906–929.

_____. (In Migne, Mark the Monk) *Opuscula 2: De His qui Putant se ex Operibus Justificari*. PG 65: 929–966.

Maximos the Confessor. *Ambigua*. PG 91:1031–1417.

_____. *Liber Asceticus*. PG 911–958.

_____. *Capita de Charitate*. PG 90: 959–1082.

_____. *Orationis Dominicae Brevis Expositio*. PG 90: 871–910.

_____. *Disputatio cum Pyrrho*. PG 91: 287–360.

_____. *Epistulae*. PG 91: 363–649.

_____. *Mystagogia*. PG 91: 658–718.

_____. *Opuscula theologica et polemica*. PG 91: 9–214.

_____. *Quaestiones et Dubia*. CCSG 10.

_____. *Quaestiones ad Thalassium*. CCSG Vol. 7; Vol. 22. Also PG 90: 244–785.

_____. *Capita Theologiae et Economiae*. PG 90: 1083–1177.

_____. *Capita Quinquies Centena* (also known as *Various Texts on Theology, the Divine Economy, and Virtue and Vice*). PG 90: 1178–1393.

Origen, *Contra Celsum*. PG 11: 641–1631.

_____. *Commentaria in Epistulam Beati Pauli ad Romanos*. PG 14: 837–1291.

_____. *Commentaria in Evangelium Joannis*. PG 14: 21–828

_____. *Commentaria in Evangelium secundum Mattheum.* PG 13: 829:1599.

_____. *Exegetica in Psalmos.* PG 12: 1053–1684.

_____. *Homiliae in Genesim.* PG 12: 145–280.

_____. *Homiliae in Leviticum.* PG 12: 405–573.

_____. *Homiliae in Numeros.* PG 12: 583–804.

_____. *Commentaria in Canticum Canticorum.* PG 13: 61–197.

_____. *De Principiis (Peri Archōn).* PG 11: 111–413.

Plotinus, *Enneades.* Loeb Classical Library. Cambridge, Mass.: Harvard University Press, 1968–88.

Plutarch. *De Iside et Osiride.* Loeb Classical Library. Cambridge, Mass.: Harvard University Press, 1936.

Pseudo-Denys. *De Coelesti Hierarchia.* PG 3: 115–368.

_____. *De Divinis Nominibus.* PG 3: 586–996.

_____. *De Ecclesiastica Hierarchia.* PG 3: 369–585.

Symeon the New Theologian. *De Fide et Profectu Libellus.* PG 120: 693–702.

Theophilos. *Epistula Paschalis.* CSEL 55: 160–165.

PRIMARY TEXTS FROM THE CHRISTIAN TRADITION IN TRANSLATION

Anselm of Aosta. *Monologion and Proslogion With the Replies of Gaunilo and Anselm.* Translated by T. Williams. Indianapolis, Ind.: Hackett Publishing Company, 1996.

Cassian, John. *The Conferences.* Translated by B. Ramsey, O.P. New York and Mahwah, N.J.: Newman Press, 1997.

_____. *The Institutes.* Translated by B. Ramsey, O.P. New York and Mahwah, N.J.: Newman Press, 2000.

_____. *On the Holy Fathers of Sketis and on discrimination.* Pages 94–108 in Geoffrey E. H. Palmer, Philip Sherrard, and Kallistos Ware, eds. *The Philokalia* (Vol. 1). London: Faber & Faber, 1979.

Cyril of Alexandria. *On the Unity of Christ.* Translated by John A. McGuckin. Crestwood, N.Y.: St. Vladimir's Seminary Press, 1997.

Evagrios Pontikos. *Contro i pensieri malvagi (Antirrhetikos).* Translated by G. Bunge and V. Lazzeri. Magnano, Comunita' di Bose: Ed. Qiqajon, 2005.

_____. *Kephalaia Gnostika. Les Six Centuries des 'Kephalaia Gnostica' d'Évagre le Pontique.* Translated from the Syriac by A. Guillaumont. Paris: Firmin Didot, 1958.

_____. *Letter to Melania.* Pages 2–38 in "Evagrius of Pontus' 'Letter to Melania'." Translated by M. Parmentier. *Bijdragen: Tijdschrift voor filosofie en theologie* 46 (1985): Part I.

_____. *Monastic mirror. Texte und Untersuchungen*, xxxix 4b. Leipzig: Gressman ed., 1913.

_____. *Outline teaching on Asceticism and Stillness in the Solitary Life*. Pages 31–37 in Geoffrey E. H. Palmer, Philip Sherrard, and Kallistos Ware, eds. *The Philokalia* (Vol. 1). London: Faber & Faber, 1979.

_____. *Praktikos*. Pages 15–42 in *The Praktikos and Chapters on Prayer*. Translated by J. E. Bamberger OCSO. Kalamazoo, Mich.: Cistercian Publ., 1981.

_____. *On Prayer: 153 Texts*. Pages 55–71 in Geoffrey E. H. Palmer, Philip Sherrard, and Kallistos Ware, eds. *The Philokalia* (Vol. 1). London: Faber & Faber, 1979.

_____. *Texts On Discrimination in Respect of Passions and Thoughts*. Pages 38–52 in Geoffrey E. H. Palmer, Philip Sherrard, and Kallistos Ware, eds. *The Philokalia* (Vol. 1). London: Faber & Faber, 1979.

Gregory of Nyssa. *Treatise on the Inscriptions of the Psalms*. Translated by R. E. Heine. Oxford: Oxford University Press, 1995.

Mark the Ascetic. *On the Spiritual Law*. Pages 109–124 in Geoffrey H. Palmer, Philip Sherrard, and Kallistos Ware, eds. *The Philokalia* (Vol. 1). London: Faber & Faber, 1979.

_____. *On those who think that they are made righteous by works*. Pages 125–147 in Geoffrey H. Palmer, Philip Sherrard, and Kallistos Ware, eds. *The Philokalia* (Vol. 1). London: Faber & Faber, 1979.

Massimo il Confessore, *Ambigua*. Translated by C. Moreschini. Milan: Bompiani, 2003.

_____. *The Ascetic Life and the Four Centuries on Charity*. Translated and introduced by P. Sherwood, OSB. London: The Newman Press, 1955.

_____. *The Church's Mystagogy*. Pages 181–225 in *Maximus Confessor: Selected Writings*. Classics of Western Spirituality. Translated by G. Berthold. Mahwah, N.J.: Paulist Press, 1985.

_____.*Centuries on Charity*. Pages 52–113 in Geoffrey H. Palmer, Philip Sherrard, and Kallistos Ware, eds. *The Philokalia* (Vol. 2). London, Faber & Faber, 1981.

_____. *Commentary on Our Father*. Pages 99–126 in *Maximus Confessor: Selected Writings*. Classics of Western Spirituality. Translated by G. Berthold. Mahwah, N.J.: Paulist Press, 1985.

_____. *Opuscules théologiques et polémiques*. Translated by É. Ponsoye. Paris: Cerf, 1998.

_____. *"Quaestions and Doubts."* Translated by Despina D. Prassas in "St. Maximos the Confessor's 'Questions and Doubts': Translation and Commentary." PhD diss., Catholic University of America, 2003.

_____. *Two Hundred Texts on Theology and the Incarnate Dispensation of the Son of God.* Pages 114–163 in Geoffrey H. Palmer, Philip Sherrard, and Kallistos Ware, eds. *The Philokalia* (Vol. 2). London, Faber & Faber, 1981.

_____. *Various Texts on Theology, the Divine Economy, and Virtue and Vice.* Pages 164–284 in Geoffrey H. Palmer, Philip Sherrard, and Kallistos Ware, eds. *The Philokalia* (Vol. 2). London, Faber & Faber, 1981.

_____. *Life of the Virgin* (contested attribution). Translated by M.-J. van Esbroeck. Louvain: Ed. Peeters, 1986.

_____. *Origen: An Exortation to Martyrdom, Prayer, and Selected Works.* With an introduction by Rowan A. Green. Classics of Western Spirituality, Mahwah, N.J.: Paulist Press, 1979.

Symeon the New Theologian. *On Faith.* Pages 16–25 in Geoffrey H. Palmer, Philip Sherrard, and Kallistos Ware, eds. *The Philokalia* (Vol. 4). London: Faber& Faber, 1999.

Thomas Aquinas. *Summa Theologiae.* Translated by the Fathers of the English Dominican Province. Westminster, Md.: Christian Classics Pub., 1981.

PRIMARY TEXTS FROM THE BUDDHIST TRADITION

Anon. *Kun bjed rgyal po.* In *The supreme source: The Fundamental Tantra of the Dzogchen Semde 'Kunjed Gyalpo'.* Translated and introduced by Chos rgyal nam kha nor bu and A. Clemente. Ithaca, N.Y.: Snow Lion Pub., 1999. Also in *The sovereign all-creating mind: The motherly Buddha, A Translation of the Kun byed rgyal po'i mdo.* Translated by Eva K. Neumaier-Dargyay. Albany, N.Y.: SUNY Press, 1992.

'Jigs med gLing pa. *Treasure Texts (The Great Perfection Tantra of the Expanse of Samantabhadra's Wisdom; The Subsequent Tantra of Great Perfection Instruction; Experiencing the Enlightened Mind of Samantabhadra; Distinguishing the Three Essential Points of the Great Perfection).* Translated by Sam van Schaik. Pages 137–165 in Sam van Schaik. *Approaching the Great Perfection: Simultaneous and gradual methods of Dzogchen practice in the Longchen Nyingtig.* Somerville, Mass.: Wisdom Publication, 2004.

_____. *Pure Visions (An Aspirational Prayer for the Ground, Path, and Result; Vajra Verses on the Natural State).* Pages 167–171 in Sam van Schaik. *Approaching the Great Perfection.*

_____. *Supporting Texts (The White Lotus; The Words of the Omniscient One; The Lion's Roar that Destroys the Deviations of Renunciants Meditating on the Seminal Heart; Seeing Nakedly the Natural State of the Great Perfection).* Pages 173–238 in Sam van Schaik. *Approaching the Great Perfection: Simultaneous and gradual methods of Dzogchen practice in the Longchen Nyingtig.* Somerville, Mass.: Wisdom Publication, 2004.

Mañjuśrīmitra ('Jam dpal bshes gnyen), *Primordial experience (Byang chub sems bsgom pa)*: *an Introduction to rDzogs chen meditation*. Also known as *rDo la gser zhun*. Translated and introduced by Namkhai Norbu and K. Lipman; Boston, Mass.: Shambala 2001.

Tsong kha pa. *Lam rim chen mo*: *The Great Treatise on the Stages of the Path to Enlightenment*. Vol. 2. Translated by the Lamrim Chenmo Translation Committee. Joshua W. C. Cutler, Editor in Chief; Guy Newland, Editor. Ithaca, N.Y.: Snow Lion Publications, 2004.

_____. *Lam rim chen mo*: *The Great Treatise on the Stages of the Path to Enlightenment*. Vol. 3. Translated by the Lamrim Chenmo Translation Committee. Joshua W. C. Cutler, Editor in Chief; Guy Newland, Editor. Ithaca, N.Y.: Snow Lion Publications, 2002. Sections 564–606 also translated by Elizabeth Napper in pages 153–214 of her *Dependent-Arising and Emptiness*: *a Tibetan Buddhist interpretation of Mādhyamika Philosophy*. Boston, Mass.: Wisdom Publications, 2003.

_____. *Legs bshad snying po* (long version). Translated by Robert A. F. Thurman. Pages 185–385 in Robert A. F. Thurman. *The Central Philosophy of Tibet—A Study and Translation of Jey Tsong Khapa's 'Essence of True Eloquence'*. Princeton, N.J.: Princeton University Press, 1984.

_____. *Legs bshad snying po* (short version). Translated by Robert A. F. Thurman. Pages 185–194 in Robert A. F. Thurman. *The Central Philosophy of Tibet*.

SECONDARY LITERATURE

Amand, David. "Fatalisme et liberté dans l'antiquité grecque." *Recueil de travaux d'histoire et philologie*, 3d series (19): Louvain, 1945.

Ames, William L. "Bhāvaviveka's own view of his differences with Buddhapālita." Pages 41–66 in Sara McClintock and Georges Dreyfus, eds. *The Prāsangika-Svātantrika distinction*: *What Difference does a Difference make?* Boston, Mass.: Wisdom Publications, 2003.

De Angelis, Bernardo. *Natura Persona e libertà: l'antropologia di Massimo il Confessore*. Quaderni dell'Assunzione. Roma: Armando Editore, 2002.

Anon. *The Rig Veda*. Trans. by Wendy Doniger O'Flaherty. London: Penguin, 1982.

Arens, Herbert. *Die Christologische Sprache Leos des Grossen: Analyse des Tomus an den Patriarchen Flavian*. Freiburger Theologische Studien, 123. Freiburg: Herder, 1982.

Aristotle, *Nicomachean Ethics*. Translated by T. Irwin. Indianapolis, Ind.: Hackett Pub., 1999.

Armantage, W. "Will the body be raised? Origen and the Origenist controversy." PhD diss., Yale University, 1970.

Armstrong, Karen. *Buddha*. London: Penguin, 2004.

Aziz, Barbara N., and Matthew Kapstein. "A rNying ma text: the *Kun byed rgyal po*." Pages 282–293 in Barbara N. Aziz and Matthew Kapstein, eds. *Soundings in Tibetan civilization*. New Dehli: South Asia Books, 1985.

von Balthasar, Hans Urs. *Kosmische Liturgie: Maximus der Bekenner*. Einsiedeln: Johannes Verlag, 1961. English translation: *Cosmic Liturgy: The Universe According to Maximus the Confessor*. Translated by Fr. Brian Daley, S.J. San Francisco: Ignatius Press, 2003.

_____. *Two Sisters in Christ*. Translated by D. D. Martin. San Francisco: Ignatius Press, 1970.

_____. *Skizzen zur Theologie* (Vol. 2). Einsiedeln: Johannes Verlag, 1971.

_____. *Theodramatik* (Vol. 3: *Die Handlung*). Einsiedeln: Johannes Verlag, 1980. English translation: *Theo-drama*, Vol. 3: *The Action*. Translated by G. Harrison. San Francisco: Ignatius Press, 1994.

_____. *Origen, spirit and fire: a thematic anthology of his writings*. Washington, DC: Catholic University of America Press, 1984.

_____. *Skizzen zur Theologie* (Vol. 5). Einsiedeln: Johannes Verlag, 1986.

_____. *Theologik* (Vol. 3). Einsiedeln: Johannes Verlag, 1987. English translation: *Theo-logic*, Vol. 3, *The Spirit of Truth*. Translated by G. Harrison. San Francisco: Ignatius Press, 2005.

_____. *Truth Is Symphonic: Aspects of Christian Pluralism*. Translated by G. Harrison. San Francisco: Ignatius Press, 1987.

_____. *Herrlichkeit-Schau der Gestalt*. Einsiedeln: Johannes Verlag, 1988. English translation: *Seeing the Form. The Glory of the Lord: a Theological Aesthetics*. San Francisco: Ignatius Press, 1982.

_____. *Theo-Drama: Theological Dramatic Theory*, Vol. 1: *Prolegomena*. San Francisco: Ignatius Press, 1988.

_____. *Presence and Thought: Essay on the Religious Philosophy of Gregory of Nyssa*. Translated by M. Sebanc. San Francisco: Ignatius Press, 1995.

_____. *Das betrachtende Gebet*. Einsiedeln: Johannes Verlag, 2003. English translation: *Prayer*. San Francisco: Ignatius Press, 1986.

Barth, Karl. *Letter to the Romans* .Oxford: Oxford University Press, 1968.

_____. *Church Dogmatics*, IV, 3, 2. Edinburgh: T&T Clark, 2004.

Bachelor, Stephen. *A guide to the Bodhisattva's way of life* (including a translation of Śāntideva's *Bodhicaryāvatāra*). 2d ed. Ithaca, N.Y.: Snow Lion Publ., 1999.

Barnes, S.J., Michael. *Theology and the Dialogue of Religions*. London: Cambridge University Press, 2002.

Barzin, Alexander. *The Validity and Accuracy of Cognition of the Two Truths in Gelug-Prasangika and Non-Gelug Madhyamaka*. Online: http://www. berzinarchives.com/sutra/sutra_level_5/validity_prasanghika_mad-hyamaka.html. *The Berzin Archive*, 2002.

Bathrellos, Demetrios. *The Byzantine Christ: Person, Nature, and Will in the Christology of Saint Maximus the Confessor*. Oxford and New York: Oxford University Press, 2005.

Bausenhart, Guido. *"In Allem uns gleich außer der Sünde"*: *Studies zum Beitrag Maximos des Bekenners zur alt-kirchlichen Christologie*. Tübinger Studien zur Theologie und Philosophie, 5. Mainz: Matthias-Grünewald-Verlag, 1992.

Bellah, Robert, Richard Madsen, et al. *Habits of the Heart: Individualism and Commitment in American Life*. Berkeley, Calif.: University of California Press, 1996.

Berkeley, George. *A Treatise Concerning the Principles of Human Knowledge*. Whitefish, Mont.: Kessinger Publications, 2004.

Berthold, George. "The Cappadocian roots of Maximos the Confessor." Pages 51–59 in Felix Heinzer and Cristoph von Schönborn, eds. *Maximus Confessor. Actes du Symposium sur Maxime le Confesseur*. Fribourg-en-Suisse: Éditions Universitaires, 1982.

Bloom, Alfred. *Shinran's Gospel of Pure Grace*. Tucson, Ariz.: University of Arizona Press, 1965.

Blowers, Paul. *Exegesis and Spiritual Pedagogy in Maximus the Confessor—An Investigation of the Quaestiones ad Thalassium*. Notre Dame, Ind.: University of Notre Dame Press, 1991.

Boulnois, Olivier. "Reading Duns Scotus: From History to Philosophy." *Modern Theology* 21.4 (2005): 603–608.

Boyancé, Paul. "Les deux démons personnels dans l'antiquité grecque et latine." *Revue de philologie* (1935): 189–202.

Boys-Stones, George. *Post-Hellenistic Philosophy—A Study of its Development from the Stoics to Origen*. Oxford: Oxford University Press, 2001.

_____. "The truest account: Origen in defense of Christian allegory." Paper delivered at the annual meeting of the SBL, San Antonio, Tex., November 21, 2004.

Bunge, Gabriel. *Geistliche Vaterschaft: Christliche Gnosis bei Evagrios Pontikos*. Regensburg: Kommissionsverlag Friedrich Pustet. 1988.

Butler, Judith. *Bodies that Matter: On the Discursive limits of 'Sex'*. London: Routledge, 1993.

Cabezon, José I. "The canonization of philosophy and the rhetoric of *siddhānta* in Tibetan Buddhism." Pages 7–26 in Paul Griffiths and John

P. Keenan, eds. *Buddha Nature: A Festschrift in Honor of Minoru Kiyota.* Los Angeles: Buddhist Books International, 1990.

Cadiou, René. *Introduction au système d'Origène.* Paris: Les Belles Lettres, 1932.

Campbell, Joseph. *The Masks of God: Oriental Mythology.* London: Penguin, 1991.

Candal, Manuel SJ. "La gracia increada del *Liber Ambiguorum* de San Maximo." *Orientalia Christiana Periodica* (1961): 131–149.

Caputo, John D. *The Prayers and Tears of Jacques Derrida: Religion without Religion.* Bloomington and Indianapolis, Ind.: Indiana University Press, 1997.

Carpenter, Rhys. *Religion in the Homeric Epics.* Los Angeles: University of California Press, 1946.

Cartwright, Nancy. *How the Laws of Physics Lie.* Oxford: Oxford University Press, 1983.

Chagdud Tulku. *Gates of Buddhist Practice: Essential Teachings of a Tibetan Master.* Rev. ed. Junction City, Calif.: Padma Publ., 2001.

Chestnut, Glenn F. *The First Church Histories. Eusebius, Socrates, Sozimen, Theodoret and Evagrius.* Macon, Ga.: Mercer University Press, 1998.

Chödrön, Pema. *Start where you are: a Guide to Compassionate Living.* Boston: Shambala, 2001.

Clarke, Elizabeth A. *The Origenist Controversy: The Cultural Construction of an Early Christian Debate.* Princeton, N.J.: Princeton University Press, 1992.

Clooney, Frank SJ. *Theology After Vedanta: An Experiment in Comparative Theology.* Albany, N.Y.: SUNY Press, 1993.

———. *Seeing Through Texts: Doing Theology among the Śrivaiśnava of South India.* Albany, N.Y.: SUNY Press, 1996.

Coakley, Sarah. *Powers and Submissions: Spirituality, Philosophy and Gender.* Oxford, U.K., and Cambridge, Mass.: Blackwell, 2002.

Colledge, Edmund, Bernard McGinn, and Houston Smith, eds. *Meister Eckhart* (Vol. 2). Classics of Western Spirituality. Mahwah, N.J.: Paulist press, 1981.

Congregation for the Doctrine of the Faith. *Letter to the Bishops of the Catholic Church on Some aspects of Christian Meditation.* Rome, Oct. 15th, 1989.

Conradi, Peter J. *The Saint and the Artist: A Study of Iris Murdoch's Works.* New York: HarperCollins, 2001.

Conze, Edward. *The Perfection of Wisdom: In Eight Thousand Lines and its Verse Summary.* San Francisco: City Lights Publications, 1973.

Cooper, Adam G. *The Body in St. Maximus the Confessor: Holy Flesh, Wholly Deified.* Oxford and New York: Oxford University Press, 2005.

Corbin, Henry. *Temple and Contemplation*. London, Islamic Publications, 1986.

Croce, Vittorio. *Tradizione e ricerca. Il metodo teologico di san Massimo il Confessore*. Milano: Vita e Pensiero, 1974.

Crouzel, Henri. *Théologie de l'image de Dieu chez Origène*. Theologie 34. Paris: Aubier/Montagne, 1956.

_____. *Origène et la 'connaisance mystique'*. Bruges: Desclée de Brouwer, 1961.

_____. *Origen*. Edinburgh: T&T Clark, 1989.

Cullmann, Oscar. *Le Christ et le temps: Temps et histoire dans le christianisme primitive*. Lausanne-Paris: Delachaux & Niestlé, 1947. English translation: *Christ and time: The primitive Christian conception of time and history*. Louisville, KY : Westminster/John Knox Press, 1950.

Cunningham, Connor. "Wittgenstein after Theology." Pages 64–90 in John Milbank, Catherine Pickstock, and Graham Ward, eds. *Radical Orthodoxy*. London and New York: Routledge, 1999.

_____. *Genealogy of Nihilism: Philosophy of nothing and the difference of theology*. London and New York: Routledge, 2002.

Cyril of Scythopolis. *The Lives of the Monks of Palestine*. Translated by J. Binns and R. M. Price. Cistercian Studies Series, No. 114. Collegeville, Minn.: Cistercian Publ., 1991

HH the Dalai Lama. *Tantra in Tibet: The Great Exposition of Secret Mantra by Tsong kha pa*. London: Allen and Unwin, 1977.

_____. *The Good Heart: A Buddhist Perspective on the Teaching of Jesus*. Somerville, Mass.: Wisdom Publications, 1996.

Daley, Brian E. "Origen's *De principiis*: A Guide to the 'Principles' of Christian Scriptural Interpretation." In John F. Petruccione, ed. *Nova et Vetera: Patristic Studies in Honor of Thomas Patrick Halton*. Washington, DC: Catholic University of America Press, 1998.

_____. *The Hope of The Early Church: A Handbook of Patristic Eschatology*. Peabody, Mass.: Hendrickson, 2003.

Dalmais, Irénée-Henri. "Saint Maxime le Confesseur, Docteur de la Charité." *Vie Spirituelle* 78 (1948): 194–201.

_____. "La Théorie des 'Logoi' des Créatures chez S. Maxime le Confesseur." *Revue des sciences philosophiques et théologiques* 36 (1952): 244–249.

_____. "La doctrine ascétique de saint Maxime le Confesseur, d'après le *Liber asceticus*." *Irénikon* 26 (1953): 25–36.

_____. "Un traité de théologie contemplative: Le *Commentaire de Pater Noster* de saint Maxim le Confesseur." *Revue d'Ascetique et de Mystique* 29 (1953): 123–139.

_____. "L'anthropologie spirituelle de Saint Maxime le Confesseur." *Recherches et Debats* 36 (1961): 202–211.

_____. "Saint Maxime le Confesseur et la crise de l'origénisme monastique." Pages 416–424 in George Lemaître, ed. *Théologie de la vie monastique: Études sur la tradition patristique.* Théologie, 49. Paris: Aubier, 1961.

_____. "La fonction unificatrice du Verbe Incarné dans les oeuvres spirituelles de saint Maxime le Confesseur." *Sciences ecclésiastiques* 14 (1962): 445–459.

_____. "L'héritage évagrien dans la synthèse de Saint Maxime le Confesseur." Studia Patristica 8 (1966): 356–363.

_____. "Théologie et mystère liturgique dans la *Mystagogie* de S. Maxime le Confesseur." Studia Patristica 13 (1975): 145–153.

_____. "Maxime le Confesseur." *Dictionnaire de spiritualité* X (1980): 836–847.

Daniélou, Jean. *Origen.* Translated by W. Mitchell. London and New York: Sheed and Ward, 1955.

_____. *Philon d'Alexandrie.* Paris, Seuil, 1958.

_____. *Platonisme et théologie mystique. Essay sur la théologie spirituelle de Gregoire de Nysse.* 2d ed. Paris : Seuil, 1953.

Descartes, René. *Discourse on Method.* Translated by D. Cress. Indianapolis, Ind.: Hackett Publishing Co., 1999.

_____. *Rules for the Directions of the Mind.* Indianapolis, Ind.: Bobbs-Merrill Co., 2000.

Derrida, Jacques. *Speech and Phenomena and Other Essays on Husserl's Theory of Signs.* Translated by D. Allison. Evanston, Ill.: Northwestern University Press, 1973.

_____. *On Grammatology.* Translated by G. C. Spivak. Baltimore, Md.: John Hopkins University Press, 1976.

_____. *Writing and Difference.* Translated by A. Bass. Chicago: Chicago University Press, 1980.

_____. *The Margins of Philosophy.* Translated by A. Bass. Chicago: University of Chicago Press, 1981.

Doctorow, Edgar L. *City of God.* New York: Random House, 2000.

Doucet, Marcel. "Vues récentes sur les 'métamorphoses' de la pensée de saint Maxime le Confesseur." *Sciences et Esprit* 31.3 (1979): 269–291.

Dudjom Rinpoche. *The Nyingma School of Tibetan Buddhism: Its Fundamentals and History.* Translated and edited by Gyurme Dorje and Matthew Kapstein. Somerville, Mass.: Wisdom Publications, 1991.

Dulles, Avery R. *Models of Revelation.* Maryknoll, N.Y.: Orbis Books, 1992.

Dupuis, Jacques. *Towards a Christian Theology of Religious Pluralism*. Maryknoll, N.Y.: Orbis Books, 1999.

Eckel, M. David. *Jñānagarbha's Commentary on the Distinction between the Two Truths: An Eighth-Century Handbook of Mādhyamaka philosophy*. Albany, N.Y.: SUNY Press, 1987.

_____. "The Satisfaction of No-Analysis." Pages 173–203 in Sara McClintock and Georges Dreyfus, eds. *The Prāsangika-Svātantrika distinction: What Difference does a Difference make?* Boston, Mass.: Wisdom Publications, 2003.

Evdokimov, Paul. *Ages of the Spiritual Life*. Crestwood, N.Y.: Saint Vladimir's Press, 1998.

Evennett, Henry Outram. "Counter-Reformation Spirituality." Pages 47–64 in David Luebke, ed. *The Counterreformation: Essential Readings*. Oxford, U.K., and Cambridge, Mass.: Blackwells, 1999.

Evola, Julius. *The Doctrine of Awakening: The Attainment of Self-Mastery According to the Earliest Buddhist Texts*. Translated by H. E. Musson. Rochester, Vt.: Inner Traditions. 1996.

Farrell, Joseph P. *Free choice in St. Maximus the Confessor*. South Canaan, Pa.: Saint Tikhon's Seminary Press, 1989.

De Faye, Eugène. *Origène, sa vie, son oeuvre, sa pensée*. Bibliothèque de l'École des Hautes Études en Sciences Religieuses, 37, 43, 44. Paris: Éditions Leroux, 1923–8

Fedwick, Paul F. *Basil of Caesarea on Education*. Toronto: Pontifical Institute of Medieval Studies, 1983.

Fee, Gordon. *The First Epistle to the Corinthians*. Grand Rapids, Mich.: Willem B. Eerdmans Publishing Company, 1987.

Feuerbach, Ludwig. *The Essence of Christianity*. Translated by G. Eliot. Amherst, N.Y.: Prometheus Book, 1989.

Florovsky, Georges. *The Byzantine Fathers of the Sixth to the Eighth century*. Crestwood, N.Y.: St. Vladimir's Seminary Press, 1987.

Foucault, Michel. *Archeology of knowledge*. Translated by A. M. Sheridan Smith. London: Tavistock, 1972.

_____. "Technologies of the Self." Pages 16–49 in Luther H. Martin, Huck Gutman & Patrick H. Hutton, eds. *Technologies of the Self: A Seminar with Michel Foucault*. Amherst, Mass.: University of Massachussets Press, 1988.

_____. *The History of Sexuality: The Use of Pleasure*. New York: Vintage, 1990.

Fox, Matthew. *A New Reformation: Creation Spirituality and the Transformation of Christianity*. Rochester, Vt.: Inner Spirituality, 2006.

Frend, W. H. C. *The rise of the monophysite movement; chapters in the history of the church in the fifth and sixth centuries.* Cambridge: Cambridge University Press, 1972.

Freud, Sigmund. *The Future of an Illusion.* Trans. by J. Strachey. New York and London: W. W. Norton & Company, 1999.

Garrigues, Jean-Michel. "L'énergie divine e la grâce chez Maxime le Confesseur." *Istina* 19 (1974): 282–84.

_____. "La Personne composée du Christ d'après Saint Maxime le Confesseur." *Revue Thomiste* 74 (1974): 181–204.

_____. *Maxime le Confesseur: La charité, avenir divine de l'homme.* Paris: Beauchesne, 1976.

Garrigou-Lagrange, Reginald, OP. *Predestination.* Rockford, Ill.: Tan Press, 1999.

_____. *Providence.* Rockford, Ill.: Tan Press, 1999.

Gauthier, René-Antoine. "Saint Maxime le Confesseur et la psychologie de l'acte humain." *Recherches de Théologie Ancienne et Mediévale* 21 (1954): 51–100.

Gavrilyuk, Paul. *The Suffering of the Impassible God: The Dialectic of Patristic Thought.* Oxford Early Christian Studies. Oxford: Oxford University Press, 2004.

Gawronski, Raymond SJ. *Word and Silence: Hans Urs von Balthasar and the Spiritual Encounter between East and West.* Edinburgh: T&T Clark, 1995.

Germano, David. "Poetic thought, the intelligent universe, and the mystery of self: the Tantric synthesis of rDzogs chen in 14th century Tibet." PhD diss., Univ. of Wisconsin-Madison, 1992.

_____, and Kevin Trainor, eds. *Embodying the Dharma: Buddhist Relic Veneration in Asia.* Albany, N.Y.: SUNY, 2003.

Gomez, Louis O. "The direct and gradual approaches of Zen master Mahāyāna." Pages 393–434 in R. Lewis Lancaster, ed. *Early Ch'an in China and Tibet.* Berkeley, Calif: Asian Humanities Press, 1983.

Gregory, Peter N. "The Place of the Sudden Teaching within the Hua-yen Tradition: an Investigation of the Process of Doctrinal Change." *Journal of the International Association of Buddhist Studies* 6.1 (1983): 31–60.

Grillmeyer, Alois. *Le Christ dans la tradition chrétienne* (II, 1). *Le Concile de Chalcédoine (451), Réception et opposition (451–513).* Cogitatio Fidei, 154. Paris: Cerf, 1990. English translation: *Christ in Christian tradition.* Louisville, Ky.: Westminster/John Knox Press, 2002.

Griffiths, Paul. *On Being Buddha: Maximal Greatness and the Doctrine of Buddhahood in Classical India.* Albany, N.Y.: SUNY, 1994.

Gross, Jules. *La divinisation du Chrétien d'après les Pères grecs.* Translated by P. A. Onica. Anaheim, Calif.: A&C Press, 2002.

Gudmunsen, Chris. *Wittgenstein and Buddhism.* London: Macmillan Press, 1977.

Guillaumont, Antoine. *Les 'Kephalaia Gnostica' d'Évagre le Pontique et l'histoire de l'Origénisme chez les Grecs et chez les Syriens.* Paris: Seuil, 1962.

Le Guillou, Marie-Joseph. "Lumière et charité dans la doctrine palamite de la divinization." *Istina* 19 (1974): 329–338.

Hacker, Paul. *Das Ich im Glauben bei Martin Luther: Der Ursprung der anthropozentrischen Religion.* Bonn: Verlag "Nova et Vetera," 1966.

Hadot, Pierre. *Philosophy As a Way of Life: Spriritual Exercises from Socrates to Foucault.* Translated by M. Chase. Oxford, U.K., and Cambridge, Mass: Blackwell Publ., 1995.

Hagberg, Garry. "Philosophy as Therapy: Wittgenstein, Cavell, and Autobiographical Writing." *Philosophy and Literature* 27.1 (2003): 196–210.

Hahm, David E. *The Origins of Stoic Cosmology.* Columbus, Ohio: Ohio State University Press, 1977.

Harl, Marguerite. *Origène et la fonction révélatrice du Verbe incarné.* Paris: Seuil, 1958.

Harris, Ian Charles. *The continuity of Madhyamaka and Yogācāra in Indian Mahāyāna Buddhism.* New York : E. J. Brill, 1991.

Harrison, Paul. "Is the *dharmakāya* the Real 'Phantom body' of the Buddha?" *Journal of the International Association of Buddhist Studies* 15.1 (1992): 44–94.

Hausherr, Irénée. *Philautie. De la tendresse de soi à la charité selon Saint Maxime le Confesseur.* Rome: Pontificium Institutum Orientalium Studiorum, 1952.

Heidegger, Martin. *Gelassenheit: A Discourse on Thinking.* Translated by J. M. Anderson and E. H. Freund. New York: Harper & Row, 1966.

Heim, S. Mark. *The Depth of the Riches: A Trinitarian Theology of Religious Ends.* Grand Rapids, Mich., and Cambridge, Mass.: Wm. B. Eerdmans Publishing Company, 2001.

Heintjes, Jan. "De opgang van den menschelijken geest tot God volgens sint Maximus Confessor." *Bijdragen van de philosophische en theologische Faculteiten der Nederlandsche Jesuïten* 6 (1943): 65–72.

Heinzer, Felix. *Gottes Sohn als Mensch: die Struktur des Menschseins Christi bei Maximus Confessor.* Freiburg, Schweiz: Universitätsverlag, 1980.

Hirakawa, Akira. *A History of Indian Buddhism from Śākyamuni to Early Mahāyāna.* Translated by P. Groner. Honolulu, Hawaii: University of Hawaii Press, 1990.

Hodge, Stephen. *The Maha-Vairocana-Abhisambodhi Tantra.* Routledge Curzon, London: Routlegde Curzon, 2003.

Hopkins, Jeffrey. *Meditation on Emptiness.* Boston, Mass.: Wisdom Publications, 1983.

_____. *Emptiness in the Mind-Only School of Buddhism: Dynamic Responses to Dzong-ka-ba's 'The Essence of True Eloquence.'* Berkeley, Calif: University of California Press, 2003.

Houston, Gary W. *Sources for a History of the bSam yas Debate. Monumenta Tibetica Historica.* Ab. 1, Bd. 2. Sankt Augustin: VGH Wissenschaftsverlag, 1980.

Huntington Jr., C. W. (Sandy). "Was Candrakīrti a Prāsangika?" Pages 67–91 in Sara McClintock and Georges Dreyfus, eds. *The Prāsangika-Svātantrika distinction: What Difference does a Difference make?* Boston, Mass.: Wisdom Publications, 2003.

von Ivanka, Endre. *Maximos der Bekenner: All-eins in Christus.* Einsiedeln: Johannes Verlag, 1961.

_____. *Plato christianus. La réception critique du Platonisme chez les Pères de l'Église.* Paris: Presses Universitaires de France, 1990.

Jackson, Roger. "Sa sKya Pandita's account of the bSam yas debate: history as polemic." *Journal of the International Association of Buddhist Studies* 5 (1982): 89–99.

Jakobson, Roman, and Moris Halle. *Fundamentals of Language.* New York: Walter de Gruyter, 2002.

James, William. *A Pluralist Universe.* Cambridge, Mass.: Harvard University Press, 1977.

_____. *The Will to Believe.* Cambridge, Mass.: Harvard University Press, 1979.

_____. *The Varieties of Religious Experience.* Cambridge, Mass.: Harvard University Press, 1985.

Johnson, Vida T. and Graham Petrie. *The Films of Andrei Tarkovsky: A Visual Fugue.* Bloomington and Indianapolis, Ind.: Indiana University Press, 1994.

Kapstein, Matthew. "Religious Syncretism in 13th century Tibet: The *Limitless Ocean* Cycle." Pages 358–371 in Barbara N. Aziz and Matthew Kapstein, eds. *Soundings in Tibetan civilization.* New Dehli: South Asia Books, 1985.

Karmay, Samten G. "A Discussion on the Doctrinal Position of rDzogs chen from the 10th to the 13th century." *Journal Asiatique* 263 (1975): 147–155.

_____. *The Great Perfection: A Philosophical and Meditative Teaching in Tibetan Buddhism*. Leiden: E. J. Brill, 1988.

Kattan, Assaad. *Verleiblichung und Synergie: Grundzüge der Bibelhermeneutik bei Maximos Confessor*. Suppl. to Vigiliae Christianae, 63. Leiden and Boston: Brill, 2003.

Kawamura, Leslie, ed. *The Bodhisattva doctrine in Buddhism*. Waterloo, Ontario: Wilfred Laurier University Press, 1981.

Keenan, John P. *The meaning of Christ: A Mahāyāna Theology*. Maryknoll, N.Y.: Orbis Books, 1989.

Kelsang Gyatso. *Meaningful to Behold: The Bodhisattva's Way of Life*. 4th ed. Boston, Mass.: Wisdom Publications, 1994.

Kerr, Fergus. *After Aquinas: Versions of Thomism*. Oxford, U.K., and Cambridge, Mass.: Blackwells, 2002.

Koch, Hal. *Pronoia und Paideusis, Studien über Origenes und sein Verhältniss zum Platonismus*. New York: Garland Publications, 1979.

Koyré, Alexandre. *From the Closed World to the Infinite Universe*. Baltimore, Md., and London: John Hopkins University Press, 1968.

Kristeva, Julia. *In the Beginning was Love: Psychoanalysis and Faith*. Translated by A. Goldhammer. New York: Columbia University Press, 1988.

_____. *Tales of Love*. Translated by L. Roudiez. New York. Columbia University Press, 1991.

Krivocheine, Archbishop Basil. *In the Light of Christ. St. Symeon the New Theologian: Life-Spirituality-Doctrine*. Crestwood, N.Y.: St. Vladimir's Seminary Press, 1986.

Küng, Hans. *A Global Ethic for Global Politics and Economics*. Oxford: Oxford University Press, 1998.

La Cugna, Catherine M. *God for us: the Trinity and Christian life*. San Francisco: Harper, 1993.

Laird, Martin. "The 'Open Country whose Name is Prayer': Apophasis, Deconstruction, and Contemplative Practice." *Modern Theology* 21 (1): 141–155.

Lamotte, Etienne. *La somme du Grand Vehicule d'Asanga*. Tome 2. Louvain, Belgium: Museon, 1938.

Lampe, Geoffrey W. H. "The Holy Spirit and the Person of Christ." Pages 125–146 in Stephen Sykes and John P. Clayton, eds. *Christ, Faith and History: Cambridge Studies in Christology*. London: Cambridge University Press, 1972.

Larchet, Jean-Claude. *La Divinisation de l'Homme selon Saint Maxime le Confesseur*. Paris: Cerf, 1996.

_____. *Saint Silouane de l'Athos*. Paris: Cerf, 2001.

Lash, Nicholas. "Where does Holy Teaching leave Philosophy? Questions on Milbank's Aquinas." *Modern Theology* 15 (1999): 433–45.

Léthel, François Marie. *Théologie de l'agonie du Christ: la liberté humaine du fils de Dieu et son importance sotériologique mises en lumière par saint Maxime le Confesseur.* Théologie historique, 52. Paris: Beauchesne, 1979.

Lonergan, Bernard. *Method in Theology.* Toronto: University of Toronto Press, 1990.

Long, Stephen S. *Divine Economy: Theology and the Market.* London and New York: Routledge, 2000.

Longchen Rabjam. *The Practice of Dzogchen.* Translated by Namkhai Norbu and Tulku Thondup. 2d ed. Ithaca, N.Y.: Snow Lion Pub., 1996.

Lopez, Donald S. *A Study of Svātantrika.* Ithaca, N.Y.: Snow Lion Press, 1987.

Lossky, Vladimir. *In the Image and Likeness of God.* Crestwood, N.Y.: St. Vladimir's Seminary Press, 1985.

_____. *The Mystical Theology of the Eastern Church.* Crestwood, N.Y.: St. Vladimir's Seminary Press, 1997.

Lot-Borodine, Myrrha. "La doctrine de la déification dans l'Église grecque jusqu'au XI siécle." *Revue de l'histoire des religions* 105 (1932): 5–43.

_____. "L'anthropologie théocentrique de l'Orient chrétien comme base de son expérience spirituelle." *Irénikon* 16 (1939): 6–21.

Louth, Andrew. *The Origins of the Christian Mystical Tradition: From Plato to Denys.* Oxford: Oxford University Press, 1981.

_____. *Maximus the Confessor. The Early Church Fathers.* London and New York: Routledge, 1996.

Lusthaus, Dan. *Buddhist Phenomenology: A Philosophical Investigation of Yogacara Buddhism and the Ch'eng Wei-shih Lun.* New York: RoutledgeCurzon, 2003.

_____. "What is and what is not Yogācāra." Online: http://www.human. toyogakuen-u.ac.jp/ ~acmuller/ yogacara/ intro-asc.htm.

MacMullen, Ramsay *Christianity and Paganism in the Fourth to Eighth Century.* New Haven, Conn: Yale University Press, 1999.

Makransky, John. *Buddhahood Embodied: Sources of Controversy in India and Tibet.* SUNY Series in Buddhist Studies. Albany, N.Y.; SUNY Press, 1997.

Mantzarides, George. *Orthodox Spiritual Life.* Brookline, Mass.: Holy Cross Orthodox Press, 1994.

Marion, Jean-Luc. *God without Being: Hors-Texte.* Translated by T. A. Carlson. Religion and Postmodernism Series. Chicago: University of Chicago Press, 1991.

McDonough, Richard. "Wittgenstein's Reversal on the 'Language of Thought' Doctrine." *The Philosophical Quarterly* 44, 177 (1994): 482–94.

McGuckin, John. *St. Cyril of Alexandria: the Christological Controversy. Its History, Theology, and Texts.* Crestwood, N.Y.: St. Vladimir's Seminary Press, 1994.

McIntosh, Mark. *Mystical Theology: The Integrity of Spirituality and Theology.* Oxford, U.K., and Cambridge, Mass.: Blackwell, 1998.

Meyendorff, John. *Christ in Eastern Christian Thought.* Crestwood, N.Y.: St. Vladimir's Seminary Press, 1997.

––––––––. *St. Gregory Palamas and Orthodox Spirituality.* Crestwood, N.Y.: St. Vladimir's Seminary Press, 1997.

Merleau-Ponty, Maurice. *Phenomenology of Perception.* Translated by P. Kegan. London and New York: Routledge, 2002.

Milbank, John. *Theology and Social Theory: Beyond Secular Reason.* Oxford, U.K., and Cambridge, Mass.: Blackwell, 1990.

––––––. *The World Made Strange: Theology, Language, Culture.* Oxford, U.K., and Cambridge, Mass.: Blackwell, 1997.

––––––––, and Catherine Pickstock. *Truth in Aquinas.* New York: Routledge, 2000.

Monk, Ray. *Wittgenstein: the Duty of Genius.* London: Penguin Books, 1990.

Murdoch, Iris. *Bruno's Dream.* London, Penguin, 1970.

––––––. *Under the Net.* New York: Penguin, 1977.

––––––. *Sartre: Romantic Rationalist.* Tonbridge, U.K.: Viking Press, 1987.

––––––. *Metaphysics as a Guide to Morals.* London: Penguin Books, 1994.

––––––. *Nuns and Soldiers.* Reprint ed. London: Penguin, 2002.

Musil, Robert. *L'uomo senza qualitá.* Translated by A. Rho. Torino: Einaudi, 1966.

Nagao, Gadjin M. "On the theory of Buddha-Body (*Buddha-kāya*)." *Eastern Buddhist* 4.1 (1973): 25–53.

Nam khas nor bu. *Dzogchen: the Self-Perfected State.* Ithaca, N.Y.: Snow Lion Publication, 1996.

Nancy, Jean-Luc. *The Inoperative Community.* Translated by P. Connor. Minneapolis, Minn.: University of Minnesota Press, 1991.

––––––. *A Finite Thinking.* Translated by S. Sparks. Palo Alto, Calif.: Stanford University Press, 2003.

Napper, Elizabeth. *Dependent-Arising and Emptiness: a Tibetan Buddhist interpretation of Mādhyamika Philosophy.* Boston, Mass.: Wisdom Publ., 2003.

Nellas, Panaghiotis. *Deification in Christ. The Nature of the Human Person.* Crestwood, N.Y.: St. Vladimir's Seminary Press, 1987.

Neumaier-Dargyay, Eva K. "The concept of a 'Creator God' in Tantric Buddhism." *Journal of the International Association of Buddhist Studies* 8.1 (1985): 31–47.

Nichols, Aidan OP. *Byzantine Gospel: Maximus the Confessor in Modern Scholarship.* T&T Clark: Edinburgh, 1993.

Nietzsche, Friedrich. *Thus Spake Zarathustra.* New York: New York Modern Library, 1995.

Norris, Frederick. *Faith gives Fullness to Reasoning: The Five Theological Orations of Gregory Nazianzen.* Supplements to *Vigiliae Christianae,* 13. Leiden: Brill Academic Publishing, 1997.

O'Keefe, John J. "Impassible Suffering? Divine Passion and Fifth-Century Christology." *Theological Studies* 58 (1997): 39–60.

O'Leary, Joseph Stephen. *Religious Pluralism and Christian Truth.* Edinburgh: Edinburgh University Press, 1996.

Pelikan, Jaroslav. *The Christian Tradition: A History of the Development of Doctrine.* Vol. 1: *The Emergence of the Catholic Tradition (100–600).* Chicago and London: University of Chicago Press, 1971.

_____. *Christianity and Classical Culture: the Metamorphosis of Natural Theology in the Christian Encounter with Hellenism.* New Haven, Conn.: Yale University Press, 1993.

Pickstock, Catherine. *After Writing: The Liturgical Consummation of Philosophy.* Oxford: Blackwells, 1997.

_____. "The Soul in Plato." Pages 115–126 in Dean-Peter Baker and Patrick Maxwell, eds. *Exploration in Contemporary Continental Philosophy of Religion.* New York: Rodopi, 2003.

Radford-Ruether, Rosemary. *Integrating Ecofeminism, Globalization, and World Religions.* Lanham, Md.: Rowman & Littlefield Publishers, 2005.

Radoslavljevic, Artemije. "Le problème du 'présupposé' ou du 'non-présupposé' de l'Incarnation de Dieu le Verbe." Pages 193–206 in Felix Heinzer and Cristoph von Schönborn, eds. *Maximus Confessor. Actes du Symposium sur Maxime le Confesseur.* Fribourg-en-Suisse: Editions Universitaires, 1982.

Rahner, Karl. "Die geistliche Lehre des Evagrius Pontikus." *Zeitschrift für Askese und Mystik* (1933): 22.

_____. "Mysticism." *Encyclopedia of Theology: The Concise 'Sacramentum mundi.'* New York: Crossroad Publishing, 1975.

_____. *Foundations of Christian Faith.* Translated by W. V. Dych. New York, N.Y.: Crossroad, 1982.

Ratzinger, Joseph (Pope Benedict XVI). *The Nature and Mission of Theology: Approaches to Understanding Its Role in the Light of Present Controversy.* San Francisco: Ignatius Press, 1995.

_____. 'Inter-religious Dialogue and Jewish-Christian Relations.' *Communio* 25, no. 1 (1998): 29–41.

_____. *Truth and Tolerance: Christian Belief and World Religions.* San Francisco: Ignatius Press, 2004.

Ray, Reginald A. *Indestructible Truth: The Living Spirituality of Tibetan Buddhism.* Boston, Mass. & London: Shambala, 2002.

_____. *Secrets of the Vajra World: The Tantric Buddhism of Tibet.* Boston, Mass. & London: Shambala, 2002.

Reale, Giovanni. "Plotino come 'Erma bifronte'." Pages xi-lxx (Introductory essay) in Plotino, *Enneadi*. Italian trans. by R. Radice. Milano: Arnoldo Mondadori ed., 2002.

Refoulé, François. "La Christologie d'Evagre et l'origénisme." *Orientalia Christiana Periodica* 27 (1961): 221–266.

_____. "Evagre fut-il origéniste?" *Revue des Sciences Philosophiques et Théologiques* 47 (1963): 247–254.

_____. "Immortalité de l'âme et résurrection de la chair." *Revue de l'historie des religions* 163 (1963): 247–254.

Renczes, Philipp Gabriel. *Agir de Dieu et liberté de l'homme: Recherches sur l'anthropologie théologique de saint Maxime le Confesseur.* Paris: Cerf, 2003.

Ridenhour, Jamieson. "'I Know the City Well': The Metaphysical Cityscape in Iris Murdoch's 'Under the Net'." Online: *Literary London Journal* 1, 1 (2003): http://homepages.gold.ac.uk/london-journal/march2003/ridenhour.html.

Ringu Tulku. "The Rime movement of Jamgon Kongtrul the Great." *Proceeds of the International Association for Tibetan Studies* 7, Vol. 2. Vienna: Verlag der Österreichischen Akademie der Wissenschaften, 1995.

Romanides, John. *The Ancestral Sin.* Brookline, Mass.: Holy Cross Orthodox Press, 1988.

Ruegg, David S. *The Literature of the Madhyamaka School of Philosophy in India.* Vol. VII, Fasc. 1. in Jan Gonda, ed. *History of Indian Literature.* Wiesbaden: Otto Harassowitz Publ., 1981.

_____. "A Tibetan's Odyssey: A Review Article." *Journal of the Royal Asiatic Society* 2 (1989): 304–311.

_____. *Buddha Nature, Mind, and the Problem of Gradualism in a Comparative Perspective.* London: SOAS Publications, 1989.

Rusch, William C. *The Trinitarian Controversy.* Sources of Early Christian Thought. Minneapolis, Minn.: Fortress Press, 1980.

Samuel, Geoffrey. *Civilized Shamans: Buddhism in Tibetan Societies.* Smithsonian Series in Ethnographic Inquiry. Washington DC: Smithsonian Pub., 1993.

Sartre, Jean Paul. *Nausea.* Translated by L. Alexander. New York: New Directions Publishing Corporation, 1969.

de Saussure, Ferdinand. *Course in General Linguistics.* Translated by R. Harris. London: Duckworth, 1983.

Savvidis, Kyriakos. *Die Lehre von der Vergöttlichung des Menschen bei Maximos dem Bekenner und ihre Rezeption durch Gregor Palamas.* St. Ottilien: Veröffentlichungen des Instituts für Orthodoxe Theologie, Bd. 5, 1997.

van Schaik, Sam. *Approaching the Great Perfection—Simultaneous and gradual methods of Dzogchen practice in the Longchen Nyingtig.* Somerville, Mass.: Wisdom Publication, 2004.

von Schelling, Friedrich W. J. *Bruno, or On the Natural and the Divine Principle of Things.* Translated by M. Vater. Albany, N.Y.: SUNY Press, 1984.

Schleiermacher, Friedrich D. E. *The Christian Faith.* Edinburgh: T&T Clark, 1999.

_____. *On Religion: Speeches to its Cultured Despisers.* Cambridge: Cambridge University Press, 1996.

Schmithausen, Lambert. *Ālayaviñāna. On the origin and the early development of a central concept of Yogācāra philosophy.* SPB IV. Tokyo: The International Institute of Buddhist Studies, 1987.

Scola, Angelo. "A style of thought." Pages 3–33 in Elisa Buzzi, ed. *A Generative Thought: an Introduction to the Works of Luigi Giussani.* Montreal: McGill-Queen's University Press, 2003.

Sedgwick, Mark. *Against the Modern World: Traditionalism and the Secret Intellectual History of the Twentieth Century.* Oxford: Oxford University Press, 2004.

Schmithausen, Lambert. "Spirituelle Praxis und philosophische Theorie im Buddhismus." *Zeitschrift für Missionswissenschaft und Religionswissenschaft* 57.3 (1973): 161–186.

Schneiders, Sandra. "Scripture and Spirituality." Pages 1–2 in *Christian Spirituality: Origins to the Twelfth Century.* Edited by Bernard McGinn, John Meyendorff and Jean Leclercq. World Spirituality 16. New York: Crossroads, 1985.

Sfameni-Gasparro, Giulia. "Aspetti di 'doppia creazione' nell'antropologia di Massimo il Confessore." Studia Patristica 18 (1986): 127–134.

Sheldrake, Philip. *Spirituality and History. Questions of Interpretations and Method.* Maryknoll, N.Y.: Orbis, 1998.

Sherrard, Philip. *Christianity and Eros: Essays on the Theme of Sex and Love.* London: SPCK Holy Trinity Church, 1976.

Sherwood, Polycarp OSB. *The Earlier Ambigua of St. Maximos the Confessor.* Studia Anselmiana 36. Rome: Herder, 1955.

Smith, J. Warren. *Passion and Paradise: A Study of Theological Anthropology in Gregory of Nyssa.* New York: Crossroads Publ., 2004.

St. Silouan the Athonite. *Wisdom from Mount Athos. The Writings of Staretz Silouan, 1866–1938.* Translated by R. Edmonds. Crestwood, N.Y.: St. Vladimir's Press, 1974.

Smith, James K. *The Fall of Interpretation: Philosophical Foundations for a Creational Hermeneutic.* Downers Grove, Ill.: InterVarsity Press: 2000.

_____. *Introducing Radical Orthodoxy: Mapping a Post-Secular Theology.* Grand Rapids, Mich.: Baker Academic, 2004.

Snellgrove, David L, and Hugh E. Richardson. *A Cultural History of Tibet.* Bangkok, Thailand: Orchid Press, 2004.

Sobrino, Jon. *Spirituality of Liberation: Toward Political Holiness.* Maryknoll, N.Y.: Orbis, 1988.

Staniloae, Dumitru. *The Experience of God—Orthodox Dogmatic Theology.* Vol. II. The World: *Creation and Deification.* Brookline, Mass.: Holy Cross Orthodox Press, 2000.

_____. *Orthodox Spirituality.* South Canaan, Pa.: Saint Tikhon Seminary Press, 2003.

Steinkerchner, Scott OP. "Painting the Clouds." PhD diss., Boston College, 2005.

Stern, David. *Midrash and Theory: Ancient Jewish Exegesis and Contempory Literary Studies.* Chicago: Northwestern University Press, 1998.

Suzuki, Daisetz T. *On Indian Mahāyāna Buddhism.* New York: Harper & Row, 1968.

Takasaki, Jikido. *A study on the Ratnagotravibhāga (Uttaratantra), being a treatise on the tathāgatagarbha theory of Mahāyāna Buddhism.* SOR 33. Roma: Istituto Italiano per il Medio ed Estremo Oriente, 1966.

Thien-An, Thich. *Zen Philosophy Zen Practice.* Berkeley, Calif.: Dharma Publishing, 1975.

Thubten Yeshe. *Introduction to Tantra: the Transformation of Desire.* Compiled by Jonathan Landlow. Somerville, Mass.: Wisdom Publications, 2001.

Thunberg, Lars. *Man and the Cosmos: The Vision of St. Maximus the Confessor.* Crestwood, N.Y.: St. Vladimir's Seminary Press, 1985.

_____. *Microcosm and Mediator: The Theological Anthropology of Maximus the Confessor.* 2d ed. Chicago and La Salle, Ill.: Open Court, 1995.

Thurman, Robert A. F. *The Central Philosophy of Tibet: A Study and Translation of Jey Tsong Khapa's 'Essence of True Eloquence.'* Princeton, N.J.: Princeton University Press, 1984.

———. *Tsong Kha Pa's Speech of Gold in the Essence of True Eloquence.* Princeton, N.J.: Princeton University Press, 1984.

———. "Tsong kha pa's integration of *sūtra* and *tantra*." Pages 372–383 in Barbara N. Aziz and Matthew Kapstein, eds. *Soundings in Tibetan civilization.* New Dehli: South Asia Books, 1985.

Törönen, Mikko K. "Union and Distinction in the Thought of Maximos the Confessor." PhD diss., Durham University, 2002.

Torrance, Iain R. *Christology after Chalcedon: Severus of Antioch and Sergius the Monophysite.* Eugene, Ore.: Wipf and Stock, 1998.

Troeltsch, Ernst. *Die Absolutheit des Christentums und die Religionsgeschichte.* München: Siebenstern Taschenbuch-Verlag, 1969.

Tulku Thondup. *Hidden Teachings of Tibet: An Explanation of the Terma Tradition of Tibetan Buddhism.* Boston, Mass.: Wisdom Publications, 1997.

Tulku Urgyen Rinpoche. *Rainbow Painting.* Hong Kong: Rangjung Yeshe Publications, 1995.

Unger, Dominic Joseph. "Christ Jesus, center and final scope of all creation according to Saint Maximos the Confessor." *Franciscan Studies* 9 (1949): 50–62.

Vatican II, Council. *Declaration on the Relation of the Church to Non-Christian Religions 'Nostra Aetate'.* Rome, 1965.

Vattimo, Gianni. *After Christianity.* Translated by L. D'Isanto. New York: Columbia University Press, 2002.

Viller, Marcel. "Aux sources de la spiritualité de saint Maxime. Les œuvres d'Évagre Pontique." *Revue d'Ascétique et de Mystique* 11 (1930): 163–166.

Völker, Walther. *Das Vollkommenheitsideal des Origenes. Beiträge zur Historischen Theologie* 7. Nendeln: Kraus Reprint, 1966.

———. *Maximus Confessor als Meister des geistlichen Lebens.* Wiesbaden: F. Steiner, 1965.

Geoffrey Wainwright, "Eschatology." Pages 113–128 in Edward T. Oakes, S.J., and David Moss, eds., *The Cambridge Companion to Hans Urs von Balthasar,* Cambridge: Cambridge University Press, 2004.

Ward, Graham. *Theology and Contemporary Critical Theory.* London: Palgrave Macmillan, 2000.

———. *Cities of God.* New York: Routledge, 2001.

Wasserstrom, Steven M. *Religion after Religion: Gershom Scholem, Mircea Eliade, and Henry Corbin.* Princeton, N.J.: Princeton University Press, 2004.

Wayman, Alex. "A Defense of Yogācāra Buddhism." *Philosophy East and West* 46 (1996): 447–477.

Wilken, Robert. "Maximus the Confessor on the Affections in Historical Perspective." Pages 412–423 in Vincent L. Wimbush and Richard Valantasis, eds. *Asceticism.* Oxford: Oxford University Press, 2002.

Williams, Anna N. *The Ground of Union: Deification in Aquinas and Palamas.* Oxford: Oxford University Press, 1999.

Williams, Paul. "Some Aspects of Language and Construction in the Madhyamaka." *Journal of Indian Philosophy* 8 (1980): 1–45.

_____. "Silence and Truth: Some Aspects of the Madhyamaka Philosophy in Tibet." *Tibet Journal* 7. 1–2 (1982): 67–80.

_____. *Mahāyāna Buddhism: the Doctrinal Foundations.* New York: Routledge, 1989.

Williams, Rowan. "Origen on the Soul of Jesus." Pages 131–137 in Henri Crouzel and Richard Hanson, eds. *Origeniana Tertia.* Rome: Edizioni dell'Ateneo, 1981.

_____. *Wound of Knowledge: Christian Spirituality from the New Testament to St. John of the Cross.* 2d ed. Cambridge, Mass.: Cowley Publications, 2003.

Wittgenstein, Ludwig. *Philosophical Investigations.* Translated by G. E. M. Anscombe. 3d ed. London: Blackwell, 2002.

Wuthnow, Robert. *The Restructuring of American Religion.* Princeton, N.J.: Princeton University Press, 1990.

Yoshimizu, Chizuku. "Tsong kha pa's Reevaluation of Candrakīrti's Criticism of Autonomous Inference." Pages 257–288 in Sara McClintock and Georges Dreyfus, eds. *The Prāsangika-Svātantrika distinction: What Difference does a Difference make?* Boston, Mass.: Wisdom Publications, 2003.

Zabala, Santiago, ed. *The Future of Religion.* New York: Columbia University Press, 2002.

Žižek, Slavoj. *Welcome to the Desert of the Real.* London, Verso, 2002.

INDEX